MARXISM AND ECOLOGICAL ECONOMICS

Historical Materialism Book Series

More than ten years after the collapse of the Berlin Wall and the disappearance of Marxism as a (supposed) state ideology, a need for a serious and long-term Marxist book publishing program has risen. Subjected to the whims of fashion, most contemporary publishers have abandoned any of the systematic production of Marxist theoretical work that they may have indulged in during the 1970s and early 1980s. The Historical Materialism book series addresses this great gap with original monographs, translated texts and reprints of "classics."

Haymarket Books is proud to be working with Brill Academic Publishers (http://www.brill.nl) and the journal *Historical Materialism* to republish the Historical Materialism book series in paperback editions. Current series titles include:

Alasdair MacIntyre's Engagement with Marxism: Selected Writings 1953–1974
Edited by Paul Blackledge and Neil Davidson

Althusser: The Detour of Theory, Gregory Elliott

Between Equal Rights: A Marxist Theory of International Law, China Miéville

The Capitalist Cycle, Pavel V. Maksakovsky, Translated with introduction and commentary by Richard B. Day

The Clash of Globalisations: Neo-Liberalism, the Third Way, and Anti-globalisation, Ray Kiely

Critical Companion to Contemporary Marxism, Edited by Jacques Bidet and Stathis Kouvelakis

Criticism of Heaven: On Marxism and Theology, Roland Boer

Exploring Marx's Capital: Philosophical, Economic, and Political Dimensions, Jacques Bidet

Following Marx: Method, Critique, and Crisis, Michael Lebowitz

The German Revolution: 1917–1923, Pierre Broué

Globalisation: A Systematic Marxian Account, Tony Smith

Impersonal Power: History and Theory of the Bourgeois State,
Heide Gerstenberger, translated by David Fernbach

Lenin Rediscovered: What Is to Be Done? In Context, Lars T. Lih

Making History: Agency, Structure, and Change in Social Theory, Alex Callinicos

Marxism and Ecological Economics: Toward a Red and Green Political Economy, Paul Burkett

A Marxist Philosophy of Language, Jean-Jacques Lecercle and Gregory Elliott

The Theory of Revolution in the Young Marx, Michael Löwy

Utopia Ltd.: Ideologies of Social Dreaming in England 1870–1900, Matthew Beaumont

Western Marxism and the Soviet Union: A Survey of Critical Theories and Debates Since 1917
Marcel van der Linden

MARXISM AND ECOLOGICAL ECONOMICS

TOWARD A RED AND GREEN POLITICAL ECONOMY

PAUL BURKETT

Haymarket Books
Chicago, Illinois

First published in 2005 by Brill Academic Publishers, The Netherlands
© 2006 Koninklijke Brill NV, Leiden, The Netherlands

Published in paperback in 2009 by
Haymarket Books
P.O. Box 180165
Chicago, IL 60618
773-583-7884
www.haymarketbooks.org
ISBN: 978-1-608460-25-0

Trade distribution:
In the U.S., Consortium Book Sales, www.cbsd.com
In the UK, Turnaround Publisher Services, www.turnaround-psl.com
In Australia, Palgrave Macmillan, www.palgravemacmillan.com.au
In all other countries, Publishers Group Worldwide, www.pgw.com

Cover design by Ragina Johnson. Cover image by Antonia Sofronova, 1933.

Printed in Canada by union labor.

This book was published with the generous support of
the Lannan Foundation and Wallace Global Fund.

10 9 8 7 6 5 4 3

Library of Congress Cataloging-in-Publication Data is available.

Contents

Preface

This book aims at instigating a dialogue between Marxist political economy and ecological economics. It shows how Marxism can help ecological economics better fulfill its commitments to methodological pluralism, interdisciplinarity, and openness to new visions of policy and of structural economic change that confront the current biospheric crisis. The potential contribution of Marxism to ecological economics is developed in terms of four fundamental issues: (i) the relations between nature and *economic value*; (ii) the treatment of *nature as capital*; (iii) the significance of the *entropy law* for economic systems; (iv) the concept of *sustainable development*.

In writing this book, I have made a conscious effort to avoid the kind of *ad hominem* argumentation that has all too often hampered the effectiveness of intellectual interchanges between Marxism and ecological economics. I have tried to engage seriously with the central features of ecological economics as a 'meta-paradigm' as well as its core theoretical constructs in the four above-mentioned issue areas. I hope that the result is a book that will be useful not only to Marxists and ecological economists interested in pursuing dialogue, but also to those just seeking a critical, but readable, introduction to the basic ideas of ecological economics. That the book was written by a relative 'outsider' to ecological economics will not, I trust, cripple its effectiveness in either function, and may even help it a bit. To risk a cliché, sometimes an outsider can better distinguish the forest from the trees.

Although my Marxist engagement with ecological economics dates to the early 1990s, the idea of this book germinated on the evening of 19 October 2001, when I had to respond to a public talk given by Herman Daly in conjunction with an interdisciplinary conference on 'Causes and Cures of Poverty', sponsored by the Center for Process Studies at the Claremont School of Theology in California. My gratitude is extended both to Herman Daly and to the audience that evening for their gracious reception of, and encouraging responses to, my comments.

I want to thank Sebastian Budgen and the rest of the *Historical Materialism* Book Series editorial board, along with Sasha Goldstein and Joed Elich at Brill, for supporting this project. Several other people provided crucial help at various stages. Alfredo Saad-Filho read an early prospectus for the book and encouraged me to pursue it to completion. Kozo Mayumi emailed several of his most recent papers on entropic economics in pre-published form, and this was especially helpful for my work on Chapter 5. Ben Fine offered incisive comments on the manuscript for Chapters 3 and 4. Chapter 2 benefited enormously from critical comments by Michael Perelman, from additional readings suggested by Patrick Bond and Larry Lohmann, and from Rick Lotspeich's insights into contingent valuation analysis. Rick's father, Frederick B. Lotspeich, donated his entire collection of the journal *Ecological Economics* to the Economics Department library at Indiana State University, which greatly facilitated my study of the discipline. Angelo Di Salvo and Mark Hudson translated the work of Sergei Podolinsky into English, and without this translation the research summarised in Chapter 6 could not have been done. Most of all, I want to thank John Bellamy Foster not only for allowing me to draw from our co-produced work on the 'Podolinsky business' for Chapter 6, but also for sharing his own insights into Marxism and ecology over the years and for his constant encouragement and support.

Several of the chapters in this book are based, in whole or in part, on articles published in scholarly journals, and I wish to thank their respective editors for considering my work and giving permission for it to reappear here in revised form: John Jermier at *Organization & Environment* (Chapter 1);[1] Malcolm Sawyer at the *International Papers in Political Economzy* (Chapters 3 and 4);[2] Sebastian Budgen at *Historical Materialism* (Chapter 5);[3] Karen Lucas at *Theory and Society* (Chapter 6).[4]

In addition, some of the arguments in different chapters were initially aired at conference sessions whose participants kindly provided important encouragement and feedback: the Marxist Sociology session at the American Sociological Association Meetings, San Francisco, 14–17 August 2004, especially

---

[1] Burkett 2003b.
[2] Burkett 2003d.
[3] Burkett 2005.
[4] Burkett and Foster 2006.

Brett Clark (Chapter 6); the Conference on 'Causes and Cures of Poverty', Center for Process Studies, Claremont School of Theology, 18–21 October 2001, especially Walt Sheasby, Herman Daly, Wes Jackson, and John Cobb (Chapter 9); and the Conference on 'The Work of Karl Marx and Challenges for the 21st Century', Havana, Cuba, 5–8 May 2003, especially Michael Lebowitz and Barbara Foley (Chapter 10).

Thanks are also due to my colleagues in the Economics Department at Indiana State University, Terre Haute, for approving the one-semester leave required to put this book together, and more generally for constructing the kind of open and non-dogmatic setting needed for heterodox scholars to get their work done. In addition, essential research support was provided by the Interlibrary Loan Department at Cunningham Library, Indiana State University. Finally, I extend loving gratitude to Suzanne Carter, who for whatever reason has put up with me for two decades now, and to Patrick and Molly Burkett for their patience with the fluctuating moods that their father exhibited during the composition of this work.

Terre Haute, Indiana
August, 2005

Introduction

This book has two purposes: to undertake the first general assessment of ecological economics from a Marxist point of view, and to show how Marxist political economy can make a substantial contribution to ecological economics. By pursuing these two goals, the book tries to lay the basis for a more substantive dialogue between Marxists and ecological economists.

In an age of worsening environmental and biospheric crises, the general importance of productive interchanges among all schools of ecological thought needs no defence. But the specific motivations for this attempt at paradigm-bridging, and the approach used in the attempt, have both been shaped by a particular understanding of ecological economics as a discipline. Accordingly, Section I of this Introduction sketches the defining characteristics of ecological economics. Since these characteristics may be interpreted as analytical aspirations, they can double as criteria for evaluating the discipline and Marxism's potential contribution to it. Section I also introduces the substantive issues through which this assessment is developed. The specific needs that can be served by such an assessment at the present time are further discussed in Section II. Without underestimating the considerable historical-intellectual barriers to a productive dialogue, it is suggested that recent developments in ecological economics and ecological Marxism have created an opportunity for these barriers to be overcome. Section III provides a brief overview of the subsequent chapters.

I. A framework for assessing ecological economics

This book's assessment is not 'general' in the sense of surveying all, or even most, of the subject matters addressed by ecological economics. There is no way that one book can evaluate all the research projects that have been undertaken by members of the discipline. Rather, the book's assessment is 'general' insofar as it is developed in terms of the methodological aspirations defining ecological economics as a field of study. Based on the pronouncements of some of its most well known synthetic thinkers, these aspirations appear to be three-fold.[1]

First, ecological economics is *multidisciplinary*. Its subject matter being the dynamic, co-evolutionary interconnections between economic systems and the natural environment, ecological economics combines elements of the physical sciences (physics, biology, chemistry, geology) with the tools of economic analysis. It is, in short, a life science that, like economic life itself, is both natural and social. Second, ecological economics has a strong commitment to *methodological pluralism*. The sheer complexity of economic-ecological systems dictates that multiple methodologies be brought to bear on the theoretical and policy problems they pose; there must be both broad discussions and intensive collaborations among the different paradigms within the 'meta-paradigm' of ecological economics. Third, given the seriousness of the environmental challenges confronting humanity, ecological economics must be *historically open* in the sense of being receptive to new visions and possibilities in the realms of economic policy and institutional change. Rather than clinging dogmatically to a single model of a sustainable future, it must draw upon its plurality of cross-disciplinary perspectives to generate a variety of institutional remedies as needed to provide space for the diverse ecological values arising out of human-natural systems.

---

[1] See, for example, Boulding 1966, and 1978; Daly 1968; Costanza 1989, and 2003; Norgaard 1989a; Proops 1989; Underwood and King 1989; Folke et al. 1994; Gowdy and Erickson 2005.

The central question this book poses is whether the methodologies and concepts employed by ecological economics are adequate to its aspirations for multidisciplinarity, methodological pluralism, and historical openness. More specifically, it is argued that Marxism's class perspective, especially its notion of class as a material-social relation of production, can help the discipline better live up to these aspirations. This thesis is developed by showing how Marxism reveals and helps resolve important contradictions, analytical silences, and unanswered questions present in ecological economics. My intent is not to add yet another school to the hyper-fragmented arena of environmental studies.[2] Rather, I want to show that Marxism can provide new pre-analytical visions and conceptual tools that further enliven and open up the meta-paradigmatic formation that is ecological economics, both theoretically and politically. For example, Marxism can help ecological economists to question the ecological adequacy of markets, and of neoclassical theories of value and economic growth, at a more fundamental level than they have done heretofore.

Such an assessment of ecological economics, and of Marxism's positive role in it, cannot remain on a purely methodological level. It requires a critical account of how ecological economics has grappled with specific substantive issues. Nonetheless, the choice of which issues to focus on should be dictated by their usefulness as indicators of the discipline's ability to live up to its methodological aspirations. For this purpose, topical issues such as global warming, wetlands protection, the political-economy of oil, and so on are not very useful. It is better to frame the assessment in terms of basic conceptual issues that reflect more directly upon the methodological pluralism, and resulting tensions, within the discipline. These conceptual issues, if well chosen, will be implicated in the analysis of most if not all of the important topical areas, regardless of how conscious and self-critical ecological economists are about their basic concepts when they undertake their theoretical and empirical research.

Therefore, the present assessment of ecological economics is couched in terms of four basic issues or concepts: (i) the relations between nature and *economic value*; (ii) the concept of *natural capital*; (iii) the applicability of the second law of thermodynamics, or the *entropy law*, to economic systems; (iv)

---

[2] Jamison 2001, pp. 24–8.

the notion of *sustainable development*. Before surveying how the book deals with each of these areas, a bit more should be said about the need for, and timing of, the present study. In sketching this background, it is necessary to anticipate certain tendencies in the development of ecological economics which are only fully documented in the subsequent chapters.

II. The need for dialogue, and why now?

As the research leading to this book began, the author was quickly confronted by three indicators of a need for a greater quantity and quality of intellectual interchanges between Marxists and ecological economists. First, a thorough survey of *Ecological Economics*, the discipline's flagship journal, starting from its initial number in 1989, revealed that Marxists had a near zero presence in it. In fact, the journal had carried only two articles espousing even a remotely Marxist perspective.[3] Apart from these two articles, the journal contained a few other references to Marx and Engels, and to Marxism in general, but these were almost always in the way of polemical, *ad hominem* dismissals which – despite the discipline's commitment to methodological pluralism – expressed blanket denials of the actual or potential usefulness of Marxist thinking for economic-ecological analysis. The same goes for the few references to Marxism by ecological economists to be found in other journals and books.[4]

Second, a somewhat less formal stock-taking of the English-language political economy journals in which Marxists have a prominent and ongoing presence – especially the *Review of Radical Political Economics*, *Capital & Class*, *Science & Society*, *Studies in Political Economy*, and the main ecosocialist journal *Capitalism, Nature, Socialism* – revealed an almost equally complete vacuum of serious Marxist engagements with ecological economics as a meta-paradigmatic discipline. In fact, one recent Marxist survey of neoclassical and heterodox views on 'the economics-environment relationship' limits itself to a discussion of neoclassical, institutional, and Marxist approaches, with ecological economics mentioned only briefly and vaguely as providing a

---

[3] Mayumi 1991; Nelson 2001.
[4] See Burkett 1996a, and 1999a; and Foster 1995, and 2000a, for broader inventories of, and responses to, the most common ecological criticisms of Marx and Engels.

'rubric' for the institutional perspective.[5] Similar to the pronouncements of ecological economists on Marxism, the relatively few Marxist references to ecological economics to be found in the literature have often been polemical in nature, even to the point of dismissing ecological economists as crackpot scientists.[6]

Third, despite the evident separation and antagonism between Marxism and ecological economics, the author found some striking suggestions that a more productive dialogue is both possible and potentially quite fruitful. One was Elmar Altvater's demonstration that thermodynamic and entropic concerns can be handled by a Marxian analysis of capitalist exploitation and accumulation.[7] Another was John O'Neill's account of how some important themes of contemporary ecological economics – especially the dependence of economic sustainability on the physical environment and the limitations of purely monetary calculation – were prefigured in the classic 'socialist calculation debate' between Friedrich Hayek and Otto Neurath.[8] Finally, there was the simple fact that despite the best efforts of mainstream 'green capitalism' theorists, both environmentalism (especially environmental activism) and Marxism continue to co-occupy a common (left) position on the political spectrum. This has recently been verified by Eric Neumayer's statistical finding, based on data from a large number of advanced and underdeveloped countries, that left-wing political parties and individuals are significantly 'more likely to embrace pro-environmental positions than their right-wing counterparts'.[9] Neumayer draws the conclusion that 'ecological economics is more likely to be supported by left-wing parties and individuals'.[10] If accurate, this conclusion reinforces the need for less acrimonious engagements between Marxists and ecological economists.

Further investigation revealed that the lack of effective communication between Marxists and ecological economists has both long-term historical and short-term conjunctural roots. Historically, ever since Malthus, Marxists have been suspicious of any theory that posits purely natural limits to human

---

[5] Adaman and Özkaynak 2002, p. 117.
[6] See, for example, Boucher 1996; Schwartzman 1996; and Harvey 1996, pp. 194–7.
[7] Altvater 1990, 1993, and 1994.
[8] O'Neill 2002, and 2004; compare Martinez-Alier 1987, pp. 212–18.
[9] Neumayer 2004, p. 167.
[10] Neumayer 2004, p. 168.

production and development. The reason is obvious: such theories tend to embody a conservative bias against all efforts to improve the human condition by fundamentally transforming class and other power relationships, or even by redistributing wealth and income. However, as Ted Benton has persuasively argued, Marxists have often over-reacted to conservative natural limits arguments.[11] Indeed, by completely dismissing the importance of natural conditions and limits – even socially mediated ones – Marxists have often lost touch with the ecologically-friendly materialist dimension which is central to Marxism.[12] Of course, these Marxist over-reactions do not excuse the tendency of many ecological economists to downplay the role of socio-economic class relations in the generation of environmental problems, in favour of more-or-less free-floating ideological and technological factors. To bridge this polarity between pure natural limits arguments and reactive Marxist retreats from materialism is, in fact, an important sub-purpose of this book.

In broader terms, what is needed is a demonstration that Marxist class analysis can help answer many of the questions raised by ecological economists, at the same time that the substantive agenda of ecological economics can enrich the materialist dimension of Marxism. This is one way of phrasing the kind of project that this book tries to initiate. That it has not been effectively initiated up til now is partly due to certain short-term developments in both ecological socialism and the discipline of ecological economics.

Since the late-1980s, the development of ecosocialism, at least so far as economic questions are concerned, has been dominated by James O'Connor's 'two contradictions' framework.[13] This framework grafts capitalism's tendency to erode its own natural and social conditions, as theorised by Karl Polanyi,[14] onto its tendency toward overproduction of commodities relative to the market (due to surplus-value growing faster than wages), as theorised by Marx. Through its promulgation by the journal *Capitalism, Nature, Socialism* and other publications, O'Connor's analysis has become the reference point for virtually all ecosocialist debates on the political economy of environmental

---

[11] Benton 1989.
[12] I disagree with Benton's contention that Marx and Engels themselves fell prey to this kind of over-reaction. See Burkett 1998a.
[13] O'Connor 1998.
[14] Polanyi 1944.

crisis. But whatever its paedagogical advantages, the dominant position of the two contradictions model has, arguably, crowded out any serious Marxist engagement with ecological economics – all the more so insofar as this model does not itself embody such an engagement.[15]

The basic idea motivating O'Connor's two contradictions framework is that Marxism does not adequately account for the natural and social conditions of production (this is merely asserted, not demonstrated). Conditions of production are, accordingly, grafted onto a Marxian model of accumulation and crisis. More specifically, any deterioration in the quality of the conditions of production is said to raise firms' costs, both directly and via the efforts of environmental movements to force firms to help finance government programmes that maintain and/or repair these conditions. This functionalist grafting approach to a red-green political economy helps explain why O'Connor's major work cites ecological economists, such as Nicholas Georgescu-Roegen and Juan Martinez-Alier, mainly in order to endorse their criticisms of classical Marxism, not to critically engage with their substantive analyses.[16] Indeed, the conventional wisdom among ecosocialists now seems to be that classical Marxism, as represented by Marx and Engels, is seriously flawed ecologically unless augmented with, and even largely supplanted by, a 'Polanyian' analysis of the conditions of production together with certain elements of green theory. The French ecosocialist Alain Lipietz thus argues that 'the general structure, the intellectual scaffolding of the Marxist paradigm, along with the key solutions it suggests, must be jettisoned'.[17] Insofar as ecosocialists have followed this advice and moved away from Marxism, the

---

[15] As one symptom of this crowding-out effect, consider that a special issue of *Capital & Class* dedicated to 'environmental politics: analyses and alternatives' found no space for any discussion of ecological economics, but did include two extended engagements with O'Connor's two contradictions framework (*Capital & Class* 2000). For my own critical appreciation of O'Connor's work, see Burkett 1999a, pp. 193–7, and 1999b.

[16] O'Connor 1998. According to John Bellamy Foster, this kind of grafting operation characterises the 'first stage' of ecosocialism, with the still germinating 'second stage' involving a more thoroughgoing reconstruction of both Marxism and ecology. Second-stage ecosocialism 'seeks to go back to Marx and to understand the ecological context of his materialism – as a means of critically engaging with and transcending existing green theory'. Foster 2001, p. 463.

[17] Lipietz 2000, p. 75. For my response to Lipietz's arguments for 'jettisoning' Marxism, see Burkett 2000.

likelihood of an in-depth Marxist engagement with ecological economics has been greatly reduced.

From the side of ecological economics, any potential dialogue has been greatly hindered by the above-mentioned tendency to exclude Marxism from the discipline almost by *fiat*. A strong force behind this exclusionary tendency has been Martinez-Alier's influential history of ecological economics, which argues that, beginning with Marx and Engels, Marxists have distanced themselves from the discipline by refusing to analyse the forces of production from an ecological, and especially energetic, point of view.[18] Martinez-Alier's critique of Marxism has become standard fare among ecological economists and even among ecosocialists – in both cases hampering a serious dialogue with Marxism.[19]

This *a priori* exclusion of Marxism from ecological economics has interacted with the pluralism otherwise practised by the discipline to produce an additional barrier to dialogue: the infiltration of neoclassical visions and concepts into ecological economics. Ecological economists have strongly criticised neoclassical theory for downplaying natural limits to growth; but the basic neoclassical supply and demand framework, with its underpinnings in marginal utility and marginal productivity theory, is still accepted (with qualifications) by many if not most members of the discipline. And even those members that reject the neoclassical market model have not subjected it to an immanent critique rooted in the organic linkages between generalised market valuation and the relations of production. The exclusion of Marxism from ecological economics (which is partly an exclusion self-imposed by Marxists, to be sure) has undoubtedly further weakened the anti-market current within the discipline compared to the pro-market current, which has, in turn, enabled neoclassical theory to gain a stronger foothold in the discipline than it would have otherwise.

Insofar as ecological economics has come under the influence of neoclassicism's undiluted allegiance to an abstract-ideal market model, the

---

[18] Martinez-Alier 1987.

[19] Martinez-Alier's influence within ecosocialist circles is reinforced by his prominent presence as an editor of, and regular contributor to, *Capitalism, Nature, Socialism*. The only serious engagement with ecological economics to appear in this journal is built around a sympathetic account of Martinez-Alier's history of the discipline (Rosewarne 1995).

discipline's commitment to a historically open approach to policymaking and institutional change has been undercut. One form this has taken is the relegation of anti-market positions to the realm of ecological ethics and politics, with the economic arena as such reserved mainly for technocratic analyses that take the market framework and monetary valuation as natural elements of reality to which ecological visions and policies must adapt themselves, however critically and grudgingly. As a result, neoclassical conceptions of the market, money, value, capital, and growth have increasingly served as the initial points of analytical departure even for anti-market and anti-neoclassical theorists; these conceptions have thus tended to channel the discipline's research agenda in certain 'safe' directions. This process has been reinforced by the ability of neoclassical theory to adapt itself to ecological considerations in relatively shallow ways that nonetheless appear to offer promising areas of research in which members of the discipline can at least 'make a difference'.[20] All of this has undercut the ability and the inclination of ecological economics to draw upon the more radical insights that Marxism can provide.

However, the same developments have also caused the tension between neoclassicism and the aspirations of ecological economics towards real interdisciplinarity, pluralism, and historical openness to become ever more glaring.[21] They have also highlighted the ecological shortcomings of neoclassical theory itself which, with its reduction of all efficiency and welfare to the uni-dimensional terms of money and 'utility', presents an incredibly impoverished vision of human development and its co-evolution with nature. And, as the systemic character of many environmental crises, and the class character of many ecological conflicts, have become more apparent, the limpness of a theoretical vision based on materially and socially ungrounded utility-maximising individuals has become ever more obvious. A growing number of ecological economists are forthrightly rejecting the neoclassical vision, together with the hegemony of market competition and monetary valuation, in favour of explicitly communal conceptions of production, resource-allocation and human development. To demonstrate the potential contribution of

---

[20] Rosewarne 1995. For a broader analysis of neoclassicism's ability to co-opt non-neoclassical economists and social scientists in general, thereby displacing alternative approaches, see Fine 2002.
[21] Spash 1999.

materialist class analysis to this growing rebellion within ecological economics is one of the prime goals of this book.

Another short-term factor that helped determine the timing of this book is the recent development of research on the ecological content of classical Marxism. This research has made it clear that Marx and Engels's engagement with the natural sciences was more intensive and extensive than anyone could have previously imagined.[22] Natural science, including what is now known as ecological analysis, played an essential role in the development of Marx and Engels's materialist approach to history in general and capitalism in particular.[23] And the most influential prejudices against Marx and Engels among ecological thinkers – that they ignored natural limits, championed human domination of nature, embraced an anti-ecological industrialism, downplayed capitalism's reliance on materials and energy, and reduced wealth to labour – have all been thoroughly debunked.[24] The air having been cleared of these quick and easy excuses for non-engagement, now is the time to initiate a real dialogue between Marxism and ecological economics.

III. An overview

The topical sequence of this book follows the four issues mentioned earlier: value, natural capital, entropy, and sustainable development. All the chapters try to demonstrate how Marxism can contribute to the aspirations of ecological economics for methodological pluralism, interdisciplinarity, and historical openness.

The first two chapters deal with the question of nature and economic value. Chapter 1 uses Marx's critique of the physiocrats to interpret alternative views on nature's value within ecological economics. The physiocrats are relevant insofar as their concept of value is a complex hybrid of the views held by different schools of thought within contemporary ecological economics. Marx's critique helps reveal a common inability of ecological economists to

---

[22] Baksi 1996, and 2001.
[23] Griese and Pawelzeig 1995; Foster 2000a; Foster and Burkett 2004; Burkett and Foster 2006. In light of recent studies, there can be no doubt that Marx and Engels would endorse Herman Daly's statement that 'the ultimate subject matter of biology and economics is *one, viz., the life process*'. Daly 1968, p. 392 [emphasis in original].
[24] Burkett 1996a, 1996b, 1997, 1998a, 1998b, and 1999a; Foster 1995.

fundamentally criticise market valuation, due to their failure to link nature's monetary valuation to the underlying relations of production. Materialist class analysis helps alleviate this problem through its distinction between value and use-value, and its clear demonstration that generalised market valuation is rooted in the commodification of labour-power based on the separation of the producers from necessary conditions of production, starting with the land.

Chapter 2 discusses how pro-ecological norms can be brought into an ecological value analysis framed by capitalism's specific class relations. The vehicle used to address this question is a qualitative survey of contingent valuation (CV) studies. In these studies, people are asked to put a price tag on certain parts of the environment, or on certain actions to maintain or improve it. The chapter first suggests that CV analysis, including its roots in neoclassical utility theory, is a form of commodity fetishism in the sense of Marx. At the same time, it is shown that a Marxist analysis of capitalistic alienation and of workers' resistance to it can help explain the resistance to monetary valuation of nature that is often revealed by peoples' individual and group responses to CV surveys. Marxism thus helps strengthen the anti-market current within ecological economics, thereby contributing to the discipline's methodological pluralism and its openness to a greater diversity of (non-market) institutions and policies, including the use of deliberative democracy and multi-criteria decision-making procedures as suggested by political-philosophical critics of CV analysis.

The next two chapters consider the lively debate among ecological economists over the concept of natural capital. This controversy is interpreted from the standpoint of the tension between methodological pluralism and neoclassical 'economic imperialism' within the discipline. Chapter 3 traces natural capital to its origins in the neoclassical sustainable growth literature, and shows that its analytical weaknesses – especially its purely instrumental treatment of natural resources, and its failure to specify production in social-relational terms – are carried over to non-neoclassical attempts to theorise sustainability as maintenance of natural capital stocks. This helps explain why natural capital has been strongly resisted by many ecological economists, despite its pedagogical convenience and despite efforts by powerful members of the discipline to make it a defining concept of ecological economics. As Chapter 4 shows, this resistance has questioned the basic building blocks of natural-capital theory: the reduction of nature to an aggregate stock of productive assets; the monetary valuation of natural resources; and the definition of sustainable development in non-social-relational terms as simply sustainable growth of wealth in general. Marxism, with its critical analysis of how the social relations of production underpin nature's capitalisation in theory and practice, can strengthen the resistance to natural capital, thereby preventing its anti-pluralistic installation as a new orthodoxy within ecological economics.

Another important controversy within ecological economics concerns the economic significance of the second law of thermodynamics, also known as the entropy law. After outlining the entropic economics of Nicholas Georgescu-Roegen and Herman Daly, Chapter 5 charts the ensuing entropy debate along four distinct sub-controversies or tracks, which respectively involve: (i) the ability of human production to purposefully 'fix' matter-energy in useful forms; (ii) the impossibility of defining the 'usefulness' of matter-energy apart from human purposes; (iii) the possibility of complete, or practically complete, recycling of material resources; (iv) the extent to which market prices reflect, or can be made to reflect, scarcities of low-entropy matter-energy. It is shown that the development of all four tracks has been hampered by the absence of a class perspective on production and its natural conditions. For example, the economic usefulness of low-entropy matter-energy depends, as a matter of definition, on the priorities served by production. In the Marxist view, the market's valuation of entropy is limited by the class-exploitative and alienated character of production, and this is reflected, paradoxically, in the system's ability to reproduce itself (with periodic interruptions due to materials-supply crises) in spite of its accelerated entropic degradation of the conditions of human development. The Marxist perspective on the economy-entropy connection thus poses a dialectical distinction between sustainable development and sustainable capitalism. This distinction provides ecological economics with a new perspective on the need for an explicit communalisation of production and its natural conditions.

Chapter 6 further demonstrates Marxism's ability to address energy and entropic questions by reconsidering Marx and Engels's reaction to Sergei Podolinsky's attempt to ground socialist theory in the first law of thermodynamics. While many ecological economists have accepted Martinez-Alier's argument that Marx and Engels ignored or dismissed Podolinsky's work, thereby setting Marxism on a course neglectful of energy and other ecological issues, recent research by John Bellamy Foster and the present author has severely undercut this argument.[25] This research is based on, among other things, the first complete English-language translation of Podolinsky's work in the form in which it was read by Engels, as well as Marx's newly discovered excerpt-notes from a draft sent to him by Podolinsky.[26] The evidence now shows that Marx and Engels took Podolinsky's seriously enough to subject it to a systematic critique. More specifically, Engels rejected the energy-reductionist elements of Podolinsky's analysis, pointed out the need to take fuller account of the depletion of non-renewable energy sources in human production, and highlighted Podolinsky's failure to fully integrate environmental and class-relational concerns. Moreover, compared to Podolinsky, who reduced production to the 'accumulation of energy on the earth', Engels's reaction is much more sensitive to entropic constraints on human production under both capitalism and socialism.

Chapter 6 goes on to explain that Marx's analysis of capitalism, especially in *Capital*, already answers the questions raised (or thought to be raised) by Podolinsky's work. First, it is shown that Marx applies a metabolic-energy approach to capitalist exploitation that recognises both conservation of energy and matter-energy dissipation. In other words, the consistency of this exploitation with the first and second laws of thermodynamics is already established by Marx. Second, it is demonstrated that open-system thermodynamic and metabolic considerations are absolutely central to Marx's analysis of machinery and large-scale industry – so central that Marx was able to provide a class-based explanation as to how and why human production definitively 'broke the budget constraint of living on solar income and began to live on geological capital'.[27] Third, Engels's criticisms of Podolinsky are shown to follow the spirit and the letter of Marx's metabolic open-system analysis of capitalist production and exploitation.

The book's final four chapters reconsider the notion of sustainable development by employing the Marxist distinction between environmental crises of capital accumulation (for example, materials-supply crises) versus

---

[25] Martinez-Alier 1987; Martinez-Alier and Naredo 1982; Foster and Burkett 2004; Burkett and Foster 2006.

[26] Podolinsky 2004; Marx forthcoming.

[27] Daly 1992a, p. 23.

crises in the natural conditions of human development. Chapter 7 uses this distinction to develop a critique of James Boyce's power-inequality model.[28] Boyce's model basically extends the Environmental Kuznets Curve (EKC), or inverted-U relation between real income per capita and pollution, by arguing that increased inequality is associated with worsening environmental conditions for any given level of real income per capita. Lyle Scruggs has argued that the connection between inequality and environmental degradation is much more complex and ambiguous than Boyce suggests.[29] From a Marxist perspective, however, the conceptual and empirical difficulties with the EKC, the power-inequality model, *and* Scruggs's critique can be traced to their common failure to root power inequalities and environmental conditions in the economy's relations of production. Indeed, all three analyses uncritically adopt the neoclassical notion of pollution as simply an external effect of market activity.

Chapter 8 intervenes in the controversy among ecological economists regarding the applicability of Sraffian modelling to ecological crises and conflicts. I argue that a Marxian focus on production relations, and the corollary distinction between crises of capital accumulation and crises of human development, sheds light on the ecological shortcomings of Sraffian analysis. The argument proceeds on two levels: a critical review of the methodological issues raised by the Sraffian theory of reproduction prices, and then a detailed critique of the influential eco-Sraffian analyses of Charles Perrings and Martin O'Connor.[30]

Chapter 9 first shows that even some Marxist analyses do not consistently distinguish the environmental conditions required by capitalism from the conditions of sustainable human development. The chapter then explains how a more holistically Marxist approach can distinguish the two kinds of environmental crisis in a way that brings in pro-ecological values, but without relying on exogenous value judgements. This involves Marx's projection of the human developmental constraints and possibilities created by capitalism's 'metabolic rift' between the producers and natural conditions.[31] This rift can

[28] Boyce 1994, and 2002.
[29] Scruggs 1998.
[30] Perrings 1987; O'Connor 1993a.
[31] Foster 2000a.

only be overcome through a revolutionary struggle by workers and their communities to establish a communal system of user rights and responsibilities *vis-à-vis* the conditions of production – one that converts these conditions into conditions of free human development. Accordingly, Chapter 10 shows how the classical-Marxist conception of communism, with its vision of production relations as relations of human development, integrates three dimensions of sustainable development that have been more or less separately envisioned by ecological economists: (i) the 'common pool' character of natural resources; (ii) co-evolution of individual human beings, society, and nature; (iii) common property management of natural resources.

Chapter One
The Value Problem in Ecological Economics: Lessons from the Physiocrats and Marx

One's view of nature's economic value helps shape one's conceptions of nature's role in production and of environmental crises. Given the difficult issues raised by the question of economic value, however, nature's value in particular has long vexed economists. This applies especially to contemporary ecological economics, which 'addresses the relationships between eco-systems and economic systems in the broadest sense'.[1] Nonetheless, from the diverse disciplinary and methodological perspectives within ecological economics, two broad positions on nature's value seem to have emerged as dominant. One ascribes value directly to natural resources. While this position has been led by the energy-value school, it also includes eco-Sraffian and ecosocialist theorists who argue that monetary exchange-values (prices and profits) largely or fully represent the values extracted from nature in general. Opposing such natural-value analyses is a second broad perspective that focuses on nature – especially low-entropy matter and energy – as an objective condition or basis for value defined as psychic income or 'enjoyment of

---

[1] Costanza 1989, p. 1.

life'. The present chapter interprets this value controversy from the standpoint of Marx's critique of the physiocrats.

Marx's engagement with the physiocrats focuses on the issue of nature and economic value; yet it has gone unnoticed by the contemporary nature-valuation debate. Accordingly, after Section I's outline of the competing views of ecological economists on nature's value, Section II recounts the basic elements of physiocratic value theory together with Marx's critique. It is shown that physiocratic value theory is a complex hybrid of the positions held by ecological economists. Interestingly, Marx criticised the physiocrats not for emphasising nature as a source of wealth or use-value, but for conflating *capitalist* value with its natural basis. Indeed, he critically incorporated important elements of physiocracy into his own analysis of value and capital accumulation.

Section III applies Marx's analysis of the physiocrats to the controversy among ecological economists regarding nature's value. It is argued that, like the physiocrats, both sides in this debate do not adequately consider the relations between use-value, capitalist production relations, and market valuation. As a result, both sides are fundamentally uncritical toward market forms of nature valuation. Section IV concludes by suggesting that Marx's class-based approach to nature, value, and use-value provides a potential way out of this analytical impasse.

I. Nature's value: views of ecological economists

Ecological economists share a deep concern with the role of limited natural conditions in human production.[2] By contrast with neoclassical economics, they insist that production is dependent on unproducible resources which cannot be substituted for by human labour and technology. The main issue in the value debate among ecological economists is whether ascribing economic value directly to nature is the most logical and useful way to build this concern with limited natural conditions into analyses of contemporary environmental problems.

---

[2] Costanza 1989; Daly 1992a; Hay 2002, pp. 233–42.

Nature as a direct source of value

One group of ecological economists treats nature as a direct source and substance of value. This line of thinking has been led by the 'embodied-energy' theorists, who argue that the 'primary input' into production is energy. Since '"free" or "available" energy' is required for the production of all goods and services, and cannot be substituted for by other inputs, it is viewed as 'the only "basic" commodity and . . . ultimately the only "scarce" factor of production':[3]

> An energy theory of value posits that, at least at the global scale, free or
> available energy from the sun (plus past solar energy stored as fossil fuels
> and residual heat from the earth's core) are the only 'primary' inputs to the
> system. Labor, manufactured capital, and natural capital are 'intermediate
> inputs'. Thus, one could base a theory of value on the use in production of
> available energy.[4]

The presumption here is that 'a production-based theory that can explain exchange-values' must grant a logical or chronological primacy to one particular input of material production.[5] It is also presumed that the main purpose of value theory is to 'explain exchange-values [market prices] in economic systems'.[6] In short, the embodied-energy theory 'is really a cost of production theory with all costs carried back to the solar energy necessary directly and indirectly to produce them'.[7] The approach closely and consciously parallels the Ricardian labour-embodied theory of value, with energy replacing labour as the primary factor of production.[8]

Given the parallel just mentioned, it is not surprising that one of the main methods used to test the energy theory has been the Sraffian input-output

---

[3] Farber, Costanza and Wilson 2002, p. 382.
[4] Farber, Costanza and Wilson 2002, p. 383. For similar statements along these lines, see Hannon 1973, pp. 139–40; Costanza 1980, pp. 1219–20, and 1981a, p. 122; Gowdy 1991, pp. 80–1; Deléage 1994, p. 44; and Salleh 1997, p. 155. Mirowski 1988 provides a critical history of energy-value theories.
[5] Farber, Costanza and Wilson 2002, p. 382.
[6] Farber, Costanza and Wilson 2002, p. 383. To anticipate, this view of the nature and purposes of value analysis is most definitely *not* shared by Marx, however much it may have affected the classical economists, including Ricardo.
[7] Costanza 1980, p. 1224.
[8] Farber, Costanza and Wilson 2002, pp. 376–7, 382–3.

analysis of price determination.[9] Indeed, Kozo Mayumi has shown that the embodied energy input-output framework is formally identical to the Sraffa system expressed in current and dated labour terms.[10] The only difference is that the energy system replaces the direct and indirect labour requirements of the various sectors' outputs with their direct and indirect *energy* requirements.[11] Applying the energy accounting framework to US data, the energy analysts have found strong statistical correlations between the monetary values of sectoral outputs and the amounts of energy directly and indirectly embodied in these outputs.[12] Other, more aggregative analyses investigate the correlation between the total energy consumed by national production (controlling for fuel quality as proxied by the shares of energy obtained from different sources) and monetary value added as measured by GDP or GNP. Such studies have found relatively stable or at least predictable ratios of aggregate energy consumption to aggregate monetary value added in the United States and other industrialised economies.[13]

Although three proponents conclude that the 'energy theory of value . . . seems to be the only reasonably successful attempt to operationalize a general biophysical theory of value',[14] the approach 'has been strongly criticized for its failure to recognize the importance of unique characteristics of matter and the operation of "other" factors in the economic system apart from energy constraints'.[15] This rejection of 'energy as the sole cause of value' has developed along three analytical tracks.[16]

Opposing the purported 'convergence between the Neo-Ricardian and embodied energy approaches to economic valuation',[17] the first track uses Sraffian input-output models to analyse the determination of market exchange-values (and related issues of distributional conflict and economic crises), but without treating any *single primary input* as the unique source of value.[18] From

---

[9] Sraffa 1960.
[10] Mayumi 2001, pp. 65–6.
[11] Compare Judson 1989, pp. 267–8.
[12] Costanza 1980, and 1981a.
[13] Cleveland et al. 1984; Kaufmann 1992.
[14] Farber, Costanza and Wilson 2002, p. 384.
[15] Judson 1989, p. 266.
[16] Judson 1989, p. 268.
[17] Judson 1989, p. 267.
[18] See, for example, Perrings 1987; Gowdy 1988; O'Connor 1993a; Martinez-Alier 1995b; Martinez-Alier and O'Connor 1996; O'Connor and Martinez-Alier 1998.

the perspective of these models, the notion of energy as *the* prime factor of production hinges on external presumptions about the reproducibility of other factors – specifically the arbitrary reduction of their reproduction to pure energetics.[19]

One cannot use Sraffian models to argue 'that labour creates value and is exploited, rather than any other input, e.g., corn, iron or energy'.[20] In the same way, Sraffian analysis provides some support for those who argue that ecological economics should 'do without a general theory of value' in the sense of uniquely ascribing value to energy or any other 'primary input'.[21] The eco-Sraffian view thus posits that production and monetary exchange-values depend upon 'labor, resources, and environmental services' in all their physical and biological diversity.[22] In this broader sense, it still treats nature as a direct source of value.

A second track is interested in generalising the Marxist theory of exploitation to include the exploitation not just of labour, but of nature as well. Since Marx's analysis of labour-exploitation is developed in terms of the category surplus-value, this ecosocialist project has necessarily involved the treatment of nature itself as a source of value and surplus-value. However, these ecosocialists, unlike the energy-value theorists, do not conceptualise natural resource use in purely energetic terms; or they, at least, argue that production is reducible to energy processing only at a highly abstract level. In their view, nature-exploitation involves the extraction of profit from biologically and physically variegated eco-systems; it thus calls not for an energy theory of value but for a genuinely 'biophysical' or 'bioenergetic' theory of value.[23]

---

[19] This conclusion may seem harsh; but consider Costanza's response to the observation that value analysis 'could do the same thing we have done with energy with any of the other currently defined primary factors. We could thus support capital, labor or government service theories of value. The answer is that on paper we could. We must look to physical reality to determine which factors are net inputs and which are internal transactions. Can any one seriously suggest that labor creates sunlight?' (Costanza 1981a, p. 140). Similarly, Hannon, after paying lip-service to the various 'natural inputs to the economy, such as water, minerals, soil (erosion) and sunlight', constructs a price analysis presuming 'only one net input, absorbed sunlight', so that 'metabolic factor costs' can be identified with 'absorbed energy units . . . per unit of product' (Hannon 1998, pp. 269, 273).

[20] Saad-Filho 2002, p. 24.

[21] Martinez-Alier and Naredo 1982, p. 219.

[22] Gowdy 1988, p. 38.

[23] Deléage 1994, pp. 48–50; Salleh 1997, p. 154.

Skirbekk, for example, argues that insofar as capitalism takes more wealth out of nature than it puts back in, it is 'an extractive form of production' in which 'value is transferred from resources to profits'.[24] He suggests that this 'extractive surplus profit' allows 'the entire production process, at all levels' to 'receive more value . . . than the labor itself has created'.[25] Such value extraction then takes the form of increased monetary incomes for capitalists and/or workers, with these higher incomes obtained at the expense of 'nature, and, indirectly, future generations'.[26] On similar grounds, Brennan argues that capitalism exploits nature whenever 'natural substances' are 'used up faster than they can reproduce themselves'.[27]

Nature as a basis for 'enjoyment of life'

The third track rejecting energy-value analysis has been led by the renowned ecological economists Nicholas Georgescu-Roegen and Herman Daly. Their critique has two components. First, like the first two tracks, Georgescu-Roegen and Daly argue against the reduction of production to energetics. They point out that production of useful goods and services involves not only energy but also qualitatively diverse material stocks and flows, and this makes variegated forms of purposeful human activity and ingenuity – of labour, science, and technology – essential elements of the process.[28] While all production requires energy, 'matter matters, too' in the irreducible sense that 'at the macro-level no practical procedure exists for converting energy into matter or matter of whatever form into energy'.[29] Secondly, and unlike the first two tracks, Georgescu-Roegen and Daly do not ascribe economic value directly to nature. Instead, they treat nature as one essential basis or condition (along with human activity and human knowledge) for the production of

---

[24] Skirbekk 1994, p. 100.
[25] Ibid.
[26] Skirbekk 1994, p. 101.
[27] Brennan 1997, p. 185.
[28] Daly 1992a, pp. 216–17. Along the same lines, Stern (1999, p. 392) argues that 'a biophysical theory of value formation needs to account for the use of knowledge in the creation of economic value and should not limit itself to the role of energy alone'.
[29] Georgescu-Roegen 1979b, p. 1040; compare Daly 1992a, p. 25.

goods and services which enhance value, with value defined in immaterial use-value terms as 'enjoyment of life'.[30]

Georgescu-Roegen and Daly develop these two points largely through an application of the laws of thermodynamics, starting with the observation that the economy 'neither produces nor consumes matter-energy; it only absorbs matter-energy and throws it out continuously'.[31] Appealing to the entropy law, they argue that production involves the conversion of matter and energy from more ordered (and thus more useful) forms into less ordered (and less useful) forms.[32] In short, 'the ultimate usable stuff of the universe is low-entropy matter-energy . . . and it exists in two forms: a terrestrial stock and a solar flow', both of which are limited (even if some stocks of low-entropy matter-energy are 'renewable on a human time scale').[33] Low-entropy matter-energy thus appears as the ultimate input of, and constraint on, production – implying that, at some point, the global economy will have to adjust to a 'steady-state' in order to ensure its own reproducibility.[34]

Georgescu-Roegen and Daly recognise that the economy, as a system of provision, cannot be reduced to purely physical, entropic, terms. As Georgescu-Roegen puts it, 'it would be a great mistake to think that [production] may be represented by a vast system of thermodynamic equations. . . . The entropic process moves through an intricate web of anthropomorphic categories, of utility and labor, above all'.[35] Similarly, Daly observes that 'all low entropy cannot be treated alike', insofar as alternative low-entropy matter-energy sources differ greatly in terms of their appropriateness for the qualitatively diverse material and energy conversions required by human production and consumption.[36]

---

[30] Georgescu-Roegen 1973, p. 53, and 1979b, p. 1042; Daly 1981, p. 168, and 1992a, p. 36.

[31] Georgescu-Roegen 1973, p. 50.

[32] 'From the viewpoint of thermodynamics, matter-energy enters the economic process in a state of *low entropy* and comes out of it in a state of *high entropy*' (Georgescu-Roegen 1973, p. 51 [emphasis in original]).

[33] Daly 1992a, p. 21.

[34] Georgescu-Roegen 1973, pp. 53–4, 58; Daly 1974.

[35] Georgescu-Roegen 1979b, p. 1042.

[36] Daly 1992a, p. 25.

Accordingly, Georgescu-Roegen and Daly do not define *value* in terms of the primacy of any one or several factors of production. For them, the value of any production derives from its satisfaction of human needs and wants, although this end-product must be adjusted for the costs of its production. From their perspective, the 'true product' of production 'is not a physical flow of dissipated matter and energy, but the enjoyment of life – account being also taken of the drudgery of labor'.[37] Value thus derives from the 'psychic income' or 'immaterial flux' generated by production, even though low-entropy matter-energy *and* purposeful human labour are its fundamental preconditions.[38] Stated differently: 'Service (net psychic income) is the final benefit of economic activity. Throughput (an entropic physical flow) is the final cost'.[39]

II. Nature, wealth and value in the physiocrats and Marx

Despite their view that 'the land is the unique source of wealth',[40] the physiocrats have received little attention in the value controversy among ecological economists. Cleveland suggests that the physiocrats' 'steadfast belief that Nature was the source of wealth became a recurring theme throughout biophysical economics'; but he does not elaborate on the parallel.[41] Georgescu-Roegen characterises physiocratic doctrine (referring specifically to Quesnay's *Tableau Économique*) as an 'analytico-physiological approach', meaning 'a manifest endeavour to submit the economic phenomena to a physiological analysis akin to that of biology'.[42] But he does not relate this methodological description to the question of nature's value. Similarly, in a sketch of 'historical roots for ecological economics', Christensen includes the physiocrats (along with other pre-classical and classical economists) among

---

[37] Georgescu-Roegen 1979b, p. 1042. 'Value derives from the enjoyment of life, and there is more to life than energy. . . . For example, there is material, there is time, there is purpose, there is beauty. These things all affect value without bearing any determinate relation to energy' (Daly 1981, p. 168).

[38] Daly 1992a, pp. 31–6; Georgescu-Roegen 1973, p. 53.

[39] Daly 1992a, p. 36.

[40] Quesnay 1963d, p. 232.

[41] Cleveland 1987, p. 50.

[42] Georgescu-Roegen 1976, p. 236.

those who showed 'an early attention to the physical side of economic activity' by using a 'reproductive' approach that 'regarded production in terms of the transformation of materials and food taken from the land'.[43] He does not consider value-theoretical questions, however, despite his assertion that Sraffian analysis is the logical heir to this earlier 'reproductive' tradition.[44]

Apart from the general view among 'most economists' that 'the Physiocrats represent an historical curiosity' and nothing more,[45] perhaps the main reason for their marginalisation from the nature-value debate is the dominant role played by thermodynamics and the energy theory of value in this debate. Indeed, that the physiocrats pre-date the development of the laws of thermodynamics may help explain why they have been largely written out of the history not only of ecological value analysis but of ecological economics in general. Thus, Martinez-Alier's influential history of ecological economics focuses exclusively on those economists who 'counted calories'; it therefore begins in the mid-1860s, 'at a time when the laws of thermodynamics had been established' – the idea being that 'not much is lost analytically by focusing on the use of energy as the central point in ecological economics'.[46] If one does not embrace this energy-reductionist view of the subject, then the physiocrats and the lessons to be learned from them could loom much larger.

The physiocrats on value and nature[47]

Physiocratic value theory was based on the land's unique capacity to generate means of subsistence.[48] For the physiocrats, non-agricultural production involves increases in the usefulness of the material means of subsistence created by agriculture – 'increase[s] brought about *by combining* raw materials with expenditure on the consumption of things which were in existence prior

---

[43] Christensen 1989, p. 18.

[44] Christensen 1989, pp. 33–4.

[45] Cleveland 1987, p. 50.

[46] Martinez-Alier 1987, p. 2.

[47] See Burkett 2003b (and references therein) for further discussion of the historical background and policy implications of physiocratic thought. Burkett 2004 offers an ecological interpretation of Quesnay's *Tableau Économique* in relation to Marx's schemes of reproduction.

[48] Christensen 1994, pp. 271–3.

to this kind of increase'.[49] In this sense, non-agricultural production is 'an *adding together* of items of wealth which are combined with one another'.[50] Agriculture, by contrast, entails an actual *'generation* or creation of wealth', insofar as it 'constitutes a renewal and *real* [material] increase of renascent wealth'.[51] In fact, the physiocrats identified both real wealth and economic value with the 'subsistence and prime materials' generated by the land.[52] As Turgot says, 'the earth . . . is always the first and only source of all wealth; it is that which as the result of cultivation produces all the revenue; it is that also which has provided the first fund of advances prior to all cultivation . . .'.[53]

From this perspective, only agriculture can produce a 'net product' or 'superfluity' of material means of subsistence over the amount required for the subsistence of the agricultural labourer.[54] However, even though this surplus is 'a pure gift' of nature, its production depends upon human labour and ingenuity.[55] The net product 'is the physical result of the fertility of the soil, and of the wisdom, far more than the laboriousness, of the means . . . employed to render it fertile'.[56] It is thus 'the labour of the Husbandman' which 'produces more than his wants' and which appears as the source of an 'independent and disposable' surplus 'which the land gives as a pure gift to him who cultivates it'.[57] The physiocrats thus treat agricultural labour as the *prime mover* of 'the sequence of the labors divided among the different members of society'.[58] This is a 'primacy . . . of *physical necessity*' in the sense that the material subsistence of non-agricultural labourers depends on the ability of the agricultural labourer to 'produce over and above the wages of his labour'.[59] Since agriculture alone can yield a surplus of material means

---

[49] Quesnay 1963b, p. 207 (emphasis in original).
[50] Ibid.
[51] Ibid.
[52] Christensen 1994, p. 272.
[53] Turgot 1898, p. 46.
[54] Turgot 1898, p. 9.
[55] Turgot 1898, p. 9. Quesnay qualifies this for the case of early peoples who 'were able to consume the spontaneous gifts of nature without making any effort', although even here such consumption had to be preceded by the labour of hunting and gathering (Quesnay 1963a, p. 60).
[56] Turgot 1898, p. 14.
[57] Ibid.
[58] Turgot 1898, p. 9.
[59] Ibid. (emphasis in original).

of subsistence, 'it is . . . the labour of the Husbandman which imparts the first impulse' to the social division of labour: that 'circulation, which, by the reciprocal exchange of wants, renders men necessary to one another and forms the bond of the society'.[60]

It is true that cultivators and non-agricultural 'artisans' are 'equally industrious'; but the cultivators' labour 'produces, or rather draws from the land, riches which are continually springing up afresh, and which supply the whole society with its subsistence and with the materials for all its needs'.[61] Artisans, on the other hand, are merely 'occupied in giving to materials thus produced the preparations and the forms which render them suitable for the use of men'.[62] In short, 'the Husbandman gathers, beyond his subsistence, a wealth which is independent and disposable, which he has not bought and which he sells', while, in material terms, non-agricultural workers produce 'only their livelihood' through their processing of the material wealth provided by agriculture.[63]

Allowing for the distinction between agricultural workers and landowners, the physiocrats' famous division of society into the productive, proprietary, and sterile classes follows immediately from their basic vision of wealth production. The productive class is, of course, 'that which brings about the regeneration of the nation's wealth through the cultivation of its territory'.[64] 'The class of proprietors' or landowners 'subsists on the revenue or *net product* of cultivation'.[65] Finally, the *'sterile class* is composed of all the citizens who are engaged in providing other services or doing other work than that of agriculture, and whose expenses are paid by the productive class, and by the class of proprietors, which itself draws its revenue from the productive class'.[66]

Quesnay presumed self-employed artisans and thus did not distinguish non-agricultural workers and capitalists. Turgot made explicit the division of the sterile or 'stipendiary' class into 'capitalist undertakers and simple

---

[60] Turgot 1898, p. 7.
[61] Turgot 1898, p. 10.
[62] Ibid.
[63] Turgot 1898, p. 9.
[64] Quesnay 1963c, p. 150.
[65] Ibid. (emphasis in original).
[66] Ibid.

workmen'.[67] Both argued on Malthusian-type grounds that competition among workers limits agricultural and non-agricultural wages to subsistence levels; hence 'the two working or non-disposable classes' receive only 'the recompense of their labour'.[68] Since, in the physiocrats' material-flows perspective, 'there is no revenue save the net produce of lands', the amount of wealth the cultivator 'causes the land to produce beyond his personal wants' is 'the only fund for the wages which [non-agricultural workers] receive in exchange for their labour. The latter, in making use of the price of this exchange to buy in their turn the products of the Husbandman, only return to him exactly what they have received from him'.[69] Similarly, all non-agricultural profit 'is either paid by the revenue, or forms part of the expenditure which serves to produce the revenue'.[70]

The physiocrats, the nature-valuation debate, and Marx

Physiocracy represents an interesting hybrid of the different views held by present-day ecological economists on nature's value. The physiocrats, like the (energy, eco-Sraffian, and ecosocialist) natural-value theorists, see nature as a direct source of economic value. On the other hand, the physiocratic notion that the land's surplus-producing capability is the prime mover of wealth production is echoed by both the energy-value theory and the Georgescu-Roegen/Daly 'enjoyment of life' approach, which find an ultimate net input in energy and 'low-entropy matter-energy', respectively. However, since Georgescu-Roegen and Daly do not see the primary net input as the sole basis of *value*, they would not endorse the physiocratic argument that agriculture is the sole source of a net *value* product. Nonetheless, both Georgescu-Roegen and Daly *and* the physiocrats see human activity as more than a separate physical input to wealth production: in both visions, human labour and ingenuity are crucial to the unleashing of nature's material-energetic productivity and its conversion into useful goods and services. It is just that the physiocrats do not originate economic value with 'enjoyment of life' but rather with material means of subsistence. In other words, they find the

---

[67] Turgot 1898, p. 54.
[68] Turgot 1898, p. 15.
[69] Turgot 1898, pp. 7–8, 96.
[70] Turgot 1898, p. 96.

proximate basis of value in the *material conditions and substance* of human life, not in this life's psychic 'enjoyment'.

What distinguishes Marx from both the physiocrats and the contemporary nature valuation debate is his definition of 'value' as capitalism's specific form of economic valuation. For Marx, *real wealth or use-value* is anything that satisfies human needs, whereas *value* is the specific social representation of use-value under capitalism, a system in which use-values are *generally* exchanged as commodities, that is, as exchange-values. Marx thus insists that value relations, including the various tensions between use-value and exchange-value, be analysed in terms of capitalism's specific relations of production. In Marx's view, capitalism reduces value to the homogenous, socially necessary labour time objectified in commodities. Marx sees this reduction as an outgrowth of the social separation of the labourers from the land and other necessary conditions of production, upon which basis social production becomes mainly organised through market relations among competing enterprises employing wage-labour for a profit. In other words, the reduction of value to labour time does not represent Marx's judgement as to which material production input is most important or 'primary' (either logically or chronologically). Marx always insists that, as far as real wealth or use-value is concerned, nature and labour are of co-equal importance.[71] That Marx finds the substance of value in abstract labour is, in short, the result of his analysis of specifically capitalist production.[72]

It follows that the reduction of value to labour time does not apply to non-capitalist forms of production in Marx's view. Just as obviously, Marx does *not* see abstract labour time as an adequate representative or measure of wealth – including the wealth of nature. Indeed, the contradiction between use-value (including its natural basis and substance) and exchange-value runs like a red thread throughout Marx's value analysis in *Capital*.[73] Marx makes no presumption that the monetary exchange-values of commodities accurately reflect wealth in all its natural and social diversity – either qualitatively or quantitatively.[74] His dialectical analysis of the value-form culminates in a

---

[71] Burkett 1999a, p. 26.
[72] Saad–Filho 2002, Chapter 3.
[73] Marx 1981.
[74] Burkett 1999a, Chapter 7.

powerful critique of the metabolic rift created by the treatment of labour and nature as means of value accumulation.[75] Marx's critique of physiocratic value theory should therefore be of special interest to those ecological economists who are most sceptical about the ability of market-oriented environmental policies to protect ecological wealth in a holistic sense.

Marx's critique of the physiocrats

Marx's main engagement with physiocracy on the question of value is in Chapter II of *Theories of Surplus-Value*.[76] What immediately strikes the reader of this chapter is that Marx's extremely high regard for the physiocrats is not limited to his well-known praise of Quesnay's *Tableau*,[77] but extends to basic features of their value analysis.[78] The 'great and specific contribution of the Physiocrats', in Marx's view, is 'that they derive value and surplus-value not from circulation but from production'.[79] For Marx, this 'contrast to the Monetary and Mercantile system' qualifies physiocratic analysis as the first attempt 'to analyse the nature of surplus-value in general'.[80] It also explains why 'the Physiocratic system is the first systematic conception of capitalist production'.[81]

Marx was especially impressed with the physiocrats'

> analysis of the various *material components* in which capital exists and into which it resolves itself in the course of the labour-process. . . . It was their

---

[75] Foster 2000a.

[76] Marx 1963, pp. 44–68. *Theories of Surplus-Value*, a massive critical history of political economy written in 1861–3, was to have been the fourth volume of *Capital*, but this plan was not fulfilled. Among Marx's other major writings on the physiocrats are the chapter he contributed to Engels's *Anti-Dühring* (Marx 1939), Chapter VI of *Theories of Surplus-Value* (Marx 1963, pp. 308–44), and Chapter XIX, Section I of *Capital*, Volume II (Marx 1981, Vol. II, pp. 435–8). But these texts all focus on the *Tableau*, not basic value-theoretic issues. A brief precursor of the discussion dealt with here appears in the *Grundrisse* (the first draft of *Capital*, compiled in the winter of 1857–8) (Marx 1973, pp. 328–30, 588).

[77] Marx 1939, p. 275; 1963, pp. 343–4; 1981, Vol. II, pp. 435–6.

[78] Even Marxologists often do not mention any dimension of Marx's engagement with the physiocrats other than his interest in the *Tableau*. See, for example, Meek 1973, p. xlii; Rosdolsky 1977, pp. 457–8.

[79] Marx 1963, p. 49. 'The Physiocrats transferred the inquiry into the origin of surplus-value from the sphere of circulation into the sphere of direct production, and thereby laid the foundation for the analysis of capitalist production' (Marx 1963, p. 45).

[80] Marx 1963, p. 49, and 1981, Vol. III, p. 919.

[81] Marx 1981, Vol. II, p. 436.

great merit that they conceived these forms as physiological forms of society:
as forms arising from the natural necessity of production itself, forms that
are independent of anyone's will or of politics, etc.[82]

However, while praising the physiocrats' focus on production's 'material
laws', Marx suggests they erred in conceiving 'the material law of a definite
historical social stage . . . as an abstract law governing equally all forms of
society'.[83] What does Marx mean by this?

The problem is that the physiocrats did not critically analyse capitalism's
own form of wealth valuation, that is, they did not consider 'value' in
historically specific, social-relational terms. As a result, they confused the
natural substance of real wealth with capitalist 'value'. Marx thus points to
the physiocrats' 'general view of the nature of value, which to them is not a
definite social mode of existence of human activity (labour) but consists of
material things – land, nature, and the various modifications of these material
things'.[84] This is a 'confusion of value with material substance, or rather the
equating of value with it', and it shapes 'the whole outlook of the physiocrats'.[85]
In Marx's view, capitalism reduces economic value to a specific social substance:
abstract (homogenous, socially necessary) labour time. So, from Marx's
standpoint, the physiocrats' confusion of value with material wealth explains
why 'they have not yet reduced value . . . to its simple substance – the quantity
of labour or labour-time'.[86] And this, in turn, explains why they 'could not
penetrate the mystery of surplus-value'.[87]

For Marx, the source of surplus-value is the ability of workers' labour-
power to produce commodities containing more value than is represented
by their wages. Such a surplus presumes, of course, that *agricultural* labour
is productive enough to produce more means of subsistence than are required
by agricultural workers themselves. Otherwise, there would be no surplus

---

[82] Marx 1963, p. 44 (emphasis in original). Marx thus credits the physiocrats with
the first serious analysis of the value of labour-power in its material aspects (Marx
1963, p. 45). He also applauds Quesnay's pioneering analysis of the distinction between
fixed capital and circulating capital (Marx 1981, Vol. II, pp. 268, 277).
[83] Marx 1963, p. 44.
[84] Marx 1963, p. 46.
[85] Marx 1963, p. 60.
[86] Marx 1963, p. 46.
[87] Marx 1981, Vol. I, p. 672.

product in agriculture and no means of subsistence for non-agricultural workers, hence no (agricultural or non-agricultural) surplus-value.[88] In this sense, surplus-value has a natural basis. Unfortunately, the physiocrats conflated this natural basis with the actual determination of surplus-value under specifically capitalist production relations:

> So what they say is not: the labourer works more than the labour-time required for the reproduction of his labour-power; the value which he creates is therefore greater than the value of his labour-power; or the labour which he gives in return is greater than the quantity of labour which he receives in the form of wages. But what they say is: the amount of use-values which he consumes during the period of production is smaller than the amount of use-values which he creates, and so a surplus of use-values is left over. Were he to work only for the time required to reproduce his own labour-power, there would be nothing left over. But the Physiocrats only stuck to the point that the productivity of the earth enables the labourer, in his day's labour, which is assumed to be a fixed quantity, to produce more than he needs to consume in order to continue to exist. The surplus-value appears therefore as a *gift of nature*, through whose co-operation a definite quantity of organic matter – plant seeds, a number of animals – enables labour to transform more inorganic matter into organic.[89]

It needs to be emphasised that Marx does not deny the natural basis of either the surplus product or surplus-value. While arguing that it is wrong to treat surplus-value as simply 'a pure gift of nature', he nonetheless says that the physiocrats were led to do this partly because 'it depends on the productivity of nature that the labourer is able to produce in his day's labour more than is necessary for the reproduction of his labour-power, more than the amount of his wages'.[90] In fact, Marx goes out of his way to excuse the physiocrats

---

[88] Marx 1963, p. 48.

[89] Marx 1963, p. 51 (emphasis in original).

[90] Marx 1963, p. 55. 'The Physiocrats were also correct in seeing all production of surplus-value . . . as resting on the productivity of agricultural labour as its natural foundation. If men are not even capable of producing more means of subsistence in a working day, and thus in the narrowest sense more agricultural products, than each worker needs for his own reproduction, if the daily expenditure of the worker's entire labour-power is only sufficient to produce the means of subsistence indispensable for his individual needs, there can be no question of any surplus product or surplus-value at all' (Marx 1981, Vol. III, p. 921).

for their confusion, on grounds that their focus on agricultural productivity was shaped by their historical circumstances. For instance, physiocracy 'considers agriculture in comparison with a still quite undeveloped state of manufacture'.[91] Besides, is it not the case that 'in agriculture, the soil itself with its chemical etc. action is already a machine which makes direct labour more productive, and hence gives a surplus *earlier*, because work is done here at an *earlier* stage with a machine, namely a *natural* one'?[92] Marx even pardons the physiocrats on the grounds that agriculture is the only 'field where the natural force of the instrument of labour [i.e., the land] tangibly permits the labourer to produce more value than he consumes':[93]

> The difference between the *value* of labour-power and *the value created* by it ... appears most palpably, most incontrovertibly, of all *branches of production*, in *agriculture*, the primary branch of production. The sum total of the means of subsistence which the labourer consumes from one year to another, or the mass of material substance which he consumes, is smaller than the sum total of the means of subsistence he produces. In manufacture the workman is not generally seen directly producing either his means of subsistence or the surplus in excess of his means of subsistence. The process is mediated through purchase and sale, through the various acts of circulation, and the analysis of value in general is necessary for it to be understood. In agriculture it shows itself directly in the surplus of use-values produced over use-values consumed by the labourer, and can therefore be grasped without an analysis of value in general, without a clear understanding of the nature of value. Therefore also when value is reduced to use-value, and the latter to material substance in general. Hence for the physiocrats agricultural labour is the only *productive labour*.[94]

For all these reasons, then, 'agricultural labour ... was bound to be considered the creator of surplus-value' by the physiocrats.[95] The down-side is that the physiocrats' limited historical-social vision prevented them from critically analysing capitalism's specific forms of wealth valuation and exploitation,

---

[91] Marx 1973, p. 588.
[92] Marx 1973, p. 588 (emphasis in original).
[93] Marx 1973, p. 328.
[94] Marx 1963, p. 46 (emphasis in original).
[95] Marx 1963, p. 48.

that is, that 'they let the form drop altogether and only look[ed] at the simple production process'.[96] As a result, they 'conceived value merely as use-value, merely as material substance, and surplus-value as a mere gift of nature':[97]

> Their error was that they confused the *increase of material substance*, which because of the natural processes of vegetation and generation distinguishes agriculture and stock-raising from manufacture, with the *increase of exchange-value*. Use-value was their starting point. And the use-value of all commodities, reduced, as the scholastics say, to a universal, was the material substance of nature as such, whose increase in the same form occurs only in agriculture. . . . Surplus-value itself is wrongly conceived, because they have a wrong idea of value and reduce it to the use-value of labour, not to labour-time, social, homogenous labour.[98]

Given the close connection between the rise of capitalism and the industrial revolution, it seems paradoxical that the physiocrats, with their emphasis on agriculture, conflated capitalist value with material wealth or use-value. In Marx's view, this paradox reflects physiocracy's historical context: that of 'the new capitalist society prevailing within the framework of feudal society . . . bourgeois society in the epoch when [it] breaks its way out of the feudal order'.[99] Hence, the physiocrats 'made of the capitalist form of production an eternal, natural form of production', but in 'the character of a bourgeois reproduction of the feudal system, of the dominion of landed property'.[100]

This 'feudal semblance' of the physiocratic system helps explain some of its limitations, especially its treatment of 'the industrial spheres in which capital first develops independently . . . as "unproductive" branches of labour, mere appendages of agriculture', and thus its failure to see non-agricultural production as a source of surplus-value.[101] For the physiocrats, '*rent* is the

---

[96] Marx 1973, p. 328.
[97] Marx 1963, p. 52.
[98] Marx 1963, pp. 62–3, 154 (emphasis in original).
[99] Marx 1963, p. 50.
[100] Marx 1963, pp. 44, 49–50. This interpretation carries no presumption of deliberate stealth campaigning on the physiocrats' part: 'The label of a system of ideas is distinguished from that of other articles, among other things, by the fact that it deceives not only the buyer, but often the seller as well. Quesnay himself, and his closest disciples, believed in their feudal signboard' (Marx 1981, Vol. II, pp. 435–6).
[101] Marx 1963, p. 50.

only form of surplus-value', and *'profit* on capital in the true sense . . . does not exist'.[102] Stated differently, the physiocrats see rent as 'the *general form of surplus-value'*, and 'industrial profit and interest [as] merely different categories into which rent is divided'.[103] In short, in physiocracy, 'the formation of surplus-value is not explained in terms of capital as such, but ascribed simply to one specific sphere of capitalist production, agriculture'.[104] It is 'explained . . . in a feudal way, as derived from nature and not from society; from man's relation to the soil, not from his social relations'.[105]

As noted earlier, the physiocrats' three-class schema assumes capitalist relations within agriculture; or as Marx puts it, 'it is taken for granted that the landowner confronts the labourer as a capitalist'.[106] In Marx's view, this presumption is what enabled at least one of the physiocrats, namely Turgot, to attain 'a correct grasp of surplus-value . . . *within the limits of agricultural labour'*, insofar as he treated the net product 'as a product of the wage-labourer's labour' which the landowner appropriates 'without an equivalent'.[107] That the physiocrats' 'landowner is in essence a capitalist' who 'confronts the free labourer as an owner of commodities' also 'hits the mark' insofar as the 'first condition for the development of capital is the separation of landed property from labour – the emergence of land, the primary condition of labour, as an independent force, a force in the hands of a separate class, confronting the free labourer'.[108]

Because they took capitalist production relations as natural givens (at least within agriculture), however, the physiocrats failed to analyse the connections between these relations and capitalism's specific forms of wealth valuation. In fact, they showed little if any interest in qualitative value-form issues. Hence, in their system, 'Value itself is resolved into mere use-value, and therefore into material substance', and 'what interests [the physiocrats] in this material substance' is not its social form but rather 'its quantity – the

---

[102] Marx 1963, pp. 46–7 (emphasis in original).
[103] Marx 1963, p. 47 (emphasis in original). Compare Marx 1981, Vol. III, pp. 919–20; Herlitz 1961, p. 51.
[104] Marx 1981, Vol. II, p. 297.
[105] Marx 1963, p. 52.
[106] Marx 1963, p. 51.
[107] Marx 1963, p. 57 (emphasis in original).
[108] Marx 1963, pp. 50–1.

excess of the use-values produced over those consumed . . . the purely quantitative relation of the use-values to each other, their mere exchange-value'.[109] The quantitative emphasis of the physiocrats' value theory is shown by their treatment of money as merely a convenient medium of exchange and measure of value, rather than in terms of what the necessity of such a general representative of value tells us about the underlying relations of production and *vice versa*.[110] Stated differently, the physiocrats treat exchange-value and money as natural forms of wealth or use-value, not as (potentially contradictory) forms of capitalist wealth valuation.[111]

Marx's critical appropriation of physiocratic ideas

Marx's historical and social-relational approach to value diverges sharply from the physiocrats' crude materialist approach. Yet, Marx's materialism enabled him to incorporate critically certain physiocratic concepts into his own analysis of capitalism. The physiocratic elements in Marx's thinking stem from his understanding of capital's material requirements: exploitable labour-power and the objectification of workers' labour in vendible use-values (commodities).[112] Insofar as nature supplies these requirements, it contributes to the accumulation of capital. As Marx says,

> The mass of labour that capital can command does not depend on its value, but rather on the mass of raw and auxiliary materials, of machinery and elements of fixed capital, and of means of subsistence, out of which it is composed, whatever their value may be.[113]

---

[109] Marx 1963, p. 52.

[110] See, for example, Quesnay 1963b, pp. 217–19.

[111] Banzhaf (2000, p. 520) is thus wrong to lump Marx in with those who fault the physiocrats for failing to distinguish the material net product from the 'value surplus', with 'value' understood simply as 'exchange-value', i.e., 'market prices'. When Marx criticises the physiocrats for conflating value and (material) use-value, he is using the term 'value' to connote the specific social substance that (in his view) regulates exchange-values, namely, social labour time in the abstract. Marx was well aware that the physiocrats used money as a measure of value and treated monetary exchange-values. In fact, he criticised Eugen Dühring for his inability to understand this basic feature of Quesnay's *Tableau* (Marx 1939, pp. 267–8). Marx's problem with the physiocrats is that they failed to reduce value to its specifically capitalist substance and were thus unable to deal with the difficult value-form issues posed by capitalist valuation and exploitation.

[112] Burkett 1999a, Chapter 5.

[113] Marx 1981, Vol. III, p. 357.

Even though the substance of capitalist value is abstract labour time, the material world must provide capital with a 'material sub-stratum . . . objective elements of capital', and these elements must 'serve to absorb additional labour, and thus additional surplus-labour also, and . . . in this way form additional capital'.[114]

Given capital's material requirements, Marx argues, 'we may say that surplus-value rests on a natural basis', namely, 'on the naturally originating productivity of labour, which produces more than the absolutely necessary subsistence of the worker, a natural productivity which of course rests on qualities of its inorganic nature – qualities of the soil, etc.'.[115] Marx's endorsement of this kernel of truth in physiocratic doctrine was discussed earlier – the point being that, without an agricultural surplus, there can be no surplus labour in agriculture and no means of subsistence for non-agricultural workers, hence no surplus-value in the economy as a whole. Marx's only complaint in this connection is that the physiocrats reduced the determination of surplus-value to this natural basis, due to their uncritical acceptance of capitalist production relations (at least in agriculture).[116]

Like the physiocrats, Marx often refers to the natural conditions of production as 'gifts' of nature. These gifts are freely appropriated by capital whenever they provide conditions enabling the extraction of surplus labour from workers and its objectification in vendible use-values, without adding to the wage-labour needed to produce commodities. Nature's gifts can serve as free gifts for capital, in other words, because even though they are not products of wage-labour, they still provide use-values that capital needs to produce and realise surplus-value. Unlike the physiocrats, Marx argues that such gifts 'create use-value without contributing to the formation of exchange-value'.[117] He sees the free appropriation of nature's gifts as a key factor in capitalist development, but in a way that recognises the essential role of capitalist

---

[114] Marx 1981, Vol. III, pp. 356–7.

[115] Marx 1981, Vol. I, p. 647, and 1994, p. 155.

[116] For details of Marx's many analyses of the natural basis of surplus-value, see Burkett 1999a, Chapter 3. As Foster (2000a, p. 167) points out, Marx applied his critique of the physiocrats to Malthus, who, at certain points, also treated surplus-value as simply a gift of nature, thereby conflating the actual determination of surplus-value with its natural basis. See Marx 1994, pp. 150–9.

[117] Marx 1981, Vol. I, p. 312.

production relations. For Marx, capitalism's conversion of nature's gifts into conditions of surplus-value production is enabled by the 'freeing' of labour-power from the land and other necessary conditions of production. The capitalisation of nature's gifts is thus both condition and result of the system's alienation of real wealth vis-à-vis the direct producers, in Marx's view.[118]

III. The nature-valuation debate revisited

Like the physiocrats, ecological economists do not root the question of nature's value in capitalism's basic relations of production: 'freeing' of labour-power from the land and other necessary conditions of production, and the reuniting of labour-power and production conditions only as wage-labour and capital producing commodities for a profit. In this sense, the nature-valuation debate has not considered the monetary valuation of nature as a specifically capitalist form of valuation. As with the physiocrats, this lack of attention to the connections between the system's internal economic relations and the way the system values nature leads to an identification of nature's value with its use-value, an acceptance of exchange-value and money as natural ways of valuing nature, and a one-sidedly quantitative perspective on nature's value. The way these tendencies work themselves out is a function of the somewhat different conceptions of use-value and exchange-value held by the respective participants in the debate.

Energy-value theory

For the energy theorists, embodied energy – the true primary input or resource – best explains the relative and total production costs of commodities. Assuming that prices reflect production costs, they see embodied energy as the real source and substance of economic value as measured by money.

The problem is that market valuations are assumed to be qualitatively and quantitatively adequate measures of the true resource costs of production. Hence, in his attack on energy-value theory, Daly points out that it implicitly assumes not only an absence of monopolistic 'imperfections' in the markets

---

[118] Burkett 1999a, Chapter 6.

for resources and produced commodities, but also that markets exist for all sources and types of energy used in production including the free solar energy that lights and heats the earth, without which production obviously could not occur.[119] Given such implausible assumptions, the statistical correlations found between embodied energy and monetary values are most likely not 'a true empirical finding', but rather an 'imposed result of the analytical framework', specifically of the presumption that there is 'only one primary input, namely energy'.[120] Worse yet, due to its search for the quantitative Holy Grail of a single primary input, the energy approach presumes that all natural resources can be reduced to pure energetic terms. Combined with the presumption that 'embodied energy values are . . . accurate indicators of market values, and vice versa', this suggests that 'market energy prices might be used to evaluate natural ecosystem structures and processes according to the amounts of energy embodied in them'.[121]

Costanza's response to Daly's critique verifies the energy theory's reductionism as well as its uncritical approach to the market. On the reduction of nature's use-value as a production input to energy, he merely restates two of the theory's assumptions in more 'material' and 'entropic' terms: (i) 'Embodied energy is the direct and indirect energy required (in combination with unstructured mass) to produce organized material structures';[122] and (ii) 'The energy embodied in material structures is taken as a measure of their degree of organization – the amount of low entropy they contain'.[123] If these two points clarify anything at all it is that the energy theory's search for a primary input is driven by its reduction of the question of value to that of finding some common measure of use-value conceived apart from historically specific social relations of production. This decision having been made, it is but a short step to the view that money and markets are just convenient social

---

[119] Daly 1981, pp. 168–9.
[120] Daly 1981, p. 167. This is most obviously the case in the input-output studies which first reduce production cost to embodied energy and then assume that prices reflect costs. But a similar spurious correlation is at work in the more aggregative studies of energy/GDP or energy/GNP ratios which employ 'adjustments for fuel quality' to strengthen the correlations between energy use and GDP or GNP. See Stern 1999 on this point.
[121] Daly 1981, p. 168.
[122] Costanza 1981b, p. 188.
[123] Ibid.

devices for registering these quantitative 'energy values' as exchange-values.

Indeed, it is difficult to avoid the conclusion that the concern of energy theorists with value quantification is largely driven by their admiration for money and monetary prices as uni-dimensional measures of use-value. Hannon, for example, makes the case for an 'energy standard of value' by analogy with the 'readily understood . . . utility of employing a common denominator, such as money' in order to 'measure value'.[124] Evidently, 'evaluative standards other than money ought to be adopted . . . to add another dimension to the traditional money standard of value'.[125] Nonetheless, this additional dimension is still purely quantitative (BTUs) and itself evaluated in monetary terms; hence Hannon makes reference to 'the dollar cost of . . . alternatives to various goods or services which use less energy'.[126]

For this kind of natural-value theory, the inadequacies of the market reduce to quantitative deviations of monetary exchange-values from energy values. Moreover, these deviations do not call for an abandonment of the market in favour of other (say, political) forms of economic decision-making, but rather a more complete and perfect marketisation of nature:

> An embodied energy theory of value postulates that a perfectly functioning market would, through a complex evolutionary selection process, arrive at prices proportional to embodied energy intensity. The transactions covered by the national input-output tables are carried on in relatively well-behaved (though not perfect) markets, and the theory predicts a good (though not perfect) empirical relation between market prices and embodied energy intensities for these sectors. This is a positive statement about how the existing market works. Given that this statement is relatively accurate, we can make a normative statement about what market (shadow) prices would be in the absence of all imperfections. Daly's criticism that an embodied energy theory of value implies the impossibility of divergence between market prices and embodied energy intensities is not accurate. To the contrary,

---

[124] Hannon 1973, p. 139.

[125] Ibid.

[126] Hannon 1973, p. 140. Hannon's more recent derivations of 'ecological prices' (really energy prices) also start from a principles-level account of money, market exchange, and prices as convenient social devices (Hannon 1998, p. 273, and 2001, pp. 19–20).

> I see large bodies of transactions (i.e., in ecological systems) where markets
> are nonexistent or incomplete. In these systems embodied energy obviously
> diverges from market price. It is just these points of divergence that are
> most interesting, since embodied energy may be useful in correcting for
> imperfect ownership and other market imperfections.[127]

For Costanza, the problem of environmental damage from market-oriented
production is not due to any fundamental tensions between natural wealth
and market valuation, but rather to the fact that markets for natural wealth
are missing, incomplete, or imperfect. Apparently, if nature's use-value were
properly reduced to embodied energy and then properly measured by money,
environmental problems would be automatically corrected. In short, as Daly
notes, the 'surprising and disturbing implication of the energy theory of
value . . . is its extension of market prices to the valuation of ecosystem services
heretofore considered outside the domain of the market'.[128] Indeed, Hannon
applies monetary categories directly to quantities of energy itself, referring
to the future 'flow' of a new 'currency . . . regulated by the amount of energy
budgeted for a given period'.[129] More recently, in an attempt to answer the
question 'how might nature value man?', Hannon analyses the 'net outputs'
of non-human ecological systems (reduced to pure energetic terms) using the
categories of market values, prices, and rates of profit.[130]

The energy theorists' uncritical stance on the marketisation of nature is also
reflected in their otherwise inexplicable appeal to neoclassical utility theory
with its correspondence between market prices and individual subjective
valuations of nature. Costanza thus claims that 'there is no inherent conflict
between an embodied energy (or energy cost) theory of value and value
theories based on utility'.[131] Evidently, utility itself is ultimately reducible to
energy flows; otherwise the appeal to 'economic principles grounded in
optimization' to show the consistency of the cost-based and utility-based
approaches makes no sense.[132] Similarly, Farber, Costanza and Wilson, after

---

[127] Costanza 1981b, pp. 189–90.
[128] Daly 1981, p. 167.
[129] Hannon 1973, p. 153.
[130] Hannon 1998, pp. 273–7.
[131] Costanza 1981a, p. 140.
[132] Ibid.

championing the energy-value theory, endorse various efforts at constructing artificial monetary valuations of natural resources, including some based on subjective valuations by survey respondents and focus groups, in cases where relevant markets do not exist.[133] All of this ignores the fact that the main purpose of Sraffa's model of reproduction prices – the basis of energy-value analysis in practice – is to demolish the neoclassical demand and supply approach to value based on marginal utilities and marginal products.[134]

Given the energy school's profoundly asocial approach to the question of value, it is not surprising that its leading member, Costanza, bases the case for a specifically ecological economics on technological pessimism, that is, a sceptical attitude toward the ability of new technologies to overcome predetermined natural limits to economic growth.[135] One should, of course, guard against the kind of social constructionism that has pro-ecological forms of production automatically flowering once market- and profit-driven production is replaced by socialist planning. The difficulty is that Costanza ignores the inner connections between capitalist relations of production, nature valuation, and the development of technologies that deplete and despoil natural wealth.

The eco-Sraffian approach

Like the energy school, the eco-Sraffian approach tends to naturalise capitalism's monetary valuation of nature, and to blame environmental problems on the fact that markets in natural resources are either missing or incomplete. The basic problem is that Sraffian input-output models cannot qualitatively distinguish the exploitation of labour from the exploitation of any other input. Treating production as a combination of discrete factors connected by given technological parameters, they do not capture capitalism's specific relation of exploitation: wage-labour. Hence, these models cannot be used to construct a critical perspective on capitalism's specific form of nature valuation.[136]

---

[133] Farber, Costanza and Wilson 2002.
[134] Sraffa 1960; Dobb 1973, Chapters 8 and 9; Sweezy 1981, p. 21.
[135] Costanza 1989, p. 4.
[136] Chapter 8 further elucidates this point in connection with ecological crises and conflicts.

Perrings, for example, tells us that the goal of his dynamic input-output analysis is 'to establish just what the price mechanism can be expected to do in an economy-environment system and what it cannot'.[137] But, rather than specifying the specific production relations underpinning (more or less) generalised market relations, he claims that 'coercive systems of production such as the slave, feudal, or corvee systems are directly analogous to the more familiar exploitation of non-human environments'.[138] As a result, he finds capitalism's 'fundamental flaws' not in the system's production relations, but rather in 'environmental external effects'.[139] The problem, evidently, is that not all 'resources . . . are subject to rights and property'; specifically, that some natural resources 'have the status of *commodities* and some . . . do not'.[140] In short, 'environmental resources . . . lie outside the price system of the economy', which results in 'persistent external effects'.[141] Presumably, if all natural resources could somehow be marketised and monetised, the problem of 'unobservability and uncontrollability of the processes of the environment through the price system' could be resolved.[142] Not surprisingly, Perrings supports the proposal of the neoclassical economist, Robert Solow, to use 'environmental bonds' as a method of attaining 'social control of external effects'.[143] Such bonds are equivalent to a natural resource user fee paid by their purchasers, with the fee to be set according to the monetary value of the social ('external') costs associated with the use of the resource in question. This instrument presumes, of course, that money is an adequate measure of natural wealth, despite all the uncertainties, qualitatively variegated benefits and costs, and human value conflicts, associated with natural resource use.[144]

---

[137] Perrings 1987, p. xii.
[138] Ibid.
[139] Perrings 1987, p. 1.
[140] Perrings 1987, pp. 10–11 [emphasis in original].
[141] Perrings 1987, p. 11.
[142] Ibid.
[143] Perrings 1987, p. 164; compare Perrings 1989; Solow 1971.
[144] This presumption is not softened one bit if the user fee is set at a level determined by 'worst case' social costs (Perrings 1987, p. 165, and 1989, p. 101; Solow 1971, p. 502). The difficulty lies in the qualitative reduction of natural wealth to homogenous monetary terms. For a discussion of other limitations of environmental bonds connected with information problems, perverse incentives, and inequalities in economic power, see Shogren, Herriges and Govindasamy 1993.

Similarly, Gowdy first presents an input-output 'growth accounting framework' that 'would show the contribution to economic growth . . . of labor, resources, and environmental services'.[145] He then endorses various efforts at empirically quantifying these kinds of models in monetary terms, and even applauds attempts 'to adjust GDP for environmental damage'.[146] Gowdy's response to those who would criticise such monetary valuation of natural wealth?: 'a wise person once said if anything is worth doing it is worth doing badly. Those concerned with the accelerating loss of global environmental quality need to begin quantifying past economic growth and productivity considering these losses'.[147] His pragmatic strategy takes the widespread monetary valuation of wealth as given, and uses it to justify protecting the environment, while still giving non-market values their due place in an overall hierarchy of value.[148] But the fact is that the monetary quantification of natural wealth carries value judgments, such as 'more is better' and the substitutability of man-made and natural wealth, which directly contradict non-market values such as bio-diversity and respect for natural limits.[149] More basically, Gowdy's perspective does not root the contemporary dominance of market valuation in the relations of production, in other words, it lacks a structural explanation of the subordinate place of non-market values in the value hierarchy of actually existing capitalism and the revolutionary changes in the class hierarchy needed to reverse this ordering.

To be clear, the intent of the present critique is not to argue against the use of input-output methods to represent biophysical and energetic production data, as a way of posing analytical questions about the environmental problems faced by 'the social institutions and signalling system of the economy'.[150] The difficulties arise when input-output systems are overlaid with monetary exchange-values which are taken as qualitatively adequate ways of representing natural 'values' (really use-values). Surprisingly, this kind of approach has been utilised even by some ecological economists who elsewhere insist on the incommensurability of natural use-values.

---

[145] Gowdy 1988, p. 38.
[146] Gowdy 1988, p. 39.
[147] Ibid.
[148] See also Gowdy 1997.
[149] On the problems with 'adjusting' GDP for environmental effects, see Norgaard 1989b; Aaheim and Nyborg 1995; Hueting 1996, p. 87; and Lintott 1996.
[150] Perrings 1987, p. 7; compare O'Connor 1993b; Rees 1999.

Martin O'Connor and Juan Martinez-Alier, for example, have strongly criticised the monetisation and capitalisation of nature, that is, its reduction to quantitative exchange-values and 'rates of return'.[151] Yet, they have also used Sraffian input-output pricing models to analyse questions of ecological sustainability and conflict. In one contribution, they identify value with exchange-value (relative price), and argue that, even though 'environmental costs cannot, in general, be convincingly translated into prices', Sraffian pricing models can still provide 'insights . . . concerning valuation of natural capital stocks and flows'.[152] Their 'Sraffian ecological economics' represents 'social conflicts of interests concerning the appropriation and use of natural capital' in 'an industrial commodity economy'.[153] Even though the economy's production relations are not clearly specified, the model presumes generalised commodity production and monetary commensurability of natural use-values. Indeed, it applies the categories of money prices and profits even to non-commodity processes such as 'insertion of economic waste . . . by economic proprietors into the environment [which] brings degradation of some ecological capital' as well as to the production of 'ecological capital' itself.[154]

Given these presumptions, 'ecological value system conflicts' are 'portrayed at two levels. The first is the definition of . . . the prevailing price system; and the second is contest over the distribution of any surplus-value defined in terms of this price system'.[155] All conflict outcomes are thus reduced to pure monetary quantities taken as accurate measures of ecological 'values', where value is identified with use-value. The influence of the model's presumptions goes well beyond the merely 'didactic'.[156] Precisely because the Sraffian framework 'does not deal with wider social/cultural issues such as political arrangements and incommensurability of values and systems of legitimacy', it is bound to shape one's basic visions of ecological sustainability and conflict.[157] For example, the assignment of monetary prices to ecological use-values, even

---

[151] O'Connor 1994; Martinez-Alier, Munda and O'Neill 1998.
[152] Martinez-Alier and O'Connor 1996, pp. 161–2.
[153] Martinez-Alier and O'Connor 1996, p. 163.
[154] Martinez-Alier and O'Connor 1996, p. 164. See also O'Connor (1993a, p. 409), where the categories of money, price, and profit rate are applied to 'a "traditional" society geared to self-reproduction'.
[155] Martinez-Alier and O'Connor 1996, p. 166.
[156] Martinez-Alier and O'Connor 1996, p. 153.
[157] Martinez-Alier and O'Connor 1996, p. 163.

when they are not priced in reality, complements the 'tragedy of the commons' notion that the *non*-pricing of natural resources and the *non*-assignment of private or state property rights to these resources explains why they are overexploited, as well as the companion notion of a 'green capitalism' which fulfills the resource-pricing and property rights functions more effectively. Hence, O'Connor and Martinez-Alier draw a positive analogy between their Sraffian approach and the 'general equilibrium methodology' which finds the roots of the environmental 'externality problem' in 'missing markets' for natural resources and resultant 'cost-shifting' by capitalist enterprises 'onto local communities, onto "the taxpayer", and onto future generations'.[158] Although they hasten to add that 'the creating of markets through defining [property] rights and subsequent "capitalization" is not necessarily a step towards social justice and sustainability', the logic of their own analysis runs against this qualification.[159]

Having bypassed the connection between the system's core production relations and its valuation of nature, it is not surprising that when not blaming environmental problems on missing markets, the eco-Sraffians appeal to more-or-less free-floating ideological, institutional, and technological factors. Hence, Gowdy refers to the 'preoccupation of modern economies with economic growth' as 'a prime example of the extractive mentality' which, together with 'certain "ceremonial" activities promoted by the dominant class [which] are environmentally wasteful', has caused civilisation to run up against natural limits.[160] Martinez-Alier blames an 'industrialist' ideology which is evidently not specific to capitalism since it also afflicted the Soviet Union and was, so the story goes, embraced by Marx and most subsequent Marxists.[161] Others ascribe environmental problems to 'ecodistributional conflicts' without rooting the structure and dynamics of these conflicts in the basic relations of production (see Chapters 7 and 8). That capitalism's social separation of workers and their communities from the land and other necessary conditions of production might have something to do with ecological crisis seems to have escaped attention, and this may have something to do with the didactic use of models that do not specify the system's class relations.

---

[158] O'Connor and Martinez-Alier 1998, p. 38.
[159] Ibid.
[160] Gowdy 1984, p. 397.
[161] Martinez-Alier 1995b.

The ecosocialist nature-exploitation view

It may seem paradoxical that, in arguing that capitalist production extracts value not just from labour-power but directly from nature, ecosocialists implicitly take an uncritical stance on capitalist valuation. The problem, however, is that this approach does not mediate capital's appropriation of natural conditions through the system's social separation of workers from these conditions and the alienated form of their unification as wage-labour and capital. As a result, the ecosocialist attempt to attribute value directly to nature runs into contradictions when it tries to explain the forms in which nature's value appears once it has been extracted.

According to Skirbekk, nature is exploited whenever 'a part of the natural resources is used without being restored, without an equal quantity of wealth being returned to nature', and 'this destructive extraction of limited natural wealth represents an impoverishment of future generations'.[162] Notice that, in using the term 'exploitation' to connote both the net extraction of natural wealth and the resulting impoverishment of future generations, this approach identifies value with use-value. One does not need a value theory to say that capitalism (or any other form of production) appropriates natural wealth. But then we have learned nothing about how capitalism's specific forms of nature-utilisation and nature-valuation differ from other historical forms.[163]

This difficulty becomes evident when Skirbekk tries to show how the exploitation of nature creates higher monetary incomes. On the one hand, he suggests that capitalists and/or workers in extractive industries (oil, for example) benefit from the sale of natural resources at prices *exceeding* their labour values, and that this represents an important source of 'extractive surplus profits'.[164] On the other hand, he argues that resource-*using* industries benefit from the *under*-pricing of natural resources and consequent lowering of their unit production costs relative to their output prices.[165] Apparently extractive surplus profits involve a simultaneous over-pricing and under-

---

[162] Skirbekk 1994, p. 99.
[163] Burkett 1999a, pp. 101–2. The same shortcoming affects Brennan's (1997) argument that capitalist production extracts value from nature by not paying for nature's reproduction time.
[164] Skirbekk 1994, p. 100.
[165] Skirbekk 1994, pp. 99–101.

pricing of natural resources compared to their labour values – but Skirbekk does not explain why the two forms of unequal exchange do not cancel each other out in the aggregate.

Stated differently, the nature-exploitation approach conflates value and exchange-value.[166] In Marx's view, for example, individual exchange-values can incorporate surplus profits from the appropriation of scarce natural conditions. However, such surplus profits represent redistributions of surplus-value in the form of rents, and are not to be confused with the production of new surplus-value.[167]

More fundamentally, the whole conception of exploitation in terms of the under- and over-pricing of natural resources presupposes that market prices and money can be qualitatively adequate representatives of nature's use-value. Presumably, if prices were 'properly' set, there would be no exploitation of nature. (But this, of course, would contradict the identification of 'exploitation' with the extraction of natural wealth (use-value).) Similar to the energy theorists and the eco-Sraffians, this conception bypasses the ecological contradictions of market prices and money as *forms* of natural wealth. As a result, the nature-exploitation approach reduces capital's destructive utilisation of nature to quantitative 'extractive' terms, which tends to obfuscate the system's various qualitative forms of ecological despoliation.

Entropy and enjoyment of life

Georgescu-Roegen and Daly see low-entropy matter-energy as a necessary condition for the production of goods and services that generate psychic income or 'enjoyment of life'. On this basis, they reject pure 'cost of production' approaches which ascribe value directly to nature. Despite this divergence, however, the Georgescu-Roegen/Daly approach also does not connect the issue of nature-valuation to capitalism's relations of production. This naturalisation of market relations leads to an arbitrary dichotomy between allocation and scale. To see how, consider that the Georgescu-Roegen/Daly critique of pure cost-based value theories can be rephrased in simple supply and demand terms, as a failure to take demand-side factors into account. As Daly says in reference to a hypothetical low-entropy theory of value:

---

[166] Burkett 1999a, pp. 102–3.
[167] Marx 1981, Vol. III, Part VI; Burkett 1999a, pp. 90–3.

Although low entropy is a necessary condition for something to have any value at all, it is not a sufficient explanation of the value of one commodity relative to another. For one thing, entropy is entirely on the supply or cost side. There is still demand to consider. Hemlock may have lower entropy than orange juice. Bathwater heated to 211°F has lower entropy than 110°F bathwater but is not more valuable.[168]

This criticism takes it for granted that the purpose of value theory is to explain relative prices, and that supply and demand analysis is the appropriate way to attain such an explanation. Apparently, market values are, or can be made to be, adequate indicators of value in the sense of enjoyment of life and the costs of obtaining this enjoyment. This implication becomes especially disturbing when one considers how far removed the Georgescu-Roegen/Daly notion of enjoyment of life is from neoclassicism's 'psychological categories of pure preference and choice'.[169] Daly's 'value' in particular sees the immaterial enjoyment of life as rooted in 'the objective needs of human beings or other species considered as biological entities bound together in ecological communities and social systems'.[170] Georgescu-Roegen draws a similar contrast between human wants and abstract utility (or revealed preference), and uses it to argue that wants are incommensurable, satiable, and 'hierarchized'.[171] According to Daly, this hierarchy can be divided into 'relative and absolute wants or needs', with the former involving subjective comparisons of one's situation with others and the latter not involving such comparisons.[172]

We will return to the use made of the relative/absolute wants distinction in a moment. The thing to emphasise here is that, even though Georgescu-Roegen and Daly point out the necessary ecological and cultural bases of enjoyment of life, they do not provide an alternative to neoclassical value theory, the core principle of which is that use-value ('utility') can be adequately represented and measured by money and market prices.[173] And the reason they are unable to provide such an alternative is that they share the neoclassical

---

[168] Daly 1992a, p. 25.
[169] Daly 1981, p. 171.
[170] Daly 1992a, p. 213.
[171] Georgescu-Roegen 1954.
[172] Daly 1992a, p. 40.
[173] Compare Mirowski 1988, pp. 825–7.

failure to relate the general marketisation of wealth – capitalism's specific form of value – to the system's core production relations.[174]

Paradoxically, that Daly sees the market as merely a convenient device for allocating resources is most clear from his environmental critique of the market. Opposing neoclassical theory, he argues that it is only relative wants that are insatiable, and that this is fortunate given the 'absolute scarcity' of the 'ultimate means' of satisfying human wants, namely, low-entropy matter and energy.[175] Unfortunately, markets are concerned only with 'relative scarcity', that is, 'the scarcity of a particular resource compared to another resource'.[176] The problem with the market system, in other words, is not that it *allocates* resources inefficiently or in anti-ecological fashion, but, rather, that it does not take absolute scarcity – the problem of *scale* – into account. Since 'scale is not determined by prices', it calls for 'a social decision reflecting ecological limits'.[177] The market 'solves the allocation problem by providing the necessary information and incentive. It does that one thing very well. What it does not do is solve the problem of optimal scale . . .'.[178]

Underpinning this allocation/scale dichotomy is the view that market allocation is more private and less social than the question of scale. This is asserted even though the *relative* wants catered to by the market involve inter-subjective comparisons. As Daly phrases it, 'Distribution and scale involve relationships . . . that are fundamentally social in nature rather than individual'.[179] He amplifies the point in a piece co-authored with Costanza:

> The cost and benefit functions relevant to the micro-allocation problem are those of individuals bent on maximizing their own private utility both as consumers and producers. The market coordinates and balances these individualistic maximizing efforts and in so doing determines a set of relative prices that measure opportunity cost. Individuals are allowed to appropriate matter-energy from the ecosystem as required for their individualistic purposes. Since the benefits of such expropriation are mostly private while

---

[174] On this point, see Altvater 1994, p. 90.
[175] Daly 1992a, p. 39.
[176] Ibid.
[177] Daly 1992b, p. 188.
[178] Daly 1991, p. 35.
[179] Daly 1992b, p. 190.

the costs are largely social, there is a tendency to overexpand the scale of the economy. . . . Therefore the macro-allocation or scale problem should be viewed as a social or collective decision rather than an individualistic market decision.[180]

The allocation/scale, private/social dichotomy thus mimics the standard 'externalities-missing markets' view of environmental problems. The only difference is that Daly conceptualises the externalities at the macro-level, as the economy's overuse of low-entropy matter-energy and overemission of high-entropy matter-energy. Like neoclassical theory, Daly treats the economy itself as a social-relational black box, its internal structural relations having been reduced to private market transactions among free-floating individuals. Not surprisingly, Daly's policy prescriptions are quite similar to those of neoclassical environmental economics. He suggests that private markets be used to price and allocate natural resource 'depletion quotas' as well as quotas on aggregate births.[181] In other words, 'Quantitative limits are set with reference to ecological and ethical criteria, and the price system is then allowed, by auction and exchange, to allocate depletion quotas and birth quotas efficiently'.[182] Daly's admiration for market devices is also reflected in his support for monetary valuation of 'natural capital' as well as for efforts to 'adjust' standard measures of national and even world income for resource depletion and other environmental costs.[183]

The crucial question haunting this entire approach, of course, is whether allocation and scale are really independent aspects of economic activity and economy-nature interaction.[184] Once one steps away from the vision of the economy as an aggregated processor of low-entropy matter-energy, it becomes clear that the setting of depletion quotas on particular (animate and inanimate) forms of matter and energy (or any birth quota applied across households of varying wealth levels and socio-ecological circumstances) is, by its nature, an allocational decision. It can hardly be otherwise, given that environmental

---

[180] Costanza and Daly 1992, p. 41.
[181] Daly 1992a, Chapter 3.
[182] Daly 1974, p. 20.
[183] Daly and Cobb 1989, pp. 401–55; Daly 1991, p. 41; Costanza and Daly 1992, pp. 41–3.
[184] For the debate on this point in the pages of *Ecological Economics*, see Prakash and Gupta 1994; Daly 1994c; Stewen 1998; and Daly 1999.

'externalities' are 'an inherent and general part of the production and consumption process' in market economies.[185] Moreover, the market allocation of said quotas, and resulting patterns of economic activity and socio-material reproduction, will naturally have various quantitative and qualitative impacts on natural and social wealth, that is, on human life in all its cultural and ecological diversity. Daly admits as much when he suggests – in what can only be regarded as a leap of faith – that with resource-depletion and birth quotas in place, 'the market will, at the micro level, come up with a different set of prices which now reflect the social value of sustainability'.[186] In short, it is impossible to separate scale from allocation unless we take the market-determination of the latter as a natural 'given' and accordingly reduce all questions of scale to aggregate (that is, global) low-entropy matter-energy use as measured by a single indicator which can only be monetary.[187]

The allocation/scale dichotomy helps explain the failure of the Georgescu-Roegen/Daly approach to come up with any meaningful explanation as to how humanity has placed itself in the environmental straits it currently finds itself. Lacking a critical perspective relating the economy's production relations and allocational mechanisms, the tendency is to appeal to exogenous technological and ideological factors. Georgescu-Roegen's reduction of economic history to 'entropic degradation of matter-energy' goes so far as to treat the discovery of fossil fuels as a kind of original sin enabling 'the modern fever of industrial development' by which people became 'addicted to industrial luxuries' – the problem being that 'Man's nature is such that he is always

---

[185] Ayres and Kneese 1969, p. 295.
[186] Daly 1986, p. 320.
[187] Responding to the argument that allocation and scale cannot be separated, Daly (1994c, p. 91) warns that 'Theorists must not allow themselves to be debilitated and rendered irrelevant by too deep a philosophical reflection on the infinite interconnectedness of all things'. Apparently, some questions are too dangerous to ask. The same kind of intellectual default led Keynes to suggest that there is 'no reason to suppose that the existing system seriously misemploys the factors of production which are in use. . . . It is in determining the volume, not the direction, of actual employment that the existing system has broken down' (Keynes 1964, p. 379). This glib reassurance comes at the end of Keynes's (1964, p. 159) demonstration that speculative financial markets had converted 'capital development' into 'a by-product of the activities of a casino'! Similarly, Daly would have us believe that the ecological irrationality of markets is purely a matter of scale, not allocation, despite his own emphasis on the materially and socially variegated character of economically useful matter-energy.

interested in what will happen until tomorrow, not in thousands of years from now'.[188]

Daly, on his part, blames the 'technological project of redesigning the world (substituting technosphere for ecosphere) so as to allow for indefinite economic growth', and says that the 'conceptual roots of [this] growthmania are to be found in the orthodox doctrines of "relative scarcity" and "absolute wants"'.[189] Even though he criticises the 'money fetishism', according to which neither the satisfaction of desires nor the multiplication of interest income has any limit, Daly does not relate the dominant power of money in capitalist society to this system's production relations (the story of Midas is quite old, after all). As a result, he does not ask whether his critique of money and interest applies equally to capital and profit in general.[190] In sum, we are counselled not to struggle against the system of market-oriented production for profit that is reeking environmental havoc (that would be too dangerous and impractical), but to attack 'the ideology of growth'.[191] Evidently, the most promising line of attack is that provided by 'traditional religions' which 'teach man to conform his soul to reality by knowledge, self-discipline, and restraint on the multiplication of desires'.[192]

IV. Conclusion

While applauding the physiocrats' materialist analysis of capitalist production, and even appropriating some of their conceptions for his own purposes (especially the concept of nature's gifts and the natural basis of surplus-value), Marx criticises physiocracy's identification of value with nature's material use-value. In his view, this identification carries with it an unfortunate naturalisation of capitalist forms of valuation (exchange-value, money, and profit) and of the class relations which underpin them. This chapter has shown that the same basic critique applies to the contemporary nature-valuation debate within ecological economics. Like the physiocrats, the debate's

---

[188] Georgescu-Roegen 1973, pp. 54, 58.
[189] Daly 1974, p. 17.
[190] Daly 1992a, pp. 45, 186–7.
[191] Daly 1974, p. 19.
[192] Daly 1992a, p. 44; compare Daly and Cobb 1989.

participants have identified value with use-value in one form or another, and have not critically addressed the qualitative issues raised by the marketisation and monetisation of wealth in general and natural wealth in particular. And, as with the physiocrats, this gap is arguably rooted in the failure of ecological economists to develop the inner connections between capitalist production relations and capitalist valuation.

For Marx, by contrast, capitalism's reduction of value to labour time is based on this system's social separation of labour-power from the land and other necessary conditions of production, and their recombination only under capital exploiting wage-labour for a profit. In this sense, capitalism's fundamental form of valuation is rooted in what John Bellamy Foster has termed a 'metabolic rift' between people and nature.[193] Capitalist valuation also manifests the material, use-value requirements of value and capital: exploitable labour-power, conditions in which this exploitation can take place, and the necessity to objectify workers' labour in vendible commodities. After all, capitalism is a social form of human-material production; hence it still has material, use-value requirements.[194] But these requirements are obviously quite minimal compared to the requirements of a healthy and sustainable interchange between economy and nature. This is precisely why it is so crucial to analytically distinguish capitalist reproduction from human-natural reproduction in general.

Marx insists, moreover, that the regulation of social production by the market (the imperative for value to be objectified in saleable commodities) is itself based on the separation of producers from necessary production conditions.[195] It is true that markets and money have existed for aeons; but the dominant position of profit-driven commodity production, and the constant

---

[193] Foster 2000a.

[194] In Marx's analysis, this role of use-value is imprinted in the definition of value itself as *socially necessary* labour time, with social necessity defined partly in terms of the demand for the commodity in question. This implies, among other things, that value and price are simultaneously determined in Marx's view. See Saad-Filho 2002, Chapters 5–7.

[195] Stated differently, the regulation of resource allocation by market prices, and the corresponding role of money as a general representative and embodiment of wealth, are necessary forms of capitalist value understood as abstract labour time. For Marx's development of this connection, see Rosdolsky 1977, Chapter 5, and Marx 1981, Vol. I, Part I.

competitive pressures on the producers, owe themselves to the commodification of 'free' labour-power and its employment by autonomous enterprises controlling the (now 'separate') conditions of production. The conversion of natural conditions into mere conditions of market- and profit-driven production (either through their free appropriation or through their formal capitalisation as rent-yielding private or state property) is, in particular, enabled by the 'freeing' of labour-power from these conditions. This process continues today whenever public or communal lands are privatised, and whenever corporations are given freer reign to exploit national forests and other natural resources.

Marx's analysis contains a powerful ecological indictment of capitalism's valuation of natural wealth.[196] It highlights the contradiction between capitalism's reduction of value to abstract labour time and nature's contribution to wealth production. (Marx has often been blamed for this contradiction, but the real culprit is capitalism.) It also emphasises the tensions between value's monetary forms on the one hand, and the natural environment on the other. Money is homogenous, divisible, mobile, and quantitatively unlimited, by contrast with the qualitative variegation, interconnection, locational uniqueness, and quantitative limits of natural and ecological wealth.[197] Capitalist environmental crises – both crises in accumulation and crises in the conditions of human development – clearly manifest these tensions.[198]

The power of Marx's analysis derives from its establishment of inner connections between market valuation of nature and capitalism's core class relation: wage-labour. The qualitative and quantitative contradictions between monetary exchange-values on the one hand, and the real wealth of nature and the conditions of its reproduction on the other, are rooted in capitalism's alienation of the producers vis-à-vis the conditions of their existence. This perspective poses a challenge to workers and communities everywhere: that of converting capitalism's alienated social forms of nature-valuation into explicitly communal forms appropriate to human beings co-developing with their environments including other species. Only through a real communality,

---

[196] Burkett 1999a, Chapters 6–8.

[197] These anti-ecological features of money are noted by Sterrer (1993, p. 195), without, however, connecting the general use of money and monetary valuation to capitalism's specific production relations and specific value-substance: abstract labour time.

[198] Burkett 1999a, Chapter 9.

in which people gain control over the social conditions of their existence (instead of placing them at the service of exploitative and anarchically competitive money-making), will society be able to regulate its metabolic interchange with nature in a healthy and sustainable way. This vision of a communal reunion of the producers and the conditions of production, based on a recognition of the historically specific, limited character of capitalism, makes Marx's perspective on nature-valuation much more 'open' than those approaches which close off both history and utopia by accepting money, capital, and the market as permanent social forms of human and natural wealth.[199]

---

[199] See Proops 1989 on the advantages of historically 'open' analysis for ecological economics as both theory and policy.

Chapter Two
Values in Ecological Value Analysis: What Should We Be Learning from Contingent Valuation Studies?

The previous chapter argued that the general failure of ecological economists to critically analyse capitalist production relations helps explain their failure to construct an immanent critique of market valuation. The corollary question of how to bring pro-ecological values into an analysis framed by capitalism's class relations was addressed only indirectly, in terms of the tension between market valuation and certain given characteristics of natural wealth.

The present chapter pursues the role of values in ecological value analysis from a somewhat different angle: how people react when they are asked to put a price tag on nature in contingent valuation (CV) surveys. Section I introduces the CV method and its basis in neoclassical utility theory. Section II gives an overview of the difficulties confronted by CV in practice, focussing on the different kinds of resistance often exhibited by people when they are asked to value nature in money terms. It is suggested that the communal dimension of the environment helps explain why there are often wide gaps observed between compensatory and contributive payment bids, and why many survey respondents do not see either kind of payment as a monetary *valuation* of nature in the sense of neoclassical theory. This interpretation has provided sufficient political-ethical grounds for many ecological economists to reject CV.

As discussed in Section III, neoclassical economists have either ignored these political-ethical problems or interpreted them in relatively shallow ways as necessary to paper over the cracks in the underlying theory. Not so the ecological critics of CV, who, as shown in Section IV, have attacked the utilitarian and monetary foundations of market-environmentalism. However, the critics have not paid much attention to the underlying production relationships of market economies. Section V accordingly explains how Marxist analysis can incorporate the grassroots anti-market values exhibited in CV surveys into a framework that roots both monetary valuation and neoclassical utility theory in capitalist production relations. This framework interprets CV as a derivative form of the commodity fetishism associated with generalised market exchange which is, in turn, underpinned by capitalism's structural separation of the producers from necessary conditions of production. The Marxist approach thus locates popular resistance to CV as part of the broader struggle of working people for improvements in the total life process of human development in, against, and beyond capitalism. In this way, Marxism reinforces the commitments of ecological economics to methodological pluralism and to historical openness in the formulation of environmental policy visions.

I. Theory and practice of contingent valuation

CV is an outgrowth of neoclassical value theory. Associating value directly with relative price, neoclassical theory uses supply and demand analysis to demonstrate the welfare-enhancing properties of well-functioning markets. Specifically, it shows that, in a system of perfectly competitive markets for all goods and services (markets in which all buyers and sellers are pure 'price takers', that is, have no influence over market prices), the relative prices of different goods and services will accurately reflect: (i) the relative preferences of consumers for different goods and services, as represented by their marginal utilities (where marginal utility is the additional utility gained by consuming one more unit of a good or service, *ceteris paribus*); (ii) the relative marginal costs of producing different goods and services. Result (i) represents the demand side of the value (relative price) analysis, and result (ii) the supply side.[1]

However, the demand-side result depends on three additional assumptions about the preferences of individual households for different goods and services (their 'utility functions'). First, these preferences must be 'complete' in the sense that any combination of goods and services can be ordinally compared with any other. Second, preferences must be 'transitive': if combination a is preferred over combination b, and b is preferred to a third combination c, then a must be preferred to c. Third, preferences cannot be such that some combination of goods and services becomes preferred to itself, for example, after the passage of time or as a result of a change in mood. This is the 'reflexivity' requirement.[2]

It must be stressed from the outset that the neoclassical efficiency results are completely imaginary, and that this is only partly due to the lack of realism of perfect competition. At a more basic level, consumer choice cannot be reduced to a purely hedonistic and timeless calculus along the lines required by completeness, transitivity, and reflexivity of preferences.[3] This is related to the broader assumptions the theory makes about the natural and social environments. Strictly speaking, its efficiency results presume that *all* goods and services consumed by individuals, and *all* goods and services used in production, are bought and sold in markets. Otherwise, one must consider the effects of market activity on non-market conditions and activities, as well as the role of non-market, for example, cultural, phenomena in shaping consumer preferences and human perceptions of production costs. The neoclassical presumption, in other words, is that the only interactions that individuals have with other individuals or with their material setting are fully marketised relations in which all resources, and all produced goods and services, are subject to well-defined individual private property rights and can be bought and sold, and adequately valued, by money.

---

[1] An additional supply-side efficiency result is that the relative prices of different production inputs (land, labour, capital) will be equalised with their relative marginal contributions to production (their 'marginal products'). Chapters 3 and 4 deal with certain aspects of this supply-side dimension in connection with the 'natural capital' concept.

[2] Varian 1978, pp. 80–1.

[3] Lee and Keen 2004, pp. 174–81.

Having implicitly expunged all non-market conditions of economic life, it is not surprising that neoclassical theory treats all unpriced costs of market activity as special exceptions to the presumptive efficiency of the market system. Indeed, it is argued that such 'external costs' are due to a failure to extend market pricing to the conditions themselves. Neoclassical theory thus strives to put a 'correct' price on all the social costs of economic activity that are not currently priced.[4]

The tension between the market system and the economy's non-market environment is clearly manifested in the need to construct artificial prices for phenomena that are not currently priced. But neoclassical theory does not investigate this tension; the possibility that the unpriced natural and social costs in question are, by nature, antithetical to one-dimensional monetary valuation is simply ignored. Instead, neoclassical theory clings to the purely pragmatic question as to how a set of artificial prices can be constructed which is consistent with utility-based value theory. In other words, it attempts to conform the real world to the abstract-ideal market model, not the other way around. The correct relative prices for market externalities would thus reflect the relative marginal utilities of lowering the external costs in question, with due allowance for any expenses involved (for example, the costs of purchasing labour and other resources needed to clean up and/or protect the environment).[5] But how can one construct such efficient prices when markets, by definition, do not exist for these external effects? The most popular technique for answering this question is the contingent valuation (CV) method, which uses surveys to ascertain how much money respondents would be

---

[4] Equivalently, the external costs of economic activity can be re-expressed as external benefits. External pollution costs, for example, may be viewed as a failure to price the benefit of a less polluted environment. Hence, correction of market externalities can be phrased in terms of the pricing of either external benefits or external costs (Mishan 1971, pp. 101–24; Nicholson 1985, pp. 695–703).

[5] The discussion in text presumes an analysis striving toward the 'general equilibrium' goal of an efficient outcome in all markets simultaneously. In practice, the question is often how to price a particular external effect (or perhaps a government project of some sort), in order to determine if its benefits exceed its costs, *ceteris paribus*, that is, taking the situation in all other markets as given. But even such 'partial equilibrium' applications of neoclassical cost-benefit analysis derive their theoretical legitimacy from the underlying utility theory (Mishan 1971, Part II). By ignoring the 'second best' problems involved in partial equilibrium analysis, we merely address the theory in its most coherent form (Mishan 1971, pp. 90–9; Nicholson 1985, pp. 663–5).

willing to pay (WTP) to obtain a given environmental improvement (that is, to reduce the external cost), or, alternatively, how much money they would be willing to accept (WTA) as a substitute for the given environmental improvement.

The origins of CV can be traced to the late-1940s work of Ciriacy-Wantrup, who observed that the benefits of reduced soil erosion often have a 'public good' (collectively consumed) character, 'and suggested that one way to obtain information on the demand for the goods would be to ask individuals directly how much they would be willing to pay for successive increments'.[6] The actual implementation of this idea did not commence until the 1960s. 'Its first appearance in the legal system came in the 1980s, as a means of valuing damages from hazardous waste contamination at Superfund sites'.[7]

The CV method can be described in terms of a five-stage procedure.[8] In Stage 1, an artificial market is created by designing a set of survey questions that reduce an environmental outcome to monetary payments by or to the prospective survey respondents in exchange for the creation or preservation of an environmental good (for example, 'how much would you be willing to contribute to preserve a wetland area?', or 'how much would you have to be paid to accept the destruction of a wetland area?'). Stage 2 then administers the survey by face-to-face interviews, phone, or mail. Stage 3 commences the analysis of the survey results by calculating average figures for WTP and/or WTA (this becomes more complex insofar as the survey questions are in the form of dichotomous 'yes or no, I will/will not contribute' type choices). Stage 4, which some analyses skip, involves the estimation of 'bid curves' measuring the statistical correlations of the WTP and/or WTA figures with a set of respondent variables, such as income, education, and age, as well as (if applicable) some measure of the amount of the environmental good being bid on. These bid curves can be used to assess the accuracy, consistency and robustness of the survey results. Finally, Stage 5 aggregates the WTP and/or WTA responses into some kind of total value figure. This involves weighting the different responses (for example, in terms of the seriousness of environmental sub-impacts of the overall prospective outcome, and the

---

[6] Ciriacy-Wantrup 1947; quote from Portney 1994, p. 4.
[7] Ackerman and Heinzerling 2004, p. 159.
[8] Hanley, Shogren and White 1997, pp. 384–92.

differing intensities with which individuals are affected by these sub-impacts), correcting for sampling biases, and choosing the time period and discount rate for future benefits and costs.

Assuming that all the technical details can be worked out, the resulting WTP and/or WTA estimates will, it is hoped, provide monetary equivalents of the total and marginal utilities attained by the respondents from the environmental good in question. Insofar as the figures for total WTP and/or WTA exceed the prospective costs of the environmental good, its production or maintenance is deemed economically justified. Application of CV-derived prices (through taxes or environmental user-fees, for example) should then improve people's welfare in utility terms. 'The underlying general assumption', of course, 'is that people do possess relatively well-defined economic preferences for a vast variety of non-marketed public goods [goods that are collectively used]'.[9] In other words, the validity of the CV figures presumes that the three properties of neoclassical preference orderings mentioned earlier – completeness, transitivity, and reflexivity – apply to all households over all the relevant combinations of private and social outcomes. Only if preferences are 'well-behaved' in this sense – and all markets perfectly competitive – are the CV results a sensible guide to environmental policy.

II. Human resistance to contingent (capitalist) valuation

With the proliferation of CV studies, starting in the mid-1970s, one problem quickly became apparent: it mattered a great deal whether the people being surveyed were asked to give a value for WTA as opposed to WTP. In study after study, the average WTA figures greatly exceeded those for WTP, *ceteris paribus*.[10] In other words, the minimum compensation needed to get people to accept an environmental cost appeared to far surpass the maximum payment people were willing to make to remove the same cost, whereas the underlying theory predicted that the two amounts should be equal, at least insofar as they were both small compared to respondents' income and wealth levels.[11]

---

[9] Svedsäter 2003, p. 122.
[10] For an overview, see Brown and Gregory 1999, p. 325, Table 1.
[11] Willig 1976.

One of the most prominent verifications of this 'WTA-WTP gap' was the series of experiments conducted by Knetsch and Sinden, which found 'a wide disparity between the two bases for measuring economic values'.[12] Surveying the results of their own, and of other, studies, the same authors observed that:

> In spite of many assurances and widely accepted practice, the possibility of a sizeable and therefore potentially important difference in the alternative measures of economic worth has been raised by the results of numerous surveys. These have consistently found that people say they would require a far larger sum to forgo their rights of use or access to a resource than they would pay to keep the same entitlement.[13]

Similarly, Hanemann noted that 'recent empirical work using various types of interview procedures has produced some evidence of large disparities between WTP and WTA measures'.[14] Bromley reported that 'it is not uncommon to find that estimates of willingness to accept compensation – or compensation required – can be three to five times larger than willingness to pay measures for the same event'.[15] Vatn and Bromley sum things up: 'The evidence is irrefutable that bids based on willingness to accept compensation (WTA) will systematically exceed – often by a large ratio – bids based on willingness to pay. . . . WTA measures generally seem to exceed the WTP measures by not less than a factor of three'.[16]

WTA-WTP gaps do not in themselves prove a failure of the underlying theory. They could, for example, be partly explained by income and wealth effects, seeing as how environmental payments might represent a financial hardship, especially for less affluent respondents and their families. But to admit that per capita external costs might be the same order of magnitude as many households' private income and/or wealth levels would threaten the presumption that such externalities are a relatively minor deviation from market efficiency. Hence, a consensus quickly emerged among CV theorists

---

[12] Knetsch and Sinden 1984, p. 516.
[13] Knetsch and Sinden 1984, p. 508.
[14] Hanemann 1991, p. 635.
[15] Bromley 1995, p. 132, citing information provided by Ward and Duffield 1992.
[16] Vatn and Bromley 1994, p. 140.

that the typical WTA-WTP gaps were much too large to be explained by income and wealth effects. As Knetsch and Sinden put it: 'Wealth positions would be expected to vary little with or without most entitlements at issue. Consequently, little or no difference between the two measures would be anticipated from this source . . .'.[17] Hanemann similarly argues that income and wealth effects would have to be 'unusual' to explain the 'significant differences between WTP and WTA'.[18]

Although the WTA-WTP gap has been the prime area of controversy among CV analysts, other unexpected problems have arisen, having to do with certain difficulties respondents have in formulating monetary bids along the lines demanded by the surveys. These difficulties emerged most clearly when environmental analysts began to record the qualitative responses people gave when asked to place a monetary value on an environmental good. For present purposes, they can be divided into four categories: (i) problems of information, uncertainty, and context; (ii) questions of fairness in the distribution of payment commitments; (iii) the feeling among many respondents that environmental decision-making should be a matter of collective, deliberative discussion rather than individualised market bidding; (iv) respondents questioning the monetary valuation of nature on ethical grounds.

The information and contextualisation problems are illustrated by Clark, Burgess and Harrison's analysis of a UK survey connected with a wildlife enhancement scheme for a wetlands area, Pevensey Levels on the south coast of England.[19] They found that

> context was clearly problematic, for when faced with the WTP question, the 21 participants in the three groups had anchored their responses in a variety of ways. One, Ray, refused to answer on the grounds that no context was given; he said he 'needed to know a lot more'. Nine reported idiosyncratic reasons for answering in the way they did. Keith and Bob both failed to find a context, cheerfully admitting that they had not really understood the question, while Daniel thought that he was contributing to environmental causes in general. Carla and Barry seem to have just come up with a number.

---

[17] Knetsch and Sinden 1984, pp. 507–8.
[18] Hanemann 1991, p. 635.
[19] Clark, Burgess and Harrison 2000.

Susan had wondered how to compare the Levels with other nature conservation areas that she was concerned about, while Norman compared his use of the Levels with his use of other areas. Malcolm tried to think in terms of the global sum that would be forthcoming if everyone contributed but Laura did not see that any money was needed in the first place – 'I thought wetlands looked after themselves' – and quite consistently bid zero extra.[20]

One very common theme in respondents' discussions 'was how to work out WTP for one project in isolation':[21]

People agreed that the value of any particular scheme could only be determined relationally. Acknowledging their lack of scientific expertise and their limited knowledge of the national picture, people felt it was impossible for them to make a meaningful judgement about the worth of the Pevensey scheme in relation to the large number of probably equally worthy schemes around the country. They were just not 'qualified', as Bob put it.[22]

The minimum lesson that can be derived from such responses is that CV survey methods only make sense 'when participants are familiar with the commodity being valued, when they have had experiences with making choices about the commodity, and when there is little uncertainty'.[23] Needless to say, in the case of many environmental 'commodities' none of these conditions is likely to hold, at least not for most respondents. Interestingly, however, many respondents who view themselves as inadequately informed seem to place a high priority on the environment, and express a strong interest in obtaining relevant information. In the Pevensey survey, for example: 'Despite having to struggle with the WTP question, group members reported that they took the survey seriously and were concerned about the truthfulness of their answers. In part, this reflected a belief that the questions being asked were important in some way for the area and/or for nature conservation . . .'.[24]

---

[20] Clark, Burgess and Harrison 2000, p. 51. Some modifiers of the respondents' names have been omitted from the quotation for brevity's sake. O'Neill (1997, p. 124) reports similar responses from the same survey.
[21] Clark, Burgess and Harrison 2000, p. 55.
[22] Ibid.
[23] Stevens et al. 1991, p. 391.
[24] Clark, Burgess and Harrison 2000, p. 55; compare O'Neill 1997, p. 124.

Similarly, in analysing responses to a CV survey on actions to prevent global warming, Svedsäter found that, given the uncertainties involved, 'many people are willing to "pay what it takes", while being reluctant to assess any specific value for the amenity on a continuous scale'.[25] As two respondents put it:

> because if global warming threatens to destroy the whole planet, then you're going to say ok, I'll pay everything, but how to assess how much it is worth to you, and maybe not going to threatens your life. You see it is not something you're used to put[ting] a value on, you're used to [putting] a value on something and then you get that thing.

> It's very difficult to, huh, to give you, you know, if you want some sort of a bold hard figure, how much is it worth to you, I mean, you know, in a touching feely sense it's worth a lot to me if it succeeds 'cause it's gonna help my children and my grandchildren and, huh, so forth, but asking me to put a figure on it, how much per year am I willing to pay is extremely difficult.[26]

Moreover, this desire for more information is often connected with respondents' wishes to contribute their 'fair share' to the environmental good. They wish to know more about the nature of the *collective* benefits and costs involved in relation to their *individual* ability to pay.[27] Svedsäter thus found that 'people are keen to reflect upon how much they otherwise spend on charitable contributions (mental accounts), they want to pay a fair share of the cost of a solution, and they tend to signal a concern for a much larger set of environmental amenities'.[28] Such ethical responses must be distinguished from monetary valuation in the sense of neoclassical utility maximisation. For instance, they often assign a *communal responsibility* to those who are able to pay:

> I don't think I can put a figure to it. I can just put a percentage of my income . . . everyone should pay but in different gradings, i.e., people who are obviously less capable of paying, due to lower income or large families,

---

[25] Svedsäter 2003, p. 130.
[26] Ibid.
[27] Clark, Burgess and Harrison, 2000, pp. 51–5.
[28] Svedsäter 2003, p. 123.

and I'm not going to be able to pay the same [amount] as people who are industrialists. . . . [What is important is] knowing that everyone else is doing the same thing, because why should it be that [only] people who believe in it [pay] and, it's very difficult to explain but, if you're paying you feel it has to be part of a joint effort with everyone else, it can't just be selectively done.[29]

In short, even insofar as people are willing to provide monetary figures for WTP or WTA, these figures often do not seem to connote an endorsement of the principle of individual monetary valuation of nature as such, but rather notions of fair contribution to a worthy communal cause. Thus, peoples' willingness to help cover the monetary *cost* of protecting natural resources does not necessarily imply their endorsement of monetary *valuation* of these resources.[30] This interpretation is reinforced by another response often observed: that the biggest payment burdens for environmental protection should be borne by those who are responsible for the 'external costs' in question. A respondent to the global warming survey thus argued that: 'The second thing that should be taken into account is the fact that industrialists, or people who are related to the industry, which is actually producing part of the problem, should probably be taxed, in quotation marks, more'.[31] As pointed out by Bromley, such a broadly shared preference for 'increasing the costs of polluting events to responsible parties' may help explain the WTA-WTP gap referred to earlier.[32] After all, even from a purely judicial standpoint,

it seems contrived – and is often illegal – to ascertain an individual's willingness to pay to avoid a welfare-decreasing event. . . . it is clearly wrong therefore to measure natural resource damages using willingness-to-pay responses from those whose welfare is reduced by these damages'.[33]

Or, as Vatn and Bromley suggest,

by striving to mimic the conventional market behaviour of individual consumers, it is apparently thought that environmental goods and services

---

[29] Svedsäter 2003, p. 129.
[30] Ackerman and Heinzerling 2004, pp. 153–78.
[31] Svedsäter 2003, p. 129.
[32] Bromley 1995, p. 129.
[33] Bromley 1995, pp. 132, 134.

can be made to seem like 'ordinary' goods and services. But of course the moral dimension intrudes into the presumed clarity of economic choice. Individuals who imagine with some conviction that, say, their drinking water should be uncontaminated, will be expected to be unimpressed, if not irate, about having to pay to prevent it from becoming even more contaminated. They will often wonder why they should have to pay to obtain a state of nature that existed prior to the advent of chemical runoff caused by someone else.[34]

In other words, WTA-WTP gaps, including those associated with 'unusual' income and wealth effects, may represent a people's protest against the violation of their communal rights in the environmental commons, and against the failure of those responsible for environmental 'externalities' to fulfill their duties to the (present and future) collective.[35] Far from corresponding to monetary valuations of nature's utility for individual human beings, WTP and WTA 'bids' may be imperfect, implicit inscriptions of people's feelings about the amounts that should be contributed to the common good.

Another communal dimension of the CV dilemma is respondent resistance to purely individualised administration of the surveys. There is a strong basis for such resistance insofar as deliberative discussions among all relevant environmental 'stakeholders', with participation (but not control) by relevant scientific experts, may encourage the exchange of important information that can help people formulate and focus their views on environmental costs. Such a result was found by Kaplowitz and Hoehn in 'the initial stage of a nonmarket valuation study of mangrove ecosystems in Mexico's Yucatan Peninsula', which 'included both focus groups and individual interviews'.[36] Commenting on the fact that the focus groups tended to raise a more variegated array of mangrove services for discussion than did the individual interviews, the authors conjecture that:

> The group dynamics of focus groups may tend to encourage speculation about information. It may be that once groups have identified the obvious routine activities that the group dynamics lead to consideration of 'what

---

[34] Vatn and Bromley 1994, p. 141.
[35] Compare Brown and Gregory 1999, pp. 327–8.
[36] Kaplowitz and Hoehn 2001, p. 239.

else'. In the case of consumptive and non-consumptive use information, the data suggest that the focus groups revealed significantly more information about intermittent consumptive use activities (e.g., crab collection, salt extraction, shrimp collection) than did the individual interviews.[37]

Clark, Burgess and Harrison's analysis of the group discussions in the Pevensey survey strongly supports the view that people tend to prefer deliberative group settings over individual interviews, and that this preference is based on both information issues and democratic values.[38] In other words, this is not so much a preference for groups per se as a feeling that groups, if set up democratically and with access to relevant information, are better suited to giving all legitimate environmental values and interests a fair hearing. This feeling was reflected in some Pevensey respondents' negative reactions to the knowledge that survey results would be used to place a price tag on nature:

> Doubts about what WTP figures would be used for, suspicion about who 'owned' the CV survey, and feelings that people had been somehow duped into taking part, grew over the life of the two in-depth groups. The questionnaire had been presented as a survey on nature and nature conservation and at the time of their interviews members of both groups took this statement at face value. . . . When the groups were told how WTP figures are analyzed and what the results might mean to economists or decision-makers, a number of individuals expressed anger and distress, feeling that they had been manipulated.[39]

A similar preference for a more open and deliberative procedure seems to underlie the reaction of one of the individual (non-local) interviewees in the Pevensey study:

> I said to the interviewer, perhaps I should read up on Pevensey. She said no, you don't need to do that, that you needed if you like uninformed

---

[37] Kaplowitz and Hoehn 2001, p. 245. At the same time, the results suggested that in some cases, individuals felt 'more comfortable volunteering controversial information unknown to researchers during individual interview sessions rather than sharing that information in a focus group setting among people from their own locale' (Kaplowitz and Hoehn 2001, p. 245). This may reflect the influences of class and gender power structures as well as competition over access to natural resources among members of the focus groups.
[38] Clark, Burgess and Harrison 2000, pp. 56ff.
[39] Clark, Burgess and Harrison 2000, pp. 56–7.

opinion to look at it in a new light. . . . So it depends on *your* approach. If
you wanted just the public reaction then that's fair enough. But if you wanted
a more informed reply, I think people have got to be put on their guard to
think about it and to study what the objectives are.[40]

This preference for group airing of information and concerns need not imply
that *all* environmental policy decisions should be subject to group deliberation
let alone a democratic vote. What is important is that all environmental
stakeholders and their values (including preservationism) be given a fair
hearing. Especially as concerns environmental questions on which most people
lack information, many of the technical issues involved in implementation,
and in some cases even prioritisations, may have to be worked out by elected
representatives acting on 'the advice of biologists and naturalists, professional
and amateur, and . . . the voice of people who have practical knowledge of
and special relations to different places'.[41] This is all part of the give and take
of the democratic process. Expert opinion is obviously needed to frame
different policy options for dealing with an environmental 'externality'.
Bromley reduces these options to three: 'restoration, rehabilitation, and
substitution', adding that the 'question of which corrective measure is to be
taken cannot be separated from the issue of compensation'.[42] But 'the most
fundamental level' of the choice among corrective goals still involves 'the
problems of the decision process – and the decision rule – that will determine
the preferred response'.[43]

In short, one should not minimise the difficulties involved in constructing
viable democratic procedures and rules for environmental policy, and in
determining the role of experts therein. But what the CV studies seem to be
telling us is that many people do not want to see individual monetary
valuations, and financial decision rules derived therefrom, displace the open
airing, reconciliation, and prioritisation of environmental values. Indeed,
many survey respondents express strong and principled opposition to the
pricing of nature as a policy guide. Apparently, these people have failed to

---

[40] O'Neill 1997, p. 124 (emphasis in original).
[41] O'Neill 1997, p. 124.
[42] Bromley 1995, pp. 130–1.
[43] Ibid.

embrace the utilitarian calculus of neoclassical theory with its treatment of nature as just another commodity.[44]

Thus, in analysing results from a CV mail-survey study of four New England wildlife species (bald eagle, Atlantic salmon, wild turkey, and coyote), Stevens, et al. show that many respondents were 'unable or unwilling to give meaningful answers to questions about the value of wildlife', due to their 'ethical or moral principles' including the notion 'that wildlife has an intrinsic right to exist, independent of human attitudes towards their existence'.[45]

> Analysis of the follow-up questions suggested that many respondents were motivated by altruism and ethical considerations. Seventy-nine percent of respondents to the salmon survey agreed with the statement that, 'All species of wildlife have a right to exist independent of any benefit or harm to people', and 70 percent of respondents gave this as one of three most important reasons for the existence of bald eagles, wild turkeys, and coyotes in New England.[46]

Many respondents specifically objected to the principle of monetary valuation. For example, while over eighty per cent 'said that bald eagles, wild turkeys, and Atlantic salmon are either very or somewhat important to them', roughly two-thirds of respondents said they 'would not pay any money' for their existence:

> When asked why, only 6 percent of those not willing to pay said that these species were worth nothing to them. Forty percent of those refusing to pay for bald eagles or wild turkeys protested the payment vehicle used; they stated that the money should come from taxes or license fees. Twenty-five percent protested for ethical reasons, claiming that wildlife values should not be measured in dollar terms.[47]

Moreover,

> 44 percent of all respondents agreed with the statement that 'preservation of wildlife should not be determined by how much money can be spent'

---

[44] Spash 2000a, pp. 197–201.
[45] Stevens et al. 1991, pp. 390–1.
[46] Stevens et al. 1991, p. 396.
[47] Stevens et al. 1991, p. 397.

and 67 percent of all respondents agreed that, 'As much wildlife as possible should be preserved no matter what the cost.' . . . Two-thirds of salmon survey respondents said trade-offs between money and wildlife did not describe their decision-making behaviour . . .[48]

Even allowing for sampling bias (environmentally-inclined people tend to be over-represented among respondents to such mail surveys), these results seem to contradict the completeness, and possibly also the transitivity, properties of preferences required by neoclassical utility theory. In fact, Stevens, et al. report that the answers provided by 70 per cent of their respondents 'appeared inconsistent with' neoclassical 'models of behavior'.[49] Similarly, in his global warming survey study, Svedsäter observes that the 'difficulty of the task' of monetary valuation

is furthermore reflected by the fact that roughly 20% of the respondents reported guessing or were just making up an answer. These results hence not only suggest that standard economic theory is insufficient to explain CV results, but also that responses seem to be arbitrarily constructed during the course of the interview.[50]

Svedsäter goes on to interpret his results as a verification that 'people are concerned about what ought to be right or wrong in society when faced with the valuation scenario', in which case even 'very large WTP estimates' may actually express peoples' opinion 'that the environment is not well represented by economic [monetary] value'.[51] This interpretation is consistent with Spash's finding, based on a survey of psychological studies of the motivations shaping CV bids, that the 'complexity of value formation and expression' in CV responses goes 'far beyond that generally accepted by economic models'.[52]

Indeed, a prime theme among respondents seems to be the gross inadequacy of money as a measure of natural wealth, given the latter's communal and

---

[48] Stevens et al. 1991, p. 398.
[49] Ibid.
[50] Svedsäter 2003, p. 123. This jibes with Diamond and Hausmans's (1994) survey of CV studies, which finds that 'contingent valuation responses are not consistent with [neoclassical] economic theory. . . . In short, we think that the evidence supports the conclusion that to date, contingent valuation surveys do not measure the preferences they attempt to measure' (p. 46).
[51] Svedsäter 2003, p. 123; compare Ackerman and Heinzerling 2004, pp. 158–9.
[52] Spash 2000b, p. 453.

inter-generational character. Here is a group-discussion from the Pevensey study:[53]

> *Malcolm*: Well, you're talking our very existence, really. [agreement] If you're talking about the environment, then there isn't a price because it is your life, really. Our future life.

> *Meg*: And, I mean, diversity is so important to nature and without diversity it will not self-perpetuate and it will become, um, sterile eventually [agreement]. And, I mean, I think that's inevitable. Well that is the reality. That's why nature is diverse, because it's, it's all built on relationships. And every time you destroy one creature, you're destroying the relationships between that and other species, and altering the micro-environment. So it's not just about the Levels. It's about much broader issues. I don't think you can put a price on that . . .

> *Carol*: Isn't this, I mean, it's a much bigger issue than all this, isn't it really? Because this money business. Now everything [emphasis] has to have a price on it [agreement]. So we're told. I mean, I think it's rubbish!

In short:

> There was a feeling of moral outrage . . . that a monetary sum was being used as a measure of what individuals saw as their ethical and moral values for nature. Group members were at pains to distinguish the economic value of land (when traded as private property or utilized for tourism, for example) from the much more significant issue of values of nature itself, and nature's contribution to quality of life, now and in the future. . . . A refusal to accept that it was proper to put a money value on nature and convictions such as the right of nature to exist and its fundamental importance for humanity, now and in the future, found consensus . . .[54]

This moral outrage seems to reflect, in part, a strong feeling that nature is 'expressive of social relations between generations . . . our relation to the past and future of communities to which we belong . . . a particular set of relations to one's children that would be betrayed were a price upon it accepted'.[55] As a Pevensey respondent put it:

---

[53] Clark, Burgess and Harrison 2000, p. 50.
[54] Clark, Burgess and Harrison 2000, p. 55.
[55] O'Neill 1997, p. 120.

it's a totally disgusting idea, putting a price on nature. You can't put a price on the environment. You can't put a price on what you're going to leave for your children's children. . . . It's a heritage. It's not an open cattle market.[56]

Similarly, when confronted with questions about the monetary value of their relationship to the land which was being threatened by a dam project, the Yavapai people of central Arizona insisted that 'it is wrong to value their land as a commodity, that money could not capture its value or compensate for its loss'.[57] 'As one Yavapia teenager put it, "This land is our mother. You don't sell your mother"'.[58] In short, many people across cultural divides seem to feel that 'the most rational response to such [CV] queries is, roughly, "what in the hell are you talking about?"'.[59] 'Even in the most commodified societies, practices of assigning prices (or otherwise commensurating) such [environmental] goods are likely to be unfamiliar, circumscribed, irrelevant or disallowed'.[60]

Such common-sense resistance to environmental monetisation may help account for the failure of many governments to follow the neoclassical advice of implementing price-based, as opposed to quantitative and non-monetary, environmental regulations on firms and other polluters.[61] Insofar as people's communal-environmental values have any influence on government policies, directly or through electoral voting patterns, the aversion to pricing nature may be manifested (imperfectly to be sure) in a government preference for pollution limits, technological restrictions, and other 'command and control'

---

[56] Ibid. A similar view was often expressed by Rachel Carson, e.g.: 'The tragedy of the oceanic islands lies in the uniqueness, the irreplaceability of the species they have developed by the slow processes of the ages. In a reasonable world men would have treated these islands as precious possessions, as natural museums filled with beautiful and curious works of creation, valuable beyond price because nowhere in the world are they duplicated' (Carson 1951, pp. 96–7).

[57] Nelson Espeland 1999, p. 10.

[58] Nelson Espeland 1999, p. 11.

[59] Lohmann 1998, p. 4.

[60] Ibid.

[61] Evidence suggests that even when market-based regulations are used, they tend to serve mainly as revenue-sources, not efficiency-enhancers, and as a supplement to non-market controls. See, for example, Huppes and Kagan 1989; Kopp, Portney and DeWitt 1990; Savornin Lohman 1994; Verbruggen 1994; Harris 1996; Lotspeich 1998; Ciorcirlan and Yandle 2003; Jordan, Wurzel and Zito 2003; Kirchgassner and Schneider 2003. Verbruggen (1994, pp. 41–2) refers to this conundrum as an 'instrument crisis' in the theory and practice of neoclassical environmental economics.

devices, in spite of their purported inefficiency compared to market-mimicking instruments.[62]

III. Neoclassical reactions to contingent valuation difficulties

The resistance of CV-survey respondents to the individualised utilitarian and monetary calculus poses a real problem for neoclassical theory. Given the paradigm's commitment to 'positive', value-free analysis, it is supposed to take people's preferences as given and then analyse market outcomes on that basis. This rules out the *imposition* of hedonistic utility-maximising behaviour where it does not exist. But the communal and anti-market preferences exhibited in CV studies nullify the theory's main claims regarding the efficiency and welfare-maximising properties of competitive markets. Not surprisingly, the neoclassical school has responded to this paradigm-threatening difficulty mainly by either ignoring or soft-pedalling the most inconvenient CV results.

For example, the most common response to the WTA-WTP gap is not to seriously consider people's concerns about communal rights and responsibilities (fairness), but simply to use the WTP numbers on grounds of practicality. As noted by Bromley, 'within the contingent valuation method, there is an overwhelming affinity among researchers for measures of *willingness to pay* as the procedure to estimate the value of natural resource damages'.[63] Indeed, even though WTP *prima facie* represents a *cost*, not a *benefit*, to people, 'it has become the accepted tradition to use willingness-to-pay estimates to derive *benefit* measures with which to inform the policy process', including, for example, 'the *benefits* of clean water'.[64] Ward and Duffield state the rationale for this tradition:

---

[62] Buchanan and Tullock 1975.

[63] Bromley 1995, p. 129 (emphasis in original). One environmental economics text goes so far as to identify the CV method with the collection and analysis of WTP figures, not even mentioning WTA. According to this text, 'the *contingent valuation* approach relies on surveys to ascertain how much respondents would be willing to pay to preserve the environment, to reduce the amount of human-induced injury to it, or to lower the various types of environmental risk posed by modern industrial society' (Tietenberg 1996, p. 73 [emphasis in original]).

[64] Bromley 1995, p. 131 (first emphasis added); compare Brown and Gregory 1999, p. 324.

In hypothetical market applications, willingness-to-accept scenarios are often implausible. Respondents simply do not have experience with or cannot realistically accept the idea of being compensated for natural resource losses. For this reason, guidelines for implementation of contingent valuation have generally recommended use of willingness-to-pay formats.[65]

The authors do not explain why lack of experience does not apply equally to both WTP and WTA numbers. After all, many people may be just as uncomfortable having to pay to prevent or repair natural resource destruction, especially insofar as they are not the ones responsible for said destruction. In either case, such inexperience appears to violate the underlying theoretical assumptions of fully informed utility maximisation and convertibility of utilities into monetary equivalents. In searching for a way out of this dilemma, some have gone so far as to interpret the 'loss aversion' evident in WTA-WTP gaps as evidence of a kind of sub-optimal behaviour. It is suggested, for example, that the observed differences between WTA and WTP reflect an asymmetry between the subjective perceptions pertaining to compensatory offers and predetermined monetary 'endowments', respectively.[66] The basic idea is that 'desirable things are considered more valuable when they are part of a person's endowment than when they are not, all else equal':[67]

Thus, money or assets that are considered by individuals to be part of their endowment seem to be valued more highly – it takes a more advantageous offer for them freely to give them up – than money or assets that are not considered to be included in their present endowment. If this is the case, evaluations will then be affected accordingly, as it would take more dollars of the latter to be equivalent to any sum of the former. . . . As with responses to changes in physical attributes, such as temperature and light, where stimulus of a change is perceived by individuals in relation to a reference point or previous adaptation level, the evaluation evidenced by offers of added money wealth seems to differ from that of giving up money wealth. . . . The observed reluctance to give up money or assets seems likely to be, at least in part, due to various cognitive biases and such motives as

---

[65] Ward and Duffield 1992, pp. 201–2.
[66] Thaler 1980; Knetsch and Sinden 1984.
[67] Brown and Gregory 1999, p. 327.

an incentive to protect against a feeling of regret that might accompany a deliberately made change in asset protection. Thus, a possible cost of future regret is imposed on making a change that is absent from maintaining the present endowments, and choices will be influenced accordingly. A similar disincentive to change may be posed by the necessity for exerting more mental effort in weighing the net benefits of changing assets that is likely to be less onerous or absent when no change is made.[68]

In short, by treating the conundrum of the WTA-WTP gap in terms of subjective individual perceptions of the best strategy for maintaining individual monetary endowments (that is, by treating human motivations as equivalent to the protection of one's initial stack of chips at the poker table), all communal aspects of natural wealth are conveniently suppressed. But the cost is irremediable theoretical incoherence, seeing as how the hypothesised subjective asymmetry clearly violates preference transitivity and reflexivity – essential presumptions of the theory. Inconsistent choices among plural or singular alternatives are now possible depending on which side of the asymmetry the individual is on.

In a more useful vein, Hanemann argues that the WTA-WTP gap manifests the non-substitutability of environmental improvements and private goods.[69] In his view, environmental improvements are 'public goods' (goods that are collectively consumed), which implies that they may have unique characteristics not replicable by private goods. Indeed,

> if the public good has almost no substitutes (e.g., Yosemite National Park, or in a different context, your own life), there is no reason why WTP and WTA could not differ vastly; in the limit, WTP could equal the individual's entire (finite) income, while WTA could be infinite.[70]

Amiran and Hagen extend this analysis to a broader class of utility functions by focussing on an important characteristic of pure public goods: 'The quantity (and not the price) of these public goods is determined exogenously to the individual'.[71] Such a quantity constraint must effectively limit substitution

---

[68] Knetsch and Sinden 1984, pp. 516–17.
[69] Hanemann 1991.
[70] Hanemann 1991, pp. 635–6.
[71] Amiran and Hagen 2003, p. 458.

possibilities, possibly leading to 'extreme differences between WTA and WTP' even without the assumption of complete non-substitutability as such.[72]

Unfortunately, these authors do not pursue the non-substitutability of the environment and private goods to the point of a full-scale critique of monetary valuation. Amiran and Hagen do indicate that 'the phenomenon underlying our results is the same as that presented by Hanemann – an inability to substitute money for a public good'.[73] But the term 'money' here serves as a mere symbol for the private goods that it can purchase. The tension between money and environmental goods involves much more than the difficulty of purchasing the latter with the former. It is also a contradiction between the variegated material-social character of natural wealth versus the purely quantitative, uni-dimensional character of monetary values, as well as a contradiction between the communality of the environment and the private power of money over that environment. These contradictions cannot be adequately addressed on the neoclassical level of representative individuals' utility functions. They call for a structural analysis of the socio-economic (class) relations that shape production and monetary wealth-valuation.[74] Still, the public good explanation of the WTA-WTP gap is about as close as neoclassical theory gets to an admission that monetary pricing of nature is structurally flawed.

Hence, the dominant tendency among CV practitioners is to ignore the questions raised by the environment's public good character, and to proceed on the basis of 'plausible' WTP estimates that commensurate the environment with Twinkies, Big Macs, cell phones, and the numerous other ecologically disastrous products generated by the market system. Any survey responses contradicting such commensuration are typically thrown out: 'protest bids together with strategic bids, "wild guesses" and the like are rejected'.[75]

---

[72] Ibid.

[73] Amiran and Hagen 2003, p. 463.

[74] For example, one should address class-based differences in the amounts, and the qualities, of environmental public goods available to different individuals. In the real world, environmental public goods are rarely *pure* – for example, the wealthy can more easily protect themselves from pollution by moving to cleaner areas and confines, and can more easily afford the amenities needed to cope with environmental problems (air conditioners, automobiles, pharmaceuticals, etc.).

[75] O'Neill 1997, p. 116.

> When survey respondents refuse to answer the questions posed to them, or when they give answers that, to the survey managers, appear to reflect unrealistically high valuations of natural resources, their responses are simply not counted. . . . When the data are analyzed, extreme values and other seemingly illogical responses are normally screened out; estimated environmental valuations are based only on those responses that appear well-behaved to the investigator.[76]

> It is standard practice in the contingent valuation literature to eliminate some responses as being unreasonably large to be the true willingness-to-pay. Thus trimming responses that are more than, say, 5 percent of income for an environmental public good that contains only nonuse value may be criticized for having an arbitrary cutoff, but not for omitting answers that are believed to be credible. Similarly, it is standard practice to eliminate some responses of zero on the basis that these are 'protest zeros', that answers to other questions in the survey indicate that individuals do put a positive value on changes in the level of the public good, and thus zero is not a credible answer.[77]

Heightening the arbitrariness of such procedures is the fact that 'in practice there does not appear to be any agreement over what constitutes a protest response let alone a comprehensive rationale'.[78] Indeed, 'the practice of censoring protest responses appears to vary across surveys using different conceptual models and in cases where the same CV model has been employed'.[79] In this way, monetary valuation of nature becomes a self-fulfilling prophecy, and analysts can focus their energies on various technical and statistical biases that leave the underlying hedonistic calculus unquestioned.[80] Besides, given that such biases 'can be kept acceptably small with suitably designed survey instruments', is not a positive monetary valuation better than no valuation at all?[81] For the technocratic environmentalist, as O'Neill

---

[76] Ackerman and Heinzerling 2004, pp. 163–4.
[77] Diamond and Hausman 1994, p. 47.
[78] Jorgensen et al. 1999, p. 133.
[79] Ibid.
[80] See, for example, Tietenberg 1996, pp. 73–4; Hanley, Shogren and White 1997, pp. 392–4.
[81] Tietenberg 1996, p. 74.

observes, the important thing is that 'the sums come out more or less right. . . . Environmental benefits outstrip costs'.[82]

IV. The political-ethical critique: scope, depth, and limits

The critics of CV are to be commended for their revelation that the neoclassical market emperor has no political or ethical clothing – that the hedonistic utility-maximising calculus and its reflection in monetary prices is not adequate to human-natural relations, which are essentially communal. As O'Neill puts it, the neoclassical approach presumes that environmental damages only occur 'because environmental goods and harms are unpriced', but this viewpoint

> runs up against a political and ethical objection that runs in the opposite direction; that our environmental problems have their source not in a failure to apply market norms rigorously enough, but in the very spread of market mechanisms and norms. The source of environmental problems lies in part in the colonization of markets, not only in real geographical terms across the globe, but also in the introduction of market mechanisms and norms into new spheres of life that previously have been protected from markets. The neoclassical project of attempting to cost all environmental goods in monetary terms becomes an instance of a larger expansion of market boundaries. The proper response is to resist that expansion.[83]

From this perspective, the protest bids and overtly anti-market ethics expressed in many CV surveys reflect people's shared feeling that there are important elements of the human life-process that are unpriceable, or which become corrupted if subjected to monetary valuations and calculations. It is therefore worth considering for a moment what the market's corrupting effects entail. Perhaps the most basic difficulty is that even insofar as they represent individual preferences as neoclassical utility theory suggests, monetary prices are 'reason-blind':

> The strength and weakness of the *intensity* of a preference as measured by a person's willingness to pay at the margin for its satisfaction do count in

---

[82] O'Neill 1997, p. 116.
[83] O'Neill 1997, pp. 114–15.

a decision; the strength and weakness of the *reasons* for a preference do not. Preferences are treated as expressions of mere taste, to be priced and weighed one with the other.[84]

In other words, CV and other monetary pricing techniques 'misconstrue the ethical aspects related to environmental choices by forcing them into becoming ordinary trade-off problems'.[85] The result is that the preferences that underpin market prices, 'far from being rational', are, 'rather, whimsical'; as one Pevensey survey respondent describes the pricing of nature:

> . . . if it goes out of fashion, it's in danger all the time, isn't it? If the price drops, nobody's going to be interested. That aspect, that way of thinking is not really on is it? You can't put it on the Stock Market really. It's our very existence. It's our future.[86]

The whimsicality of market pricing poses especially large dangers to the natural environment, given the complexities, uncertainties, and irreversibilities attached to ecological phenomena and the corresponding difficulty (indeed, impossibility) of capturing all relevant environmental use-values (or costs) using monetary prices which are by definition one-dimensional.[87] This problem should be familiar to neoclassical economists from the work of Tinbergen, which shows that any given set of policy goals is unfeasible if the number of policy instruments is less than the number of goals.[88] Similarly, the singular instrument of a money price is insufficient to register the multiple, overlapping, interacting, and highly uncertain environmental use-values (goals) bound up with any particular natural phenomena to which the price is applied.

Market pricing, and the utility theory underpinning it, are particularly ill-equipped to deal with large-scale and structural changes in the system of production and its interaction with the environment, as opposed to small, marginal changes within a given system.[89] And it is the large-scale changes that are likely to have the biggest environmental and social consequences,

---

[84] O'Neill 2002, p. 144 (emphasis in original).
[85] Vatn 2000, p. 493.
[86] O'Neill 1997, p. 123.
[87] Hueting 1996, p. 87; Gustafsson 1998; Vatn 2000; Nunes and Van der Bergh 2001.
[88] Tinbergen 1970.
[89] Bergström 1993.

shaking up variegated human transactions with nature in a way that generates more widespread and intense distributional and value conflicts.[90] As observed by O'Neill:

> Market approaches offer conflict resolution without rational assessment and debate. However, since environmental conflicts are open to reasoned debate which aims to change preferences rather than simply recording them, it follows that different institutional forms are required for their resolution. Where conflict is open to reasoned adjudication, discursive institutions are the appropriate form for resolution.[91]

This perspective suggests that the purported advantage of markets – their reduction of various conflicting wants and needs to a system of uni-dimensional money prices to which people adapt their individual optimising behaviour – in fact favours the view that environmental phenomena 'are issues for political debate and judgement, not for pricing'.[92] Environmental issues are best addressed not by 'the market picture of democracy as a procedure for aggregating and effectively meeting the given preferences of individuals', but rather by 'democracy as a forum through which judgements and preferences are formed and altered through reasoned dialog'.[93] In this way, the political-ethical critique stands the famous Arrow Impossibility Theorem on its head.[94] According to Arrow's Theorem, it is impossible to construct a social preference ordering out of given individual preferences without violating a minimal set of conditions, including the condition that 'social choice should display the same properties that neo-classicists routinely ascribe to individual choice'.[95] This theorem has generally been used to argue against non-market forms of decision-making; but, once one recognises the limitations of neoclassical utility theory and market pricing in the environmental arena, the opposite conclusion can be drawn. Vatn and Bromley put it this way:

> In a new domain of collective choice – and many novel issues related to the management of environmental goods and services certainly qualify as a

---

[90] Neefjes 1999; Campos 2002.
[91] O'Neill 2002, p. 144.
[92] O'Neill 1997, p. 126.
[93] O'Neill 2002, p. 143; compare Anand 2000.
[94] Arrow 1963.
[95] Stirling 1997, p. 190.

new domain – the most basic question concerns the development of societal norms and standards. The collective choice problem is, first of all, about advancing common ways of understanding what the pertinent issues are about. Only then can we develop a basis for collective choice predicated upon the elicitation of individual choice. It is axiomatic – and also well known since Arrow's seminal work – that coherent collective choice cannot be made on the basis of some simple aggregation of individual preferences alone.[96]

In other words, environmental issues demand that the domain of individual choices be restricted through the forging of consensus (social choice) regarding certain standards of behaviour and the kinds of decision-making rules that should be applied in different situations.[97] Such a consensus-forging lightens 'the heavy hand of Arrow's Impossibility Theorem' through reasoned open deliberations in which people are informed and their preferences reshaped.[98]

For present purposes, a crucial point is that the consensus behavioural standards must involve individual user rights and responsibilities vis-à-vis natural resources. Indeed, as discussed in Chapter 10, it is precisely such systems of communally agreed upon rights and responsibilities that comprise the common property alternative to private and/or state property with market relations. There is a clear parallel here between the inversion of Arrow's Theorem, and the debunking of those versions of the 'tragedy of the commons' metaphor which fail to distinguish common property from open, free access to natural resources.[99] The real tragedy of the commons has been the depletion and despoliation of communal resources by private, market-driven economic activity, that is, the inadequate recognition and enforcement of communal property in the form of strict user rights and responsibilities.[100] Some free-market environmentalists would try solving the problem by privatising more natural resources – as if the mere act of privatising communal wealth makes it (and the damages from its exploitation) any less communal.[101] In any case, the results of CV studies suggest that many people see privatisation as a

---

[96] Vatn and Bromley 1994, p. 142.
[97] Norton and Toman 1997, pp. 561–5.
[98] Fine 2001, p. 181.
[99] Gordon 1954; Hardin, 1968; compare Harris 1996, p. 160.
[100] Burkett 1999a, p. 95.
[101] See, for example, Smith 1995.

violation of the public-good and common-pool characteristics of natural resources as conditions of human development now and in the future. This latent common property element of the political-ethical critique is a potentially useful ideological weapon in the hands of the growing number of working peoples' communities worldwide that are resisting the corporate privatisation and marketisation of land, water, and biological resources.[102]

It remains to address the exact menu of decision-making rules that will operate within the structure of behavioural standards, that is, within the system of communal property rights. Here, the political-ethical critics envision heavy reliance on 'multi-criteria mapping' that gives due weight to the different use-values represented by natural wealth.[103] Without getting into technical details, the basic idea of such mapping, well described by Victor Wallis,

> is to definitively reject the conflation of need with the market-oriented concept of 'demand'. Once need is no longer calibrated in accordance with purchasing power, however, new criteria are required. Ecological concerns can here take their place side by side with long-recognized fundamental rights in the economic, educational, and cultural spheres. These will then serve as the guidelines under which productive activities are sponsored. The application of such guidelines will require that any particular project be considered in relation to the totality of other commitments and of available resources, taking into account also, of course, the variety of possible ways in which such factors can be combined. In ecological parlance, this is known as a holistic approach. In political economy, it is known as planning.[104]

As previously noted, the political-ethical critics also would delegate a certain amount of authority over both formulation and implementation of policy options to environmental experts and to those most affected by particular policies – within the broader consensus formed in open and deliberative fashion.

With all its insights, however, the political-ethical critique remains an ahistorical mirror of the neoclassical approach – more ethical and socially conscious, to be sure, but equally lacking in the way of establishing any direct

---

[102] Churchill 1993; Foster 1994, Chapter 7; Guha and Martinez-Alier 1997; Bond 2000, and 2002; Johnston 2003.
[103] Stirling 1997; Gowdy and Erickson 2005, pp. 213–14.
[104] Wallis 2004, p. 43.

connections between the market and monetary valuation on the one hand, and the social relations of production on the other. In fact, despite its emphasis on the environmental havoc wrought by market-driven productive activity, the development of production, both materially and socially, is not an important element in the critique. This development is surely shaped not just by market competition but more basically by the relations of the direct producers to both the conditions of production and to the competing market operators (capitalists and functionaries) who control, manage, and abuse these conditions. The critique rightly rejects the notion that there is no alternative to the market, but it says little about how the dominant position of the market and monetary values came about, and the changes in the class structure that are needed to overcome this domination. While lamenting the widespread perception that market relations are the natural way of doing things, the critique has no explanation as to why markets and money appear so natural to so many people (and not just to neoclassical economists).

V. Contingent valuation as commodity fetishism

Marx argues that the dominant position of commodity exchange and monetary valuation in resource allocation is itself an outgrowth of the dominant position of the wage-labour relation in the system of production, which represents, in turn, an historically extreme social separation of workers from necessary conditions of production. Only insofar as labour-power is itself a commodity, which workers are forced to sell to the owners and operators of necessary means of production, does commodity exchange necessarily become the main way in which individual people and enterprises gain access to use-values needed for their consumption and production. In short, the dominance of 'private' market activity and monetary valuation over social production is endogenous to the basic class structure of capitalism. Ditto the tendency of people to think of markets and money as the natural way of doing things, even to the point where they lose consciousness of the communal character of production and of its material conditions. And why not? The 'sphere of commodity exchange . . . is in fact a very Eden of the innate rights of man . . . the exclusive realm of Freedom, Equality, Property and Bentham'.[105]

---

[105] Marx 1981, Vol. I, p. 280.

Neoclassical theory and CV analysis faithfully mirror this inversion of reality, in which the real social relations of human production appear as free private exchanges among otherwise isolated individuals. Even more, insofar as the theory reduces individual motivations and behaviour to uni-dimensional utility orderings of different combinations of commodities, it, like capitalism, effectively represents 'the definite social relations' of production in 'the fantastic form of a relation between things'.[106]

As Veblen puts it, the neoclassical 'theoretical scheme' reduces the 'human relations governed by use and wont in whatever kind and connection' to 'ownership and free contract' as mediated by money.[107] 'The immediate consequence is that the resulting economic theory is of a teleological character'.[108] Its efficiency postulates only make sense if one accepts the reduction of human welfare to the singular property of 'utility' together with the parsimonious and ahistorical institutional setting that said reduction requires. The theory *must* reduce individuals' preferences to a single quantitative ordering of a predetermined set of feasible outcomes expressed in terms of a single measure (utility), and individual behaviour to a cold, calculating maximisation over this ordering (utility maximisation). If people think and behave in this simple way, the theory holds by definition.

Expressed in terms of the category of money, neoclassical utility theory 'is really only a disguised value notion which presupposes the money form, and thus cannot be used to give a noncircular explanation of capitalist production'.[109] The theory reduces human valuation to a crude mimicking – as one-dimensional 'utility' – of the monetary calculus.[110] Yet it treats money as simply a convenient

---

[106] Marx 1981, Vol. I, p. 165.

[107] Veblen 1990, pp. 235–6.

[108] Veblen 1990, p. 237; compare Linder 1977, p. 122.

[109] Linder 1977, p. 135.

[110] Marx and Engels's comments on an early version of utility analysis are *apropos* here: 'The apparent absurdity of merging all the manifold relationships of people in the *one* relation of usefulness, this apparently metaphysical abstraction arises from the fact that in modern bourgeois society all relations are subordinated in practice to the one abstract monetary commercial relation. . . . The material expression of this [utility] is money which represents the value of all things, people and social relations' (Marx and Engels 1976, pp. 433–4 [emphasis in original]). They rightly add: 'The economic content gradually turned the utility theory into a mere apologia for the existing state of affairs, an attempt to prove that under existing conditions the mutual relationships of people today are the most advantageous and generally useful. It has this character among all modern economists' (Marx and Engels 1976, pp. 437–78). See also Marx's commentary on Bentham in Volume I of *Capital* (Marx 1981, Vol. I, pp. 758–9).

means of exchange and measure of utility, not as a social relation in its own right, and commodity production and exchange as merely a natural activity by given individuals with no social bonds other than property, exchange, and contract.[111] It has nothing to say about the underpinnings of generalised commodity exchange and monetary valuation in the real relations people have with one another and with nature – in the actual life process of society as it has developed historically.

In short, neoclassical value theory is an analytical form of what Marx termed the 'fetishism of the world of commodities', or the mystification of the social character of human productive activity by commodity exchange.[112] That market valuation is a specific, historically limited form of valuation does not enter the neoclassical picture. All alternatives to the market are therefore viewed as pre-civilised savagery, anarchy, or as artificial infringements (usually by government) on the natural condition of competitive exchange and private property rights.

The Marxist approach accounts for the dominance of neoclassical theory in the economics discipline, and the expansion of the realm of monetary valuation with CV and other techniques, as two very important forms of the fetishism inherent to generalised commodity exchange based on wage-labour. Marxism also provides a structural explanation as to why many CV-survey respondents *do not* overtly or covertly rebel against environmental pricing but instead try to provide more-or-less accurate monetary estimates of how much environmental improvements are 'worth' to them. Such an explanation is missing from the political-ethical critique of CV analysis.

In the Marxist view, the monetary valuation of nature, that is, its effective reduction to a private good, indirectly manifests working people's alienation from the essentially communal conditions of social production. Given this alienation, communal ethics and values tend to be relegated to realms that are external to productive activity and social intercourse insofar as these latter are dominated by commodity production and exchange. For example, communality 'take[s] flight into the misty realm of religion', where it becomes 'the sigh of the oppressed creature, the heart of a heartless world, . . . the spirit

---

[111] Marx 1971, pp. 131–2; Veblen 1990, p. 248.
[112] Marx 1981, Vol. I, p. 165.

of a spiritless situation . . . the *opium* of the people'.[113] Any *practical* communality,
that is, any overt communality in the economic realm, comes for the most
part to be seen as a completely unworkable 'tragedy' of which anarchy,
barbarity, and ultimate breakdown are the inevitable results. This is especially
the case in the most recent neoliberal stage of capitalism.[114]

The producers' alienation from natural conditions is not static. It constantly
evolves with its material-social basis, namely, the capitalist development of
industry. Under capitalism, the means of production and the productive
division of labour, in short the producers' entire metabolic interaction with
nature, are scientifically developed and socialised. But, since this development
is driven not by the goal of sustainable improvements in human development
(through production of environmentally friendly use-values and increased
free time, for example) but by competitive monetary accumulation, the
productive forces of nature and social labour appear as alien forces holding
power over the workers, in fact as productive powers of capital itself. In this
way, commodity fetishism takes the form not just of a masking of class
exploitation by 'free' commodity exchange, but also of a *growing powerlessness*
of the producers vis-à-vis the conditions they themselves have helped create:

> Hence the rule of the capitalist over the worker is the rule of things over
> man, of dead labour over the living, of the product over the producer. For
> the commodities that become the instruments of rule over the workers
> (merely as the instruments of the rule of *capital* itself) are mere consequences
> of the process of production; they are its products. Thus at the level of
> material production, of the life-process in the realm of the social – for that
> is what the process of production is – we find the *same* situation that we
> find in *religion* at the ideological level, namely the inversion of subject into
> object and *vice versa*.[115]

It is impossible to overestimate the crucial role of natural conditions and of
natural science in this historical process of 'inversion', in Marx's view. As he
indicates, the 'conditions of labour' become 'an *alien circumstance* to the
workers', as 'the social character of their labour confronts them to a certain
degree as capitalized', and 'the same naturally takes place with the forces of

---

[113] Marx 1981, Vol. I, p. 165, and 1955, p. 42 (emphasis in original).
[114] Dickens 2004, pp. 135, 141.
[115] Marx 1977, p. 990 (emphases in original).

nature and science', which 'confront the labourers as powers of capital'.[116] Capital's appropriation of nature and science is thus integral to the 'reduction of individual labour to the level of helplessness in face of the communality represented by and concentrated in capital'.[117]

Moreover, insofar as nature and natural science become specialised powers of capital, they become not just inaccessible to the direct producers but also increasingly isolated from social science.[118] Ecological economics, with its unique combination of natural- and social-scientific perspectives, therefore has an exceptional potential for serving the struggle against the capitalistic alienation of nature.[119] Marxism can help here through its notion of capital as a material-social relation: separation of workers from necessary conditions of production, and their reuniting only in production driven by competing capitalists seeking to maximise their monetary capital values. For instance, the capitalist alienation of nature and of natural science provides essential background to the information and contextualisation problems evident in many CV surveys.

The structural powerlessness of working people vis-à-vis the capitalistically developed conditions of production also helps explain the limited ability of non-class political and ideological struggles to defend pro-ecological values against the market, by influencing government policies, for example. This is not meant to minimise the importance of anti-privatisation struggles as well as efforts to maintain and improve environmental regulations; but these struggles will remain rearguard actions as long as they do not strive toward a disalienation of working people and their communities vis-à-vis the main conditions of production. Conversely, the inability or unwillingness of many governments to abide fully by the neoclassical advice to fully marketise their environmental regulations should be seen as an important, but partial, victory for an ecological socialism, just as Marx saw the successful struggle for government restrictions on working time as a qualified victory for socialism over capitalism and the market.[120]

---

[116] Marx 1991, p. 480, and 1963, p. 391 (emphasis in original); compare Burkett 1999a, pp. 77–8.
[117] Marx 1973, p. 700.
[118] Burkett 1999a, pp. 158–63.
[119] Underwood and King 1989.
[120] Burkett 1999a, pp. 140–43, and 2003–4, p. 460.

In this last connection, Marxism can incorporate pro-ecological values into its structural analysis of capitalistic alienation in a way that accounts for, and lends assistance to, political and ideological struggles against the marketisation of nature. In addition to an awareness of the structural alienation that these struggles must confront and overcome, hence of the general shape of the value conflicts involved, Marxism provides a perspective on the potential development of the class agency needed to drive these struggles forward.

On the level of value conflicts, Marxism highlights the material basis of pro-ecological struggles in the structural contradiction between the conditions required and produced by capital accumulation on the one hand, and the natural conditions required for a sustainable and healthy human development on the other. Marx provides the tools for this analysis in *Capital*, beginning in Chapter 7 of Volume I, where he treats the capitalist labour process as a dialectical unity between the production of value (abstract, socially necessary labour times as represented by money) and the general requirements for production of use-values by human labour and its natural conditions (applicable to all modes of production).[121] In Marx's view, the conditions required by human production and development are in no way, not even partially, *external* to the market-oriented sphere where surplus-value is produced and realised. They are part of an overall process in which use-value (human need satisfaction and development through the metabolic interaction of labour and nature) is subsumed under, and becomes a means of, the class-exploitative and competitive process of value accumulation. In Marx's dialectical view, the ecological and other social costs of capital accumulation are internal to the general metabolic process of human-natural reproduction (co-evolution) in its specifically capitalist form.[122]

But where do the conditions required by human production and development in general come from in Marx's perspective? Partly, this involves the natural-scientific study of human production and its natural conditions across different modes of production, and not just capitalism. Natural sciences, especially agricultural chemistry, human and animate physiology, and physics, played a crucial role in Marx's conception of the sustainability requirements of human

[121] Marx 1981, Vol. I, pp. 283–306.
[122] Burkett 1998b, pp. 133–9.

production and development, and of capitalism's systemic violations of these requirements.[123] This is evident from his analyses of: (i) capital's tendency to broach the minimum value of labour-power and maximum worktime consistent with labour-power's healthy reproduction; (ii) the contradiction between capitalist production and a 'rational agriculture', defined as one that does not violate the metabolic reproduction requirements of soil fertility ('the eternal natural condition for the lasting fertility of the soil');[124] (iii) capitalism's creation, through its urbanised concentration of mechanised manufacturing and its industrialisation of agriculture, of 'an irreparable rift in the interdependent process of social metabolism, a metabolism prescribed by the natural laws of life itself'.[125]

Marx's ecological criticisms of capitalist economy do not, of course, rely solely on natural-scientific knowledge. He was keenly aware of the historically relative, value-laden character of natural science, and, insofar as possible, he adjusted his applications accordingly. His criticisms are therefore largely based on capitalism's inability to fulfill the sustainable human development potential that it creates. In other words, capitalism shaped Marx's conception of the requirements of sustainable human development in the more positive sense of potentiating an *explicitly communal economy* in which these requirements would be more effectively met.

Through capitalism's socialisation of production, and its development of an ever broader and more intensive human-natural metabolism (albeit in the service of private profit), the communal character of the conditions of production becomes ever more evident. (In this sense, one can even say that the ecological and certainly the biospheric way of thinking are in part products of capitalism itself.) The rising 'external costs' (vitiation of communal wealth) that the system produces, and the impossibility of dealing with these costs through the market and private profit-making, make it more and more apparent that production and its necessary conditions should be explicitly communal. As Marx indicates with regard to the metabolic rift created by the system's factory farms and mechanised manufacturing,

---

[123] Griese and Pawelzeig 1995; Baksi 1996, and 2001; Foster 2000a; Foster and Burkett 2004; Burkett and Foster 2006.
[124] Marx 1981, Vol. III, p. 216, and 1981, Vol. I, p. 637.
[125] Marx 1981, Vol. III, p. 949.

by destroying the circumstances surrounding that metabolism, which originated in a merely natural and spontaneous fashion, it compels its systematic restoration as a regulative law of social production, and in a form adequate to the full development of the human race.[126]

Today's worsening biospheric crisis – global warming, ozone holes, nuclear and other non-biodegradable pollution, and skyrocketing cancer rates worldwide, to list a few indicators – highlights this communal imperative that can no longer be hidden by the fetishism of commodity exchange and class alienation of productive forces.

That this Marxist, materialist analysis of capitalism's environmental contradictions creates a space for ecological ethics is clear from Marx's projection that:

From the standpoint of a higher socio-economic formation, the private property of particular individuals in the earth will appear just as absurd as the private property of one man in other men. Even an entire society, a nation, or all simultaneously existing societies taken together, are not the owners of the earth. They are simply its possessors, its beneficiaries, and have to bequeath it in an improved state to succeeding generations, as *boni patres familias* [good heads of the household].[127]

Evidently Marx would support the replacement of private property and markets by multi-criteria decision-making within a system of user rights and responsibilities (communal property) in order to manage the environmental commons, as suggested by the political-ethical critics. However, Marx does not present the need for such an explicit communalisation of the environment in terms of a generalised stance of 'people and nature versus the market'. Rather, he identifies a potential agency of such communalisation within capitalist society: the working people currently alienated from necessary conditions of production, but whose productive activity is objectively communalised, and increasingly so, by capitalism itself.[128]

Given the need for explicit communal recognition of all important aspects of nature's use-value, what is needed is an agency whose structural position within capitalism orients it toward use-value. Capital itself (capitalist enterprises,

---

[126] Marx 1981, Vol. I, pp. 637–8.
[127] Marx 1981, Vol. III, p. 911.
[128] Burkett 2003a.

their owners and managers) obviously does not qualify for this position. But the working class and its communities do.[129] For workers, the goal of entering into the wage-labour relationship is not monetary accumulation, but rather the commodified use-values (necessary means of human reproduction and development) that are only obtainable with the wage. For capital, all that matters is monetary value; but, for workers, the money wage is only needed to purchase use-values. True, the workers still need money in order to live. *But every single day, week, year, and lifetime, workers make the eminently practical distinction between having to pay money for something versus valuing it monetarily*; in other words, they routinely experience and act upon the fact 'that there are values in pursuit of which we must spend money while unable in principle to capture or prioritize them in those terms'.[130] Their structural position is such that they cannot reduce all use-values to one-dimensional utility (in reality, money) terms; hence their life-processes mimic, but in a practical way, the stance taken by the political-ethical critique of environmental pricing.

It is quite a distance from this structural parallel to the development of a communal environmentalism integrated into a movement by the workers to take, hold, operate, and redevelop the currently capitalised means of production.[131] But, as capitalism's class-exploitative and ecologically unhealthy socialisation of production creates more and more individual and collective problems for workers that simply cannot be addressed within the wage-labour relation, workers naturally begin to look beyond wage-labour for new, more communal and self-created, forms of human production and development.[132] Marxists and other ecological economists should take part in these struggles, learn as much as possible from them about emergent non-capitalist alternatives, and contribute new ideas and analyses to them as circumstances warrant. There is a special place here for natural scientists, who can help workers overcome their alienation from ecological knowledge, thereby reducing their reliance on 'experts' both now and under the future system of communal property and multi-criteria decision-making. The Marxist vision thus provides an eminently practical contribution to the methodological pluralism and policy openness of ecological economics.

---

[129] Lebowitz 1992.
[130] Foster 1997, p. 7.
[131] Burkett 1999a, Chapter 13.
[132] Dickens 2004, Chapter 8 and *passim*.

Chapter Three
Natural Capital in Ecological Economics

An interesting tension lies at the heart of ecological economics. Given that its subject matter 'is too big and complex to touch it all with one limited set of perceptual tools', ecological economics rejects the notion that there is 'one *right* approach or paradigm'; it therefore strives for 'a large measure of "conceptual pluralism"'.[1] This openness to 'a diversity of methodologies' means that 'pressures to eliminate methodologies for the sake of conformity should be avoided'.[2] At the same time, the commitment to pluralism means that ecological economics encompasses, and is heavily influenced by, neoclassical environmental economics as one of its 'subsets'.[3] And it is well known that neoclassical economics accepts only 'one pattern of thinking . . . the market model'.[4] Neoclassical economics not only rejects methodological pluralism, but increasingly extends the reach of its positivist and methodological-individualist methods into 'non-economic' issue-areas.[5] Insofar as this tendency to reduce phenomena to forms treatable with neoclassical market concepts

---

[1] Costanza 1989, p. 2 (emphasis in original).
[2] Norgaard 1989a, p. 37.
[3] Costanza 1989, p. 1.
[4] Norgaard 1989a, p. 37.
[5] Lazear 2000; Fine 2001, and 2002.

operates within ecological economics, other, less reductionist, approaches may be crowded out, undercutting the discipline's commitment to methodological pluralism.

This chapter uses the concept of 'natural capital' as a window on the tension between methodological pluralism and neoclassical 'economic imperialism' within ecological economics. There are at least two strong reasons for using the environment-as-capital approach as a case study of this tension.

First, although the origins of natural capital are unambiguously neoclassical, ecological economists have been at the forefront in developing and popularising its usage. Indeed, some leading lights of the discipline have sought to pose natural capital as a core paradigmatic concept. Although this dynamic would seem to be a striking illustration of the conformist pressures that ecological economics is supposed to avoid, its proponents see it as a way to highlight the ecological shortcomings of neoclassical theory and the need for alternatives. In short, they see natural capital as a useful metaphor for legitimising ideas that are pro-ecological. By dissecting this argument, the present chapter reveals the theoretical contradictions generated by the uncritical adaptation of neoclassical concepts to ecological purposes and vice versa.

Second, and more specifically, different views on natural capital correspond to different conceptions of 'sustainable development'. The dominant neoclassical position is that there is considerable scope for substituting produced capital for natural capital, and this leads to the notion of 'weak sustainability' under which economies can continue to grow indefinitely even as the stock of natural capital shrinks. By contrast, the ecological economists who support the natural-capital metaphor see natural and produced capital as complements, so, in their view, production is ultimately constrained by the 'strong sustainability' condition that the stock of natural capital be non-decreasing. The present chapter shows that, despite the apparent contrast between weak sustainability and strong sustainability, neither neoclassical nor ecological natural-capital approaches are able to distinguish sustainable development from sustainable capitalism.

Section I traces natural-capital thinking to the neoclassical sustainable growth literature. The adoption of natural capital by ecological economics is critically surveyed in Section II. Section III gives a preliminary evaluation of the extent to which ecological natural-capital perspectives overcome the difficulties with neoclassical sustainable growth theory. The resistance to natural capital within ecological economics, and the contribution that Marxism can make to this resistance, are treated in Chapter 4.

I. Primitive (neoclassical) accumulation of natural capital

Beginning in the early 1970s, oil and other materials price shocks combined with resurgent environmental movements to produce a growing concern with natural limits to economic growth. Such limits were the subject of two controversial reports to the Club of Rome, which forecast the time frames over which stocks of renewable and (especially) non-renewable resources would be depleted under alternative production and population scenarios.[6] Limits-to-growth ideas represented a challenge to neoclassical economics, whose growth theory had heretofore been completely unconcerned with natural resources. Nonetheless, neoclassical economists almost universally rejected limits-to-growth arguments. Neoclassical 'resource optimism' was based on the automatic working of market mechanisms to promote resource substitution and technological advance. Shortages of particular resources would cause their prices to rise, leading to a substitution of less scarce resources as well as a shift of final demand toward products that are less intensive in the scarcer resources. Rising resource prices would also encourage recycling and other improvements in the efficiency of resource use. Finally, increased resource prices would accelerate the search for additional resource supplies.[7]

Weak sustainability and natural capital

As part of the mainstream reaction to natural-limits arguments, the aggregate production functions employed in neoclassical growth models were extended to incorporate an exhaustible natural resource alongside labour and 'capital' – with capital defined as a homogenous manufactured good whose services contribute to the production of goods and services.[8] Using this kind of framework, Solow demonstrated that an economy can indefinitely maintain a positive level of consumption by investing its savings in capital, so long as

---

[6] Meadows et al. 1972; Mesarovic and Pestel 1975.
[7] Solow, 1976; Neumayer 2000.
[8] For detailed surveys of this literature, see Dasgupta and Heal 1979; Hanley 2000.

capital can be substituted for the natural resource.[9] As Hartwick observed, Solow's result can be expressed as the use of the rents from the exhaustible resource for investments in capital:

> Invest all profits or rents from exhaustible resources in reproducible capital such as machines. This injunction seems to solve the ethical problems of the current generation shortchanging future generations by 'overconsuming' the current product, partly ascribable to current use of exhaustible resources. Under such a program, the current generation converts exhaustible resources into machines and 'lives off' current flows from machines and labor.[10]

However, this strategy, now known as the Hartwick rule, is crucially dependent on the assumption that capital can always be substituted for the natural resource, even though production requires at least some natural resource input. Stated differently, the 'productivity of the natural resource' (output compared to the resource input) is assumed to rise as the resource input is reduced (and capital input increased).[11] This is equivalent to the assumption that the required resource input approaches zero without ever quite getting there, while the capital input increases over time with the continuous investment of resource rents. At the same time, technological change, by increasing the productivity of the inputs, can raise the level of infinitely maintainable consumption or lower the capital investment needed to maintain a given consumption path.[12]

Because the Hartwick rule 'only requires that a generalized capacity to produce [be] maintained, rather than any particular resource', it could be interpreted as a 'constant capital' or 'weak sustainability' criterion.[13] As Solow explained:

> The policy of investing resource rents in reproducible capital suggests irresistibly that some appropriately defined stock is being maintained intact,

---

[9] Solow 1974b.

[10] Hartwick 1977, p. 972.

[11] Hanley 2000, p. 17.

[12] Stiglitz 1974 formalised this result for the case where technological advance is not embodied in particular inputs, and thus generates increases in total factor productivity rather than in the productivity of individual factors. Pearce, Atkinson and Dubourg (1994, p. 464), on the other hand, emphasised the possibilities for increases in the productivity of manufactured capital connected with technological changes directly embodied in capital investments.

[13] Pearce, Atkinson and Dubourg 1994, pp. 463–4.

and that consumption can be regarded as the 'interest' on that stock. . . . Under Hartwick's rule net accumulation [of manufactured plus natural capital] is zero all the time . . . a reminder of the old-fashioned obligation to 'maintain capital intact'.[14]

In this interpretation, 'the stock that is being maintained intact can be . . . interpreted to include the initial endowment of resources and, if there is any, of capital'.[15] It is then but a short step to dub the resource stock itself as 'natural capital', so that weak sustainability becomes the case where total capital is maintained regardless of what happens to the stock of natural capital.[16]

Overall, the initial response of neoclassical growth theory to limits-to-growth arguments was to trivialise and minimise natural limits by treating nature as a substitutable productive asset. As Solow put it:

The finite pool of resources . . . should be used up optimally according to the general rules that govern the use of reproducible assets. In particular, earlier generations are entitled to draw down the pool (optimally, of course!) so long as they add (optimally, of course!) to the stock of reproducible capital.[17]

In essence, then, the procedure was to adapt material reality to abstract theory. This explains the appeals to factor substitutability and technological change as necessary to discount the constraint imposed on production by natural conditions. Solow thus stated:

If it is very easy to substitute other factors for natural resources, then there is in principle no 'problem'. The world can, in effect, get along without natural resources, so exhaustion is just an event, not a catastrophe. . . . at some finite cost, production can be freed of dependence on exhaustible resources altogether.[18]

---

[14] Solow 1986, pp. 146, 148–9.

[15] Solow 1986, p. 148.

[16] Solow's interpretation had actually been foreshadowed by Hartwick himself: 'Under such a program, one might assume that in some sense the total stock of productive capital was never depleted since ultimately the exhaustible resources stock will be transmuted into a stock of machines and, given that machines are assumed not to depreciate, no stock either of machines or of exhaustible resources is ever consumed'. Hartwick 1977, p. 972.

[17] Solow 1974b, p. 41.

[18] Solow 1974a, p. 11.

and Stiglitz explained:

> Even with no technical change, capital accumulation can offset the effects
> of the declining inputs of natural resources. . . . With technical change, at
> *any* positive rate, we can easily find paths along which aggregate output
> does not decline. For so long as the input of natural resources declines
> exponentially, no matter at how small a rate, provided the initial level of
> input is set correctly, *we will just use up our resources.* And the technical
> change can offset the effects of the slowly declining input of natural resources.[19]

The reduction of the human environment to a substitutable resource thus
goes hand-in-hand with the reduction of sustainable development to sustainable
capital accumulation.

Critical natural capital and strong sustainability

The obvious shortcomings of weak sustainability theory eventually spurred
some neoclassical economists to develop the 'strong sustainability' approach,
which models feasible paths of economic growth subject to the constraint
that at least some portion(s) of natural capital be preserved. As Pearce and
Atkinson specify it, 'A *strong* sustainability indicator would involve identifying
and measuring "critical" natural capital such that *any* positive depreciation
would be a sign of non-sustainability'.[20] In order to qualify as 'critical', however,
a stock of natural capital must 'provide non-substitutable services ("keystone
processes") to the economy':[21]

> It is the maintenance of ecosystem goods and services – assimilative capacity
> for industrial wastes, supply of biological diversity, role in modulating
> climate and maintaining clean air and water, maintenance of fertile soil,
> etc. – that give the greatest cause for concern. Ecologists tend to see these
> as primary characteristics of the natural world, for which there are no real
> substitutes. In essence, these are the life-support systems as we know them.[22]

Similarly, Hanley suggests that critical natural capital encompasses

---

[19] Stiglitz 1974, p. 131 (second emphasis added).
[20] Pearce and Atkinson 1993, p. 106 (emphasis in original).
[21] Hanley 2000, p. 21.
[22] Pearce, Atkinson and Dubourg 1994, p. 469.

the processes responsible for regulation of atmospheric conditions, the spiritual values provided by wildlife, and nutrient cycles. If humans need the services of ecosystems, then it is important to maintain these ecosystems in a functioning state. This in turn means protecting their natural resilience (ability to withstand shocks), which may be achieved by ensuring that certain species ('keystone species') are preserved . . .[23]

The use of ecological and aesthetic grounds to argue for preservation of certain elements of natural capital represents a definite advance over weak sustainability analyses. But strong sustainability theory maintains the notion that investments in manufactured capital can continuously reduce an economy's reliance on natural resources. If a natural capital asset is not 'critical', that is, if it does not provide (productive or aesthetic) services for which acceptable substitutes are deemed unavailable, then it will not be protected. Thus, Solow's notion that we can 'get along without natural resources' still applies to non-critical natural capital.[24]

This, of course, raises the question how it should be decided which natural-capital services are substitutable (non-critical) and which are not. It is not very helpful to define 'criticality' in terms of such general categories as irreversibility, uncertainty, and aversion to loss – all of which could conceivably apply to virtually all natural as well as manufactured capital.[25] On the other hand, the literature's emphasis on basic life-support systems and aesthetic generalities suggests considerable scope for discretion in favour of defining resources as non-critical and thus for continued depletion of natural capital in the name of strongly sustainable growth.

The ambiguity may explain attempts to pose weak sustainability as a pre-condition for strong sustainability. El Serafy, for example, argues that 'income (sometimes called weak) sustainability . . . should be considered as a step leading ultimately to an ecological (or stronger) sustainability'.[26] As Hanley observes, 'The argument made is that if countries fail this weak test of sustainability, they will not pass a sterner test'.[27] But this is misleading insofar

[23] Hanley 2000, p. 21.
[24] Solow 1974a, p. 11.
[25] Pearce and Atkinson 1995, pp. 169–70; compare Holland 1994, pp. 170–1; Gutés 1996, p. 151.
[26] El Serafy 1997, p. 217.
[27] Hanley 2000, p. 18.

as accumulation of manufactured capital (net of depreciation of non-critical natural capital) may proceed on the basis of an absolutely smaller depreciation of critical natural capital, in which case weak sustainability may actually be enhanced by strong non-sustainability. To ignore this possibility, and to treat weak sustainability as a necessary condition for strong sustainability, is to implicitly presume that growth of manufactured capital (net of non-critical natural capital) is never constrained by the stock of critical natural capital. It is, in short, to smuggle neoclassical optimism about factor substitution in through the backdoor.

The danger of a 'slippery slope' from strong to weak sustainability is illustrated by the World Bank's 2003 *World Development Report*:

> Limits-to-growth type arguments focus on strong sustainability, while arguments in favour of indefinite growth focus on weak sustainability. So far the former arguments have not been very convincing because the substitutability among assets has been high for most inputs used in production at a small scale. There is now, however, a growing recognition that different thresholds apply at different scales – local to global. Technology can be expected to continue to increase the potential substitutability among assets over time, but for many essential environmental services – especially global life support systems – there are no known alternatives *now*, and *potential technological solutions* cannot be taken for granted.[28]

The decision as to which natural resources are essential and which are expendable is thus reduced to 'the mix of assets that supports improvements in human well-being' – a mix 'likely to change over time, as people's preferences and technologies change'.[29] So it turns out not only that critical natural capital is currently represented by a relatively narrow range of 'environmental assets', but that no elements of natural capital are permanently inviolate. Similarly, two prominent environmental economists reject the very possibility of natural limits to economic growth ('the finitude of the environment, broadly defined') on grounds that 'we do not know the character of new, future technologies, which may, in some part, be extraterrestrial in character'.[30]

---

[28] World Bank 2003, pp. 14–15 (emphasis added).
[29] World Bank 2003, p. 15.
[30] Burness and Cummings 1986, p. 323.

The basic problem here is that the strong sustainability approach does not relate the criticality of natural capital to the economy's relations of production. Like the weak sustainability framework, strong sustainability theory does not specify the material requirements of wage-labour in particular – simply because it has no social-relational conception of capital or of production. As a result, decisions on critical versus non-critical natural capital are taken exogenously, in asocial terms, and no distinction is made between sustainable human development and sustainable capitalism.

II. Accumulation of natural capital in ecological economics

Despite the shortcomings of neoclassical sustainability analysis, leading ecological economists have embraced natural capital in the belief that it 'signals an intention to create an alternative paradigm that includes values and concerns that cannot be characterized in the mainstream paradigm'.[31] This helps explain why ecological economists have done far more than neoclassicals to develop the conceptual underpinnings of natural capital. In order to infuse natural capital into the normal science of ecological economics, it must be clearly distinguished from other, less natural, forms of capital, and the different components or elements of natural capital themselves differentiated, but in a way that makes it plausible to refer to nature as 'capital' in some overarching sense. Further, natural capital stocks must be related to flow concepts such as income, investment, and depreciation. In terms of intellectual legitimation, the capitalisation of nature within ecological economics depends on the presentation of natural capital as an outgrowth of a long tradition of like-minded thinkers, that is, on the recasting of the history of ecological economics itself.[32]

The movement to make natural capital a core construct of ecological economics seems to have started around 1989 or 1990 when (allowing for publication lags), three of its formative articles were written.[33] In August, 1992 the International Society for Ecological Economics (ISEE) held a conference in Stockholm dedicated to 'the major characteristics of the rapidly evolving

---

[31] Norton 1995, p. 119; compare Åkerman 2003, pp. 435–8.
[32] Kuhn 1970.
[33] Daly 1990; El Serafy 1991; Costanza and Daly 1992.

field of ecological economics, with particular emphasis on the concept of natural capital, and its maintenance and enhancement'.[34] The volume generated by this conference was advertised as a full-scale attempt to define and operationalise natural capital as a central paradigmatic concept.[35] The ISEE *imprimatur*, and the fact that none of the papers in the volume put forth any criticisms of natural capital, suggest a narrowing (however unintended) of the methodological pluralism supposedly defining the discipline. A second ISEE-sponsored book emphasising the centrality of natural capital in ecological economics appeared just a year later.[36] 'Thereafter the concept has been constantly used as a label for ecological economics'.[37] By 2003, the editor's introduction to a special number of *Ecological Economics* entitled 'Identifying Critical Natural Capital' asserted without qualification that 'Natural capital is a key concept in ecological economics'.[38]

Clarifying and refining natural capital

The definition of capital adopted by ecological/natural-capital theorists is neoclassical: any 'stock of real goods, with power of producing further goods (or utilities) in the future'.[39] Although 'real goods' would seem to suggest that capital must take the form of material stocks, ecological economists also apply the capital term to individual and collective human productive capabilities, that is, 'human capital' and 'cultural capital'.[40] As Folke et al. phrase it,

> Ecological economists speak of natural capital, human capital (and/or cultural capital), and manufactured capital when categorizing the different kinds of stocks that produce the range of ecological and economic goods and services used by the human economy.[41]

The flow of goods and services yielded by capital stocks is labelled 'income'.[42]

---

[34] Folke et al. 1994, p. 1.
[35] Jansson et al. 1994.
[36] Prugh 1995.
[37] Åkerman 2003, p. 435.
[38] Ekins, Folke and De Groot 2003, p. 160.
[39] El Serafy 1991, p. 168.
[40] Berkes and Folke 1992.
[41] Folke et al. 1994, p. 4.
[42] Costanza and Daly 1992, p. 38.

The next step in the argument is to offer 'compelling reasons why nature should be treated as capital' in this general sense.[43] On one level, the answer is trivial: nature, considered 'as part of the stock of real goods', is 'capable of producing further goods ... both as a source of raw materials and as a receptor of wastes generated in the course of economic activity'.[44] Nature is capital insofar as it produces a flow of 'natural income' that can be divided into 'resource' and 'service' components.[45] The point is illustrated by Costanza and Daly:

> For example, a stock or population of trees or fish provides a flow or annual yield of new trees or fish, a flow that can be sustainable year after year. The sustainable flow is 'natural income'; the stock that yields the sustainable flow is 'natural capital'. Natural capital may also provide services such as recycling waste materials, or water catchment and erosion control, which are also counted as natural income.[46]

On another level, however, it must be demonstrated that the goods and services yielded by nature are in some sense unique compared to the incomes generated by other forms of capital. Otherwise, it is not clear why natural capital cannot be theoretically subsumed under other factors of production.[47] This is where non-substitutability of natural capital begins to enter the argument. The basic vision is one in which, 'as a part of nature, humans with our skills and manufactured tools not only adapt to but modify natural capital, just like any other species in self-organizing ecosystems'.[48] In other words, production always involves an amalgam of natural, manufactured, human, and cultural capital. Equivalently, 'It is not possible for human ingenuity to create human-made capital without support from natural capital', so natural capital must be explicitly recognised theoretically.[49]

Nature's productivity is then specified in terms of the distinction between 'renewable' and 'non-renewable' natural capital:

---

[43] El Serafy 1991, p. 170.
[44] El Serafy 1991, p. 169.
[45] Daly 1994b, p. 30.
[46] Costanza and Daly 1992, p. 38.
[47] El Serafy 1991, p. 170.
[48] Folke et al. 1994, p. 4.
[49] Berkes and Folke 1992, p. 1.

Renewable natural capital is active and self-maintaining using solar energy. Ecosystems are renewable natural capital. They can be harvested to yield ecosystem goods (such as wood) but they also yield a flow of ecosystem services when left in place (such as erosion control and recreation). Nonrenewable natural capital is more passive. Fossil fuel and mineral deposits are the best examples. They generally yield no services until extracted.[50]

Renewable and non-renewable natural capital are further distinguished through the argument that the category of depreciation applies to the former but not the latter. As El Serafy argues:

I find no fault in applying the accounting convention of depreciation of assets that wear out in the process of production to those environmental assets which are renewable. For renewability gets such assets very close to buildings and machines that can be renovated or replaced. In respect of resources such as forests and fish, sustainable yields can be calculated, and exploitation over and above such yields may be considered as comparable to depreciation. . . . Where I think depreciation is not applicable is in the case of nonrenewable natural resources such as fossil fuels that cannot be recycled or reused once they have been combusted. . . . [I]n their case, we need to adjust gross income itself and not just net income.[51]

Or, as Costanza and Daly put it, 'Renewable natural capital is analogous to machines and is subject to . . . depreciation; nonrenewable natural capital is analogous to inventories and is subject to liquidation'.[52]

One difficulty is that the concept of 'investment', in the sense of human processing of material resources into increased capital stocks, does not directly apply to either renewable or non-renewable natural capital. After all, 'how do we invest in something which by definition we cannot make? If we could make it, it would be manmade capital!'.[53] As an alternative, Daly appeals to a 'classical notion' of investment as '"waiting" or refraining from current consumption'.[54] 'For renewable resources', in particular, 'we have the possibility

---

[50] Costanza and Daly 1992, p. 38.
[51] El Serafy 1991, p. 173.
[52] Costanza and Daly 1992, p. 38.
[53] Daly 1994a, p. 186.
[54] Daly 1994b, p. 29.

of fallowing investments, or more generally "waiting" in the Marshallian sense – allowing this year's growth increment to be added to next year's growing stock rather than consuming it'.[55] 'Investment in natural capital, both maintenance and net investment, is fundamentally passive with respect to natural capital which is simply left alone and allowed to regenerate'.[56]

Unfortunately, for non-renewables, even simply 'waiting' is not an option: 'We can only liquidate them' at greater or lesser rates:[57]

> Non-renewable natural capital cannot be increased either actively or passively. It can only be diminished. We can only divest non-renewable natural capital itself, even though we invest in the man-made capital equipment that hastens its rate of extraction and divestment. Non-renewable natural capital is like an inventory of already-produced goods, rather than a productive machine or a reproducing population. For non-renewable natural capital the question is not how to invest, but how to best liquidate the inventory, and what to do with the net wealth realized from that liquidation.[58]

Further complexities arise from 'the mixture of natural and manmade capital' or 'cultivated natural capital' present in agriculture, fish farming, livestock raising, forestry, and other activities where the materials and processes 'are not really man-made, but are significantly modified from their natural state by human action'.[59] Although investment in cultivated natural capital 'also involves waiting, . . . it is never really left alone. Even during the waiting period some tending and supervision is required'.[60] Hence, while 'investment in renewable natural capital must be only passive . . . more active investment is possible in cultivated natural capital'.[61] While allowing that the latter 'hybrid' investments 'substitute for natural capital proper in certain functions', Daly

---

[55] Daly 1994a, p. 186.
[56] Daly 1994b, p. 31.
[57] Daly 1994a, p. 186.
[58] Daly 1994b, p. 32.
[59] Daly 1994a, p. 186, and 1994b, p. 30.
[60] Daly 1994b, p. 31.
[61] Ibid. It is evidently with reference to such 'active' investments in cultivated natural capital that El Serafy (1991, p. 173) suggests that '"Positive depreciation" may be possible if replanting or restocking exceeds exploitation, but this should more appropriately be treated as capital formation'.

argues that such substitution is ultimately limited by the 'strong complementary relation between the natural and man-made components of cultivated natural capital'.[62]

The adoption of strong sustainability

As observed earlier, the neoclassical weak sustainability criterion posits that economic growth can continue so long as the total (natural plus manufactured) stock of capital is maintained, even if the natural component of capital becomes very small compared to the manufactured component. However, this presumes that the productivity of natural capital rises as natural capital decreases – with productivity approaching infinity as natural capital approaches zero. Ecological/natural-capital theorists have rejected weak sustainability on grounds that it presumes an unreal degree of substitutability of manufactured capital (and labour) for natural capital, in effect violating the material constraints on production. Daly, for example, suggests that, while the standard neoclassical production function (with only labour and manufactured capital as inputs) completely ignores nature, the addition of natural resources to 'this type of production function simply sweeps the contradiction under the rug without removing it'.[63] His critique follows Georgescu-Roegen's earlier argument (with 'capital' denoting manufactured capital only):

> On paper, one can write a production function any way one likes, without regard to dimensions or to other physical constraints. . . . In reality, the increase of capital implies an additional depletion of resources. And if [the capital stock approaches infinity], the [resources] will rapidly be exhausted by the production of capital. Solow and Stiglitz could not have come out with their conjuring trick had they borne in mind, first, that any material process consists in the transformation of some materials into others . . . and second, that natural resources are the very sap of the economic process.

---

[62] Daly 1994a, p. 186, and 1994b, p. 30. Similarly, Guha and Martinez-Alier (1997, pp. 116–17) refer to the 'complementary relationship between wild and agricultural biologic diversity. Agricultural genetic resources could be called "cultivated natural capital". They cannot be fully substituted by the capital goods, including "improved" seeds, used in modern agriculture. This cultivated natural capital must be complemented by natural capital, the wild relatives of cultivated plants'.

[63] Daly 1997, p. 262.

They are *not* just like any other production factor. A change in capital and labor can only diminish the amount of waste in the production of a commodity; no agent can create the material on which it works. Nor can capital create the stuff out of which it is made.[64]

Or, as Costanza and Daly state it: 'Manufactured capital is itself made out of natural resources, with the help of human capital (which also consumes natural resources). Creation of the "substitute" requires more of the very thing that it is supposed to substitute for!'.[65] Similarly, referring to the production of human capital, Folke et al. emphasise that 'there will always be a minimum or critical amount of natural capital needed to sustain any individual of the human species'.[66] Given its essential human element, 'Production of goods and services cannot be decoupled from its biophysical reality'.[67]

Nor can technological advance negate these basic material constraints, given the first and second laws of thermodynamics: 'In some cases, it may also be that the same service can be provided by a design that requires less matter and energy. But even in this direction there exists a limit, unless we believe that the ultimate fate of the economic process is an earthly Garden of Eden'.[68] To assume that 'worsening natural resource scarcity could be offset by technical progress' is to ignore the limits to increasing natural resource productivity 'within a natural world'.[69] Against such technological optimism, ecological economists favour a more cautionary approach recognising 'that our planet's capacity to absorb our wastes and to provide raw materials and energy is limited, and that this limitedness cannot be assumed away in the belief that advances in technology are bound to ease out the constraints'.[70] Besides, if the technological optimists are wrong, 'repairing the damage would be far more costly than attempting to avert it before it has taken place'.[71]

Indeed, many ecological economists see 'natural capital . . . increasingly becoming the limiting factor for further development' as human production

---

[64] Georgescu-Roegen 1979a, pp. 97–8 (emphasis in original).
[65] Costanza and Daly 1992, p. 41.
[66] Folke et al. 1994, p. 6.
[67] Ibid.
[68] Georgescu-Roegen 1979a, p. 98.
[69] England 2000, p. 426.
[70] El Serafy 1991, p. 170.
[71] El Serafy 1991, p. 171.

and consumption grow 'relative to the natural environment'.[72] Daly explains:

> Once the complementarity of natural and manmade capital is accepted then
> it becomes clear that development is limited by the one in shortest supply.
> In the past era of 'empty-world economics' manmade capital was limitative.
> We are now entering an era of 'full-world economics' in which natural capital
> will be increasingly limitative.[73]

In this way, the ecological/natural-capital synthesis makes a case for a variant
of strong sustainability requiring that the total size of the natural capital stock
(not just 'critical' components) be maintained intact.[74] 'Hence constancy of
total natural capital . . . is the key idea in sustainability of development'.[75]
With natural capital the limiting asset, sustainability requires that we live off
the flow of income or 'interest' from this asset without eroding the stock or
'principal'. This requires, among other things, that we 'stop counting the
consumption of natural capital as income'.[76]

This is, of course, the same logic as for neoclassical weak sustainability
only applied to natural capital instead of total capital. It is thus unsurprising
that precursory statements can be found in the works of earlier neoclassical
economists such as Alfred Marshall, who referred to the 'impoverishment'
of the 'large element of capital' represented by the 'properties of the soil' and
other 'free gifts of nature'.[77] An even more striking forerunner is Sir John
Hicks, who 'supplied an excellent definition of sustainability by defining
income'.[78] Specifically, Hicks defined income as 'the maximum amount that
a community can consume over some time period and still be as well off at
the end of the period as at the beginning'.[79] Such constant welfare requires
maintenance of productive capacity, which means 'maintaining capital intact'.
Adding the role of natural capital as a limiting element of total capital gives
the conclusion that the strong sustainability criterion is 'explicit in this Hicksian

---

[72] Folke, et al. 1994, p. 5.
[73] Daly 1990, pp. 3–4.
[74] Daly 1990, p. 4.
[75] Costanza and Daly 1992, p. 39.
[76] Daly 1994a, p. 183; compare El Serafy 1991, pp. 171–2.
[77] Quoted in El Serafy 1991, p. 169.
[78] El Serafy 1991, p. 171.
[79] Quoted in Daly 1994b, p. 23.

definition of income'.[80] With natural capital as a limiting factor, 'natural income must be sustainable; that is, any consumption that requires the running down of natural capital cannot be counted as [Hicksian] income'.[81]

Because some depletion of *non-renewable* natural capital is unavoidable, however, the constant *total* natural capital rule is not sufficient to sustain production. Renewable natural capital must be increased *in forms that can substitute for the non-renewable natural capital that is used up.* Hence, 'The general rule would be to deplete non-renewables at a rate equal to the development of renewable substitutes'.[82] In this strategy, 'extractive projects based on non-renewables must be paired in some way with a project that develops the renewable substitute'.[83] Meanwhile, renewable natural capital, 'in both its source and sink functions, should be exploited on a profit-maximizing sustained-yield basis', such that 'harvest rates should not exceed regeneration rates' and 'waste emissions should not exceed the renewable assimilative capacity of the environment'.[84] At the same time, 'indirect active investment in measures to increase throughput productivity' may, where feasible, maintain and even raise production in utility terms ('make waiting (throughput reduction) easier').[85]

Measuring (qualifying?) natural capital

Those ecological economists supporting 'constant natural capital' have recognised the severe measurement problems the construct poses. Costanza and Daly note that 'natural capital and natural income are aggregates of natural resources in their separate stock and flow dimensions, and forming these aggregates requires some relative valuation of the different types of

---

[80] Daly 1994b, pp. 23–4; compare Daly 1994a, p. 183.

[81] Costanza and Daly 1992, p. 39.

[82] Daly 1994b, p. 32.

[83] Ibid.

[84] Costanza and Daly 1992, p. 44. 'For renewable resources (exploited populations of fish, cattle, trees, etc.) it has long been known that there is a stock size that gives maximum yield per time period. Although this biological maximum coincides with the economic (profit-maximizing) optimum only in the case of constant costs of harvest or capture there seems to be no reason not to follow the profit-maximizing criterion in choosing the levels at which to maintain constant natural capital intact'. Daly 1990, p. 2.

[85] Daly 1994b, p. 33.

natural resource stocks and flows'.[86] El Serafy points out that a full-scale dynamic estimation of natural capital and income would require

> a totally integrated system starting with a complete inventory of environmental assets, and setting money values on these in order to construct a balance sheet of all assets, whether nature- or man-made. Changes in such a balance sheet from year to year, as a result of degradation, renovation, locating new deposits, as well as economic exploitation, would be reflected in the end-period balance sheet. The impact on the flow of income would simply be derived from the change in wealth from one balance sheet to the next.[87]

He concludes that such an application is impossible: 'It should be obvious that no balance sheet can be constructed which would not only cover the totality of natural assets in quantity and quality, but also put a money value on all these assets'.[88] Costanza et al. argue that the practical unmeasurability of natural capital stems from its non-substitutability:

> Zero natural capital implies zero human welfare because it is not feasible to substitute, in total, purely 'non-natural' capital for natural capital. Manufactured and human capital require natural capital for their construction. Therefore, it is not very meaningful to ask the total value of natural capital to human welfare, nor to ask the value of massive, particular forms of natural capital. It is trivial to ask what is the value of the atmosphere to humankind, or what is the value of rocks and soil infrastructure as support systems. Their value is infinite in total.[89]

The measurement problem is accentuated by the great heterogeneity of natural capital. England observes that natural capital is 'amazingly diverse' in terms of 'the sheer number of non-produced biological populations and inert physical stocks' and the material 'dimensionalities' in which their productive contributions operate.[90] Drawing a parallel to 'the Cambridge Capital controversy' over 'how to aggregate physically heterogeneous inputs of capital

---

[86] Costanza and Daly 1992, p. 38.
[87] El Serafy 1991, p. 172.
[88] Ibid.
[89] Costanza, et al. 1997, p. 255.
[90] England 1998b, pp. 261–2.

and labour', he suggests that 'ecological economists could easily be drawn into a similar technical debate about how to measure the aggregate value of the natural capital stock, a debate which would consume a great deal of intellectual effort'.[91]

England concludes that 'although natural capital is a powerful metaphor worthy of retention by ecological economists, its precise measurement should not be at the top of our collective agenda'.[92] Natural capital should be retained only 'as a pedagogical device and as a component of our preanalytic vision of how humanity fits into nature'.[93] This leaves the question as to how empirical work is to be related to the pre-analytical vision. Here, England suggests that 'priority should be given to' efforts to adjust national income and product accounts for environmental impacts of production – and he refers to the Index of Sustainable Economic Welfare (ISEW) developed by Daly and Cobb as an example worth 'improving and then widely disseminating'.[94] Along similar lines, El Serafy rejects the 'holistic approach' (direct and comprehensive measurement of natural capital and income) in favour of *partial* adjustments to income' using 'satellite accounts' *à la* those 'developed under the United Nations System of National Accounts'.[95]

III. A preliminary evaluation

How well has the adaptation of natural capital by ecological economists overcome the difficulties with neoclassical sustainable growth theory? At this point, we limit our answer to some basic methodological points and obvious contradictions in ecological/natural-capital analysis. Methodologically, the main shared limitation of the neoclassical and ecological natural-capital approaches is the absence of a systemic, social-relational conception of capital, which results in a failure to distinguish sustainable development and sustainable

---

[91] England 1998b, p. 264.

[92] England 1998b, p. 262.

[93] England 1998b, p. 264.

[94] Ibid. (referring to Daly and Cobb 1989). The ISEW is actually a consumption-based measure of welfare with adjustments for inequality, household labour, consumer durables and public goods services as well as for pollution costs and natural-capital depletion. See Daly and Cobb 1989, pp. 401–55; England 1998a, pp. 97–101.

[95] El Serafy 1991, pp. 172–3 (emphasis in original).

capitalism. For example, the association of Hicksian (sustainable) income with 'constant natural capital' does not come to grips with the fact that, under capitalism, the goal of competing enterprises is not ecological sustainability but, rather, sustained (and maximal) accumulation of capital (money invested to make more money) for its own sake. Stated differently, the material requirements of capital accumulation may not encompass ecological sustainability in the sense of maintaining natural conditions as conditions of human development. But, instead of delving into the underlying production relations that shape productive priorities, the ecological/natural-capital theorists merely graft the strong sustainability criterion onto the neoclassical conception of capital which is a social black box.

More basically, the notion of natural capital as 'limiting factor' seems to reflect the neoclassical division of the conditions of production into separate natural and non-natural (human-made) factors. This dualistic image undercuts the ecological economists' materialist critique of the neoclassical production function, where it is rightly pointed out that labour and manufactured capital both have a natural (material) substance. Indeed, the complementarity of natural resources and other productive factors implies that the whole edifice of neoclassical value theory must be rejected. If the employment of manufactured capital (or of labour) requires the employment of natural resources and vice versa, then the respective 'marginal products' of the production factors – essential concepts in the neoclassical theory of value and distribution – are meaningless, since they can only be individually defined under the assumption that all other factors are held constant. Yet, the ecological/natural-capital theorists have not proposed any coherent alternative value analyses (see Chapter 1). Apart from the resulting absence of any logical means for aggregating the natural-capital stock that comprises the core of the synthesis, what we are left with is a purely external, not immanent, critique of the neoclassical approach, one that hinges on empirical interpretations of the degree of substitutability of different resources and/or appeals to exogenous ethical values not related to the system's core socio-economic relations. Hence, Daly criticises the 'money fetishism' according to which 'exchange value grows by itself, it earns interest' apart from its limited material conditions.[96]

---

[96] Daly 1992a, p. 186.

But he does not root this fetishism in the underlying relations of production that allow money-making to become the main determinant of resource use, and even the main determinant of what are considered to be productive resources. Far from extending his critique of interest to other forms of profit-making, Daly suggests 'living off interest' as a guide to the sustainable use of natural capital. His critique of money fetishism thus rings hollow.

That the ecological/natural-capital hybrid is more neoclassical than ecological is shown by the roster of precursors referred to by its adherents. For the ecological/natural-capital school, the history of ecological economics *is* largely the history of neoclassical economics so far as the concept of capital is concerned. El Serafy may be stretching the consensus within this school with his suggestion (based on Hicks's notion of income and a few lines on land-as-capital in Marshall) that 'there is much in modern economics that is in harmony with environmental thinking'.[97] But there can be no doubt that the push to employ the natural-capital metaphor both reflects and contributes to a strong pressure to re-root ecological economics in neoclassical theory. This is a clear weakening of the discipline's commitment to methodological pluralism.

In the practice of ecological economics, the neoclassical shortcomings of natural capital are partly manifested in the use of the term as a convenient slogan providing a shallow unity among various analyses applying disparate methods to a variety of issues. Here, natural capital serves to create an artificial ecumenicism among the variegated population of ecological economists, not all of whom are conversant in, or in agreement with, neoclassical economics.[98] Hence, in the aforementioned ISEE-sponsored volume *Investing in Natural Capital*, the term is employed mainly in a loose way, roughly equivalent to 'natural resources', to cover such phenomena as biospheric carrying capacity, eco-system life-support properties, biotic diversity, agricultural inputs, energy, coastal wetlands, fisheries, and so on, and in connection with a variety of social issues for which the theory behind natural capital seems to add very little to the analyses – including ecological footprints, ethics, justice, security, and consumption norms.[99] Even in these cases, however, natural-capital

[97] El Serafy 1991, p. 171.
[98] Åkerman 2003, p. 438.
[99] Jansson et al. 1994, *passim*.

thinking is, arguably, doing damage to the discipline. Insofar as the paedagogy of ecological economics becomes dominated by natural capital – as a 'key word', so to speak – non-neoclassical approaches that utilise somewhat different terminologies (or interpret the same terms differently) may not get as fair a hearing. When the less capital-theoretical members of the discipline join in the collective adoption of the natural-capital term (however shallow their use of it may be methodologically), they may close themselves off from alternative ways of thinking about capital.[100]

Unfortunately, such shows of paradigmatic consensus around natural capital lend it a spurious legitimacy that expands out of academia into environmental organisations and back again. And why not? If one does not think about it too deeply, natural capital seems to usefully reconcile ecological values and 'practical' economic concerns. As Harrison, Burgess and Clark put it, 'natural capital appears to place nature on an equal footing with economic interests in debates about development. In addition, the concept proves attractive because it gains authority and legitimacy through association with the discipline of economics'.[101] It has thus 'proved influential within country agencies, . . . local planning authorities and in voluntary sector organizations'.[102] Especially in a political setting like the United States (that most commodified and capitalised of all modern societies), where money and the thirty-second soundbite have all but displaced serious analysis and discourse, at least in mainstream circles, the underlying ecological and social tensions encapsulated by natural capital may appear to be a matter of only high-browed intellectual interest. Fortunately, the environment-as-capital metaphor has not gone unchallenged in ecological economics.

---

[100] Åkerman 2003, p. 444. A striking instance of such premature analytical closure is Wackernagel, et al.'s (1999, p. 377) acceptance of natural capital, including its monetary valuation, as 'an excellent approach for awareness building' even though they strongly criticise the 'misleading' nature of monetary valuation of ecological resources and services. One wonders what kind of awareness can be generated by a misleading indicator, and why the authors do not seek out a less misleading approach to nature and capital.

[101] Harrison, Burgess and Clark 1999, p. 85.

[102] Harrison, Burgess and Clark 1999, p. 95.

Chapter Four

Marxism and the Resistance to Natural Capital

Despite the growing popularity of the environment-as-capital metaphor, many ecological economists have resisted it on grounds that it is irreparably anti-ecological. In their view, natural capital lends a spurious legitimacy to the commercialisation of nature and its reduction to a productive input. These theorists reject the treatment of nature as an aggregate stock of productive assets, the valuation of nature by money and the market, and the conflation of sustainable development and sustainable capitalism – all the hallmarks of natural-capital thinking. Sections I–III of the present chapter survey these three critical elements of the resistance to natural capital. Section IV argues that the resistance has been weakened by its failure to critically analyse the social relations of production. Section V sketches a Marxist perspective on natural capital that treats separation of the producers from necessary conditions of production as the core characteristic of capitalism. The Marxist approach is shown to strengthen the resistance to natural capital. The chapter concludes with a brief reflection on the methodological relationship between Marxism and the pro- and anti-natural-capital camps within ecological economics.

I. Rejecting the environment-as-capital parable

The resistance to natural capital sees the 'aggregation of incommensurate physical units' not just as a technical measurement issue, but as symptomatic of 'a major problem with this approach', namely, that it is highly misleading to conceptualise nature's use-value in aggregative 'stock' terms.[1] As Hinterberger, Luks and Schmidt-Bleek put it:

> Adding oil fields, butterflies, the functions of the atmosphere and wetlands (can they be substitutes for each other, and if yes, to what extent?) and 'controlling' these entities – in the sense of keeping them constant – is, to our mind, impossible.[2]

Because 'the different categories of natural capital play radically different functions within the economy', says Gutés, it is doubtful whether they can 'be compounded into a unique category'.[3]

Much earlier, Georgescu-Roegen questioned the constant natural-capital rule on grounds that the 'basic concept of a capital stock that remains constant in amount but may nevertheless undergo qualitative changes' is 'in great need of clarification'.[4] He also pointed out that the dynamic aggregation problem applies even to particular resources that come in varying grades, such as mineral ores and (especially) eco-system resources.[5] Moreover, to be meaningful, the constant natural-capital criterion must be applied over long time spans over which the stock's composition is very unlikely to remain constant.[6]

The strategy of avoiding the natural-capital aggregation problem by using ecologically adjusted income measures is doubtful at best.[7] How can aggregate natural income be definable or measurable if natural capital is not? While the definition and measurement of total natural capital requires an adding up of disparate resource-stocks, natural-income aggregation involves adding up the even more variegated services produced by these disparate stocks.

---

[1] Harte 1995, p. 159.
[2] Hinterberger, Luks and Schmidt-Bleek 1997, p. 7.
[3] Gutés 1996, p. 151.
[4] Georgescu-Roegen 1979a, p. 103.
[5] Georgescu-Roegen 1979a, p. 105.
[6] Georgescu-Roegen 1979a, p. 103.
[7] This is the strategy suggested by England 1998b, p. 264.

There is a definite tension between the constant natural-capital concept and the cornerstone of the ecological critique of neoclassical sustainable growth theory: the non-substitutability of natural resources. Constant natural capital requires substitution of renewable for non-renewable natural capital, which is really a variant of the neoclassical distinction between critical and non-critical natural capital: if non-renewable natural capital can be substituted for, it must not be 'critical'. The difficulties with defining resource criticality thus apply here as well. As Victor states:

> In the absence of renewable and non-renewable resources which are perfect
> substitutes, there are obvious difficulties in determining whether the creation
> of a renewable resource is in fact adequate to offset the exploitation of a
> non-renewable resource.[8]

This is not to flatly deny that such substitution occurs in reality. The problem is that the ecological/natural-capital synthesis does not relate 'substitution' to the social relations of particular economic systems and the resultant distinction between systemic reproduction requirements and the requirements of sustainability in some broader ecological and human developmental sense. Instead, substitution possibilities are conceptualised in a purely natural or technological way (crude materialism) or in terms of what is 'economical' according to a hypothetical competitive market uncontaminated by 'external effects' (idealism).[9] The anthropomorphic element of 'substitutability' is recognised in the determinant role of human needs and productive capabilities (human and cultural capital); but it is not developed in systemic social-relational terms.

That the capital-stock analogy actually weakens the insistence on nature's non-substitutability is clear from the notion that depreciation applies to renewables but not to non-renewables.[10] The argument is that renewability implies replaceability (if only by 'waiting') while non-renewable connotes irreplaceable, so that depreciation applies to renewables while only liquidation applies to non-renewables. This seems to make sense, until one notices that the destruction of renewable species and eco-systems must be treated as

---

[8] Victor 1991, p. 210.
[9] Daly 1994b, pp. 31–3.
[10] El Serafy 1991, p. 173; Costanza and Daly 1992, pp. 38–9.

liquidation not just depreciation. Renewability does not preclude extinction or exhaustion; hence it need not connote replaceability.

Accordingly, Hinterberger, Luks and Schmidt-Bleek question whether nature's 'exploitable resources and buffering capacities' can be treated as replaceable assets 'like a savings account'.[11] Contrary to what the capital-depreciation metaphor seems to suggest, 'The ecosphere cannot be "repaired" by human effort: while we can "invest in natural capital" by introducing soil conservation measures, planting trees and the re-establishments of wetlands, human activities are never capable of truly repairing nature, for all changes lead to (often irreversible) consequences' that are frequently 'impossible to predict'.[12] In short, 'the notion of capital indicates that nature can be reproduced by humans, which is clearly a wrong perspective'.[13] Similarly, Victor argues that

> since an essential feature of capital is that it is reproducible by human action, there is a danger in the use of this term to describe the environment. In referring to the environment as capital, there is an implicit assumption that it can be substituted by other forms of capital, that it is reproducible and that it is there to be managed in much the same way as manufactured capital.[14]

But the concept of investment in renewable natural capital by 'waiting' carries other quandaries. For one thing, it does not apply to manufactured capital. As Keynes emphasised, in a monetary economy abstinence from consumption only implies saving, not real capital investment.[15] So, we have a definition of investment that applies to renewable natural capital but not to the manufactured capital from which the capital analogy was originally drawn! In reality, however, investment as mere waiting is problematic even for renewable natural capital. Given technological change, resource substitution (however imperfect) and changes in market conditions, even unutilised natural capital can depreciate in the monetary/market terms employed by the ecological/

---

[11] Hinterberger, Luks and Schmidt–Bleek 1997, p. 4.
[12] Ibid.
[13] Hinterberger, Luks and Schmidt–Bleek 1997, p. 7.
[14] Victor 1991, p. 210.
[15] Keynes 1964, pp. 166–7, 180.

natural-capital synthesis. Hence, waiting may have a negative market value even if it results in a physical accumulation of renewables. Note that such market depreciation may also apply to non-renewables, contradicting the theory. Inventories are, after all, subject to depreciation not just liquidation.

Once the market context of natural capital is fully recognised, the Cambridge capital debate is seen to have implications that go beyond mere aggregation problems. This debate revealed that outside of a one-good economy, the quantity of capital cannot be defined independently of the composition of output or its distribution among factor owners.[16] Obviously, a one-good economy contradicts the qualitative differentiation (not to speak of the non-substitutability) of natural and human-made capital. Victor's comment that the 'London School' of weak sustainability theory 'has not faced these issues' applies with equal force to ecological/natural-capital theorists.[17]

The resistance to natural capital has also drawn attention to the parable's contextual inadequacies from ecological and co-evolutionary perspectives. Drepper and Månsson argue that the capital-stock analogy is an impoverished way of interpreting nature as a basic material *and aesthetic* condition of human life.[18] The productive instrumentalism toward nature built into natural-capital thinking is ill-suited to important 'existence values' generated by human-natural relations. Gowdy similarly observes that nature's biological support functions, being collective and co-evolutionary, are not adequately captured by 'treating isolated pieces of the environment (natural capital) as a "factor of production"'.[19]

Hinterberger, Luks and Schmidt-Bleek suggest that to treat nature as a capital asset is to metaphorically downgrade the 'naturally ever-changing' character of the 'ecological environment, which is being assaulted by technical intrusions with increasing speed'.[20] Environmental degradation involves disruptions of complex eco-system dynamics, not simply depletion or depreciation of qualitatively unchanging assets. Harte adds that eco-system '"integrity" . . . the ability of living systems to maintain their self-organising

[16] Weeks 1989, Chapter 10.
[17] Victor 1991, pp. 205–6.
[18] Drepper and Månsson 1993, p. 57.
[19] Gowdy 1994b, p. 47.
[20] Hinterberger, Luks and Schmidt-Bleek 1997, p. 4.

ability when subject to changing environmental conditions', is hardly captured by 'the notion of a constant resource stock'.[21]

It goes without saying that such ecological dynamics are 'anything but context independent' either materially or socially.[22] After all, 'humans are incapable of developing technologies that do not in some way change the environment', often in ways 'we are not capable of predicting'.[23] One troubling result of the contextuality of eco-systems is that 'ecology has neither unambiguous definitions of basic concepts such as species, niche, or ecosystem, nor a testable general theory capable of providing predictive or prescriptive guidance to environmental managers and analysis'.[24] It follows that 'ecological economists . . . can no longer rely on the authority of ecology to legitimize normative use of concepts such as natural capital'.[25] These concepts must be defined and utilised with explicit reference to 'human preferences for various ecosystem states' together with 'the cultural processes giving rise to environmental preferences'.[26] Since human preferences may differ, such a relational framework should recognise the dependence of natural-resource definitions and valuations on the distribution of wealth and power within and across generations. It is hard to see how the 'constant stock' parable employed by ecological/natural-capital theorists would survive the analytical transition.

The complex material-social context of natural wealth also throws doubt on the distinction between cultivated natural capital and renewable natural capital.[27] Given the alteration of the biosphere by human intervention, human-natural dichotomies no longer apply to living and climatic elements of the environment (although it may still make some sense to treat such non-renewables as unexplored mineral deposits as physically 'natural').[28] The fact

---

[21] Harte 1995, pp. 160, 162.

[22] Harte 1995, p. 160.

[23] Hinterberger, Luks and Schmidt-Bleek 1997, p. 4.

[24] Harte 1995, p. 160.

[25] Ibid.

[26] Harte 1995, p. 162. Douguet and O'Connor 2003 use survey data from France to illustrate the social contextuality of critical natural capital, emphasising that people's perceptions of the need for environmental preservation are informed not only by nature's basic biophysical life-support functions but also by 'collective cultural meanings' associated with the 'site and scenery functions' of the land (p. 233).

[27] Åkerman 2003, p. 444.

[28] McKibben 1990; Stokes 1994.

is that the entire biosphere is constantly cultivated and renewed just as human development is cultivated or renewed: by the material-social relations of production and the dynamics they generate. This is not to deny that human production is subject to definite physical laws; it is only to suggest that the categories cultivability and renewability – as well as others like utility (use-value), substitutability, limiting factor, and sustainability – are anthropomorphic and thus subject to both social-systemic and human-developmental determinations which cannot be presumed identical unless one adopts the idealism of 'end of history' thinking. Outside a social-relational vacuum, the issue is not how natural we want to be, but whether we are willing to fight for the kind of social system that promotes a healthier, more well-rounded form of human-ecological cultivation and renewal, that is of human development.

II. Opposing the monetisation and marketisation of nature

With practical qualifications, the ecological/natural-capital synthesis endorses monetary and market-based valuation as a way of aggregating the disparate resource stocks and service flows respectively comprising natural capital and natural income. By contrast, the resistance to natural capital detects a fundamental 'contradiction' between 'a world governed by biophysical laws and . . . a world governed by the laws of market capitalism'.[29] Foster argues that the imposition of money prices on nature is a 'dangerous misrepresentation' that marginalises important 'frames of reference' on the environment.[30] In his view, monetary values do not provide a 'standard or criterion of comparison for environmental value which inherently transcends the perspective of a particular cultural understanding of nature and our relation to it'.[31]

Indeed, a general theme in the critique of natural capital is that the uni-dimensionality of money precludes market prices from capturing nature's multi-dimensional use-value. Although markets may assign (or be made to assign) monetary values to non-produced resources such as land or even clean air (witness markets for pollution credits), these prices do not capture

---

[29] Gowdy 1994b, p. 43.
[30] Foster 1997, p. 8.
[31] Foster 1997, p. 10.

nature's true use-value in a holistic intergenerational sense. Leff thus observes that the 'task' of monetary valuation of nature

> is not an easy one given the codependence, incommensurability, and externality of the environment and the economy. There are limits to [the] ability to translate nature into market (or planning) prices, especially of ecological processes such as the resilience, regeneration, and recovery of ecosystems in the face of capital intervention, as well as nature's capacity and potential to contribute to the production of use-values.[32]

Rees and Wackernagel argue that 'Price is invariably an incomplete representation and often reflects only ecologically superficial qualities of the real thing (a log for market has none of the key biophysical properties of the forest or even the tree from which it is cut)'.[33]

Within this general framework, five specific ecological tensions in market pricing and monetary valuation have been highlighted. First, unlike money, 'Nature cannot be disaggregated into discrete and homogenous value units'.[34] There is a basic tension between monetary aggregation and the complementarity of various elements of natural wealth:

> Monetary analyses generally do not distinguish between substitutable goods and complementarity goods. On the balance sheet, all prices are added or subtracted as if goods that are priced the same have equal absolute importance to human life. However, many of nature's goods and services are essential to life even in small quantities and, therefore, not truly commensurate with manufactured capital.[35]

A second difficulty with market pricing is its inadequate accounting for the irreversible character of many natural processes. As John Bellamy Foster explains for the case of redwood forest depletion,

> The market has no internal mechanism that recognizes that the results of such decisions are irreversible within the normal human time span (it would take many generations to repair the damage, even if the system would allow

---

[32] Leff 1996, p. 146.
[33] Rees and Wackernagel 1999, p. 47.
[34] Leff 1996, p. 146.
[35] Rees and Wackernagel 1999, pp. 49–50.

such an enormously costly – in terms of market exchange – process of restoration).[36]

Even if a resource's price rises as it becomes scarce, by the time this happens it may be irreversibly depleted and/or degraded. That resource scarcity is partially reflected in higher prices is small solace to those concerned about the tendency of market-driven production and consumption to make resources scarce.[37]

The third problem with the monetary marketisation of nature is the tension between money's quantitative limitlessness and the limits to natural wealth of any given material qualities.

> The apparently unlimited potential for money growth – money has no relevant physical dimensions – obscures the possibility that there are physical limits to material growth. This encourages the human enterprise to expand further even as it exceeds global carrying capacity.[38]

Within any given time period, production driven by the unlimited motivation of money translates into temporal imbalances between productive throughput and ecological processes, degrading the latter. As Leff indicates, 'Gradual regenerative processes that allow biotic resources to recuperate and to grow cannot keep pace with accelerated capital reproduction cycles'.[39] A related problem is that market prices – and price-guided patterns of resource-use – often fluctuate more than the 'intrinsic' (*sans* human intervention) ecological dynamics of natural wealth. Clearly, 'the inherent biophysical properties of the land and its natural income generating potential (e.g. material contribution to food security) are endogenous qualities that are relatively fixed and independent of current prices'.[40] Hence, it is often impossible for the market to 'assimilate the multiple natural cycles to capital cycles' without degrading the former.[41]

Fourth, the price of a resource stock is not determined solely by its absolute size; hence this price may not rise as depletion occurs:

---

[36] Foster 2000b, p. 145.
[37] Rees and Wackernagel, 1999, p. 51.
[38] Rees and Wackernagel 1999, p. 50.
[39] Leff 1995, p. 24.
[40] Rees and Wackernagel 1999, p. 49.
[41] Leff 1996, p. 146.

Other factors also have more effect on biophysical resource prices than does stock size. These include variable demand, the intensity of competition among suppliers, the price of substitutes processing and transaction costs, etc. For example, as long as fishing remains economic in markets where the price of fish is suppressed by the prices of such substitutes as pork and chicken, it will not adequately reflect the decline of fish stocks. In these circumstances, over-harvesting might occur even if the dynamics of stock decline were smooth and continuous. . . . If the contribution of stock depletion to price is relatively small, markets will provide a weak signal of incipient biophysical scarcity and unsustainability.[42]

If, 'in the case of natural resources, prices are far from reflecting true scarcities', then 'nothing will ensure that economic resources will be invested in developing techniques that are biased into saving natural capital'.[43]

Fifth, higher resource prices may actually accelerate a resource's depletion by spurring technological advances that reduce extraction costs and/or lower the amount of the resource needed per unit of final goods, thereby encouraging its further use to increase total output.[44] Also, even if final goods prices rise with resource costs, higher-income markets may be found. As Rees and Wackernagel observe,

Suppose price does rise beyond the reach of most potential consumers. In an increasingly global market, the number of rich consumers who have access to the relevant goods – and for whom mere money has a low marginal value – is also constantly increasing. Rising demand reduces the conservation effect of high prices so that valued species may be driven below some critical population level or density needed to ensure survival. Many organisms are being over-harvested as a result of this problem – various turtles (for their meat and eggs), bears (for their gall bladders) and rhinos (for their 'horns') are cases in point.[45]

That rising prices of resources may not prevent further depletion poses a serious difficulty for ecological/natural-capital theorists. If natural capital is

---

[42] Rees and Wackernagel 1999, p. 48.
[43] Gutés 1996, p. 154.
[44] These effects form the basis of the well-known 'Jevons paradox' for coal and other fossil fuels. See Clark and Foster 2001.
[45] Rees and Wackernagel 1999, pp. 48–9.

valued with reference to market prices, then 'constant natural capital' becomes consistent with an actual depletion of natural resources. Specifically, 'a sharp reduction of the "natural capital" can be outweighed by higher prices'.[46] Insofar as manufactured capital and natural capital are complements, 'an explosion in technology coupled with a relatively static [or declining] physical stock of natural assets' may be registered as 'a dramatic rise in natural capital'.[47] In this case, it becomes impossible to distinguish strong sustainability from weak sustainability, 'for the criterion of the constancy of natural capital effectively dissolves into the criterion of the constancy of total capital'.[48] Harte adds that this paradox applies not just to natural-capital stocks but also to natural-income flows, since in the latter case, too, 'quantity can decline as long as prices increase, thus keeping value constant'.[49]

Accordingly, some critics of natural capital have concluded that the marginalisation of ecological use-values by monetary valuation applies in particular to attempts to adjust national income and product accounts for changes in natural capital (or natural incomes). For example, the Index of Sustainable Economic Welfare (ISEW) is based on the money value of private consumption net of monetary, market-based estimates of pollution costs and natural-capital depletion.[50] In other words, the ISEW and similar measures 'correspond to a *very weak version* of sustainable development' which 'effectively treats investment in manufactured capital as a substitute for keeping natural capital intact (and indeed treats output growth as a substitute for reducing environmental costs)'.[51] To support strong sustainability *and* environmentally adjusted income aggregates is thus to be caught in a contradiction. This further undercuts England's suggestion that natural capital be maintained as paedagogy and pre-analytical vision, but replaced on the level of 'empirical work' by the ISEW.[52]

Having demonstrated the ecological inadequacies of market pricing and monetary valuation, opponents of the ecological/natural-capital synthesis

---

[46] Hinterberger, Luks and Schmidt-Bleek 1997, p. 7.
[47] Holland 1994, p. 172.
[48] Holland 1994, p. 173.
[49] Harte 1995, p. 159.
[50] England 1998a.
[51] Lintott 1996, p. 18 (emphasis in original).
[52] England 1998b, p. 264.

have proposed greater reliance on multi-criteria decision-making procedures. Rejecting the 'attempt to measure all effects in monetary units', such 'non-monetary evaluation utilises a wide variety of measurement units to assess the effects' of human activity on the environment.[53] Given the likelihood that 'an action *a* may be better than an action *b* according to one criterion and worse according to another', this approach relies heavily on 'compromise solutions' to reconcile competing values.[54]

Multi-criteria evaluation provides a framework within which the different dimensions of nature's use-value can be openly compared (not quantitatively commensurated), which means an open clash of competing social frames of reference on the environment instead of an attempt to subsume them under the uni-dimensional (and inegalitarian) balance-sheets of monetary 'wealth'.[55] In other words, it rejects the search for an 'analytical fix' that somehow bypasses conflicting values, and 'offers to help structure and render more transparent, a discourse over the real issues in social choice . . . to articulate the interpenetrating domains of analysis and political judgement'.[56] Above all, the multi-criteria approach recognises that 'most aspects of the environment . . . are public goods' and thus legitimate objects of collective, democratic deliberation.[57] By contrast, both the natural capital metaphor and its operationalisation by monetary, market-based valuation tend to legitimize the treatment of nature as private property, that is, as a set of possessions whose appropriation, use, and alienation should be insulated from non-market social 'interference'.

III. Contesting sustainable development

Given the influence of natural-capital and pro-market approaches to the environment, it is not surprising that 'the commitment to sustainable development can be entirely hollow, often cynically manipulated, often merely meaningless'.[58] As Carlos Castro observes, however:

---

[53] Munda, Nijkamp and Rietveld 1995, p. 145; compare Gowdy and Erickson, 2005, pp. 213–14.

[54] Munda, Nijkamp and Rietveld 1995, p. 147.

[55] Martinez-Alier, Munda and O'Neill 1998.

[56] Stirling 1997, pp. 194–5.

[57] Jacobs 1997, p. 211.

[58] Hay 2002, p. 217; compare Jamison 2001, Chapter 1.

Sustainable development is still a contested concept. There are grassroots organizations and radical theorists who use the concept in a root critique of the established order. . . . Some organizations operating in the Third World are working on issues of sustainable development from a progressive perspective. These organizations are trying to exercise social control over capital using the concept of sustainable development.[59]

Hay is surely right to argue that 'we should not throw the concept out just because it is contestable'.[60] Clearly, 'more critical perspectives are needed if any kind of meaningful sustainable development – which has to be about sustaining the environment even more than sustaining economic development – is to be achieved'.[61] Accordingly, the resistance to natural capital has expended considerable energy exploring the more radical, pro-ecological potential latent in 'sustainable development'.

Jacobs argues that sustainable development has helped define four major 'faultlines' on the environment question: (i) how much environmental protection is needed, and what priority it should have compared to other goals such as economic growth; (ii) the meaning of environmental equity and environmental justice; (iii) the role of a more inclusive and participatory policymaking process in formulating, implementing, and legitimising environmental goals; (iv) the scope of the policy actions and institutional changes needed to move toward a more environmentally-friendly economic system.[62] Even though conservative, market-oriented interpretations have tended to dominate each of these four areas in mainstream circles, more ecological and radical-democratic conceptions have at least begun to find a voice and to operate as a kind of intellectual glue holding together environmental movements.

Similarly, Hayward suggests that sustainable development has highlighted the fact that 'environmental degradation' is 'inseparable from issues of justice within generations, between generations and also perhaps between species'.[63] Here, Dobson observes that the application of distributive justice to the environment immediately raises concerns about the comparability,

---

[59] Castro 2004, p. 220.
[60] Hay 2002, p. 217.
[61] Castro 2004, p. 220.
[62] Jacobs 1999.
[63] Hayward 1997, p. 14.

commensurability, and substitutability of environmental use-values.[64] In effect, the question *what* is to be sustained may be inseparable from the question *how* it is to be distributed.

The distributional dimension of sustainability is quite relevant to the natural-capital debate. As Holland points out, even strong sustainability 'by no means entails the protection of natural capital as such' on the micro-level relevant to particular individual and group frames of references on the environment.[65] Instead, it merely preserves *total* natural capital as needed to maintain *aggregate* welfare across generations, as measured by per capita monetary income (with some adjustments for inequality and natural-capital depletion). From the standpoint of 'a commitment to nature' in all its intrinsic and anthropomorphic diversity, 'the commitment to natural capital is therefore hollow' in both its weak and strong forms.[66]

These perspectives highlight the poverty of natural-capital approaches to sustainable development which, even in their strongest ecological form, rely on the substitution and market valuation of different natural-capital assets (specifically renewables vis-à-vis non-renewables). Any such market-based substitution is bound to marginalise important ecological use-values not registerable in money prices. And, given inequalities in monetary income and wealth, it will inevitably affect the distribution of environmental use-values. As the environment is subsumed under the market and treated as private property, the non-wealthy who rely more on uncapitalised environmental commons are immiserated compared to the wealthy who can at least purchase an environmentally adequate (if still psychologically and spiritually impoverished) existence.

The resistance has been at its strongest when emphasising how natural-capital *discourse* rationalises and legitimises pro-market conceptions of sustainable development. A basic point is that, in positing a policy primacy for maintaining some aggregate stock of capital, both weak and strong sustainability incorporate the environment into the economic system, not vice versa.[67] O'Connor and Martinez-Alier elucidate this critique:

---

[64] Dobson 1999.
[65] Holland 1999, p. 55.
[66] Holland 1999, p. 52.
[67] Hay 2002, p. 215.

The prominence in academic writing of the term 'natural capital' coincides with the real social and political process of *capitalization of nature*. This refers to a pattern of response of business, within the logic of capitalist economic relations, to the *supply problem* of depletion of natural resources and degradation of environmental services required for support of commodity production. . . . By capitalization and commodification of nature, we mean first of all the *representation*, for political and commercial purposes, of the biophysical milieu (nature) and of non-industrialized economies and the human domestic sphere (human nature) as reservoirs of 'capital'; and thereafter the *legal codification* of these stocks as property tradeable 'in the marketplace', meaning saleable at a price.[68]

In this view, natural-capital thinking provides ideological and analytical support for the expanded commercialisation of nature associated with both capitalist economic globalisation and attempts to internalise environmental management within market competition.[69] The result is that 'the modus operandi of capital as an abstract system undergoes a logical mutation'.[70] Instead of nature being 'treated as an *external* and exploitable domain', it is conceived as 'self-management and conservation of the *system of capitalized nature* closed back on itself'.[71] In this way, 'the *reproduction of capital*' becomes '*synonymous with saving nature*'.[72]

Given the aforementioned ecological inadequacies of market regulation and monetary valuation, however,

this rhetorical harmonization does not in any way guarantee the conservation of specified productive or reproductive potentialities of a society or ecosystem, nor does it assure the sustaining of the particular interests, communities, or ecologies thus valorized. In practice, the main effect of all the identifying of 'at-risk' heritages, stocks, and capitals is the better and better alignment – in ideology, though not necessarily in fact – of this participant nature (and human nature) to the norms of capital's own enlargement and reproduction.[73]

---

[68] O'Connor and Martinez-Alier 1998, pp. 37–8 (emphasis in original).
[69] Barry 2001, pp. 384–5.
[70] O'Connor 1994, p. 126.
[71] O'Connor 1994, p. 126 (emphasis in original).
[72] O'Connor 1994, pp. 132–3 (emphasis in original).
[73] O'Connor 1994, p. 133.

In short, 'There will be no actual net accumulation of natural capital; rather, nature will increasingly be converted into money or abstract exchange, subject to the vicissitudes of Wall Street'.[74]

IV. Limitations of the resistance to natural capital

How is it that nature has come to be treated as merely one among a portfolio of capital assets? To answer this question, and to effectively struggle against nature's capitalisation in theory and practice, one needs a critical analysis of capitalist production relations. This analysis must explain how capitalism generates specific material dynamics that are not only anti-ecological but also potentiate new forms of development that are pro-ecological. Sustainable development needs to be seen as development in, against, and beyond capitalism.

Because it has not rooted itself in production relations, the resistance to natural capital has not developed such a perspective. As a result, its critique of natural capital suffers from a kind of historical shallowness. Despite its emphasis on the social contextualisation of nature, its critique of market dynamics and monetary valuation relies heavily on intrinsic characteristics of natural wealth – resilience, irreversibility, carrying capacity, uncertainty, and so forth. These characteristics are not directly compared or contrasted with capitalism's own material requirements, since the latter remain largely, if not fully, unspecified. It is one thing to point out formal contradictions between nature's material forms and capitalism's monetary and market forms; it is quite another (but equally necessary) to establish tensions between capitalism's own material requirements and the reproduction of natural wealth. The latter task demands that the ecological critique of money and markets be grounded in a critique of wage-labour and capital.

The flip-side of the resistance's over-use of asocial ecological categories is its tendency toward ahistorical social contextualisation of natural wealth. Crucial socio-ecological concepts such as environmental equity, justice, and conflicts are taken in the abstract, that is, not rooted in a critique of the system's core production relations and the tensions they generate. The sustainable

---

[74] Foster 2000b, p. 145.

development issue is thus framed in terms of the ontological primacy of the economy (mainly the market) *or* nature, rather than the tension between capitalism's specific material requirements and the material-social requirements of a healthy co-evolution of humanity and nature.[75] The crucial issue, 'sustainable development of what?', is posed mainly as a kind of free-floating ethical question or at best in non-class cultural terms – a terrain on which nature's capitalisers, with their control over means of production, their powerful tools of indoctrination and repression, and their constant appeals to short-term economic practicality, are likely to have the upper hand.[76]

Correspondingly, real-world conflicts over nature's capitalisation are located either at the internal/external level of 'resistance by communities and whole societies to the ecological and cultural costs associated with the "commodification" of nature by expanding industrial societies' or at the level of competition among generic 'particular interests and capitals' *within* market societies.[77] Structurally rooted working-class struggles in and against capitalism are thereby marginalised as a force in the resistance to and movement beyond nature's capitalisation. Instead, deliberative democracy and multi-criteria evaluation are abstractly counterposed to money and the market, and the endogenous historical dynamics and human-social agency for the needed transformation inadequately addressed.

All of this produces a bias favouring environmental and cultural preservationism and interest-group politics in the depiction of resistance movements; it also tends to paint a picture of grassroots working people and their communities as passive victims (like nature itself) of nature's commercialisation, rather than active subjects of history in the historically open sense of human development in and through productive activity and struggle. Certainly, the effect is to downplay the connections between exploitation of labour and exploitation of nature as twin components of capital accumulation – which is strange, given the key role of labour in activating production as an interchange between society and nature, and especially strange for an ecological perspective that, presumably, must insist on the natural basis and substance of human labour.

---

[75] Compare Stokes 1994.
[76] Foster 1996.
[77] O'Connor and Martinez-Alier 1998, pp. 37–8; see also O'Connor 1994.

V. Natural capital from a Marxist perspective

A more effective resistance to natural capital would centre on the historically specific social relations that mediate and shape human-natural relations in production. Marxism, by emphasising class as a material-social relation of production, provides such a perspective.

Natural capital and wage-labour

Marxists find that the general treatment of productive factors as 'capital' (income-yielding assets) implicates the definite class relations, in particular wage-labour, under which production occurs. Tools, machines, human productive capabilities, and most certainly nature itself, are not intrinsically capital. Under feudalism and other precapitalist systems, not only were productive implements, land, and labourers *not* separable capital assets in the sense they are under capitalism (on which more presently), but 'the economy' itself was not seen as a separate, let alone dominant, sphere of human activity. Instead, the economy was an embedded function of natural, cultural, and political processes. This embeddedness corresponded to an epoch where social reproduction was more directly constrained by natural wealth in its given form, unprocessed by human labour.[78] In this situation, any significant 'ecological footprints' often signalled the imminent demise of the society leaving them.[79]

Under capitalism, things have been different. To see why, one must first recognise that the core relation of capitalism is not the market and monetary exchange, even though markets and money are necessary for capitalism. What distinguishes capitalism is the social separation of workers from necessary conditions of production – starting with the land – which means that workers can only make a livelihood by selling their labour-power to the (private or state) capitalists who own and control these necessary conditions, and by using the wage so obtained to purchase means of subsistence on the market. In this system, labour, nature, and produced means of production appear as 'separate' conditions of production that are only reunited in profit-driven production of commodities by wage-labour.

---

[78] Stokes 1994, pp. 4, 9–10.
[79] Wackernagel and Rees 1996.

From this core class relation derives the necessity for 'private' market exchange among economically autonomous but interdependent firms and households, in order for social (that is, communal) production and reproduction to take place. This alienated form of exchange only becomes dominant on the basis of workers' three-fold alienation: from necessary production conditions (including the land), from the production process itself, and from its products. Competitive market exchange and monetary valuation are not just matters of 'convenience' in capitalist society.[80] They are necessary social forms of material wealth in a system where workers are socially separated from necessary conditions of production to the point where they must become wage-labourers (work for money) in order to live. Wage-labour is a holistic class relation that cannot be reduced to commodity exchange; but commodity exchange (social separation of producers from other producers) is an essential mechanism by which wage-labour (separation of the producers from necessary conditions of production) is reproduced. It is only in this situation that the economy becomes an apparently autonomous, self-regulating sphere vis-à-vis the natural, cultural, and political dimensions of social reproduction and human development.

From a human standpoint, as Parlato and Ricoveri observe, the system's treatment of labour-power and natural conditions as separate capital assets appears as a 'loss of control over our own lives, which necessarily includes our relationship with nature'.[81]

> Put another way, just as labour-power is treated as if it is a commodity, so does 'capitalist nature' mean that nature is commodified, hence alienated from us, and ultimately reified into a 'thing'. And just as the capital-labour relation should be seen in qualitative terms, that is, as loss of power, alienation, and so on, so should the capital-nature relation be interpreted as powerlessness, and alienation.[82]

In this view, the conversion of human labour-power and natural conditions into capital is not just a way of thinking, not just ideological, not just a legal-juridical construct, and not even just a commodification of the conditions of

---

[80] *Pace* Rees and Wackernagel 1999, p. 47.
[81] Parlato and Ricoveri 1996, p. 236.
[82] Ibid.

human existence: it is a fundamental condition (and contradiction) of capitalism at the level of production relations. Marxism does not see mainstream 'natural-capital' theory simply as a mistake, but as an analytical reification of capitalism's alienation and exploitation of labour and nature. Under capitalism, human labour-power and nature really are socially separate means of competitive profit-driven production.

Value, market prices, and nature

Marxism deepens the critique of monetary and market valuation by rooting it more firmly in the relations of production. In the Marxist view, not only are generalised market exchange and monetary valuation a function of the separation of workers from necessary conditions of production, but the same separation enables market prices to be regulated by the abstract, (homogenous) labour time objectified in commodities. Only with social production mainly organised through market relations among competing enterprises employing 'free' labour-power for a profit is the substance of value reduced to socially necessary labour time. This specifically capitalist substance of value qualitatively abstracts from the necessary contribution of nature to wealth production – as if labour could produce wealth without nature.

The Marxist view recognises that capitalism does not convert all necessary conditions of production into commodities, and that the social separation of labour-power from necessary conditions of production does not formally apply to *all* necessary conditions (including, for example, sunlight, the air, or perhaps even a small parcel of land not sufficient for subsistence). Nonetheless, based on labour-power's *effective* separation from necessary conditions of production (enough to force workers to become wage-labourers), capitalist enterprises are able to freely appropriate many unmonopolisable natural conditions and convert them into means of exploiting labour-power for a profit. The free capitalisation of such 'common pool resources' is, in fact, a crucial dimension of Marx's analysis of capitalist exploitation, alienation, and accumulation.[83] Capitalism's exploitation and alienation of nature has a far larger scope than the monetary and market spheres alone suggest.

---

[83] Burkett 1999a, Chapter 6, and 1999c.

This is not to say that market valuation is not itself profoundly anti-ecological, in the Marxist view. As demonstrated by Saad-Filho, the formation of commodity values involves three distinct reductions of concrete labour into abstract labour: (i) *normalisation* of current individual labours producing the same commodity; (ii) *synchronisation* of individual labours producing the same commodity but at different times, under changing material and social conditions; (iii) *homogenisation* of different labours producing different commodities.[84]

In the present context, what is crucial about this three-fold reduction is that it must take place partly *through* the formation of market prices. To reduce concrete labour to abstract labour is to convert labour into a form which can be represented in a purely quantitative way by money; but the conversion itself requires the monetary valuation of labour's products. Given the separation of workers from necessary production conditions and attendant system of competitive market relations among firms and households, this is the only way that necessary labour times – capitalism's basic regulator of social reproduction – can be formed and represented. It follows that the anti-ecological characteristics of money and market prices, emphasised by the resistance to natural capital, are functional requirements of capitalism's core production relation: wage-labour.[85] This suggests that any large-scale displacement of the market by non-monetary, multi-criteria decision-making will have to challenge the wage-labour relation. Only by overturning this core relation can society apply deliberative democracy to production informed by direct measures of material stocks and flows, ecological processes, and human health.

Capitalist sustainability versus sustainable human development

The resistance to natural capital has not developed the important connections between conflicting environmental values and the wage-labour relation. Marxism does this through its analysis of the tension between the material requirements of capitalist production and the requirements of a healthy and sustainable human development.

---

[84] Saad-Filho 2002, Chapter 5.
[85] Burkett 1999a, Chapters 5 and 7.

Capitalism's material requirements follow directly from the wage-labour relation. They include exploitable labour-power and conditions under which its labour can be objectified in saleable use-values (commodities). Although these requirements directly involve natural conditions, they obviously leave a lot of space for historical contingency in terms of the exact ways they are fulfilled. They could, in principle, be met by any natural conditions capable of supporting human life. In terms of natural-capital categories, the flexibility of capitalism's material requirements implies a high degree of substitutability among the elements that can potentially serve as critical natural capital.

This shows the pitfalls in Daly's notion that natural capital increasingly becomes the 'limiting factor' in economic development.[86] Actually, the opposite is the case, and this is precisely why capitalism is such an ecologically damaging system. Unlike earlier modes of production, whose reproduction was often tied to particular local or regional eco-systems, capitalism can afford to ruin eco-systems – leaving deep and broad 'ecological footprints' in its wake – and then move on over time and space in slash-and-burn fashion.[87] Daly's limiting factor analysis is unable to detect this crucial feature of capitalism, the problem being that his adoption of neoclassicism's asocial concept of capital leads to a purely external, abstract-material conception of natural limits.

Given that capitalism's material requirements fall far short of those needed for healthy and sustainable human development, the system's environmental resiliency is no source of comfort to Marxists. Many elements of natural wealth that are critical for human development are not critical for capitalism. Human-natural relations have, in many ways, been degraded as a result of capitalism's substitution of commodified use-values for the 'non-critical' natural use-values from which it has alienated workers and communities – a process that has taken on more-or-less immiserating forms depending on one's position in the global capitalist system.[88]

Accordingly, environmental crises of capitalist reproduction should be distinguished from capitalistically-induced crises in the conditions of human development. The first kind of crisis mainly involves the tendency of capital

---

[86] Daly 1990, pp. 3–4.
[87] Wackernagel and Rees 1996; Burkett 1999a, pp. 67–8.
[88] Foster and Clark 2004.

accumulation to deplete and/or despoil particular resources which have become critical for capitalism at a particular stage of its development. Production driven by competitive pursuit of profit tends specifically to outrace supplies of critical *raw materials* whose economic availability is more-or-less limited by natural conditions. Marx analysed nineteenth-century cotton crises in these terms; more recently, capitalist reproduction has been disrupted by 'oil shocks' partly rooted in physical limits on economically exploitable supplies. It is not necessary to appeal to asocial natural limits to see that natural conditions play a role in such crises. Capital can only accumulate in value and money terms insofar as it is objectified in an ever-growing mass of material use-values (both consumer goods and means of production). Adding the quantitative limitlessness of monetary accumulation and the anarchic character of capitalist competition, it becomes clear that materials-supply disturbances are inevitable.[89]

However, given capitalism's innovative capacities and the flexible character of its material requirements, environmental crises of accumulation tend to be periodic and to not in and of themselves seriously threaten the system's reproduction. Short of human extinction, there is no sense in which capitalism can be relied upon to permanently 'break down' under the weight of its depletion and degradation of natural wealth.

Things are different with capitalism's second kind of environmental crisis, which involves a unitary, global, and permanent tendency toward qualitative deterioration in the natural conditions of human development – one actually worsened by the system's efforts to innovate around natural limits. Trends such as global warming, declining diversity of plant and animal species, the build-up of carcinogens and other poisons in the environment, the greater and greater reliance on pharmaceuticals and other drugs to mentally and physically cope with life, and ongoing mass hunger and disease in peripheral countries, all implicate the ecological contradictions of capital, value, markets, and money. In classical-Marxist terms, they represent the tension between capitalist production relations and sustainable development of human-natural productive forces.[90]

---

[89] Burkett 1999a, pp. 108–19.
[90] Hughes 2000, Chapter 5.

Capitalism's ability to continue growing despite these trends may illustrate a phenomenon noted by Gowdy, who observes that, due to

> political pressures from élites bent on preserving their power at all costs . . . a 'natural' mechanism to halt environmental degradation is not present in post hunter-gatherer human societies. There is evidently no negative feedback mechanism in complex societies which limits the destruction of natural capital . . .[91]

I disagree with Gowdy's contention that the absence of a feedback mechanism limiting 'environmental degradation' always 'leads to social disintegration' in the sense of a collapse of the system's core production relations.[92] Capitalism, in particular, is able to reproduce itself (short of human extinction) despite its depletion and degradation of natural resources. Nonetheless, Gowdy's 'feedback' argument, if adjusted a bit, really does apply to capitalism. Given capitalism's ability to reproduce itself on the basis of a degraded environment, the crisis in the natural conditions of human development can only be resolved through a direct confrontation with the system's core relations: wage-labour, production for profit, market competition, and monetary valuation. It is unlikely that the system's 'élite' (the capitalist class and its state functionaries) will support such a confrontation. But there is some hope that working people and their communities will provide the necessary *trans-systemic* 'feedback mechanism'. In this sense, the crisis in the natural conditions of human development does ultimately threaten the reproduction of capitalism, not with 'social disintegration', but with communist revolution.

Class struggle and sustainable human development

The Marxist analysis of wage-labour sheds light on the plausibility of worker-community struggle from below as a trans-systemic feedback mechanism promoting sustainable human development. It sees the emergence of more co-evolutionary frames of reference on nature as a potential outgrowth of workers' struggles to defend and improve their work and living conditions in and against their own alienation from necessary conditions of production.

---

[91] Gowdy 1994b, p. 45.
[92] Ibid.

From capital's standpoint, use-value or wealth, including both natural wealth and the individual and collective capabilities of workers and communities, is an instrument or vehicle of competitive monetary accumulation. But, for workers, the goal of the exchange of labour-power for a wage is not money itself, but the use-values that can be obtained with that money and which serve (along with domestic and other social activities) as conditions of their reproduction and development as human beings. Workers' use-value orientation is thus structurally opposed to capital's orientation simply and solely toward maximum monetary accumulation. In fact, this opposition is nothing but the tension between human development and capitalism's alienation of material conditions. It is the contradiction between use-value (human need satisfaction broadly defined) and value (capitalism's *abstract* form of wealth). It is, in short, the fundamental contradiction of capitalism: production for profit versus production for human needs.[93]

This contradiction elicits two forms of struggle. In the sphere of wage-labour proper, there is a constant tension between capital's efforts to intensify exploitation and workers' resistance to that exploitation. Here, workers struggle for higher wages, safer and less burdensome work procedures, reduced working times, and even for more co-operative and democratic forms of ownership and management. At the same time, the capitalisation and marketisation of natural and social conditions constantly generates new needs, new problems for workers that cannot be adequately addressed by struggles within the wage-labour relation, but, rather, call for worker-*community*-centred management of communal conditions as conditions of human development. The struggle against capital's degradation of nature is largely located here, beyond wage-labour, in the broader struggle for less money- and market-driven forms of economy, politics, and culture.[94]

Although they overlap, combine, and even clash in complex ways, the ultimate success of either mode of struggle in displacing the power of capital arguably depends on the other. Both forms of struggle point towards the disalienation of production and its necessary conditions. But it is only when the two kinds of struggle are brought together and become mutually constituted

---

[93] Lebowitz 1992.
[94] Burkett 1999a, Chapter 13.

that human development, seen as the growth of individual and collective capacities for self-expression and relationship-building, based on the sustainable development and utilisation of productive forces, is capable of making sudden great leaps. In short, workers' struggles, both inside and outside the workplace, contain a powerful pro-ecological potential insofar as they contest all forms of money-driven exploitation of labour and nature. The goal must be general disalienation, not more tolerable forms of alienation.[95]

The Marxist perspective thus endogenises human frames of reference on nature and sustainable development with respect to economic dynamics and struggles, but in a historically open way, as determined by more-or-less successful efforts of workers and communities to fulfill their needs and develop themselves as human beings in, against, and beyond capitalist relations. While recognising that workers often struggle in ways that do not fundamentally question wage-labour and the capitalisation of nature, Marxism detects a radical potential for worker-community movements to fight for new relations of production that treat human-natural relations as ends in themselves rather than instruments of alienated production and profit-making.

VI. Epilogue: Marxism, natural capital, and ecological economics

The present and previous chapters may seem to suggest that Marxism has a closer kinship with the anti-natural-capital position than to the pro-natural-capital position within ecological economics. However, this impression is mainly due to the sequence in which the argument was developed, moving from neoclassical natural capital to the adaptation of natural capital by ecological economists, and, only then, to the revolt against natural capital within ecological economics followed by the demonstration of how Marxism can enhance the analytical depth and political significance of anti-natural-capital arguments. Stepping back from this sequence, one can see that the relationship of Marxism to ecological economics is more complex than a simple rejection of the pro-natural-capital view and critical deepening of anti-natural-capital thinking. What Marxism really does is overcome the material-social dualism represented by the natural capital debate within ecological economics.

---

[95] Parlato and Ricoveri 1996, pp. 236–7.

While endorsing the materialist element in the ecological/natural-capital synthesis, Marxism points out that its effectiveness is undercut by the failure to analyse production as a social (class) phenomenon. To treat nature as simply a capital asset in a production function, conceived as a social-relational black box, is to adopt the abstract-ideal method of neoclassical economics. The external imposition of natural limits on this framework only leads to an abstract-material view of the economy-nature relation. The economy is thus interpreted in crude materialist *and* idealist terms, as shown by various analytical limitations and contradictions that all boil down to the failure to distinguish sustainable development and sustainable capitalism.

The resistance to natural capital tries to pose an alternative to sustainable capitalism through its critique of the monetisation, marketisation, and capitalisation of nature. It certainly provides some elements of the social deconstruction of natural capital that the ecological/natural-capital synthesis so sorely lacks. However, its deconstruction is insufficiently materialist insofar as it is not rooted in the core relation of capitalism, that is, wage-labour, considered as both a material and a social relation (social separation of the producers from necessary material conditions of production). As a result, it does not achieve a complete break with the asocial conception of nature and ahistorical view of market relations employed by natural capital thinkers.

Marxism's material-social perspective on production and capital accumulation overcomes the divide between the abstract-material idealism of the pro-natural-capital position and the abstract-social idealism of the anti-natural-capital camp. It thus provides a framework within which the real strengths of the two positions can be debated and mutually reconstituted, thereby strengthening the commitment of ecological economics to methodological pluralism. Such a reconstituted debate could lead to a politically more resonant deconstruction of natural capital – one that can effectively engage with peoples' struggles against the capitalisation of nature.

Chapter Five

Entropy in Ecological Economics: A Marxist Intervention

One of the most lively debates in ecological economics concerns the significance of the second law of thermodynamics, also known as the entropy law. The present chapter critically surveys this debate and develops a Marxist perspective on the economy-entropy relationship.

Entropy is a measure of the total disorder, randomness, or chaos in a system: increased entropy implies greater disorder. The second law says that the entropy of an isolated thermodynamic system is strictly non-decreasing, that is, that energy is only transformed from more ordered to less ordered forms. Heat, for example, can only dissipate: it will not flow spontaneously from a cold to a hot object or area in an isolated system.[1] If one interprets the orderliness of energy as a measure of its availability or usefulness to humans, then the entropy law implies that all energy transformations convert energy into less available and less useful forms. Energy cannot be transformed into work without some of the energy being dissipated as unrecoverable heat. An engine cannot operate at 100 per cent efficiency, that is, on a cycle whose only effect is to convert energy into work. A refrigerator will not operate unless it is plugged in.

---

[1] Fermi 1956, p. 30; Van Ness 1983, p. 54.

The economic importance of the entropy law was first argued systematically by Nicholas Georgescu-Roegen and Herman Daly. Section I outlines their analysis, including their application of the entropy law to the materials (not just energy) used in human production. Section II sets out four 'tracks' or sub-controversies within the ensuing debate, respectively concerning whether: (i) the purposeful character of human production negates the applicability of the entropy law: (ii) the economically relevant concept of entropy is definable apart from human purposes and technologies; (iii) solar energy can be used to achieve a complete, or practically complete, recycling of material resources; (iv) market prices already reflect (or can be made to reflect, using government policies) all economically relevant entropic phenomena. While pointing out the insights generated by each of the four tracks, I argue that the entropy debate suffers from the absence of a class perspective on nature and human production. From a Marxist standpoint, entropy as order or usefulness is, indeed, an anthropomorphic category, but this needs to be developed in terms of the class relations that shape the productive use of nature. The neglect of class is reflected in the uncritical views on market valuation of nature espoused in the entropy-economy debate. The failure to root the market in production relations also explains the debate's reliance on artificial dichotomies between allocation and scale on the one hand, and between material conditions and human values and purposes on the other.

Section III amplifies the Marxist view by considering capitalist relations as material and social relations. This opens up a dialectical perspective on entropy encompassing the close connections among wage-labour, market valuation, and the qualitative deterioration of natural wealth. Since this approach is materialist, it recognises that the entropy law does apply in terms of any given quality of materials and energy available for human production. But it also suggests that, short of human extinction, capitalist reproduction in no way hinges on the maintenance of natural wealth of any given entropy level. In other words, capitalistically-induced crises in the conditions of human development do not necessarily mean crises of capitalist reproduction. Capitalism's entropic dynamics thus pose a challenge to all who would champion ecological values: to envision new communal and non-market institutions to regulate the use and valuation of natural wealth. And the most effective answer to this challenge is not to superimpose ecological values on idealised models of capitalism, but to develop and concretise these values through a critical engagement with the struggles of workers and communities to defend and improve their conditions in opposition to capitalism's exploitation of social labour and nature. Section IV summarises the whole argument.

I. Entropy and the economic process: Georgescu-Roegen and Daly

Georgescu-Roegen and Daly begin with the observation that production depends upon materials and energy that are provided by nature. The 'economic process . . . neither produces nor consumes matter-energy; it only absorbs matter-energy and throws it out continuously'.[2] Then, appealing to the second law of thermodynamics, they argue that 'matter-energy enters the economic process in a state of *low entropy* and comes out of it in a state of *high entropy*'.[3] Production combines human labour with low-entropy forms of matter and energy to produce useful goods and services, but only at the cost of a one-way conversion of materials and energy from more ordered (and thus more useful) forms into less ordered (and less useful) forms. The increase in entropy occurs both in production itself (dispersal of heat and material pollutants), and through the disposal of products once they are used. From this perspective, 'the Entropy Law is the taproot of economic scarcity'.[4] The total supply of 'low-entropy matter-energy . . . exists in two forms: a terrestrial stock and a solar flow', both of which are limited even if particular sources of low-entropy matter-energy are 'renewable on a human time scale'.[5] 'Low entropy is' thus 'the ultimate supply limit, the source of absolute scarcity'.[6]

The key assumption of this analysis is that the entropy law applies not just to energy but also to matter, that is, that '*matter, too, is subject to an irrevocable dissipation*'.[7] Indeed, given that the earth is open to massive solar energy inflows but basically closed materially, it is not surprising that low-entropy matter, not energy, emerges most clearly as the ultimate constraint on human production.

---

[2] Georgescu-Roegen 1973, p. 50.
[3] Georgescu-Roegen 1973, p. 51 (emphasis in original); compare Daly 1974, p. 15.
[4] Georgescu-Roegen 1975, p. 353.
[5] Daly 1992a, p. 21.
[6] Daly 1992a, p. 25.
[7] Georgescu-Roegen 1975, p. 352 (emphasis in original).

Specifically, Georgescu-Roegen and Daly develop a two-step argument on the applicability of the entropy law to material production. The first step is to reiterate that production of goods and services requires not just energy but also qualitatively diverse materials – materials whose usefulness for production and consumption hinges on their specific patterns of material order or non-randomness. This dependence of production on low-entropy matter is irreducible insofar as 'at the macro-level no practical procedure exists for converting energy into matter or matter *of whatever form* into energy'.[8] Indeed, all production involves a conversion of energy into useful work, and such a conversion must always employ some material tool or apparatus possessing specific, non-random properties. 'We can never handle energy without a material lever, a material receptor, or a material transmitter. We ourselves are material structures without which no biological life can exist'.[9] In short, 'we have to spend some work and materials in order to tap a store of available energy'.[10]

The second step concerns the inevitable *dissipation and dispersal* of matter into less ordered and less useful forms. The materials used in production are subject to wear and tear not only by organic decomposition and corrosion by natural forces but also by the various kinds of *friction* produced by the material mechanisms needed to convert energy into work. As Georgescu-Roegen puts it, 'friction robs us of *available matter*':[11]

> All over the material world there is rubbing by friction, cracking and splitting by changes in temperature or evaporation, there is clogging of pipes and membranes, there is metal fatigue and spontaneous combustion. Matter is thus continuously displaced, altered, and scattered to the four corners of the world. It thus becomes less and less available for our own purposes.[12]

Friction also explains why 'available energy cannot be completely converted into *useful* work', but is always partly 'converted into irrecuperable heat'.[13]

---

[8] Georgescu-Roegen 1979b, p. 1040 (emphasis added); compare Daly 1992a, p. 25.
[9] Georgescu-Roegen 1979b, p. 1027.
[10] Georgescu-Roegen 1975, p. 354.
[11] Georgescu-Roegen 1979b, p. 1033 (emphasis in original).
[12] Georgescu-Roegen 1979b, p. 1034.
[13] Georgescu-Roegen 1979b, p. 1033 (emphasis in original).

Georgescu-Roegen is so concerned about the prior neglect of material entropy that he proposes a fourth law of thermodynamics.[14] This law has three alternative formulations, the common basis of which is the inevitability of friction, corrosion, and decomposition: (i) 'A closed system cannot perform work indefinitely at a constant rate'; (ii) 'In a closed system, available matter continuously and irrevocably dissipates, thus becoming unavailable'; (iii) 'Complete recycling is impossible'.[15]

Daly shares the view that 'terrestrial low entropy takes two forms: material and energy', both of which place an absolute limit on human production.[16] However, he goes further than Georgescu-Roegen in articulating a vision of a 'steady-state economy' that would enable humanity to more sustainably accommodate itself to these entropic limits. Such an economy

> is defined by constant stocks of physical wealth (artifacts) and a constant population, each maintained at some chosen, desirable level by a low rate of throughput – i.e., by low birth rates equal to low death rates and by low physical production rates equal to low physical depreciation rates, so that longevity of people and durability of physical stocks are high.[17]

By 'throughput', Daly means 'the extraction (depletion) of low entropy resources' and their use in production and consumption, which results in 'an equal quantity of high entropy waste (pollution) at the output end'.[18] In a steady-state economy, this throughput is 'minimized subject to the maintenance of a chosen level of stocks'.[19] Toward these ends, Daly would impose quotas on both resource depletion and aggregate human births, and then allow the market system, 'by auction and exchange, to allocate depletion quotas and birth quotas efficiently'.[20] This strategy reflects the view that whereas the market 'solves the allocation problem by providing the necessary information and incentive. . . . What it does not do is solve the problem of optimal scale', the difficulty being that there is no market for the most basic common pool

---

[14] Georgescu-Roegen 1979b, p. 1032, and 1981, p. 54.
[15] Georgescu-Roegen 1981, pp. 59–60.
[16] Daly 1992a, p. 25.
[17] Daly 1974, p. 15.
[18] Ibid.
[19] Daly 1974, p. 15.
[20] Daly 1974, p. 20.

resource: total available low-entropy matter-energy.[21] It is thus necessary to impose quantity constraints on resource extraction. To enhance flexibility, however, Daly's quotas would allow non-renewable resources to be exploited 'at a rate equal to the creation of renewable substitutes'.[22] Meanwhile, renewable resources are to be 'exploited on a profit-maximizing sustained yield basis', meaning that 'harvesting rates should not exceed regeneration rates; and . . . waste emissions should not exceed the renewable assimilative capacity of the environment'.[23]

II. The entropy-economy controversy: four trails to a dialectical perspective

The debate over the Georgescu-Roegen/Daly analysis can be divided into four crucial tracks or issue areas, all of which point to the need for a structural class perspective on entropy and economic valuation.

Entropy and the purposefulness of human production

Khalil argues that the entropy law only pertains to 'mechanistic systems' not designed or driven by 'purposeful agency'.[24] Insofar as the economy 'is about the production of goods by purposeful activity', it follows that 'the economic process is not governed by the entropy law'.[25] More precisely, the purposeful character of human production means that the usefulness of matter-energy is determined not only by its degree of orderliness, but also by the technologies employed. Hence, 'resources are not absolute à la the entropy law, but relative according to the technological potency of the purposeful agency of production'.[26] There is thus no one-to-one correspondence between rising entropy in the purely physical, objective sense and resource degradation in the sense of reduced economic usefulness. The latter can only be 'defined in relation to

[21] Daly 1991, p. 35.
[22] Daly 1991, p. 45.
[23] Ibid. For a detailed presentation of the steady-state economy proposal, see Daly 1992a, Chapters 2–4.
[24] Khalil 1990, pp. 163–4.
[25] Khalil 1990, p. 164.
[26] Ibid.

the organization which is undertaking the activity', and this 'organization could as well reverse the deterioration, after some innovations in technology and institutions are introduced'.[27]

This analysis could have opened up an interesting debate on the historical relativity of entropy as an economic concept. Unfortunately, this useful element of Khalil's argument was fogged over by his assertion that the entropy law is wholly inapplicable to purposeful processes including human production. Here, Khalil drew an analogy between human production and the Carnot reverse cycle – named after the early-nineteenth-century French engineer, Nicolas Sadi Carnot. The Carnot cycle involves a piston-cylinder engine that uses the temperature differential between two heat reservoirs to keep itself going by sequentially using heat to do work (lowering the piston) and work to transfer heat (raising the piston).[28] This cycle produces not just greater entropy (outside the limiting case of 100 per cent efficiency) but also positive net work or 'free energy'. 'In fact', says Khalil, 'the Carnot cycle is designed *purposefully* to produce free energy', which 'sets it apart from the non-purposeful, mechanistic entropy law'.[29] This is shown, he suggests, by the theoretical possibility of a 100 per cent efficient Carnot cycle that does not increase entropy at all. Since human production is also purposeful, Khalil concludes that 'the economic process should be conceived after the Carnot cycle, and not the entropy law'.[30]

The effect of this argumentative strategy is to conflate the anthropomorphic *relativity* of entropy as economic usefulness with a blanket denial that entropy plays *any role* in determining the productive usefulness of matter and energy. Not surprisingly, the responses to Khalil's article focus on the second element in this conflation, ignoring the conflation itself. After all, Khalil's misapplication of the Carnot cycle provides a more inviting target than having to grapple with the more difficult historical questions raised by entropy's relativity with respect to human purposes.

---

[27] Khalil 1990, p. 174.
[28] The temperature differential between the two reservoirs is maintained by the recirculation of heat from the cold to the hot reservoir, using the work done by the engine. For details, see Fermi (1956, pp. 31–5) and Van Ness (1983, pp. 36–40).
[29] Khalil 1990, p. 170 (emphasis in original).
[30] Khalil 1990, p. 171.

The counterattack begins with Lozada, who describes Khalil's argument as 'basically an "ultravitalist" attempt to deny that living, purposeful beings are completely subject to all laws of elementary matter such as the entropy law'.[31] Khalil mistakenly treats the entropy law as if it assumes away all purposeful conversions of energy into work; but all the law says is that energy cannot be converted into work with 100 per cent efficiency. The 100 per cent efficient Carnot cycle is only an ideal benchmark for gauging the efficiency of real world engines: 'No Carnot engine has ever existed nor will ever exist, because the Carnot cycle is reversible and therefore requires perfectly frictionless machinery and infinitely slow operation'.[32] Similarly, Williamson argues that the Carnot cycle 'incorporates *both the first and the second* laws of thermodynamics', even though it 'does indeed describe (and quantitatively so) the way in which a purposeful agency may be interposed in an otherwise spontaneous (or natural) process so as to produce useful work'.[33] The 100 per cent efficient Carnot cycle merely defines 'the *upper limit to the potency which any purposeful agency can achieve*'.[34] Khalil's error, in Williamson's view, is to interpret this upper limit as implying that 'purposeful agency in economic activity may be of unlimited potency'.[35]

More interestingly, Biancardi, Donati and Ulgiati criticise Khalil's 'risky thesis' that 'the Carnot cycle . . . has *the same form* as the economic process'.[36] 'Economic production is actually characterized by physical and/or bio-chemical processes which may or may not be cycles, depending on whether or not heat engines are used'.[37] Hence 'each economic process can be regarded as an irreversible transformation', that is, one that – unlike the Carnot cycle – never 'returns to the starting conditions' including the initial stock of resources.[38]

Unlike Carnot's ideal frictionless engine which is a closed thermodynamic system, the human economy is, from a biospheric standpoint, an open system that metabolically co-evolves with its natural environment. True, the earth as

---

[31] Lozada 1991, p. 157.
[32] Lozada 1991, p. 159.
[33] Williamson 1993, pp. 70–1 (emphasis in original).
[34] Williamson 1993, p. 71 (emphasis in original).
[35] Ibid.
[36] Biancardi, Donati and Ulgiati 1993a, p. 9 [emphasis added].
[37] Biancardi, Donati and Ulgiati 1993a, p. 10.
[38] Ibid.

a whole can 'be regarded as a big (closed) Carnot engine with the sun (a heat-reservoir at a higher temperature) and the outer-space (a heat-reservoir at lower temperature)'.[39] But the interaction of the economy with the terrestrial environment is one in which the former constantly draws matter and energy from, and emits matter and energy waste into, the latter. It is precisely through this irreversible metabolic interaction that human life (like other forms of life) consumes the low-entropy matter-energy needed for its reproduction and development. Indeed, an entire neo-Darwinian evolutionary wing of the entropy literature tries to explain the expansion and decline of different species, eco-systems, and even economic systems in terms of their relative efficiency in absorbing low-entropy matter-energy and expelling high-entropy matter-energy.[40]

This crucial *form-divergence* between the economic process and the Carnot cycle leaves quite a lot of space for various degrees of tension between human production and its environmental conditions. Is this indeterminacy not somehow connected with the *relativity* of matter-energy usefulness with respect to the purposeful character of production to which Khalil's analysis points? Presumably, the extent to which an economy accelerates entropy in 'one-way' fashion depends on the particular purposes driving production. This, naturally, points to the social relations that shape and constrain productive priorities, and that determine the way natural resources are valued economically.

The relativity of entropy

A year or so after Khalil's contribution, an article by Jeffrey Young focussed the debate more clearly on the relativity of entropy as an economic concept.[41] Unfortunately, Young prefaced his arguments on relativity with the controversial claim that entropy applies only to energy and not to matter. Young's notion that the entropy law 'can only be extended to matter by *analogy*' rests on the presumption that entropy is only definable for *homogenous* entities (entities

---

[39] Mayumi 1993, p. 353.
[40] See, for example, Binswanger 1993; Rebane 1995. The concept of entropy has, of course, been used in various, often contradictory, ways across the natural and social sciences. See Proops 1987 and Mayumi and Giampietro 2004 for surveys that do much to alleviate the resulting confusion.
[41] Young 1991.

measurable in common units – like BTUs for energy).[42] In short, the claim is that there is

> an aggregation problem in applying entropy to matter which does not exist
> for energy. Without some neutral aggregation principle it is impossible to
> tell whether a resource system is becoming more or less orderly if there is
> more than one type of material resource.[43]

Young's critics make short work of this claim. Daly points out that 'Physicists routinely apply entropy to matter, and although this extension may involve some difficulties, it is far more than a mere analogy'.[44] Townsend observes that

> entropy is a concept that applies as readily to matter as it does to energy.
> Students of physics, chemistry, and engineering routinely calculate the
> changes in entropy resulting from phase changes in ordinary materials, such
> as the fusion of water from a solid to a liquid. A cursory glance at texts on
> thermodynamics . . . reveals that the concept of entropy characterizes
> spontaneous changes in all systems, regarding matter and energy equally.[45]

Part of the difficulty is that Young's argument conflates the problem of aggregation with that of conceptualisation. After all, there are serious aggregation problems in all kinds of scientific theories including mainstream economics with its notions of aggregate real output, employment, and price level. Would Young abandon the concept of real GDP because one cannot add apples and steel in purely physical terms?

At a more basic level, Young should have noticed that non-homogeneity of energy (not just matter) is implied by the entropy law itself, since this law makes no sense unless we have already defined more and less ordered forms of energy. From a dialectical perspective, energy, too, is non-homogenous insofar as different energy sources are more or less ordered and available, due, for example, to their embodiment or immersion in different quantities and forms of matter. On this basis, Young could then have pointed out that

---

[42] Young 1991, p. 169 (emphasis in original).
[43] Young 1991, p. 178.
[44] Daly 1992c, p. 91.
[45] Townsend 1992, p. 97.

any economic interpretation of 'more and less ordered', or 'available', is by
necessity anthropomorphic, whether we are talking about energy or matter –
and regardless of whether we are dealing with particular sources of matter-
energy or matter-energy in the aggregate. This would have pre-empted Daly's
query as to 'why his [Young's] arguments' concerning the economic relativity
of entropy 'do not apply to energy as well as to matter'.[46]

Despite these problems, Young and his critics clarify the anthropomorphic
element in any entropic interpretation of the economic process. Incorporating
entropic dissipation of matter and energy into a simple Ricardian growth
model, Young argues that there are two kinds of technological change that
can operate as 'a counterforce to diminishing returns'.[47] The first kind is
'resource augmenting technological change which increases the output per
unit of matter and/or energy input'; but this only causes 'dissipation to
proceed at a slower pace'.[48] The second kind of technological change 'create[s]
resources out of noneconomic material' by discovering new matter-energy
stocks or new uses of previously known stocks.[49] It is this second kind of
technological change that most clearly poses the question: 'Is [entropy] not
in fact an anthropomorphic concept intimately associated with what is useful
and, therefore, defined by current technology?'.[50] Young answers affirmatively,
using his model to demonstrate that 'it is very possible for entropy . . . as
disorderliness or unavailability, to be decreasing even though the system is
closed'.[51] In short, 'available matter is dependent on the existence of appropriate
technologies. It is not a purely physical concept'.[52] Given this technological
relativity, Young concludes that 'the entropy law is not particularly relevant
to the economics of long-run resource scarcity'.[53]

Young is right to raise the question of the anthropomorphic relation of
entropy to economic usefulness. However, Georgescu-Roegen and Daly
themselves do not assume a simple one-to-one correspondence between

[46] Daly 1992c, p. 91.
[47] Young 1991, p. 176.
[48] Young 1991, p. 177.
[49] Ibid.
[50] Ibid.
[51] Young 1991, p. 178.
[52] Ibid.
[53] Young 1991, pp. 178–9.

economic usefulness and low entropy. Rather, they treat low-entropy matter-energy as one condition for the production of useful goods and services – with human labour, ingenuity, and tastes also playing essential roles. They do not reduce production to pure entropic terms (see Chapter 1).

Thus, in his response to Young, Daly is able to grant the point that matter-energy usefulness is anthropomorphic, while arguing that the 'absolute scarcity' of low-entropy matter-energy still imposes an 'optimal sustainable scale' on 'the economic subsystem as a part of the overall ecosystem'.[54] Here, Daly clarifies the distinction between low entropy in the purely physical sense and low entropy as usefulness, with the latter, more purposeful concept determined in part by science and technology:

> If we discover a novel resource, b, or even if we just discover more deposits
> of the same resource, a, the result is the same – namely, we must redescribe
> the state of the system, taking account of the new knowledge. That new
> description, based on new knowledge, would record a stock of low-entropy
> materials greater (and likewise in the case of energy) than in the previous
> inventory. This does not mean that the economic process is not entropic or
> even that knowledge is anti-entropic – it only means that our description
> of the initial stock of low-entropy materials was incomplete in the light of
> new knowledge. Perhaps the upward bookkeeping revision of inventory of
> low-entropy materials might be greater in a given year than the physical
> increases in entropy from resource extraction and use. That hardly reverses
> the entropic direction of economic activity.[55]

Moreover, new knowledge may itself lead to increased entropic degradation (as when the discovery of the 'usefulness' of certain gases for air conditioners, refrigerators, and aerosol spray cans led to worsening ozone depletion and greenhouse effects). It may also 'reveal new limits'.[56]

> The hole in the ozone layer is new knowledge. To suppose, as is usually
> done, that new knowledge will always expand the resource base and never

---

[54] Daly 1992c, p. 94.
[55] Daly 1992c, p. 92. Townsend (1992, pp. 98–9) makes essentially the same point, referring to 'improvements in efficiency that alter the rate of entropic change of the system without increasing the availability of resources. These may be presumed to have existed, whether or not people possessed knowledge of them'.
[56] Daly 1992c, p. 92.

contract it is to overspecify the content of new knowledge, which must always be something of a surprise – and not always a pleasant one.[57]

By recognising the role of human knowledge in determining the economic limits (or lack thereof) imposed by the entropy law, both Young and Daly point to the historical contingency of the natural limits to human production. But neither author considers the implication that the social (class) relations of production, and historically specific resource-allocation mechanisms, help define these effective limits and determine the extent to which they tend to be exceeded. Both authors treat production, knowledge, and economic limits as if they develop in a social-relational vacuum. Historically contingent natural limits are posed, but no tools of social-relational analysis are provided with which to analyse critically this contingency in particular economies and societies. The anthropomorphic character of entropy in the sense of economic usefulness is recognised, yet neither author considers the extent to which usefulness is largely defined by instrumental and/or functional goals connected with the social relations of production.[58]

For example, neither author asks whether a system of production driven by the quantitatively unlimited goal of capital accumulation has a specific tendency to accelerate entropy and overstretch its natural environment and, if so, whether this tendency in any way threatens the reproduction of such a system. How is it possible for capitalism to reproduce itself despite its continuous degradation of the natural conditions of human development? To

---

[57] Ibid.

[58] Mayumi (1993, p. 356) observes with regard to the entropy of matter: 'The proper initial state . . . is deeply related to our multi-dimensional value system: to what state should we transform the degraded matter?' Mayumi and Giampietro (2004, pp. 15–16) apply the same reasoning to energy: 'The definition of what should be considered "useful energy" in ultimate analysis depends on the goals of the system operating within a given context' (compare Giampietro and Pimentel 1991). Norgaard (1986, p. 327) also argues that 'alternative measures of the amount of entropic change seem inextricably linked to human values. Better knowledge of this phenomena may shed light on our understanding of objectivity in economics'. But such knowledge and understanding could presumably include some awareness of how social relations of production shape the economic valuation of matter-energy both qualitatively and quantitatively. And although many ecological economists recognise that 'no definite [i.e., transhistorical] law exists that relates economic value and common thermodynamic functions' (Amir 1998, p. 213), the discipline on the whole has tended to treat market valuation as a natural and self-evident phenomenon. See Chapter 1 of the present work.

address these issues, one must analyse the tensions between nature as a condition of capitalist production and nature as a condition of human development, and this requires that capitalist relations be clearly specified both materially and socially.

The recycling controversy

Georgescu-Roegen's fourth law rejects 'the axiom that recycling of matter can, in principle, be complete'.[59] This rejection is based on the observation that recycling 'must necessarily involve some material instruments':[60]

> Because there are no perdurable material structures these instruments will necessarily wear out. They will have to be replaced by others produced by some other instruments, which will also wear out and will have to be replaced, and so on, in an unending regress. This regress is a sufficient ground for denying the possibility of complete recycling . . .[61]

It is true that 'if we have enough energy, we could even separate the cold molecules of a glass of water and assemble them into ice cubes'; but 'in practice . . . such operations are impossible . . . because they would require a practically infinite time'.[62] This problem applies in particular to those 'elements which, because of their nature and the mode in which they participate in the natural and man-conducted processes, are highly dissipative' and/or 'found in very small supply in the environment'.[63] In short, 'the somber message of the second law (that dissipation of matter and energy are unavoidable consequences of their use) mutes the seemingly optimistic message of the first law (that matter and energy are not literally consumed in their use)'.[64]

While taking an agnostic stance on the *physical impossibility* of complete matter-recycling, Daly is also 'prepared to believe in common-sense evidence that for all practical purposes complete recycling is impossible'.[65] Like

---

[59] Georgescu-Roegen 1979b, p. 1034.
[60] Ibid.
[61] Ibid.; compare Georgescu-Roegen 1981, pp. 60–1.
[62] Georgescu-Roegen 1975, p. 356.
[63] Ibid.
[64] England 1994, pp. 200–1.
[65] Daly 1992c, p. 92.

Georgescu-Roegen, he points to 'the physical fact that enormous amounts of energy, as well as of other materials, are required to recycle highly dispersed matter'.[66] It thus 'remains clear that complete materials recycling would require ruinous amounts of energy and time'.[67] In sum, recycling cannot remove 'the inevitable cost of arranging greater order in one part of the system (the human economy)', namely, 'creating a more than offsetting amount of disorder elsewhere (the natural environment)'.[68] Even with maximum recycling, 'absolute scarcity' eventually 'makes growth impossible'.[69]

The critics of Georgescu-Roegen's fourth law recognise that complete materials recycling would require extremely large inputs of low-entropy energy and the conversion of this energy into higher-entropy forms. They only question whether complete recycling is *impossible* abstracting from energy constraints. Biancardi, Tiezzi and Ulgiati, for example, argue that 'complete recycling is physically possible if a sufficient amount of energy is available'.[70] However, 'such an expenditure of energy would involve a tremendous increase in the entropy of the environment, which would not be sustainable for the biosphere'.[71] Similarly, Kümmel suggests that 'dissipation of matter' can 'in principle, . . . be avoided at the cost of increased energy input and heat production', even though the cost 'may become forbiddingly high, if one would try to recollect the last atom'.[72]

By highlighting the entropic implications of material recycling operations, these analyses provide a useful antidote to the treatment of recycling as a kind of ecological panacea. But there is still a serious difficulty with these criticisms: they downplay the crucial roles of friction and matter-dissipation in Georgescu-Roegen's fourth law. In this regard, Biancardi, Tiezzi and Ulgiati try to translate friction and matter-dissipation into pure energy terms.[73]

---

[66] Daly 1992c, p. 93.
[67] Daly 1992c, p. 91.
[68] Daly 1992a, p. 24.
[69] Daly 1992a, p. 43.
[70] Biancardi, Tiezzi and Ulgiati 1993b, p. 5.
[71] Ibid.
[72] Kümmel 1994, p. 195. See also Månsson (1994, p. 192), who argues that 'it is technically quite possible to achieve recycling in the weak sense of reproducing certain objects using material *from any source'*, even though the energy-entropy cost 'may sometimes be too high' (emphasis added).
[73] Biancardi, Tiezzi and Ulgiati 1993b.

Specifically, they assert that the 'wasting and mixing of material' during recycling merely 'involves a passage from an ordered energy form (mechanical, electrical, chemical) to a less ordered one (heat)'.[74] This assumption occludes the qualitative material requirements of human production in Georgescu-Roegen's argument. Along the same lines, Kümmel argues that any 'emissions of noxious substances can be transformed into emissions of heat', so that matter-dissipation is already 'included in the Second Law'.[75] But this logic seems to neglect the limits that friction and matter-dissipation themselves place on the conversion of matter into pure energy, not to mention the adverse material effects of waste heat on the eco-systems into which it is emitted.[76] Georgescu-Roegen's dictum that 'matter matters, too' is not so easily dismissed.[77]

By contrast, two letters to the editor by Converse emphasise the material requirements of recycling operations, thereby opening up some important ecological issues.[78] His first letter uses mass-transfer theory to argue that any attempt to 'separate a homogenous mixture into its components requires that one of the components move across a phase boundary or membrane that is able to reject the other components'.[79] Since the required membrane area approaches infinity as the full removal of the single component is approached, 'complete separation of a mixture is impossible, even though it is not denied by thermodynamic considerations'.[80]

Converse's second letter theorises recycling technologies that use 'holding tank[s] into which waste is discharged, transformed by the application of energy, and then recycled'.[81] Although he describes such operations as 'complete recycling', they are not really complete insofar as, at any given time, the 'concentration of waste' in the holding tanks themselves is not 'driven to zero'.[82] Indeed, his analysis is more accurately read as setting out the limits

---

[74] Biancardi, Tiezzi and Ulgiati 1993b, p. 5.
[75] Kümmel 1994, p. 195.
[76] Compare Huesemann 2001, p. 276.
[77] Georgescu-Roegen 1979b, p. 1039.
[78] Converse 1996, and 1997.
[79] Converse 1996, p. 193; compare Middleman, 1997.
[80] Converse 1996, p. 193.
[81] Converse 1997, p. 1.
[82] Ibid.

of expanded recycling operations consistent with any given quality of natural wealth. As Converse says, 'There is, of course, the problems of sequestering anthropogenic waste in the man-made holding tank from the general environmental holding tank and achieving acceptable costs'.[83] These difficulties are clearly accentuated insofar as there is a growing amount of throughput to be recycled, especially if the throughput is of the high-dissipation type, in which case a growing share of resources (including environmental space) will need to be allocated toward the manufactured holding tanks for any given environmental quality goals.[84]

Even Ayres, who is generally optimistic on recycling possibilities, admits that 'even the most efficient conceivable recycling process will generate wastes'.[85] He suggests that the 'wastebaskets' in which these effluents accumulate can themselves be treated by recycling processes 'given the postulated availability of energy'.[86] But 'the wastebasket[s] can never be eliminated altogether' and their size will be a positive function of the amount of material throughput employed in production, the degree of recycling efficiency, and the diffusiveness of the materials to be recycled.[87]

All of this suggests that a 'sustainable society' cannot rely on recycling alone, but must also reduce its reliance on matter-energy throughput while shifting its production toward 'materials that yield wastes that can be tolerated at a finite level in the environment'.[88] Ayres thus emphasises the need for a 'dematerialization' of production through a movement toward services combined with greater 're-use, renovation, recovery and recycling'.[89] On this basis, he rejects Georgescu-Roegen's hypothesis that the 'economic system is . . . doomed to "run down" as the low entropy material resources on earth are dissipated and become unavailable'.[90]

However, Ayres's optimistic projection presumes that increasing services production does not require a growing material base, that is, that there is no

[83] Converse 1997, p. 2.
[84] Mayumi 1993, pp. 359–61.
[85] Ayres 1997, p. 286.
[86] Ibid.
[87] Ayres 1997, p. 287. For the details of this analysis, see Ayres 1998, and 1999, and Kåberger and Månsson 2001.
[88] Converse 1997, p. 2.
[89] Ayres 1997, p. 286.
[90] Ibid.

'finite upper limit to the service output of a given material'.[91] As Huws observes, the current production of ever greater amounts of information and entertainment (the main locus of today's service economy) is dependent on the growing matter-energy throughput associated with computers, scanners, printers, mobile phones, media players, disks, and so forth, which are subject to more and more rapid rates of obsolescence – not to mention 'the many components and accessories involved in their manufacture'.[92] The recycling of these high-tech instruments, parts, and auxiliaries is, at best, a highly partial operation that leaves in its wake degraded environments (and poisoned recycling workforces), especially in the Third-World regions and other poor areas where such 'wastebaskets' are normally located.[93] Overall,

> the propagation of information processing machines may increase the consumption of available matter and/or energy in the economy, instead of decreasing it. This may result in the intensification of underground materials' pollution, from which the said information society is hoped to be free.[94]

The recycling optimists also have not adequately confronted the inapplicability of recycling to biological and eco-system resources.[95] Craig, for example, recognises 'our inability to recreate biological and ecological elements of our life-support system',[96] observing that:

> Ecologists know how important it is to keep ecosystems intact. Once dismantled, they are at best difficult and usually impossible to reassemble. . . . Once lost, a species is gone forever.[97]

Yet the same author asserts that 'the theoretical limit' to materials recycling 'is minute'.[98] Such a dichotomy between recycling and eco-system reproduction is completely foreign to Georgescu-Roegen's fourth law analysis, which recognises 'that what is true for one dead lake is not true for all dead lakes'.[99]

---

[91] Ibid.
[92] Huws 1999, p. 49; compare Konrad 2005.
[93] Fairlie 1992; Shabi 2002; Joffe-Wait 2005.
[94] Tsuchida and Murota 1987, p. 27.
[95] Cleveland and Ruth 1997, p. 212; Huesemann 2001, pp. 275–9.
[96] Craig 2001, p. 381.
[97] Craig 2001, pp. 376, 381.
[98] Craig 2001, p. 374.
[99] Georgescu-Roegen 1975, p. 358.

As Lawn points out, that recycling *may* ensure 'a large quantity of low entropy' on the source- or supply-side of productive throughput is only one side of the sustainability equation.[100] One must also avoid compromising the environment's 'limited sink and life-support services'.[101] The relegation of ever-more environmental space to recycling holding-tank status obviously would not bode well in this connection. In addition, any large-scale conversion of natural eco-systems into recycling wastebaskets is likely to vitiate the aesthetic quality of life. Daly, for example, recognises that in Ayres's recycling/dematerialisation scenario, 'the materials and energy intensity of an average dollar's worth of GNP forever declines, approaching zero'; but he nonetheless finds it distinctly unattractive: 'We will all eat high-tech sandwiches consisting of ever thicker slices of information (much of it indigestible) between increasingly thin slices of silicon'.[102] Many will share his revulsion.

The limitations of recycling have led some to argue that 'modern science and technology have very limited potential to alleviate . . . environmental problems', and to find the solution in a rejection of the 'materialistic values' that are purportedly 'the root cause of the environmental crisis'.[103] However, this parachuting in of exogenous values only highlights the failure of the entire recycling controversy to take seriously the social character of economic activity. With production treated as a social-relational black box, it is not surprising that ecological economists have debated the limits of recycling in alternately thermodynamic and moralistic terms. Employing a material-social dualism in which the social side takes the form of exogenous ethical values, they have not provided any social-form analysis of material production itself. Yet any serious consideration of recycling possibilities must include the role of the social relations of production, and corresponding priorities, in enabling and delimiting the set of feasible options. Otherwise, there may be a tendency to limit these possibilities to whatever technologies are available on the market at any given time. This would be tantamount to constraining recycling techniques to those consistent with the competitive maximisation of private profit.

---

[100] Lawn 1999, p. 7.
[101] Ibid.
[102] Daly 1992a, p. 205.
[103] Huesemann 2001, pp. 283, 285.

Ayres, Ferrer and Van Leynseele, for example, emphasise the potential for 'double dividends' from recycling, meaning 'increased profits for the firm combined with environmental improvement'.[104] The determination of which forms of recycling are 'economic', and the levels of different throughputs to be recycled, are taken as given from the market. That the general failure to reduce throughput might be rooted in production relations (for example, competitive employment of wage-labour for maximum monetary accumulation) is simply not addressed. In this way, technocratic recycling optimism can lead to a position similar to that of neoclassical economics, for which market incentives generally reflect (or can be made to reflect, using an appropriate system of resource-property rights) the environmental costs of economic activity and thereby promote environmental sustainability.

Entropy and the market

Indeed, some neoclassical economists have argued that, insofar as entropy determines the usefulness of matter and energy in production, then it should already be reflected in firms' costs and thus fully accounted for by standard supply-and-demand theory. Even if the increases in entropy resulting from production are not privately priced, they can be treated under the familiar category of 'external costs'. Such gaps between private and social costs can be corrected by taxing the externality-producing activities. Alternatively, property rights can be assigned to, and markets created for, the externalities *within* some aggregate constraint on their levels. In either case, so the argument goes, entropy as such adds nothing substantial to the analysis.

Burness et al., for example, argue that in a market system, 'energy is valued only in terms of its inputs to the production of goods and services that satisfy the wants of individuals', so that 'the value of energy or the value of any other factor of production or consumption good derives from its productivity or usefulness in this regard'.[105] They apply the same argument to 'sources of low entropy' in general:[106]

---

[104] Ayres, Ferrer and Van Leynseele 1997, p. 557.
[105] Burness et al. 1980, p. 7.
[106] Ibid.

So long as markets are reasonably competitive, the thermodynamic laws are indeed reflected in markets. Marginal costs of the outputs of land (including low entropy resources), labor and capital will reflect the opportunity cost of these factors: in the case of gas, the marginal value product of gas in producing work must be reflected in its cost as an input in home heating. As the scarcity of 'work' increases, the opportunity cost of gas for home heating will rise and, ceteris paribus, one would expect a shift in factor combinations away from the use of gas in nonwork types of uses. Increases in the scarcity value of work lead to increased capital intensity, thereby altering systems to the end of performing more work for a given entropic change as well as reducing rejected heat. . . . Of course, distortions in the rate of extraction of exhaustible resources due to market imperfections . . . are reasonably well-known in economics, and policies recommended by economic studies point to the obvious need for prices which reflect scarcity.[107]

Similarly, Young suggests that

if entropy became an important constraint in a given system, then price would rise as the finite stock runs out. As technology redefines the system boundaries, price would signal any change in relative scarcity from one state of the world to another. In an ideal world of perfect markets, and all that this implies concerning government regulations and property institutions, price would be a superior indicator of scarcity since it incorporates both entropic constraint (foregone future use) and the effects of the technological redefinition of the system.[108]

In this view, the Georgescu-Roegen/Daly application of the entropy law to economic processes is merely 'a rephrased expression of the exhaustible resources problem in the economics literature'.[109] Insofar as entropy is just another term for changes in matter-energy 'endowments' that influence production costs, it 'adds nothing to traditional models based on the tension between depletion- and pollution-induced scarcity and certain scarcity mitigating factors'.[110]

---

[107] Burness et al. 1980, p. 6.
[108] Young 1994, p. 213.
[109] Burness et al. 1980, p. 6.
[110] Young 1991, p. 179.

If entropy adds nothing to economic analysis, it follows that the adoption of an explicitly entropic approach must be based on value judgements, not scientific criteria. For neoclassical economists, market prices reflect (or can be made to reflect) the preferences of individuals and the costs of serving these preferences. The imposition of additional, entropically informed, values must therefore involve an overriding of consumer sovereignty. As Burness et al. put it:

> But unless one wishes to argue for a fundamental change in our system of
> values, it is not clear that thermodynamic considerations are inappropriately
> reflected in prices. . . . Within a value system where consumer preferences
> play the role of guiding output/input decisions, it is simply not clear as to
> how thermodynamic concepts . . . are to be used in enriching the promulgation
> of public policy.[111]

Any concern with entropy as such is, in short, a 'concern with *ethical* issues rather than . . . the *allocative efficiency* of markets'.[112]

In reply, Daly reasserts the relevance of the entropy law as the ultimate basis of resource scarcity. The neoclassicals err in assuming that relative scarcity (scarcity of particular resources compared to other resources) is the only kind of scarcity that matters. For Daly, the absolute scarcity of total low-entropy matter-energy places 'a previously neglected aggregate constraint on the physical scale of the economy'.[113] Daly does not deny that market prices reflect (or can be made to reflect) relative scarcities. The problem is that this 'optimality of allocation is independent of whether or not the scale of physical throughput is ecologically sustainable'.[114]

Absolute scarcity must, therefore, be registered through 'a collectively enacted constraint on the aggregate flow (throughput) of matter and energy from the ecosystem through the economy, and back to the ecosystem'.[115] This constraint, taking the form of quotas on resource-depletion and human births, would reflect the fact that 'we collectively value sustainability, a value which,

---

[111] Burness et al. 1980, p. 8.
[112] Burness and Cummings 1986, p. 324 (emphases in original).
[113] Daly 1986, p. 320.
[114] Ibid.
[115] Ibid.

like that of justice, is not expressible at the level of individual choices in a competitive market'.[116] Once the quotas are in place 'the market will, at the micro level, come up with a different set of prices which now reflect the social value of sustainability'.[117]

Daly is right to reject the facile identification of environmental efficiency with market efficiency. Unfortunately, he does not inquire into the social-relational origins of the dualism between allocation and scale, that is, between private and collective values. How is it that people have become so alienated from nature that their dominant form of exchange, the market, places no value on environmental sustainability? Daly's failure to address this question weakens his response to the neoclassical critics in three closely related ways.

First, he treats the allocation/scale dualism as a stark dichotomy rather than a dialectical unity-in-difference, and this leads to problems. Consider Daly's attempt to specify the allocation/scale relationship in micro/macro terms:

> The market is sensitive to scale issues at the micro level, but is insensitive to the macro level scale of the whole economy relative to the ecosystem. The fact that the market can substitute relatively abundant resources for relatively scarce ones is a great virtue, but does not remove the entropic constraint. Substitutability among various types of low entropy does not mean that there can be a substitute for low entropy itself.[118]

The problem is that, precisely insofar as markets are 'sensitive to scale issues at the micro level', there does not have to be a substitute for low entropy as such in order for markets to promote its economisation. As emphasised by Young, low-entropy matter-energy can only exist in particular, more-or-less useful, forms.[119] If specific low-entropy resources become relatively scarce, and thus relatively high priced, this should – in the neoclassical view – encourage greater efficiency in the use and recycling of these resources. Whether such market-driven responses are ecologically adequate is an issue to be investigated; but Daly's analysis provides no tools for such a critical

---

[116] Ibid.
[117] Ibid.
[118] Daly 1986, p. 320.
[119] Young 1991, and 1994.

investigation. Indeed, he says that prices *will* register the social value of sustainability once his resource-depletion and birth quotas are implemented. If this is the case, neoclassical economists can justifiably ask why the same quantities cannot be generated by letting the market (supplemented by tax/subsidy schemes as external effects warrant) set the proper scarcity prices. For any given set of market demand schedules, the results should be identical.

Second, Daly's resource-depletion quotas would necessarily take the form of specific limits on the use of particular forms of low-entropy matter-energy. For non-renewables, Daly's quotas would be geared to the availability of renewable substitutes which would obviously differ case-by-case. Even renewables quotas would differ according to their differential regeneration rates (see Section I). Resource-depletion quotas would, thus, be allocational by their very nature, even prior to their allocation by the market. (Such quotas are a standard weapon in the arsenal of neoclassical environmental *micro*economics, after all.) The market's reallocation of both birth quotas and resource-depletion quotas among different households and firms would also place its own stamp on the overall rate and pattern of low-entropy matter-energy depletion. Here, too, a social-relational perspective on material production and productive priorities is needed to specify and evaluate the system's likely ecological impacts.

Third, Daly's treatment of the economy as a social-relational black box is shown by his failure to provide a systemic explanation of environmental crisis. His analysis posits that markets are only allocational devices that do not determine the scale of production; but this leaves the scale itself unaccounted for. He is thus forced to appeal to exogenous values, especially consumerism and 'growthmania', to explain the failure to control matter-energy throughput.[120] The path to a sustainable system is likewise sought not in a transformation of socio-economic relations, but rather in a change of values guided by 'traditional religions' which 'teach man to conform his soul to reality by knowledge, self-discipline, and restraint on the multiplication of desires'.[121] In this respect, the neoclassical critics are right: Daly merely adds another layer of exogenous, subjectively determined preferences to the given consumer preferences of mainstream theory.

---

[120] Daly 1974, pp. 17–19.
[121] Daly 1992a, p. 44; compare Daly and Cobb 1989.

III.   A Marxist approach to the economics of entropy

For Marxists, the economy's production relations shape its relations of exchange
and distribution, as well as the priorities served by production. Accordingly,
a Marxist analysis of the economy-entropy nexus begins by specifying these
production relations materially and socially.

Capitalism, nature, and the market

Capitalism is defined by the complete social separation of the producers from
necessary material conditions of production, starting with the land, and the
recombination of the 'freed' labour-power and material conditions as wage-
labour producing commodities for a profit. Only under capitalism does *capital*
(the advancement of money to obtain more money) dominate and constantly
reshape production, as opposed to operating on the edges of production in
the sphere of exchange. For present purposes, two aspects of this system are
absolutely crucial.

   First, the dominant position of the market in capitalist society is an outgrowth
of the wage-labour relation. With workers socially separated from productive
wealth, their reproduction requires that they sell their labour-power for a
wage used to purchase means of subsistence on the market. True, markets
and money have existed for millennia as means of exchanging surplus products
among different households and communities. But the generalisation of profit-
driven production for the market, the never-ending pressure of competition
on the producers, and the constant need for money in order to live, all owe
themselves to the commodification of 'free' labour-power and its employment
by autonomous enterprises controlling 'separate' conditions of production.
It is on this basis that the commodification of the means of production develops
historically. In short, the market system is best viewed as an outgrowth of
the alienation of the producers from the material conditions of production.
Alienation from nature and marketisation of exchange are two sides of the
same coin.[122]

---

   [122] Precapitalist societies have their own forms of alienation from nature (and
consequently their own forms of environmental crisis). In all class societies, the
producers' access to natural conditions is restricted by the requirements of exploitation.
Under feudalism, for example, much of the land and its products was reserved for
the lords. But, under capitalism, the producers' restricted relation to nature takes the

Second, capitalism's reproduction requirements are autonomous from the sustainable reproduction of labour-power and natural conditions considered as ecologically co-evolving entities.[123] For capitalist production, all that matters is that labour-power and material conditions be separately available in forms that can be combined as commodity production by wage-labour. Given this precondition, capitalist reproduction does not depend upon any particular limit to the entropy level in its matter-energy environment.

Nature, entropy, and capitalist valuation

As Marx demonstrated, capitalism reduces the substance of economic value to the abstract (homogenous, socially necessary) labour time objectified in commodities. This value-substance is specific to capitalism because it depends on the social separation of labour-power from other 'inputs' and its employment by competing enterprises as wage-labour. There is an obvious tension between this reduction of value to abstract labour and the fact that production requires not just labour but also other forms of low-entropy matter-energy. This contradiction explains capitalism's unique tendency to freely appropriate natural conditions as valueless goods.[124] To have value, labour must be objectified in use-values whose production requires specific forms of low-entropy matter-energy. Yet, from the standpoint of the system as a whole, these requisite natural resources have no value.

Saad-Filho has demonstrated that the formation of commodity values (reduction of concrete labours to abstract labours) occurs partly through the formation of market prices (and of price-value deviations).[125] This is one way of establishing the necessity of money as a form of value under capitalism. It is thus important to consider the adequacy of money prices as social representatives of natural wealth. After all, even if *values* do not adequately

---

form of a historically extreme social separation from material conditions of production and correspondingly extreme dominance of production itself by capital (money-making).

[123] This is not true of precapitalist systems, where socio-economic reproduction is typically more dependent on the reproduction of particular (local and/or regional) eco-systems, precisely because of the non-separation of producers and production conditions compared to capitalism. For further discussion, see Burkett 1999a, Chapter 5.

[124] Burkett 1999a, Chapter 6, and 1999c.

[125] Saad-Filho 2002, Chapter 5.

reflect nature's productive contributions, are not these contributions captured by market rents – at least insofar as natural resources are both scarce and (under an appropriate property rights regime) monopolisable? This question is considered later in terms of the adequacy of market regulation as a way of constraining resource-exploitation. Here, we draw attention to certain qualitative characteristics of money vis-à-vis natural wealth from an entropic perspective.

To begin with, money, unlike low-entropy matter-energy, is quantitatively unlimited. Capitalist production, driven as it is by the goal of maximum monetary accumulation – a goal forced on any recalcitrant enterprises by the pressure of competition – thus has an in-built tendency to overstretch its limited natural conditions. At the same time, money prices, like the labour values they mediate, are reversible. And, although the values of commodities may go up or down depending on developments in the productivity of labour, the general tendency is for values to fall (see below). Such quantitative reversibility does not, of course, apply to the increases in environmental entropy brought about by production.

Nor are these the only entropic contradictions of capitalist valuation. Money, like value itself, is a completely homogenous entity: its main function is to operate as pure quantity (to reduce all differences among commodities to purely quantitative differences). The natural conditions of production, on the other hand, are hardly homogenous – and hardly commensurable. Production depends on the qualitative variegation of low-entropy matter-energy. In addition, monetary values are completely divisible, unlike natural wealth which is composed of highly interconnected and interdependent material, biological, and thermodynamic systems of varying entropy levels. Finally, monetary claims on wealth – currency, bank accounts, stocks, bonds, and so forth – are highly mobile, directly contradicting the locational specificities often characterising natural eco-systems, mineral deposits, and so on.

In sum, money and money prices are homogenous, divisible, mobile, reversible, and quantitatively unlimited, by contrast with the qualitative variety, indivisibility, locational uniqueness, irreversibility, and quantitative limits of low-entropy matter-energy. It follows that production driven and shaped by monetary valuation is fundamentally antagonistic towards the natural conditions of human production and human development.

Capitalist throughput, recycling, and entropic degradation

The anti-ecological character of capitalist production should not be identified with a simple maximisation of matter-energy throughput. Capitalism has its own rules governing waste and recycling. Competition among firms penalises any 'above normal' throughput by not recognising the labour time objectified in it as socially necessary, value-creating labour. The 'normal' waste, the labour objectified in which does enter into commodity values, does not include any discarded materials or instruments that could have been profitably employed under current material-social conditions. Individual enterprises also have a motive to reduce matter-energy waste to sub-normal levels in order to enjoy lower unit costs and thus surplus profits and/or rising market shares. This incentive encompasses the development of more efficient and profitable methods of recycling the matter-energy byproducts of production.[126] Insofar as supplies of low-entropy matter-energy yield rents to their sellers, the firms employing these supplies have an obvious incentive to economise on their use. Contrary to Daly, the scale of capitalist matter-energy throughput cannot be analytically divorced from the system's allocational mechanisms, that is, from market valuation.

But the scale/allocation dialectic is a two-edged sword. Although capitalism's competitive allocation in its own way limits matter-energy waste and promotes recycling, it does so *within* a general tendency toward the conversion of matter and energy into commodities on an ever greater scale. Capitalist production is driven by the goal of monetary value accumulation; and since value must be represented in use-values (commodities) embodying both labour and natural resources, this accumulation translates into a processing of growing quantities of low-entropy matter-energy. Competition also presses individual firms to increase the productivity of their labour forces, which means increases in the matter and energy processed per hour of labour (reductions in the unit values of commodities). Although firms feel a competitive pressure to keep matter-energy throughput at or below the competitive norm, the norm is itself a function of the more basic pressure and profit incentive to boost output per labour hour (hourly throughput). Throughput is further accelerated insofar

---

[126] Burkett 1999a, pp. 110–11.

as the antagonism between managers and workers at the point of production dictates the installation of more mechanised, matter-energy intensive technologies to wrest control of the labour process away from skilled workers.

Market allocation hardly ensures an ecologically sustainable level and pattern of matter-energy use. Individual firms may economise on particular resource-inputs as their prices rise, but rising resource prices only encourage the search for additional exploitable supplies of the resource in question and for substitute resources. In cases where renewable resources are monopolisable, private profit maximisation cannot be relied upon to maintain sustainable extraction or harvesting rates – especially insofar as future profits are discounted in favour of current profits.[127] Indeed, the competitive search for resource rents is a prime mechanism by which capitalism overuses, homogenises, divides, and relocates various animate and inanimate forms of low-entropy matter-energy.[128]

That the system's allocation *and* scale mechanisms are both objectively anti-ecological helps explain why market-driven recycling and waste-management have themselves produced a 'fresh expenditure of energy and materials', thus becoming 'a constitutive part of the problem'.[129] The same goes for capitalist efforts at 'environmental restoration', such as the replacement of harvested forests with tree farms, strip-mined lands with ecologically impoverished 'parks', and plundered maritime eco-systems with artificial fisheries – all designed to create opportunities for the profitable processing of additional low-entropy matter-energy into commodities.

While ecological economists blame materialistic and consumerist values for the system's production and disposal of ever greater quantities of anti-ecological goods and services, the firms selling them know that they (and the wants they satisfy) are produced for one reason and one reason only: the competitive pursuit of profit. The notion that the capitalist economy can operate with a quota on its total use of low-entropy matter-energy is a pipe-dream. Any market economy in which production is motivated by profit must rely on growth, since money-making only makes sense if the amount of money made is greater than the amount of money advanced. As Altvater observes:

---

[127] Clark 1973.
[128] Perelman 2003.
[129] Altvater 1993, p. 213; compare Fairlie 1992.

The 'steady-state principle' is thus rational within the ecological system. . . . And yet, what is rational in the ecological system is irrational in terms of market economics: an economy without profit. The logic of the market makes it necessary to aim for a money surplus, without which a microeconomic unit (a firm) has to admit defeat and declare itself bankrupt. . . . High rates of profit and accumulation (in terms of values or prices) usually indicate a high throughput of materials and energy: that is, in a closed system, high rates of entropy increase.[130]

In sum, capitalism's 'normal' matter-energy throughput is driven first and foremost by the anti-ecological imperative of maximum capital accumulation. This imperative is enforced by the system's monetary forms of valuation – forms which themselves encourage the entropic degradation of matter and energy. It is only within these broader systemic parameters that recycling and anti-waste incentives operate.

Capitalism, environmental crisis, and ecological values

It is important to distinguish two kinds of environmental crises stemming from capitalism's use and abuse of ever greater quantities of low-entropy matter-energy. The first type involves crises of capital accumulation, as the demand for materials (including energy sources) periodically outstrips supplies – leading to rising costs, falling profits, and even physical disruptions of production due to the non-availability of essential raw and auxiliary materials. Such materials-supply disturbances reflect an inner tension between the value-creating and material dimensions of capitalist production. With booms in production driven by competitive monetary accumulation, materials shortages become inevitable, especially when the production of these materials, dependent as it often is on specific natural conditions and/or large fixed investments, cannot be rapidly increased over short periods of time. This applies especially to agricultural and mineral products. Such shortages are hastened by labour productivity growth, which increases the demand for low-entropy matter-energy per dollar of money capital invested.[131]

---

[130] Altvater 1993, pp. 202–3.
[131] Burkett 1999a, pp. 108–19.

Materials-supply disturbances tend to be periodic and do not, in and of themselves, pose a serious threat to the reproduction of the system. As long as sufficient low-entropy matter-energy is available to reproduce exploitable labour-power (and to objectify its labour in vendible commodities), capital can continue to accumulate on the basis of a degraded environment. Indeed, the production of goods and services designed to manage and cope with environmental degradation can itself be a profitable area of capital investment. Witness the rapid growth of the waste management and pollution control industries, or the massive profits earned on the newfangled pharmaceuticals peddled to asthmatics suffering from urban air pollution. Global warming adds to the market for air conditioners.

Capitalism's ability to survive and even prosper on its own money-making terms despite its degradation of nature directly defines a second kind of environmental crisis: the crisis in the *quality* of natural wealth as a condition of human development. Unlike materials-supply disturbances, this crisis is permanent and ever intensifying. And it cannot be resolved, or even temporarily softened, without a direct infringement on private profit and competition in favour of human-social needs as the main priority behind the organisation of production. The crisis in the natural conditions of human development implicates the fundamentally anti-ecological characteristics of wage-labour and market valuation. To effectively limit entropic degradation would require an economy not shaped by money and monetary prices, one not based on the goal of ever growing capital values. This necessarily involves non-market systems of egalitarian user rights and responsibilities that respect the communal character of natural wealth as a condition of human development within and across generations.

We will not get from here to there by superimposing ecological values on abstract-ideal models of the capitalist system – models that ignore or downplay the connections between wage-labour, the dominance of money and markets over material and social life, and the system's destructive ecological-entropic dynamics. What is needed is a critical engagement with the ongoing struggles of workers and communities everywhere to defend and improve their material-social conditions, and to forge new forms of human development. The new socio-economic institutions and ecological values needed to effectively limit entropic destruction can only develop out of collective struggles to disalienate the conditions of human production, to convert them from conditions of exploitative money-making into conditions of sustainable human development. A red and green political economy can assist this process by analysing capitalism's specific ecological contradictions, and by demonstrating that socialist forms of production and resource allocation are more consistent with the ecological values emerging out of worker-community struggles.

IV. Conclusion

After sketching the Georgescu-Roegen/Daly argument on the economic relevance of the entropy law, the ensuing debate was surveyed along four distinct tracks. Each of the four tracks was found to shed important light on the economy-nature relationship. At the same time, their analytical power is limited by their failure to consider the social relations of production as a factor shaping the use (and abuse) of natural conditions. The absence of a materialist class perspective is reflected in the uncritical, unsystematic stances on market valuation held by the various participants in the entropy debate, as well as in their common appeal to exogenous human purposes and values.

From a Marxist perspective, the inadequacies of the market as a form of entropy valuation, both allocatively and scale-wise, are rooted in the separation of producers from natural conditions that is central to the wage-labour relation. While recognising the objective reality of the entropy law, this viewpoint also reveals the crucial divergence between capitalism's entropic requirements and the entropic requirements of sustainable human production and development.

Capitalism experiences periodic accumulation crises rooted in the tensions between capital accumulation and its natural (human and environmental) conditions. But the crucial insight of the Marxist perspective is that, even apart from accumulation crises, capitalism's ecological-entropic dynamics produce a never-ending crisis in the natural conditions of human development. This permanent crisis can only be overcome through an explicit communalisation of production and its material conditions by the producers and their communities. Rather than preaching autonomous changes in human values, Marxism challenges each and every one of us to join in the struggle for collective-democratic forms of production and resource-allocation more appropriate to human development as a material-social process.

Chapter Six

Energy, Entropy and Classical Marxism: Debunking the Podolinsky Myth

Prominent among the wedges driven between Marxism and ecological economics is the notion that Marx and Engels responded indifferently or even negatively to Sergei Podolinsky's attempt to introduce certain elements of thermodynamics into socialist theory. Initially set out by Martinez-Alier and Naredo, the standard interpretation of this episode can be summarised in the form of three basic points.[1] First, in the early 1880s, Podolinsky published an energetic analysis of human labour and tried to reconcile Marx's labour theory of value with the first law of thermodynamics (conservation of energy). Second, when confronted with Podolinsky's analysis, Marx simply ignored it, while Engels abruptly dismissed it without giving it serious thought – even though Podolinsky had personally contacted them seeking their comradely opinions and approval. Third, Marx and Engels's negative reaction to Podolinsky helps explain, and is symptomatic of, a broader tendency for Marxism to neglect ecological issues in general and thermodynamics in particular.

Variously repeated, the above narrative is now a key element of the conventional wisdom among

---

[1] Martinez-Alier and Naredo 1982. See also Martinez-Alier 1987.

ecological economists and other environmental thinkers that Marxism suffers from inherent ecological deficiencies.[2] Section I summarises a recent study of the 'Podolinsky business',[3] by Foster and Burkett, that throws the first two elements of the standard narrative into serious doubt.[4] A subsequent study by the same authors establishes that Marx and Engels's own analyses of capitalism already contain positive responses to the specific ecological concerns raised (or thought to be raised) by Podolinsky's analysis.[5] This more affirmative study is summarised in Section II. The chapter concludes with a brief discussion of the relations between Marx and Engels's historical and dialectical frameworks, their grasp of complex ecological systems, and ecological economics. For Marx and Engels, the emphasis was on irreversible change and qualitative transformation, making their historical materialism a precursor of contemporary complexity theory.[6] This explains why they were able to appreciate the significance of energy and the first law of thermodynamics, while rejecting energy-reductionism in favour of a socio-metabolic and entropic conception of capitalist industrialisation, environmental crisis, and the necessity of socialism.

I. What remains of the Podolinsky myth?

When we first became aware of the importance that had become attached to the Podolinsky episode, we were admittedly sceptical about the claim that, by not developing an energetic basis for the labour theory of value, Marx and Engels had revealed an indifference to environmental issues and thermodynamics specifically.[7]

---

[2] That Podolinsky's work elicited an indifferent or dismissive reaction from Marx and Engels is cited as an established fact by, among others, Kaufmann 1987, p. 91; Bramwell 1989, p. 86; Deléage 1994, p. 49; Hayward 1994, p. 226; Pepper 1996, p. 230; Salleh 1997, p. 155; Hornborg 1998, p. 129; O'Connor 1998, p. 3; Barry 1999, pp. 277–8; Cleveland 1999, p. 128; Martinez-Alier 2003, p. 11.

[3] To use Engels's description of the issues raised by Podolinsky's work, in his 19 December 1882 letter to Marx (Marx and Engels 1992, p. 410).

[4] Foster and Burkett 2004.

[5] Burkett and Foster 2006.

[6] Prigogine and Stengers 1984.

[7] This section and the next, are phrased in the first person plural to indicate that they summarise research that was a collaborative effort by John Bellamy Foster and the present author.

We already knew that Marx and Engels had both filled multiple notebooks with extracts from, and commentaries on, the leading natural-scientific writers of their time. We also knew that these notebooks covered a wide range of scientific fields – physics, chemistry, physiology, geology, and agronomy – in each of which the analysis of energy dynamics occupied an important if not central position. In fact, as we studied the matter further we discovered that Marx and Engels had some familiarity with and in some cases closely studied the works of many of the scientists involved in the development of thermodynamics (both the first and second laws) – including Hermann von Helmholtz, Julius Robert Mayer, James Prescott Joule, Justus von Liebig, Jean-Baptiste Joseph Fourier, Sadi Carnot, Rudolf Clausius, William Thomson and Peter Guthrie Tait. In addition, we knew that Marx had attended numerous public lectures on natural science in the years leading up to and following the publication of *Capital*, Volume I in 1867, and that among these was a series of lectures by the English physicist John Tyndall, author of *Heat Considered as a Mode of Motion*.[8] Tyndall, a major figure in the developing physics in his own right, was the principal advocate of the ideas of J.R. Mayer – one of the codiscoverers of the conservation of energy (the first law of thermodynamics). Marx followed Tyndall's research on the sun's rays, particularly as it related to heat. Marx and Engels were also close students of the development of knowledge about electricity, including the work of Michael Faraday who invented the first electric motor. In 1882, Marx followed closely the results of the French physicist Marcel Deprez, whose research was directed at the distant transmission of electricity. In the same year, Marx also read Édouard Hospitalier's *Principal Applications of Electricity*, on which he took extensive notes.[9]

Given this interest in both theoretical physics and practical energetic questions, it seemed unlikely to us that Marx and Engels would have exhibited an unreceptive let alone deaf ear to any new work by Podolinsky that represented a potential breakthrough in the importation of thermodynamic concepts into socialist theory. Besides, it simply was not like Marx and Engels

---

[8] Tyndall 1863.

[9] See Baksi 1996, and 2001; Foster 2000a, Chapters 5 and 6 on these and other aspects of Marx and Engels's natural scientific studies.

to be indifferent or silent about contemporary writings that referred to their own works in any way.

Our scepticism only grew as we delved into the chronological development of Podolinsky's work as it related to the working lives of Marx and Engels. What we discovered was that Podolinsky's analysis had been published in four different languages over the years 1880–3, and that there were significant differences among the four versions. Importantly, the version of Podolinsky's analysis that served as the basis for the argument of Martinez-Alier and Naredo, although used to criticise Marx for his supposed neglect of Podolinsky's argument, had been published in the German socialist journal *Die Neue Zeit* in 1883, only after Marx's death.[10] Moreover, Engels's comments on Podolinsky, in two letters sent to Marx in December of 1882 (less than three months before Marx's death), were based on the version published in the Italian journal *La Plebe* in 1881 – a version that was much less extensive than the *Neue Zeit* article of 1883.[11] The *Plebe* piece itself was more extensive than an earlier version published in the Parisian *La Revue Socialiste* in June 1880.[12]

All of this took on added significance when we became aware of the fact that Marx had actually taken detailed extracts from Podolinsky's work, but only with reference to a French-language version that Podolinsky had mailed to him in early April, 1880.[13] This version seems to have been an early draft of the *Revue Socialiste* article.[14] Unfortunately, although we know from Podolinsky's own correspondence that Marx wrote back to him at least once, neither that letter nor any other letter that Marx sent to Podolinsky has

---

[10] See Podolinsky 1883. This is the version discussed by Martinez-Alier and Naredo 1982, and Martinez-Alier 1987.

[11] Podolinsky 1881; Marx and Engels 1992, pp. 410–14.

[12] Podolinsky 1880.

[13] Marx forthcoming. These extracts, roughly 1,800 words long, are to be published sometime in the next few years in Volume IV/27 of *Historisch-Kritische Gesamtausgabe*, commonly known as MEGA, the plan of which is to provide the first truly comprehensive collection of Marx and Engels's writings in their original languages. We are grateful to Kevin B. Anderson, David Norman Smith, Norair Ter-Akopian, Georgi Bagaturia and Jürgen Rohan, the editors of this MEGA volume, for allowing us access to these notes for our research.

[14] A much longer rendition of Podolinsky's analysis was published in the Russian journal *Slovo* in 1880. Recently reprinted (in Russian) in book form (Podolinsky 1991), this version contains more extended discussions of energetics and of the general importance of plants, animals, and human beings for the terrestrial distribution of energy.

survived. Still, it seems likely that Marx sent comments on the draft to Podolinsky some or all of which were incorporated into the published French version. (The most likely reason no copy of Podolinsky's original draft was found in Marx's papers and that all we have are extensive verbatim extracts from Marx's notebooks is that Marx, as was customary and expected in those days without copying machines, sent the manuscript back to Podolinsky with marginal notes on the manuscript.) Interestingly enough, the text of the *Revue Socialiste* article, as far as we can deduce from Marx's extracts from the draft-version sent by Podolinsky, contains significant additions to the earlier draft sent to Marx. Among these additions are the main reference to Marx's concept of surplus labour, the calculation of energy equivalents for agricultural labour and its output, and the attempt to analyse the energy efficiency of labour utilisation under the feudal, slave, capitalist, and socialist modes of production.[15]

Although all of this clearly undercut the standard view that Marx and Engels did not take Podolinsky seriously, a full evaluation of this view required a closer look at Podolinsky's analysis. Only then could we determine whether Engels had treated Podolinsky fairly in his letters to Marx. More specifically, only then could we determine whether Podolinsky's analysis provided important new insights that could and should have been adapted by historical materialism in general, or Marxist value analysis in particular, in ways that Marx and Engels (and later Marxists) were unable or unwilling to undertake, due to their own ecological shortcomings. We therefore arranged for a full English-language translation of the *Plebe* version of Podolinsky's work – the one read and commented upon by Engels.[16]

What we discovered was that Podolinsky had not even come close to establishing a plausible thermodynamic basis for the labour theory of value that could have been adopted by Marx and Engels. In fact, Podolinsky's analysis, although leading off with the question of how accumulation of surplus labour is consistent with the first law of thermodynamics (see below), goes on to make claims that contradict the reality of entropy and its limitations on human action. Podolinsky's analysis has nothing to say that is of direct relevance to the determination of value and surplus-value in their specifically

---

[15] This is based on our comparison of Marx's notes to an unpublished English translation of the *Revue Socialiste* article by our colleague Mark Hudson.

[16] Podolinsky 2004.

Marxist meaning as abstract (homogenous, socially necessary) labour times. Instead, Podolinsky's main themes are that: (i) human labour is uniquely gifted in its ability to accumulate energy in useful forms on the earth; (ii) this unique capability implies that the labouring human being fulfills (or even more than fulfills) the thermodynamic requirements of a 'perfect machine' as theorised by Carnot;[17] (iii) the superiority of socialism over capitalism and other class societies can be conceptualised in terms of socialism's greater potential for maximising the accumulation of energy on earth by providing the best conditions for utilising the muscular labour of the perfect human machine. Even Podolinsky's calculations of the energy productivities of different kinds of agricultural labour, we discovered, were not presented as a basis for value analysis, but, rather, as a demonstration of the greater energy-accumulation capabilities of the human machine compared to plants and animals.

We found these contents of Podolinsky's analysis quite surprising in light of how it had been used to criticise purported ecological shortcomings in Marxism. Podolinsky's framework was not only energy-reductionist, but also made the logical error of directly applying idealised concepts applicable only to a closed, isolated system (Carnot's perfect-machine concept) to the more complex reality of far-from-equilibrium, non-isolated, non-closed systems such as life in general and human society/labour more specifically. The only way that human labour can be viewed as a form of Carnot's perfect machine is if one ignores such factors as friction, that is, the natural materiality of labour, along with the inherently biochemical or metabolic nature of the human labouring organism and its interaction with the natural environment.

The limitations of Podolinsky's perfect-machine argument will be familiar to most ecological economists from the reaction generated by Khalil's suggestion that 'the economic process should be conceived after the Carnot cycle, and not the entropy law'.[18] Similar to Podolinsky, Khalil argued incorrectly that, insofar as human labour and the Carnot cycle are both 'designed *purposefully*' to produce net work or 'free energy', neither one is limited by 'the non-purposeful, mechanistic entropy law'.[19] The basic problem, as Biancardi, Donati

---

[17] Carnot 1977.
[18] Khalil 1990, p. 171; see Chapter 5 of the present work for further discussion.
[19] Khalil 1990, p. 170 (emphasis in original).

and Ulgiati observed, was with Khalil's (and, we might add, Podolinsky's) assumption that 'the Carnot cycle has *the same form* as the economic process'.[20] Unlike Carnot's ideal frictionless engine, which was conceived as a closed thermodynamic system, the human economy is a dissipative system that both draws upon (in fact mines) and dumps waste back into its natural environment. By neglecting this crucial form-divergence, both Khalil and Podolinsky confused the fact that the reproduction of human life feeds upon the (temporary) fixation of low-entropy matter-energy in useful forms, with the fantastic notion that this need not involve increasing entropy from the standpoint of the total biospheric system with which the system of human reproduction co-evolves.

Imagine our astonishment, then, when we realised that Engels's main criticisms of Podolinsky already focus precisely on some of the limitations adumbrated above. Engels not only rejects Podolinsky's energy-reductionist conception of human labour, posing a more metabolic alternative, but also emphasises the failure of Podolinsky's energy-productivity calculations to take into account the great extent to which human production has heretofore operated as 'a squanderer of *past* solar heat', especially by 'squandering our reserves of energy, our coal, ore, forests, etc.'.[21] Engels's discussion of Podolinsky had apparently been elicited by some comments by Marx on Engels's essay 'The Mark'. This essay, which was published as an appendix to the German edition of Engels's *Socialism: Utopian and Scientific*, examines socio-ecological pressures on German peasant farmers stemming from the growing influence of landed property and capitalist competition – for example, reduced peasant access to common lands and the resulting difficulty of maintaining peasant production without access to cattle manure.[22]

In short, our re-examination of the context and substance of Engels's comments, in light of our study of Podolinsky's *La Plebe* article, revealed that Engels's responses were far more advanced ecologically than Podolinsky's

---

[20] Biancardi, Donati and Ulgiati 1993a, p. 9 (emphasis added).

[21] Engels to Marx, 19 December 1882, in Marx and Engels 1992, p. 411 (emphasis in original).

[22] Engels 1978. That Marx would raise ecological, including metabolic, issues at this time is unsurprising in light of his reaffirmation, less than two years earlier in his *Notes on Adolph Wagner*, of the open-system character of his own analysis of capitalism. Referring to the method used in *Capital*, Marx wrote: 'I have employed the word [*Stoffwechsel*] for the "natural" process of production as the material exchange . . . between man and nature' (Marx 1975, p. 209). *Stoffwechsel* translates as *metabolism*.

analysis (however bold and important the latter's contribution was). Moreover, the fact that Engels's criticisms do not directly address value questions can now be seen as a quite logical non-reaction, given that Podolinsky had nothing significant to say on value theory as such. Indeed, to interpret Podolinsky's energy-productivity calculations as a potential basis for value analysis is not only to embrace a kind of energy-reductionism that has been strongly opposed by some of the major figures in ecological economics, including Georgescu-Roegen and Daly,[23] but also to conflate Marx's class-based theory with a Smith-Ricardo (that is, crude materialist) 'embodied-labour' approach to value.[24]

So what, then, remained of the Podolinsky myth? First, there was the issue as to whether Marx and Engels provided an adequate answer to Podolinsky's initial question bearing on the consistency of surplus-value with the first law of thermodynamics. As Podolinsky put it:

> According to the theory of production formulated by Marx and accepted by socialists, human labour, expressed in the language of physics, accumulates in its products a greater quantity of energy than that which was expended in the production of the labour-power of the workers. Why and how is this accumulation brought about? . . . In accepting the theory of the unity of physical forces or of the constancy of energy, we are also forced to admit that nothing can be *created*, in the strict sense of the word, through labour . . .[25]

Notice that even this statement does not speak of surplus-value, but, rather, of the energy equivalent of surplus *labour* in a more general sense applying across different modes of production. Still, insofar as the standard interpretation treats it as a challenge to Marx's value analysis, we considered it essential to investigate whether and how Marx answers Podolinsky's question for capitalism's specific form of surplus labour.

Second, even though we had established that Engels's comments on Podolinsky embody metabolic-energy and other ecological concerns, there remained the question as to how well these concerns are methodologically infused into Marx and Engels's analysis of capitalism. The debunking of the

---

[23] Georgescu-Roegen 1975, and 1976; Daly 1981.
[24] Saad-Filho 2002; Burkett 2003b.
[25] Podolinsky 2004, p. 61 (emphasis in original).

Podolinsky myth may not be sufficient to overturn the conventional wisdom that, as a general rule, Marx and Engels treat the economy as a self-reproducing system not dependent on its natural environment. Although we had demonstrated the considerable ecological content of Marx and Engels's thinking in earlier related works,[26] we felt it was important to reconsider the extent to which energy and entropic considerations are incorporated into Marx's *Capital*, and whether this incorporation is consistent with Engels's criticisms of Podolinsky. Only then could we determine the real lessons that the Podolinsky episode holds for the relationship between Marxism and ecological economics.

II. Marx's metabolic-energy analysis of wage-labour and capitalist industrialisation

As we re-investigated *Capital*, it quickly became clear that the place of energy and entropic issues in Marx's analysis was inseparable from his treatment of human labour as 'the universal condition for the metabolic interaction of man and nature'.[27] More specifically, we found that Marx's conception of labour and production as a metabolic people-nature relation serves three functions in his analysis. First, it highlights the fact that capitalism is just as much subject to nature's laws as any other form of human production. 'It would', as Marx says, 'be absolutely mistaken to attach mystical notions to this spontaneously developed productivity of labour, as is sometimes done'.[28] Marx had nothing but contempt for those who would 'fancifully' ascribe '*supernatural creative power*' to labour'.[29] This contempt extended to those who would deny that human labour is constrained by the conservation of matter and energy. As Marx indicated, 'When man engages in production, he can only proceed as nature does herself, i.e. he can only change the form of the materials. Furthermore, even in this work of modification he is constantly helped by natural forces'.[30] Driving the point home, Marx approvingly quotes the Italian political economist Pietro Verri, who had insisted that:

---

[26] Burkett 1999a; Foster 2000a; Foster and Burkett 2000, and 2001.
[27] Marx 1981, Vol. I, p. 290.
[28] Marx 1981, Vol. I, p. 647.
[29] Marx 1966, p. 3 (emphasis in original).
[30] Marx 1981, Vol. I, pp. 133–4.

All the phenomena of the universe, whether produced by the hand of man or by the universal laws of physics, are not to be conceived as acts of creation but solely as a reordering of matter. Composition and separation are the only elements found by the human mind . . . whether earth, air and water are turned into corn in the fields, or the secretions of an insect are turned into silk by the hand of man, or some small pieces of metal are arranged together to form a repeating watch.[31]

Such passages make it clear that Marx applies metabolic-energy categories *quite literally* to human production, not as a mere *analogy*. As noted by Griese and Pawelzeig,

what is involved here is no picture, no metaphor for visualization, but rather a rich concept. The exchange of matter by living organisms, according to the physiologists' definition, remains for Marx what it is, neither watered down nor 'generalized', as is often done. Exchange of matter is taking up, reshaping, storing, and giving up of matter with an exchange of energy taking place simultaneously. The same content applies – and here lies the discovery of Marx – not only to living but also to social systems, insofar as social life is also actually life in the physiological sense, arising out of social life and developing further its material basis.[32]

Second, Marx's treatment of labour and production as a socially organised exchange of matter *and* energy between people and nature enabled him to avoid energy-reductionism. This is evident from his close study of Liebig, under whose influence Marx explored in great detail the metabolic rift between nature and society manifested in the extraction of nutrients (such as nitrogen, phosphorus and potassium) from the soil in the form of food and fibre and their transportation hundreds and thousands of miles to urban centres where they eventually took the form of human and animal wastes – breaking the natural cycle that returned the nutrients to the soil. In this way, Marx explored problems of the human dependence on nature, which, while not independent of energy issues, could not be reduced to pure energetics.[33] Marx's adamant

---

[31] Pietro Verri, *Meditazione sulla Economia Politica*, quoted in Marx 1981, Vol. I, pp. 133–4. The significance of this passage was suggested to us by Altvater 2003, p. 7.
[32] Griese and Pawelzeig 1995, pp. 132–3; see also Foster 2000a, pp. 157–8.
[33] Mayumi 1991; Foster 2000a.

refusal to embrace energy-reductionism seems to foreshadow Georgescu-Roegen's famous dictum that 'matter matters, too'.[34] It also makes Marx a legitimate conceptual forerunner of contemporary 'industrial metabolism' analyses which chart both the material and the energy flows sustaining economic reproduction.[35]

Third, Marx definitely applied his metabolic conception of human production in general to capitalist commodity production in particular – and not as a mere afterthought or minor tangent. It shaped his analysis of commodities not just as *use-values* (utilities) but also as *exchange-values* (use values that fetch a price in the market) and as *values* (repositories of abstract, socially necessary labour). Marx thus considers commodity exchange as a 'process of social metabolism', and 'the value form of the commodity' as the 'economic cell form' of this metabolism.[36] A commodity is, of course, a useful good or service that is put up for exchange. Recognising that this 'use-value . . . is conditioned by the physical properties of the commodity', Marx sees commodity use-values as 'the material content of wealth' under capitalism.[37] Accordingly, he insists that both nature and human labour contribute to the production of all these use-values.[38] In analysing commodities and money, he emphasises that 'the physical bodies of commodities, are combinations of two elements, the material provided by nature, and labour'.[39] Importantly, Marx also insists that 'nothing can be a value without being an object of utility. If the thing is useless, so is the labour contained in it; the labour does not count as labour, and therefore creates no value'.[40] Stated differently: 'Value [as abstract labour] is independent of the particular use-value by which it is borne, but a use-value of some kind must act as its bearer'.[41] In sum, because commodities, like all use-values, are products of both labour and nature, and because labour is itself an interaction with nature, the production and exchange of commodity

---

[34] Georgescu-Roegen 1979b, p. 1039.
[35] Fischer-Kowalski 1997; compare Foster 2000a, pp. 162–3 and Dickens 2004, pp. 60–2.
[36] Marx 1981, Vol. I, pp. 198, 90.
[37] Marx 1981, Vol. I, p. 126.
[38] Burkett 1999a, p. 26.
[39] Marx 1981, Vol. I, p. 133.
[40] Marx 1981, Vol. I, p. 131.
[41] Marx 1981, Vol. I, p. 295.

values is both a social (people-people) and a metabolic (people-nature) relation. The dialectic of value and use-value is not a simple dichotomy in Marx's conception, but, rather, a unity-in-difference or moving contradiction.

Indeed, the more we re-read *Capital* in light of the 'Podolinsky business', the more we saw capitalism as fraught with contradictions stemming from an underlying rift between the material requirements of capital (value) accumulation and the metabolic character of labour, the labourers, and the natural conditions of production.

The value of labour-power

Upon rereading Marx's discussion of labour-power and its value, we were struck by the strong presence of metabolic-energy themes. To begin with, Marx defines 'labour-power, or labour-capacity' as 'the aggregate of those mental and physical capabilities existing in the physical form, the living personality, of a human being, capabilities which he sets in motion whenever he produces a use-value of any kind'.[42] Labour-power 'is a natural object, a thing, although a living, conscious thing'.[43] It is, 'above all else, the material of nature transposed into a human organism'.[44] The metabolic-energy content of Marx's conception is evident not just from his choice of the term labour-power, but also from an alternative (and more descriptive) translation of the definition just quoted: 'Labour-power itself is energy transferred to a human organism by means of nourishing matter'.[45]

Energy considerations are, accordingly, central to Marx's analysis of the value of labour-power. As is well known, Marx identifies labour-power's value with the value of the commodities entering into the consumption of workers and their families. Two portions of this consumption are distinguished: a physical subsistence component and 'a historical and moral element'.[46] Our main concern here is with the physical subsistence element. This begins, of course, with the worker's 'natural needs, such as food, clothing, fuel and housing' – needs which 'vary according to the climatic and other physical

---

[42] Marx 1981, Vol. I, p. 270.
[43] Marx 1981, Vol. I, p. 310.
[44] Marx 1981, Vol. I, p. 323.
[45] Marx 1967, p. 215.
[46] Marx 1981, Vol. I, p. 275.

peculiarities of his country'.[47] Even at this basic level, Marx recognises not just the energy requirements of the individual worker's reproduction, but also the role of matter-energy dissipation. Precisely because 'labour-power exists only as a capacity of the living individual', it is by nature (regardless of what happens in the labour-process) subject to 'wear and tear . . . and death'.[48] 'The owner of labour-power is mortal', and must therefore 'perpetuate himself . . . by procreation'.[49] Hence, the value of labour-power includes the value of commodities 'necessary for the worker's replacements, i.e. his children, in order that this race of peculiar commodity-owners may perpetuate its presence on the market'.[50]

But the metabolic dimension only becomes fully apparent with Marx's consideration of the connections between the worker's labouring activity and labour-power's value. 'The use of labour-power is', after all, 'labour itself', and 'the purchaser of labour-power consumes it by setting the seller of it to work'.[51] This is true whether labour is considered as production of use-values or as production of values. Even though the substance of value is abstract labour ('homogenous human labour, . . . human labour-power expended without regard to the form of its expenditure'), the 'creation of value' still requires 'the transposition of labour-power into labour', that is, 'a productive expenditure of human brains, muscles, nerves, hands, etc., of the labour-power possessed in his bodily organism by every ordinary man'.[52] Conservation of labour's value-creating power therefore imposes additional maintenance requirements on the worker:

> However, labour-power becomes a reality only by being expressed; it is activated only through labour. But in the course of this activity, i.e. labour, a definite quantity of human muscle, nerve, brain, etc. is expended, and these things have to be replaced. *Since more is expended, more must be received.* If the owner of labour-power works today, tomorrow he must again be able to repeat the same process in the same conditions as regards health and

---

[47] Ibid.
[48] Marx 1981, Vol. I, p. 274.
[49] Marx 1981, Vol. I, p. 275.
[50] Ibid. Compare Marx 1976b, pp. 39, 57.
[51] Marx 1981, Vol. I, p. 283.
[52] Marx 1981, Vol. I, pp. 128, 323, 134–5.

strength. His means of subsistence must therefore be sufficient to maintain him in his normal state as a working individual.[53]

An alternative translation of the italicised sentence is: 'This increased expenditure demands a larger income'.[54] Here, Marx is employing an 'energy income and expenditure' framework adapted from the work of the great German energy physiologist Ludimar Hermann. We know that Marx studied Hermann's *Elements of Human Physiology*, which treats energy flows in human labour from a biochemical standpoint.[55] In Hermann's analysis, 'energy income' connotes consumption of energy sources convertible into work, while 'energy expenditure' refers to the loss of energy to the labourer when work is done. Marx evidently found Hermann's approach quite useful for determining the 'ultimate or minimum limit of the value of labour-power', that is, 'the value of the commodities which have to be supplied every day to the bearer of labour-power . . . so that he can renew his life-process' in something more than 'a crippled state'.[56]

Marx follows Hermann in *not* reducing the content of the energy income and expenditure process to pure energetic terms. For Hermann, the biochemical compositions of energy income and expenditure, and their degree of compatibility with nutritional and other metabolic functions, help determine whether any given work process is consistent with the healthy reproduction of the labourer.[57] Different kinds of labour (in terms of type and intensity) require different biochemical forms of energy income, and this relationship is also affected by how well rested the worker is from past labours. Path dependency effects are crucial to this metabolic process. The worker cannot be treated like a steam engine that will just keep running as long as adequate coal is shovelled in. Marx applies this aspect of Hermann's approach when dealing with the relation between the value of labour-power and the length of daily worktime:

> When the working day is prolonged, the price of labour-power may fall below its value, although that price nominally remains unchanged, or even

---

[53] Marx 1981, Vol. I, pp. 274–5 (emphasis added).
[54] Marx 1967, p. 171.
[55] Hermann 1875; Baksi 2001, p. 378.
[56] Marx 1981, Vol. I, pp. 276– 7.
[57] Hermann 1875, pp. 199–200, 215–25.

rises. The value of a day's labour-power is estimated . . . on the basis of its normal average duration, or the normal duration of the life of a worker, and on the basis of the appropriate normal standard of conversion of living substances into motion as it applies to the nature of man. Up to a certain point, the increased deterioration of labour-power inseparable from a lengthening of the working day may be compensated for by making amends in the form of higher wages. But beyond this point deterioration increases in geometrical progression, and all the requirements for the normal reproduction and functioning of labour-power cease to be fulfilled. The price of labour-power and the degree of its exploitation cease to be commensurable quantities.[58]

In a footnote to the passage just cited, Marx provides a quotation from a work by the 'father of the fuel cell', the English jurist and physical chemist Sir William Robert Grove, entitled *On the Correlation of Physical Forces*, which states: 'The amount of labour which a man had undergone in the course of 24 hours might be approximately arrived at by an examination of the chemical changes which had taken place in his body, changed forms in matter indicating the anterior exercise of dynamic force'.[59] Marx and Engels had, in fact, read Grove's book with deep interest as early as 1864–5 as part of their studies of the mechanical theory of heat and the convertibility of different forms of energy.[60] They were familiar with the fourth edition of Grove's work, published in 1862, in which Grove had already provided a detailed discussion of the second law of thermodynamics.[61] Marx obviously found these studies directly relevant to his analysis of the value of labour-power.[62]

At this point, our investigation had revealed that Marx's metabolic analysis of the value of labour-power clearly incorporates the conservation of energy as well as the inevitability of matter-energy dissipation, but without falling prey to energy-reductionism. We were not very surprised, then, to find that Engels had criticised the crude mechanistic and energy-reductionist purposes to which thermodynamics had been put in some analyses of human labour. As he wrote in *The Dialectics of Nature*:

---

[58] Marx 1981, Vol. I, p. 664.
[59] Quoted in Marx 1981, Vol. I, p. 664.
[60] Marx and Engels 1985, pp. 551–3.
[61] Grove 1864, pp. 227–9; Marx and Engels 1975, p. 162.
[62] Stokes 1994, pp. 52–3; Baksi 2001, p. 385.

Let someone try to convert any skilled labour into kilogram-metres and then to determine wages on this basis! Physiologically considered, the human body contains organs which in their totality, *from one aspect*, can be regarded as a thermodynamical machine, where heat is supplied and converted into motion. But even if one presupposes constant conditions as regards the other bodily organs, it is questionable whether physiological work done, even lifting, can be at once fully expressed in kilogram-metres, since within the body *internal* work is performed at the same time which does not appear in the result. For the body is not a steam-engine, which only undergoes friction and wear and tear. Physiological work is only possible with continued chemical changes in the body itself, depending also on the process of respiration and the work of the heart. Along with every muscular contraction or relaxation, chemical changes occur in the nerves and muscles, and these changes cannot be treated as parallel to those of coal in a steam-engine. One can, of course, compare two instances of physiological work that have taken place under otherwise identical conditions, but one cannot measure the physical work of a man according to the work of a steam-engine, etc.; their external results, yes, but not the processes themselves without considerable reservations.[63]

Seven years after the above commentary was written, Engels was confronted with Podolinsky's naïve attempt to calculate 'the physical work of a man according to the work of a steam-engine', that is, by simply comparing the caloric food intake of the labourer to the calories embodied in the physical output of the (agricultural) labour process.[64] Conveying his opinion of Podolinsky's energy-accounting exercises to Marx, Engels reprised his critique of energy-reductionism. He pointed out that Podolinsky's calculations took no account of the complexities introduced by 'the *fresh* cal' that the worker 'absorbs from the radiation of the sun'.[65] Engels also observed that the food-calories consumed by a worker (a figure of 10,000 calories per day is used)

are known in practice to lose on conversion into other forms of energy as a result of friction, etc., a portion that cannot be put to use. Significantly so

---

[63] Engels 1964a, pp. 315–16 (emphases in original).
[64] Podolinsky 2004, pp. 64–5; Foster and Burkett 2004, pp. 39–40.
[65] Engels to Marx, 19 December 1882, in Marx and Engels 1992, p. 411 (emphasis in original).

in the case of the human body. Hence the *physical* labour performed in economic labour can never = 10,000 cal; it is invariably less.[66]

Along with this initial clear recognition of matter-energy dissipation, that is, of entropy, Engels considered further qualifications to Podolinsky's calculations stemming from the metabolic workings of the labouring organism. For example, he pointed out how Podolinsky assumed that all 'physical labour is *economic labour*', when, in reality, much of the energy expenditure of the worker is 'lost in the increased heat given off by the body, etc., and such useful residue as remains lies in the fertilising property of excretions'.[67]

In short, our research led us to conclude that compared to Podolinsky's energy-reductionist framework, Engels's metabolic approach – consistent with Marx's analysis of the value of labour-power – is more sensitive to the ecological complexities and entropic nature of the labour process.

How Marx answers Podolinsky's question

Our investigation also revealed that, at several points in *Capital* and its preparatory works, Marx considers the creation of surplus-value in terms of the difference between: (i) the energy equivalent of the value of labour-power, as determined by the labour required to produce the means of subsistence purchased with the wage, and (ii) the energy expended by labour-power, insofar as it corresponds to the energy content of the commodities in which value is objectified. But we knew, given the inability of the commodity- (value-) form to capture the metabolic-energetic requirements of labour-power and the work it performs, that it would be as incorrect to identify the energy equivalent of labour-power's value with *all* the energy that enters into the reproduction of labour-power as it would be to identify the energy content of commodity values with *all* the energy entering into their production.

---

[66] Engels to Marx, 19 December 1882, in Marx and Engels 1992, p. 410 (emphasis in original). The figure of 10,000 calories of daily food intake per worker seems to have been chosen by Engels without much thought. It is hard to see how even a worker engaged in extremely heavy labour for 16 hours per day could approach such an energy requirement. But the validity of Engels's point does not hinge on the accuracy of his illustrative numbers.

[67] Engels to Marx, 19 December 1882, in Marx and Engels 1992, p. 410 (emphasis in original).

Podolinsky's opening question, as to how the first law of thermodynamics is consistent with an excess of energy-product over the energy 'expended in the production of the labour-power of the workers', thus struck us as grossly misconceived insofar as it was meant to refer to Marx's theory.[68] Nonetheless, we found that, by considering Marx's application of the energy income and expenditure approach to the production of surplus-value, the thermodynamic consistency of his theory could be demonstrated.[69]

For Marx, the possibility of surplus-value stems from labour-power's 'specific use-value . . . of being a source not only of value, but of more value than it has itself'.[70] And this use-value is, in turn, explained by two facts. First, given capitalism's reduction of value to abstract labour time, 'the use value of labour capacity, as value, is itself the value-creating force; the substance of value, and the value-increasing substance'.[71] Second, 'the past labour embodied in the labour-power and the living labour it can perform, and the daily cost of maintaining labour-power and its daily expenditure in work, are two totally different things'.[72] While the value of labour-power is determined by the value of workers' commodified means of subsistence,

> the *use* of that labouring power is only limited by the active energies and physical strength of the labourer. The daily or weekly *value* of the labouring power is quite distinct from the daily or weekly exercise of that power, the same as the food a horse wants and the time it can carry the horseman are quite distinct. The quantity of labour by which the *value* of the workman's labouring power is limited forms by no means a limit to the quantity of labour which his labouring power is apt to perform.[73]

In energy terms, 'What the free worker sells is always nothing more than a specific, particular measure of force-expenditure'; but 'labour capacity as a

---

[68] Podolinsky 2004, p. 61.
[69] Throughout this discussion we follow Marx's assumptions, in Volume I of *Capital*, that commodity prices = commodity values, and that competition among firms has converted all concrete labours into abstract labour simultaneous with the formation of commodity prices (Saad-Filho 2002, Chapter 5). Our treatment of the energetics of surplus-value builds upon the work of Altvater 1990, pp. 20–5; 1993, pp. 188–92; 1994, pp. 86–8.
[70] Marx 1981, Vol. I, p. 301.
[71] Marx 1973, p. 674.
[72] Marx 1981, Vol. I, p. 300.
[73] Marx 1976b, p. 41 (emphases in original).

totality is greater than every particular expenditure'.[74] 'In this exchange, then, the worker . . . sells himself as an effect', and 'is absorbed into the body of capital as a cause, as activity'.[75] The result is an energy subsidy for the capitalist who appropriates and sells the commodities produced during the portion of the workday over and above that required to produce the means of subsistence represented by the wage. The apparently equal exchange of the worker's labour-power for its value thus 'turns into its opposite . . . the dispossession of his labour'.[76] Marx develops this point in terms of the distinction between surplus labour and the 'necessary labour' objectified in workers' commodified means of subsistence:

> During the second period of the labour process, that in which his labour is
> no longer necessary labour, the worker does indeed expend labour-power,
> he does work, but his labour is no longer necessary labour, and he creates
> no value for himself. He creates surplus-value which, for the capitalist, has
> all the charms of something created out of nothing.[77]

Of course, this value (energy) surplus is not really created out of nothing. Marx was well aware that neither wage-labour nor any other kind of labour creates any brand new matter-energy. Rather, matter and energy take on new forms as a result of labour, in Marx's view. Hence, when analysing the factors determining the size of the surplus product under different modes of production, Marx emphasises that 'in no case would this surplus product arise from some innate, occult quality of human labour'.[78] And, in his initial discussion of the rate of surplus-value in *Capital*, Marx tells us that 'what Lucretius says is self-evident: "*nil posse creari de nihilo*", out of nothing, nothing can be created'.[79] Obviously, if surplus-value abides by the fundamental principle of conservation of matter-energy, it must represent capital's appropriation of part of the *potential* work embodied in labour-power as a result of the metabolic regeneration of this power largely during non-worktime. And this is only possible insofar as the regeneration of labour-power, in both

---

[74] Marx 1973, p. 464.
[75] Marx 1973, p. 674.
[76] Ibid.
[77] Marx 1981, Vol. I, p. 325; compare Marx 1973, pp. 324, 334.
[78] Marx 1981, Vol. I, p. 651.
[79] Marx 1981, Vol. I, p. 323.

energy and biochemical terms, involves not just consumption of calories embodied in the commodities purchased with the wage, but also fresh air, solar heat, sleep, relaxation, and various domestic activities necessary for the cleaning, feeding, clothing, and housing of the worker. Insofar as capital forces the worker to labour beyond necessary labour time, it encroaches on the time required for all these regenerative activities. As Marx observes,

> But *time* is IN FACT the active existence of the human being. It is not only the measure of human life. It is the space for its development. And the ENCROACHMENT OF CAPITAL OVER the TIME OF LABOUR is the appropriation of the *life*, the mental and physical life, of the worker.[80]

Viewed in this way, Marx's metabolic-energy analysis of surplus-value is an essential foundation for his analysis of capital's tendency 'to go beyond the natural limits of labour-time' – a tendency 'that forcibly compels even the society which rests on capitalist production . . . to restrict the normal working day within firmly fixed limits'.[81] Unless forcibly constrained from doing so, capitalist production encroaches not just on the time the worker needs 'to satisfy his intellectual and social requirements', but also on 'the physical limits to labour-power'.[82] Capital's in-built drive to extend worktime beyond labour-power's metabolic-energetic limits is, in fact, one of the major themes in Volume I of *Capital*. But the more basic point is that Marx's analysis of surplus-value already answers Podolinsky's question: it is completely consistent with not only the first but also the second law of thermodynamics.

Thermodynamics of industrial capital accumulation

In light of the conventional wisdom that Marx's analysis of capitalist industrialisation ignores energy issues,[83] we were stunned to find that thermodynamics – the conservation of energy, its entropic dissipation through friction in particular, and the correlation of physical forces – are central to Marx's treatment of 'Machinery and Large-Scale Industry' in Chapter 15 of *Capital*, Volume I. This chapter represents the core of Marx's analysis of

---

80 Marx 1991, p. 493 (emphases and capitalisations in original).
81 Marx 1991, p. 386.
82 Marx 1981, Vol. I, p. 341.
83 Martinez-Alier 1987, 1995b, and 2003; Martinez-Alier and Naredo 1982.

industrial development under capitalism. Together with Marx's broader discussion of labour productivity and raw materials processing, it explains the massive acceleration of matter-energy throughput generated by this mode of production.

Marx treats the industrial revolution in terms of a model of machinery systems consisting of 'three essentially different parts, the motor mechanism, the transmitting mechanism and finally the tool or working machine'.[84] He analyses machine-based production as a transfer of force from one part of the system to another – starting from the motor mechanism which 'acts as the driving force of the mechanism as a whole', on through the transmission mechanism which 'regulates the motion, changes its form where necessary, and divides and distributes it among the working machines', and finally to the working machine which 'using this motion . . . seizes on the object of labour and modifies it as desired'.[85] This entire framework is clearly informed by an extensive theoretical and practical study of both energy conservation and the mechanics of energy transfer.[86]

In an 1863 letter to Engels outlining his research for 'the section on machinery', Marx wrote that he had not only 're-read all my note-books (excerpts) on technology', but was 'also attending a practical (purely experimental) course for working men given by Prof. Willis'.[87] The lecturer was the Reverend Robert Willis (1800–75), the brilliant British architect and mechanical engineer (and, from 1837 onward, Jacksonian Professor of Natural and Experimental Philosophy at the University of Cambridge). The mechanics of energy transmission were a central theme in these lectures, as is clear from the working models that Willis himself designed and integrated into an instructional system.[88] When combined with Marx's theoretical and historical studies, such practical instruction led him to argue that the industrial revolution started not with the motor mechanism and its energy sources but rather with the tool or working machine – specifically with the mechanisation of the portion of labour that involved working directly on the principal material(s). As explained in *Capital*,

---

[84] Marx 1981, Vol. I, p. 494.
[85] Ibid.
[86] Baksi 1996, pp. 274–8.
[87] Marx to Engels, 28 January 1863, in Marx and Engels 1985, p. 449.
[88] Willis 1851; Parkinson 1999.

the entire machine is only a more or less altered mechanical edition of the old handicraft tool. . . . The machine, therefore, is a mechanism that, after being set in motion, performs with its tools the same operations as the worker formerly did with similar tools. Whether the motive power is derived from man, or in turn from a machine, makes no difference here.[89]

This argument 'establish[ed] a connection between human social relations and the development of these material modes of production'.[90] After all, the ability of the capitalist to separate the tool from the worker and install it in the machine – and the subsequent application of science to the technical improvement of machinery on the capitalist's profit-making behalf – presumed that the worker had already been socially separated from control over the means of production.[91] But this historical primacy of social relations, and corresponding primacy of machine-tools over energy sources and mechanisms, hardly prevented Marx from emphasising the crucial enabling role of power supply and transmission in the industrial revolution. For one thing, the mechanisation of tools means they are freed from the limitations of the individual worker's labour-power as the direct motive force. As Marx indicates, 'assuming that [the worker] is acting simply as a motor, that a machine has replaced the tool he is using, it is evident that he can also be replaced as a motor by natural forces'.[92] Once installed in machines, tools may be driven by a greater variety of power sources and on a much larger energy-scale. Indeed, the growing scale of machinery itself precludes the continued use of labour-power as motive force.

An increase in the size of the machine and the number of its working tools calls for a more massive mechanism to drive it; and this mechanism, in order to overcome its own inertia, requires a mightier moving power than that of man, quite apart from the fact that man is a very imperfect instrument for producing uniform and continuous motion.[93]

The replacement of labour-power with other motive forces starts with 'a call for the application of animals, water and wind as motive powers', but soon

---

[89] Marx 1981, Vol. I, pp. 494–5.
[90] Marx to Engels, 28 January 1863, in Marx and Engels 1985, p. 450.
[91] Burkett 1999a, pp. 158–63.
[92] Marx 1981, Vol. I, p. 497.
[93] Ibid.

graduates to the development of coal-driven steam-engines and, eventually, (as Marx projected) electric power mechanisms.[94] It is here, with the development of motor mechanisms and their power sources in response to the energy demands of increasingly complex and large-scale machine-tool systems, that Marx emphasises the role of friction as a fundamental entropic process. Hence, in explaining that the 'increase in the size of the machine and its working tools calls for a more massive mechanism' and motor force to drive it, Marx observes that the question of force (or energy) became critical when water power, which, in Britain, had hitherto been the main source of power, no longer seemed adequate:

> The use of water-power preponderated even during the period of manufacture. In the seventeenth century attempts had already been made to turn two pairs of millstones with a single water-wheel. But the increased size of the transmitting mechanism came into conflict with the water-power, which was now insufficient, and this was one of the factors which gave the impulse for a more accurate investigation of the laws of friction.[95]

Marx goes on to observe that with 'tools . . . converted from being manual implements of man into the parts of a mechanical apparatus', it became possible to reduce 'the individual machine to a mere element in production by machinery'; but this presumed that the motive mechanism was 'able to drive many machines at once'.[96] Thus, the required 'motor mechanism grows with the number of the machines that are turned simultaneously, and the transmitting mechanism becomes an extensive apparatus'.[97] Insofar as 'the object of labour goes through a connected series of graduated processes carried out by a chain of mutually complementary machines of various kinds', the power-source must meet demanding scale, flexibility and transmission requirements.[98] In the industries using machines to produce precision machines, especially, an 'essential condition . . . was a prime mover capable of exerting any amount of force, while retaining perfect control'.[99] The material nature

---

[94] Marx 1981, Vol. I, p. 496.
[95] Marx 1981, Vol. I, pp. 497–8.
[96] Marx 1981, Vol. I, p. 499.
[97] Marx 1981, Vol. I, p. 499.
[98] Marx 1981, Vol. I, p. 501.
[99] Marx 1981, Vol. I, p. 506.

of water power precluded its use for such purposes beyond a certain level and locality, given problems of friction, containment, storability and transportability:

> The flow of water could not be increased at will, it failed at certain seasons of the year, and above all it was essentially local. Not till the invention of Watt's second and so-called double-acting steam-engine was a prime mover found which drew its own motive power from the consumption of coal and water, was entirely under man's control, was mobile and a means of locomotion, . . . and, finally, was of universal technical application and little affected in its choice of residence by local circumstances.[100]

Obviously, 'matter matters, too' in *Capital*'s analysis of the energetics of capitalist industrialisation. One can then understand why Marx paid such close attention to the physical wear and tear of machinery. In the chapter on machinery and large-scale industry, we are told that:

> The physical deterioration of the machine is of two kinds. The one arises from use, as coins wear away by circulating, the other from lack of use, as a sword rusts when left in its scabbard. Deterioration of the first kind is more or less directly proportional, and that of the second kind to a certain extent inversely proportional, to the use of the machine.[101]

Such physical deterioration is central to the analysis of the costs of fixed capital replacement and repair in Volume II, Chapter 8 of *Capital*, where Marx again distinguishes between wear and tear from 'actual use' and 'that caused by natural forces', showing through various real-world examples how the labour necessitated by each type enters into the values of commodities.[102]

Aside from friction, another reason why Marx eschewed energy-reductionism in his analysis of industry was his awareness that capitalism's 'development of the social powers of labour' involved not just machines and their motive forces, but also 'the appliance of chemical and other natural agencies' in a way that is not reducible to pure energy-transmission.[103] This is most evident

---

[100] Marx 1981, Vol. I, p. 499.
[101] Marx 1981, Vol. I, p. 528. Compare Ibid., pp. 289–90.
[102] Marx 1981, Vol. II, pp. 248–61.
[103] Marx 1976b, p. 34.

from Marx's analysis of capitalist agriculture, where the 'conscious, technological application of science' in the service of profit-making confronts a barrier in 'the fertility of the soil' with its necessary basis in 'the metabolic interaction between man and the earth'.[104] But there is an irreducible biochemical element in any kind of production where something is 'added to the raw material to produce some physical modification of it, as chlorine is added to unbleached linen, coal to iron, dye to wool'.[105] 'In all these cases', as Marx puts it when considering their effect on value accumulation, 'the production time of the capital advanced consists of two periods: a period in which the capital exists in the labour process, and a second period in which its form of existence – that of an unfinished product – is handed over to the sway of natural processes, without being involved in the labour process'.[106] Such biochemical production processes obviously reduce the relevance of purely energetic analysis.[107]

By comparison to Marx's analysis, Podolinsky's treatment of labour as a perfect machine greatly downplayed the biochemical and entropic dimensions of real world production. Podolinsky's calculations of energy productivities were thus simplistic to an extreme, failing to account for the full complexity of the problem, especially when applied to industry.[108] As Engels pointed out in his commentary on Podolinsky's work:

> In industry all [such] calculations come to a full stop; for the most part the labour added to a product simply does not permit of being expressed in terms of cal. This might be done in a pinch in the case of a pound of yarn by laboriously reproducing its durability and tensile strength in yet another mechanical formula, but even then it would smack of quite useless pedantry and, in the case of a piece of grey cloth, let alone one that has been bleached, dyed or printed, would actually become absurd. The energy value conforming to the production costs of a hammer, a screw, a sewing needle, is an impossible quantity.[109]

---

[104] Marx 1981, Vol. I, pp. 637–8.
[105] Marx 1981, Vol. I, p. 288.
[106] Marx 1981, Vol. II, p. 317.
[107] Benton 1989 terms these kinds of processes 'eco-regulated'. For a detailed rebuttal of his claim that Marx's analysis fails to take them into account, see Burkett 1998b, pp. 125–33, and 1999a, pp. 41–7.
[108] Podolinsky 2004; Foster and Burkett 2004.
[109] Engels to Marx, 19 December 1882, in Marx and Engels 1992, p. 411.

Hence, in a manner similar to Marx, Engels's argument against energy-reductionism emphasises the irreducible biochemical character of human labour and its products, and the fact that use-value is not reducible to pure energy. In this, Engels's argument is consistent with that of many later ecological economists.[110]

Moreover, while rejecting Podolinsky's energy-reductionism, Marx and Engels's analysis sheds new light on a crucial question in ecological economics, namely, how human production 'broke the budget constraint of living on solar income'.[111] Daly, for example, limits this post-solar income regime to 'the last 200 years', but does not venture a structural explanation for it, that is, an explanation combining specific socio-economic relations with the development of specific technologies relying on fossil fuels and other 'geological capital'.[112] Marx's analysis of machinery and large-scale industry provides the foundation for just such an explanation. However, this explanation must go beyond Marx's analysis of the transition from animal and water power to coal-fired machine-systems. It must also be informed by Marx's broader argument that capitalism's development of 'the productive powers of labour' is dependent on 'the *natural* conditions of labour, such as fertility of soil, mines, and so forth'.[113] Capitalist industrialisation, in Marx's view, is a process in which 'science presses natural agencies into the service of labour' under the pressures of private profit-making and competition.[114] In this process, nature provides capitalist enterprise with use-values that act not only as bearers of value, but also as 'free natural productive power[s] of labour'.[115]

One of Marx's main themes in this connection is that capitalism's development of machine-based production, and of a complex division of labour among competing enterprises, generates unprecedented increases in labour productivity, which necessarily involve equally unprecedented growth in the use of raw materials. As he says, 'the increasing productivity of labour is expressed precisely in the proportion in which a greater quantity of raw material absorbs a certain amount of labour, i.e. in the increasing mass of raw

---

[110] Georgescu-Roegen 1975, and 1976; Daly 1981; Burkett 2003b.
[111] Daly 1992a, p. 23; compare Altvater 2003, pp. 19–21.
[112] Daly 1992a, p. 23.
[113] Marx 1976b, p. 34 (emphasis in original).
[114] Ibid.
[115] Marx 1981, Vol. III, p. 879; see Burkett 1999a, Chapter 6, and 1999c.

material that is transformed into products, worked up into commodities, in an hour, for example'.[116] 'The growth of machinery and of the division of labour has the consequence that in a shorter time far more can be produced', so that 'the part of capital transformed into raw materials necessarily increases'.[117] As labour productivity grows, so grows the quantity of materials that capital must appropriate and process in order to achieve any given expansion of value. Value must, after all, be objectified in material use-values.

As shown earlier, Marx is also well aware of the crucial importance of power supplies for capitalist industry. Accordingly, he includes energy sources in capital's growing demand for 'auxiliary' or 'ancillary' materials, defined as those materials which, while not forming part of 'the principal substance of the product', are nonetheless required 'as an accessory' of its production.[118] They provide heat, light, chemical and other necessary conditions of production distinct from the direct processing of principal materials by labour and its instruments. Obviously, consumption of energy sources ('coal by a steam-engine . . . hay by draft-horses', or 'materials . . . for heating and lighting workshops') looms large in such ancillaries usage.[119] As Marx observes, 'After the capitalist has put a larger capital into machinery, he is compelled to spend a larger capital on the purchase of raw materials *and the fuels required to drive the machines*'.[120] In short, capitalist industrialisation results in 'more raw material worked up in the same time, and therefore a greater mass of raw material *and auxiliary substances* enters into the labour process'.[121]

Moreover, capitalism generates additional matter-energy throughput due to the 'moral depreciation' of fixed capital brought on by the development of more advanced machinery and structures and by rising labour productivity in the industries producing them.[122] Through such loss of capital values objectified in machinery and buildings, 'competition forces the replacement of old means of labour by new ones before their natural demise' – a clear

---

[116] Marx 1981, Vol. III, p. 203.
[117] Marx 1976a, p. 431.
[118] Marx 1981, Vol. I, p. 288.
[119] Ibid.
[120] Marx 1976a, p. 431 (emphasis added).
[121] Marx 1981, Vol. I, p. 773 (emphasis added).
[122] Marx 1981, Vol. I, p. 528, and Vol. II, pp. 208–9.

acceleration of material throughput and hence of environmental degradation.[123] The constant threat of moral depreciation also compels individual firms to speed up the turnover of their fixed capital stocks by prolonging worktime and intensifying labour processes, further magnifying the system's matter-energy throughput.[124] Advanced capitalism's extension of such accelerated turnover to consumer 'durables' (personal computers, televisions, audio equipment, kitchen appliances, and so on) only worsens these entropic dynamics.[125]

This background sheds further light on Engels's critique of Podolinsky's attempts to calculate the energy productivity of agricultural labour. In Marx's view, capitalist development of productive forces translates into a growing throughput of matter and energy per labour hour. This explains Engels's claim that 'whether the *fresh* cal stabilised by the expenditure of 10,000 cal of daily nourishment amount to 5,000, 10,000, 20,000 or a million is dependent solely upon the level of development of the means of production'.[126] In other words, the amount of energy that each hour of labour (temporarily) stabilises depends on the total amount of matter-energy processed per hour as well as the amount of ancillary energy utilised per unit of output – both of which reflect the development of production. Given that the increase in labour productivity under capitalism is generally accompanied by increases in material throughput, Podolinsky's failure to include non-labour inputs in his calculations is a serious omission indeed, seeing as how 'the energy value of auxiliary materials, fertilisers, etc., must . . . be taken into consideration' – and increasingly so.[127] The general lesson, Engels tells his life-long comrade (in a statement already referred to above), 'is that the working individual is not only a stabiliser of *present* but also, and to a far greater extent, a squanderer of *past*, solar heat. As to what we have done in the way of squandering our reserves of energy, our coal, ore, forests, etc., you are better informed than I am'.[128]

In short, our re-investigation of Marx's *Capital* revealed that, far from dismissing energetic considerations, Engels's comments – informed by Marx's

---

[123] Marx 1981, Vol. II, p. 250; compare Horton 1997.

[124] Marx 1981, Vol. III, pp. 208–9.

[125] England 1987, pp. 131–3.

[126] Engels to Marx, 19 December 1882, in Marx and Engels 1992, p. 411 (emphasis in original).

[127] Marx and Engels 1992, p. 411.

[128] Ibid. (emphases in original).

analysis of capitalist productivity growth – show a healthy awareness of how a faulty specification of the relevant dimensions of energy use can generate misleading results.[129]

III. The metabolic rift, entropy, materialist ecology and ecological economics

'The idea of a history of nature as an integral part of materialism', the winner of the 1977 Nobel prize in chemistry, Ilya Prigogine, has written,

> was asserted by Marx and, in greater detail, by Engels. Contemporary developments in physics, the discovery of the constructive role played by irreversibility, have thus raised within the natural sciences a question that has long been asked by materialists. For them, understanding nature meant understanding it as being capable of producing man and his societies.
>
> Moreover, at the time Engels wrote his *Dialectics of Nature*, the physical sciences seemed to have rejected the mechanistic world view and drawn closer to the idea of an historical development of nature. Engels mentions three fundamental discoveries: energy and the laws governing its qualitative transformations, the cell as the basic constituent of life, and Darwin's discovery of the evolution of species. In view of these great discoveries, Engels came to the conclusion that the mechanistic world view was dead.[130]

Unfortunately, many nineteenth-century materialists and socialists were reluctant to let go of the mechanistic worldview. They were not aware, as Marx and Engels were, that the rigid, mechanistic approach to nature had been displaced by a natural science that was increasingly historical in character (concerned with irreversible processes). So-called 'scientific materialism' (or mechanism) lacked a sufficiently dialectical approach to materialism. It should come as no surprise then that, among the first reactions to Carnot's advances in thermodynamics, in which he had presented an idealised model of engine efficiency in a closed, reversible system, was to see the work of animals and human beings in the terms of the steam engine. This first took the form in

---

[129] Compare Giampietro and Pimentel 1991, p. 119.
[130] Prigogine and Stengers 1984, pp. 252–3.

many cases of concrete comparisons of human labour-power, horsepower and steampower – studies with which Marx and Engels were, of course, familiar.[131]

Podolinsky made a bold departure in applying Carnot's model directly, claiming that human labour was the 'perfect machine' – a kind of steam engine able to restart its own firebox. But although drawing out some important relationships, he fell prey to crude mechanism and energy-reductionism.[132] The question of labour-power was divorced from its historical and social context and from all qualitative transformations of nature and the human relation to nature and became a purely mechanistic and quantitative relationship. Appearing to believe that he had unlocked the physical basis of the labour theory of value, Podolinsky in fact lost sight of the qualitative relations between nature, labour and society that underlay Marx's value theory. As Engels put it, 'Podolinsky went astray' when, bypassing the alienated character of machinery and mechanised labour under capitalism, he 'sought to find in the field of natural science fresh proof of the rightness of socialism', and thereby 'confused the physical with the economic'.[133] Ironically, by applying Carnot's closed, reversible model of the machine (that abstracted from all irreversible processes) to the actual world of human labour, Podolinsky essentially denied that such labour was tied up with irreversible processes and hence, in effect, denied that entropy was applicable to human labour. At the same time, he left out of his analysis the full complexity of human-nature transformations and even many aspects of the more quantitative/energetic relations, such as the solar budget, the use of coal, fertilizers, and so on.

Although contemporary ecological economics does not (for the most part) champion socialism, it, arguably, suffers from a similar tendency to confuse the physical with the economic, due to its failure to grapple with the deep material-social contradictions of capitalist relations of production and monetary valuation. One hopes that the debunking of the Podolinsky myth will help clear the air for a more productive dialogue between Marxism and ecological economics on the changes in socio-economic relations needed to live within solar income and other environmental conditions.

---

[131] See, for example, Morton 1859, and the reference to Morton's work in Marx 1981, Vol. I, pp. 497–8.

[132] Foster and Burkett 2004.

[133] Engels to Marx, 19 December 1882, in Marx and Engels 1992, p. 412.

To sum up, our investigation of the 'Podolinsky business' has revealed that the criticisms of Marx and Engels for not endorsing Podolinsky's efforts to apply quantitative energetics to human labour (and by implication value) should not be taken too seriously. The fact that the founders of historical materialism failed to embrace such notions is not an indication of their rejection of thermodynamics or their lack of sophistication where issues of energy were concerned. On the contrary, they followed the development of the physical sciences extremely closely and made sure that their analyses were consistent with the latest developments in energetics. Yet, their dialectical instincts and emphasis on the qualitative rather than simply quantitative nature of energy transformations, together with their wider metabolic approach, kept them from falling into crude energetics.

Marx and Engels saw the capitalist economy as an open system reliant on environmental inputs of labour-power and non-human matter-energy. They emphasised capital's tendency to deplete and despoil the land, while exploiting the worker. In their view, the metabolic systems that reproduce the productive powers of labour and the land are continuously subjected to adverse shocks from the system of industrial capital accumulation with which they are conjoined. Translated into today's language, they argued that capitalism's uncoupling of production from the solar budget constraint, and its tremendous acceleration of matter-energy throughput, had led to an entropic degradation of natural conditions – a metabolic rift between human reproduction and the conditions needed for this reproduction to be healthy and sustainable.

It is no accident that Marx chose the final section of his chapter on machinery and large-scale industry as the place to develop an initial synthesis of capitalism's tendency to 'simultaneously undermin[e] the original sources of all wealth – the soil and the worker'.[134] This was, for Marx, a major result of the industrialisation of agriculture, which led to the systematic and intensive robbing of the soil, as well as exploitation of the worker. Here, Marx utilises Liebig's theory of biochemical reproductive cycles to argue that capitalism 'disturbs the metabolic interaction between man and the earth'.[135] Specifically,

---

[134] Marx 1981, Vol. I, p. 638. For fuller discussions, see Burkett 1999a, Chapters 9–10, and Foster 2000a, Chapter 5.
[135] Marx 1981, Vol. I, p. 637.

capitalism concentrates population and manufacturing industry in urban centres in a way that 'prevents the return to the soil of its constituent elements consumed by man in the form of food and clothing; hence it hinders the operation of the eternal natural condition for the lasting fertility of the soil'.[136] In short, the capitalist division of town and country disrupts the soil's reproductive cycle, and this disruption is accentuated by the tendency of industrial capitalist agriculture towards 'robbing the soil' and 'ruining the more long-lasting sources of [its] fertility'.[137]

Marx returned to his critique of the metabolic rift associated with capitalist industrialisation when analysing the origins of agricultural land rent in Volume III of *Capital*, where he argues that

> large landed property reduces the agricultural population to an ever decreasing minimum and confronts it with an ever growing industrial population crammed together in large towns; in this way it produces conditions that provoke an irreparable rift in the interdependent process of social metabolism, a metabolism prescribed by the natural laws of life itself. The result of this is a squandering of the vitality of the soil, which is carried by trade far beyond the bounds of a single country.[138]

The metabolic rift between town and country created by the industrial capitalist system vitiates the reproduction of both labour-power and the land, two things that in reality constitute a unified metabolic system, however much capital may treat them merely as separable external conditions. To quote Marx once again,

> large landed property undermines labour-power in the final sphere to which its indigenous energy flees, and where it is stored up as a reserve fund for renewing the vital power of the nation, on the land itself. Large-scale industry and industrially pursued large-scale agriculture have the same effect. If they are originally distinguished by the fact that the former lays waste and ruins labour-power and thus the natural power of man, whereas the latter does the same to the natural power of the soil, they link up in the later course of development, since the industrial system applied to agriculture also

---

[136] Marx 1981, Vol. I, p. 637; see also Marx 1981, Vol. III, p. 195; Engels 1979, p. 92.
[137] Marx 1981, Vol. I, p. 638.
[138] Marx 1981, Vol. III, p. 949.

enervates the workers there, while industry and trade for their part provide agriculture with the means of exhausting the soil.[139]

Marx's analysis is fully consistent with the central concept of Liebig's agricultural chemistry paradigm: 'the cycle of processes constitutive for the reproduction of organic structures'.[140] This concept is not energy-reductionist, but it does abide by the first and second laws of thermodynamics. As Krohn and Schäfer describe it,

> plant and animal life, together with meteorological processes, jointly circulate certain 'substances'; apart from the irreversible transformation of energy into heat, living processes do not 'use up' nature, but reproduce the conditions for their continued existence.[141]

Capitalism's assault on the biochemical processes sustaining the human-land system does not create or destroy matter-energy, but it does degrade it. It degrades the metabolic reproductive capabilities of both labour-power and the land. This degradation of reproductive powers can clearly be seen as a form of entropic matter-energy dissipation. And, in Marx's view, this phenomenon – to some extent inherent in production – is dramatically worsened by capitalism's specific form of industry, which is based on the social separation of the producers from the land and other necessary conditions of production. Hence, it is possible for society to achieve a 'systematic restoration' of its reproductive metabolism with the land 'as a regulative law of social production, and in a form adequate to the full development of the human race'.[142] But this requires 'co-operation and the possession in common of the land and the means of production', based on 'the transformation of capitalist private property . . . into social property'.[143]

In conclusion, what Marx and Engels generated in their historical-dialectical materialism was a theory of the capitalist labour, production and accumulation process that was not only consistent with the main conclusions of thermodynamics originating in their time, but also extraordinarily open to

---

[139] Marx 1981, Vol. III, pp. 949–50.
[140] Krohn and Schäfer 1983, p. 32.
[141] Ibid.
[142] Marx 1981, Vol. I, p. 638; compare Marx and Engels 1976, p. 72; Engels 1939, p. 323, and 1979, p. 92.
[143] Marx 1981, Vol. I, pp. 929–30; see Burkett 2003c.

ecological laws. Although paying close attention to the quantitative aspects of energy transfers, they nonetheless emphasised, dialectically, the qualitative transformations such transfers involve. All tendencies toward mechanism or reductionism were excluded from their analysis. At the same time, Marx developed a sophisticated theory of the metabolic character of the human labour process and of the metabolic rift that appears under capitalism. This analysis not only recognised that 'matter matters' but was sensitive to the biochemical processes of life itself and to emerging evolutionary theory. In other words, classical Marxism, contrary to widespread myth, has much to contribute to ecological economics.

Chapter Seven
Power Inequality and the Environment

That power and conflict are important elements of the economy-environment relationship is increasingly recognised within ecological economics. Gale, for example, argues that it is not enough to support 'the establishment of social institutions that promote the goal of strong sustainability'.[1]

> To make a difference, ecological economics must identify the major institutional obstacles to the achievement of this goal, challenge the agents that benefit from and support existing, unsustainable social structures, and offer theoretical support to those social forces constructing sustainable alternatives.[2]

Similarly, Martinez-Alier suggests that

> if the growth of the economy implies a heavier weight on ecosystems, then environmentalism should be understood as the product of ecological distribution conflicts: i.e., conflicts on the social, spatial, temporal inequalities in the use of natural resources and services and in the burden of pollution.[3]

---

[1] Gale 1998, pp. 131–2.
[2] Gale 1998, p. 132.
[3] Martinez-Alier 1995a, p. 5.

Naturally one's analysis of ecological conflicts is shaped by one's basic vision of the economy-environment relationship. Different perspectives on socio-economic relationships, the material requirements of their reproduction, and what it means for them to undergo a crisis, yield different views on the nature of ecological power and conflicts. But an ecological political-economy should definitely move ecological economics beyond the limited focus of 'the literature of environmental economics', which 'tends to ignore the social organization of production and look for solutions to environmental problems in the sphere of market exchange'.[4]

This chapter and the next address efforts by non-Marxist ecological economists to rise to this analytical challenge. It is suggested that the absence of class analysis has softened the critical edge of non-Marxist models of ecological conflicts and crises. (The Marxist approach is developed further in Chapter 9.)

The present chapter considers James Boyce's analysis of inequality and environmental outcomes.[5] As shown in Section I, Boyce's 'power-inequality model' may be viewed as an extension of the Environmental Kuznets Curve (EKC). While EKC analysis posits an 'inverted U' relationship between pollution and real per capita income, Boyce essentially argues that increased inequality can delay the turning point at which economic growth is associated with improvements in environmental quality. His model emphasises the conflicting environmental preferences of relatively powerful and powerless groups. Section II discusses Lyle Scruggs's critique of the power-inequality model.[6] Scruggs argues that the inequality-environment relationship is more complex and ambiguous than Boyce suggests. Section III observes that neither the power-inequality framework nor Scruggs's critique connects environmental degradation to the economy's relations of production. Like neoclassical economics, they both treat environmental degradation as just an external effect of market activity. As a result, when analysing changes in environmental costs and environmental quality, they do not distinguish the standpoint of systemic reproduction from the standpoint of human development.

---

[4] England 1986, p. 235.
[5] Boyce 1994.
[6] Scruggs 1998.

I. The power-inequality model and the environmental Kuznets curve

Kuznets posited that, starting at low per capita income levels, income inequality tends to rise as an economy grows, but then eventually reaches a turning point beyond which inequality falls as per capita income rises.[7] The 1990s witnessed an explosion of Environmental Kuznets Curve (EKC) studies hypothesising a similar inverted U relationship between pollution and per capita income. Several factors have been cited that might cause pollution to turn down as countries achieve higher levels of per capita income, the most prominent being: (i) changes in the sectoral composition of production away from 'dirty' heavy industries and toward 'cleaner' high-tech manufacturing and services; (ii) improvements in technical efficiency that reduce industrial pollution; (iii) stronger household preferences for pollution reduction (compared to other goods and services) at higher income levels where most citizens' basic subsistence is pretty much assured, so that they tend to push for stronger environmental regulations to reduce sub-optimally high 'external costs' of market activity; (iv) the shifting of polluting activities to poorer countries, partly in response to the 'not in my backyard' effects associated with (iii).[8]

Although numerous tests appear to support the existence of EKC effects, the hypothesis remains controversial. Most criticisms of the EKC hypothesis have focussed on shortcomings in the empirical testing procedures.[9] Typically, the tests do not allow any feedback from pollution to per capita income, the implicit presumption being that limited natural resources do not constrain production possibilities. Also, due to data constraints, empirical studies most often utilise cross-section data, that is, single observations for a large number of countries rather than time-series data on particular countries, leading to further inaccuracies. For example, it must be presumed that per capita income is normally distributed across rich and poor countries (obviously false, given the growing per capita income gaps between most rich and poor countries)

---

[7] Kuznets 1955.

[8] Vogel 1999, Chapter 6; Cavlovic et al. 2000 p. 32; Dinda 2004, pp. 432–40.

[9] Useful surveys of the empirical EKC literature are provided by Cavlovic et al. 2000; Dasgupta et al. 2002; Copeland and Taylor 2004. The following list of criticisms is based on Stern, Common and Barbier 1996; Ekins 1997; Arrow et al. 1995; and Dinda 2004.

and that the long-term relationship between pollution and per capita income is the same across all the countries tested (even though different countries often reach similar per capita incomes, if at all, in completely different historical, technological, and environmental contexts). Finally, EKC tests mostly look at the statistical connection between national per capita incomes and national environmental concentrations of individual pollutants. They do not consider the depletion of non-renewable resources and ecological carrying capacities at the global level, let alone broader aspects of environmental quality connected with the intrinsic values of species as well as aesthetic phenomena.[10]

Another line of criticism accepts the basic EKC framework, but suggests that it needs to be extended to incorporate the environmental effects of economic inequality. Boyce's power-inequality model develops this criticism as a two-step argument.[11] The first step is the truism that environmental degradation tends to be greater, the more powerful are the 'winners' from environmentally degrading activities (those whose wealth, income, and consumption benefit from these activities, and who are often able to escape the worst effects of the degradation) compared to the 'losers' (those who bear most of the health and other costs of environmental degradation while receiving lower shares of the wealth, income, and consumption benefits of the degrading activities). In short, 'if the winners are relatively powerful, and the losers relatively powerless, more environmental degradation will occur than in the reverse situation'.[12]

The second step in the argument posits three specific channels through which increases in power-inequality tend to promote environmental degradation, especially insofar as power is associated with wealth and income: (i) *asymmetric effects* of social decisions regarding the level of environmentally degrading activities; (ii) the effects of power inequality on the *social valuation* of the environment; (iii) the impact of power inequality on the *rate of time preference*, that is, the rate at which social decision-making discounts future welfare compared to present welfare.

---

[10] Dinda 2004, p. 448.
[11] Boyce 1994. See Boyce 2002 for a useful collection of writings. Although Boyce 1994 does not depict his analysis as an extension of the EKC hypothesis, it is presented as such in subsequent applications including Torras and Boyce 1998; Boyce 2002, Chapter 5, and 2004.
[12] Boyce 1994, p. 170.

212 • Chapter Seven

Each of the three channels involves various sub-arguments, but the crucial assumption that underpins all three is that the relatively rich and powerful benefit more from environmentally degrading activities than do the relatively poor and powerless. Given this assumption, it follows, according to Boyce, that increases in power inequality will tend to worsen the rising and irreversible marginal environmental costs of polluting activities (the asymmetries effect). Greater power inequality may also lead to higher social valuations of the benefits of environmentally degrading activities and lower valuations of their costs. Here, Boyce argues that wealth and income 'endowments' influence market prices, both directly (via unequal effective demands in the market) and indirectly (as the rich and powerful influence society-wide preferences, for example, through advertising, fashion, and control of media and political discourse). In this way, market prices come to reflect the interest of the rich and powerful in maintaining a lucrative (for them) but environmentally degrading régime. Moreover, the rich and powerful can also influence social valuations by channelling technological development in more environmentally degrading directions that maintain or increase their wealth, income, and power. Witness the continued dominance of the automobile-petroleum complex in the United States.

Finally, Boyce argues that increased power inequality tends to raise the rate at which future social welfare is discounted in favour of present social welfare, thereby encouraging environmentally degrading activities. This time preference effect involves two sub-hypotheses. First, the poor and powerless may be forced to engage in environmentally degrading activities in order to maintain their subsistence. For example, resource-poor peasants may undertake farming in ways that erode the soil. Second, there is the 'insecure dictatorship syndrome' in which the rich and powerful take a 'cut and run' approach to their local environment, due to their fears about pent-up opposition from the poor and powerless. Increases in political and economic inequality tend to make the rich and powerful even more insecure about the future, thereby increasing their 'rate of time preference with respect to the country's natural resources'.[13]

---

[13] Boyce 1994, p. 177.

II. A mainstream critique of the power-inequality model

In his multi-layered critique, Scruggs first argues that Boyce's power-inequality model stands or falls on the presumption that 'the wealthy and powerful prefer more environmental degradation at the margin than the poor'.[14] This presumption is problematic insofar as environmental quality is viewed as an amenity the taste for which increases once income exceeds subsistence levels.[15] Scruggs points to survey results showing that 'even in some of the poorest regions of Western Europe (e.g. Eastern Germany and Northern Ireland) education and wealth are positively associated with more pro-environmental preferences and behavior'.[16] He also cites evidence suggesting that 'environmental protest movements . . . are usually composed of middle and upper middle-classes, not the poor'.[17] The notion that the demand for environmental quality at some point begins to rise faster than income is, of course, basic to the EKC hypothesis. This throws doubt on all the channels through which power inequality purportedly leads to environmental degradation. If the rich and powerful are not biased in favour of environmentally degrading activities, then the impact of their preferences via asymmetries in, and social valuations of, environmental costs and benefits may even lead to less, not more, environmental degradation. Boyce's 'insecure dictator' effect on time preference is also weakened insofar as powerful élites themselves have a positive preference for environmental quality.

Scruggs also questions the logical coherence of the asymmetries argument even for the case where the rich and powerful favour environmentally degrading activities.[18] If reductions in inequality cause the poor and powerless to become wealthier and more powerful, their own preferences could, by the logic of Boyce's argument, become slanted more toward environmentally degrading activities, in which case irreversibilities and rising marginal costs of environmental degradation should become just as relevant as for the case where the rich and powerful become richer and more powerful – especially with a larger initial number of poor and powerless.

---

[14] Scruggs 1998, p. 261.
[15] Scruggs 1998, p. 262.
[16] Scruggs 1998, p. 263.
[17] Ibid.
[18] Scruggs 1998, pp. 260–1, footnote 1.

214 • Chapter Seven

Scruggs goes on to deny the relevance of the insecure dictatorship model where the only two alternatives are imposition of the dictator's interests without compromise – hence increased environmental degradation – or the dictator taking flight in the face of revolt by the poor and powerless. On a global scale, the relatively wealthy comprise a majority of people in the developed countries, who 'are more likely to consider environmental problems' not as insecure dictators but, rather, 'in precisely the more long-term "public good" view'.[19] Moreover, the rich and powerful may not be able to evade all the costs of environmental degradation by moving, and their 'defensive' private expenditures to lower their own personal costs from pollution are hardly free (everything has an opportunity cost). One may add that, if a dictator is insecure about popular revolts against inequality and environmental degradation, and has such complete control over relevant short-term economic and political decisions as is presumed by Boyce's model, then she has an obvious incentive to compromise a bit rather than following a simple cut-and-run strategy. A compromise scenario, in which élites use short-term security and control as a means of reinforcing their long-term security, seems all the more likely insofar as pure dictatorships are (thankfully) not universal. In the real world, grassroots legitimacy is often as important a source of power as are brute force and wealth ownership. In any case, there is a tension between Boyce's image of the rich and powerful as insecure dictators and his notion that they can willfully shape social preferences and social valuations of the environment.

Scruggs sums up his critique as follows:

> It is impossible to make generalizations about the effect of income [or power] distribution on environmental degradation without knowing more about preferences. . . . Environmental outcomes are due to the complex interplay of individual and group preferences and the institutional situations in which those preferences are aggregated into social choices. . . . [R]esearch on the political economy of environmental degradation should pay more careful attention to why and how individuals or groups promote environmental conservation, as well as how income and power are related to preferences for public goods.[20]

---

[19] Scruggs 1998, p. 262.
[20] Scruggs 1998, pp. 263, 271–2.

III. A Marxist perspective on the power-inequality debate

Scruggs's critique is fair. The relationship between inequality and environmental degradation does seem to be more complex and ambiguous than Boyce's power-inequality model allows. From a Marxist perspective, moreover, this relationship cannot be adequately conceptualised on the level of generic (non-systemic) preferences, markets, and inequalities. Instead of questioning whether the rich and powerful necessarily *prefer* environmentally degrading activities, one should ask whether and why inequalities in wealth and power are *systematically dependent* on environmentally degrading activity. The real problem, in other words, is that Boyce's model treats environmental degradation as a direct outcome of the interests of the rich and powerful, without explaining why it is that the kind of economy that generates inequalities in wealth and power must also degrade the environment.

In fact, the system of production, considered as a historically specific set of material and social relations, plays no role at all in Boyce's analysis. Instead, he takes environmental degradation as a given outcome of market-oriented economic activity. More specifically, Boyce follows the neoclassical convention of treating environmental degradation as an 'external cost' of production for the market, that is, a cost not taken into account by private producers and consumers because it is not explicitly priced.[21] This framework takes as given an 'optimal' level of environmental degradation, starting from which the benefits of any reduction in the degradation are not worth the costs (with both benefits and costs naturally measured by money). The whole purpose of the power-inequality hypothesis is to explain not why environmental degradation is a necessary outcome of a market system, but, rather, why it is often increased to levels above this given optimum.

Like neoclassical theory, Boyce presumes that environmental quality (or reduced environmental degradation) can be treated as a commodity for which supply and demand schedules exist that accurately reflect social benefits and costs. The job of the economist is to ensure that society reaches the intersection of these two predetermined schedules. However, Boyce argues that the true supply and demand schedules for environmental quality are not properly

---

[21] Boyce 1994, p. 170.

registered due to the biases imparted to social decision-making, valuation, and time preference by power inequality. As depicted on a graph with monetary costs and benefits measured on the vertical axis and the level of environmental degradation on the horizontal axis, these biases artificially raise the level of the downsloping demand (marginal benefits) curve and artificially lower the level of the upsloping supply (marginal cost) curve, resulting in an equilibrium with an above-optimal level of degradation.[22]

This framework relates neither power inequality nor the necessity of 'optimal' environmental degradation (in other words, the basic priorities served by production) to the social organisation of production itself. It does not explain why economic activity in general, and the costs and benefits of environmental degradation in particular, are (or should be) measured in monetary terms. It assumes that the above-optimal level of degradation directly reflects the preferences of the rich and powerful, yet, at the same time, treats the existence of this degradation as an unavoidable external cost of market activities undertaken by competing firms and households. The necessity of such socially short-sighted competition, and the forms of valuation associated with it, are not rooted in production (class) relationships. Instead, they are taken as given, natural elements of reality equally applicable to all societies.

More basically, despite the emphasis on divergent environmental preferences between the powerful and the powerless, the power-inequality model presumes that there is a single 'environmental degradation' that means the same thing to all members of society. No attempt is made to define the environmental conditions required for the reproduction of the wealth and power of élites, as opposed to those required to improve the quality of life (and human development) of the poor and powerless. This distinction is not rigorously made because the model does not specify the reproduction requirements of the economy in social-relational terms.

The downgrading of production relationships is also manifested in Boyce's vague conception of 'globalization as a process of economic integration that embraces governance as well as markets'.[23] Lacking a treatment of the specific environmental requirements of capitalist production, Boyce not surprisingly

---

[22] Boyce 1994, p. 175.
[23] Boyce 2004, p. 123.

denies that any 'inexorable logic' (for example, of capital accumulation) determines global environmental outcomes. Since his model contains no concept of structural or systemic forces shaping environmental options, his global projections remain on the level of unsystematic contingencies. He thus suggests that biospheric conditions 'will depend on how the new opportunities created by the globalization of markets and governance alter balances of power, both within countries and among them'.[24] The 'countervailing forces that could bring about a greener and less divided world', like the forces degrading the environment, are not rooted in the system's specific production relations.[25]

One can understand why statistical tests of the power-inequality model exhibit shortcomings similar to those afflicting the empirical EKC literature. The failure to root environmental problems in historically specific production relationships is reflected in the notion that the same indicators of environmental degradation (or environmental quality) apply across all cross-section or historical time-series observations.[26] And the chosen indicators often have a tenuous relationship with environmental quality holistically considered. Measures of individual pollutants like sulfur dioxide, smoke, and heavy particles are highly inadequate in this regard.[27] Attempts have been made to find correlations between power-inequality measures and outcomes more directly connected with human welfare, such as access to safe water and sanitation services, public health indices, or even indicators of the strength of government environmental policies.[28] Such proxies are best viewed as

---

[24] Boyce 2004, p. 124.

[25] Ibid.

[26] As with the EKC literature, tests of the power-inequality hypothesis have mostly been limited to cross-section data, usually for countries but sometimes for states and cities. Such tests assume that the structural connections between power inequality and environmental degradation are the same across all the individual cross-sections.

[27] Torras and Boyce 1998, p. 157. A similar *caveat* applies to Torras 2002, which attempts to adjust poverty and inequality indicators for environmental damages, under alternative assumptions concerning the distribution of such damages. Here, annual environmental damage costs are identified with the imputed monetary values of selected kinds of resource depletion: oil, forests, and soil for Indonesia and fisheries, forests, and soil for the Philippines (Torras 2002, pp. 96–7). Such depletion does represent future losses of welfare insofar as it exceeds annual renewal rates, but it hardly comprises a holistic measure of environmental degradation, even if one ignores the difficulties with its monetary valuation.

[28] Torras and Boyce 1998, p. 157; Boyce et al. 1999; Torras 2006.

complex amalgams of environmental degradation and the social responses to it, and, as such, their relevance is determined by the general historical development of the country (or state, or city) observations in question. A tangled web of submerged joint hypotheses becomes unavoidable here.

The absence of a base in production relationships is also reflected in the use of tenuous proxies for the all-important, but unobservable, power-inequality variable. One popular proxy is income inequality, as measured by the Gini coefficient. The implicit presumption this carries of a quantitative symmetry in the two-way relationship between income and power does not seem to have been noted. Other proxies include broader measures of socio-economic and political conditions, such as literacy rates, average educational attainment levels, voter participation rates, indices of civil liberties, and even internet-user density.[29] At least two studies have used the level of per capita income as an inverse proxy for power inequality, based on the (unexplained) notion that any given degree of income inequality – as measured, say, by the Gini coefficient – generates wider disparities in power at lower average income levels.[30]

At the same time, tests of the power-inequality hypothesis typically assume no feedback from environmental degradation to the level of income or its distribution.[31] The lack of feedback from pollution to income *distribution* seems especially strange insofar as the theory posits that environmentally degrading activities are a prime channel by which élites maintain and increase their power and wealth. Torras, for example, argues that 'Rather than there existing an "equity-environment trade-off", the reverse appears to hold'.[32] This hypothesis directly implies that regression analyses which treat power inequality as exogenous with respect to environmental degradation are misspecified.

For all these reasons, statistical exercises purporting to show that variations in power-inequality account for differences in environmental degradation can be taken no more seriously than the empirical EKC literature. The bottom line is that the power-inequality model cannot explain the level and pattern of environmental degradation, because it does not address how and why

---

[29] Torras and Boyce 1998, p. 151; Boyce et al. 1999, pp. 132–3; Torras 2006, pp. 11–12.

[30] Torras and Boyce 1998, p. 151; Boyce et al. 1999, p. 129.

[31] Torras and Boyce 1998, p. 151; Boyce et al. 1999, p. 132; Torras 2006, pp. 12–13.

[32] Torras 2002, p. 101.

production degrades the environment. Such an explanation must be rooted in production relationships considered as both material and social relations, and needs a critical analysis of the forms of valuation that grow out of these specific production relations.

Chapter Eight

Sraffian Models of Ecological Conflict and Crisis

This chapter evaluates the Sraffian approach to ecological conflict and crisis. In the 'eco-Sraffian' literature, the 'production of commodities by means of commodities'[1] is extended to incorporate the dependence of production on limited natural resources. Sustainability and conflict are studied from the standpoint of the economy's reproduction requirements as dictated by physical input/output relations, under alternative assumptions concerning the ownership and pricing (or non-ownership and non-pricing) of resources.

The usefulness of Sraffian models remains highly controversial among ecological economists. Accordingly, Section I considers the most popular rationales for applying Sraffian techniques to ecological conflicts and crises, together with the most common criticisms of these rationales. Sraffian models are found wanting insofar as they do not specify production relations in material-social terms and are therefore unable to explain the origins of either the economy's surplus product or the structural bases of ecological conflicts. Sections II and III apply this general critique to the seminal models constructed by Charles Perrings and Martin O'Connor.[2] The

---

[1] Sraffa 1960.
[2] Perrings 1985, 1986, and 1987; O'Connor 1993a.

shortcomings inherent to the eco-Sraffian approach are shown to manifest themselves in different ways, depending on how each model relates the economy/environment distinction to the division between market and non-market spheres. Perrings defines the external environment of capitalism as a non-market sphere, and environmental crises as a problem of external effects or 'missing markets'. O'Connor, on the other hand, specifies the environment as the 'ecological capital' required by, but not producible by, an industrial market economy, and he assumes that this ecological capital may take the form of commodities produced and sold by a non-industrial economy. He then interprets ecological conflicts and crises under alternative assumptions about the terms of trade for ecological capital compared to industrial capital.

However, the technical conception of production employed by both Perrings and O'Connor precludes the drawing of structural linkages between the marketisation of nature and the relations of production, and this hampers their respective critiques of market valuation and their accompanying conceptions of ecological conflicts. In fact, both theorists assume that distributional outcomes (economic and ecological) are determined outside their respective models. The lack of a material-social specification of production also explains why neither analysis is able to broach the possibility that the kind of economy-environment interaction reproduced by capitalism may not directly threaten capitalist reproduction even if it does threaten the conditions of sustainable human development.

I. Sraffian analyses: general methodological considerations

Sraffa analysed the determination of long-run equilibrium prices, defined as the set of prices consistent with the reproduction of the economy as a physical system of input-output relations.[3] In the presence of physical surpluses of different commodities (production above that required to maintain current production levels), this set of 'reproduction prices' is the one consistent with an equalisation of the rate of profit across all industries.[4] Sraffa's analysis had two purposes: (i) to revive the classical-Ricardian tradition of deriving long-

---

[3] Sraffa 1960.
[4] Sraffa 1960, p. 6.

run equilibrium prices without reference to either 'marginal utilities' of different goods and services for consumers or the 'marginal products' of different inputs to production; (ii) to demonstrate that, outside of a one-good economy, the real value of capital is not independent of the distribution of income between wages and profits. In this way, he aimed to establish the unviability of the neoclassical theory of distribution, according to which factor owners are rewarded in line with the marginal products of 'real' increments to the factors.

As important as Sraffa's project was and is, however, it remains a 'prelude to a critique of economic theory'.[5] The use of his input/output pricing framework as a basis for a new system of thought applicable to different fields of political economy has been fraught with controversy.[6] There remains much disagreement among economists as to whether, and how, Sraffa's reconstruction of Ricardian theory needs to be extended to take better account of exhaustible resources, and on the feasibility of any such extension.[7] Accordingly, as preparation for the eco-Sraffian models discussed below, this section considers six rationales that have been voiced for applying the technique of 'reproduction prices' to ecological crises and conflicts.

Arguments favouring Sraffian models

The pro-Sraffian arguments can be evenly divided into ecological- and conflict-based rationales, although the two kinds of motivation are often combined in practice. The ecological motivations for adopting Sraffian techniques are as follows:

(i) Because 'they are formulated to ensure the replication of the components of the social-economic system through time', Sraffian reproduction prices have 'an intrinsic determination shaped by the internal physical requirements of replacing commodities and services used up in production and consumption'.[8] Unlike neoclassical price theory, with its subjective marginal valuations and ecologically closed view of production, the Sraffian input/output approach, if specified

---

[5] This is the subtitle to Sraffa 1960.
[6] Compare Roosevelt 1977; Steedman 1977; Sweezy 1981.
[7] See *Metroeconomica* 2001 for a range of views.
[8] Christensen 1989, p. 33.

comprehensively, is consistent with the conservation of matter and energy, and is thus a superior 'methodology for extending the range of price calculations . . . to environmental resources and services'.[9]

(ii) The Sraffian emphasis on 'production of commodities by means of commodities' enables a firm and consistent grasp of production as 'a process of allocating and organizing *flows* of resources'.[10] By contrast, neoclassical theory 'has never managed to break away from a marginal analysis based on the allocation of preexisting *stocks* of resources' – an analysis in which 'pure exchange is central' and production holds 'a secondary position'.[11]

(iii) Sraffa's concept of 'joint production' is useful for analysing the environmental impacts of production. Although Sraffa himself 'strays from a potentially environmentalist course by using joint production as a means to analyze fixed capital goods instead of waste residuals', there is no reason why the concept cannot be used to highlight the fact that the 'fruits of productive activity . . . are both sweet and bitter' from an ecological perspective.[12] In short, 'it is readily possible to "ecologize" the Sraffian approach, through a generalization of joint production theory to include ecological production and economy-ecosystem exchanges of natural resources, environmental services, and waste products'.[13]

The conflict-based rationales for using Sraffian analysis comprise more of a logical sequence:

(iv) Insofar as Sraffian reproduction prices are influenced by the distribution of income between wages and profits, they may be viewed as indicators of conflict outcomes. The input/output pricing framework can thus be extended and/or respecified to include the market outcomes of 'conflicts of "ecological distribution"', that is, conflicts over access to, and use of, natural resources and over 'the burdens of pollution'.[14]

---

[9] Christensen 1989, pp. 33–4.
[10] Gowdy 1991, p. 80 (emphasis in original).
[11] Ibid. (emphasis in original).
[12] England 1986, pp. 236–7.
[13] Martinez-Alier and O'Connor 1996, p. 163.
[14] Martinez-Alier 1995b, p. 80; compare Martinez-Alier 1995c, p. 517.

(v)   Sraffa's demonstration that the value of the manmade capital stock is influenced by the distribution of income between wages and profits applies *a fortiori* to 'natural capital', which is 'still more heterogeneous' than manmade capital.[15] A 'Sraffian ecological economics' would first 'decide which items belong to "natural capital" (i.e. are appropriated and by whom), and then show how their valuation depends on the distribution of income'.[16]

(vi) In the Sraffian view, 'the value of the [manmade] capital stock . . . depends on the "class struggle"', in other words, on 'the results of distributional conflict between wage-workers and capital owners'.[17] But, by uncoupling the theory of income distribution from neoclassical marginal productivity theory, and locating the outcomes of distributional conflict in the context of reproduction prices, Sraffian political economy broadens the possibilities for 'models which show social conflicts of interests concerning the appropriation and use of ecological capital'.[18] Such conflicts may involve not just workers and capitalists, but also 'different societies . . . and groups within society', and may be centred either on resource access, depletion, and destruction per se, or on less narrowly economic concerns such as 'which cultural projects will or will not be served by appropriation of environmental services and resources such as biodiversity'.[19] In short, once the Sraffian approach is extended to include 'irreplaceable natural resources and environmental amenities', then the classical concern with conflict over 'produced economic surplus' can be generalised to encompass all kinds of 'value system conflicts associated with incompatible uses of such resources'.[20]

All of the above rationales are have been questioned, however. Let us reconsider them in turn, beginning once more with the ecological themes.

---

[15] Martinez-Alier 1995b, p. 79.
[16] Ibid.; compare Martinez-Alier 1995c, p. 518.
[17] Martinez-Alier 1995b, pp. 78–9.
[18] Martinez-Alier and O'Connor 1996, p. 163.
[19] Ibid.
[20] O'Connor 1993a, pp. 398–9.

Criticisms of Sraffian modelling

(i)   Both the Sraffa model and the standard neoclassical general equilibrium model depict self-reproducing circular flows of production, income, and expenditure; hence both can be criticised for ignoring the dependence of the economy on the natural environment. Indeed, Patterson argues that 'the very essence of the Sraffa (1960) model is circular flow' and that this model 'produces a surplus from nowhere', directly contradicting 'a biophysical perspective'.[21] It is not clear why, compared to neoclassical theory, the Sraffa model can be any more or less easily extended to encompass non-circular 'biogeochemical cycles'.[22] Why cannot neoclassical supply and demand theory be extended to take account of 'the full cost of the use of resources or environmental systems'?[23]

True, neoclassical price theory has a more overt reliance on subjective preferences (marginal utilities), but it is not clear why this is a handicap insofar as environmental costs cannot be defined apart from human needs and human preferences. (One may opt for a less purely psychological, and more culturally and ecologically informed, conception of human needs than that normally allowed for in neoclassical utility theory.) Besides, it is not clear that the qualitative structure of the Sraffa model (as opposed to the quantitative determination of reproduction prices) completely escapes dependence on subjective demand-side factors. The model does presume universal commodity exchange, which, arguably, must involve some sense of subjective commensurability of commodities. Must not 'each equation in the Sraffa system' represent 'what one party is willing to give up in order to receive some other commodity'?[24] If so, then the model may still presume 'a subjective process, whereby the consumer/producer weighs up his/her own preferences based on his/her perception, tastes and knowledge'.[25] In sum, as long as one presumes that the main purpose of ecological value analysis is to extend the range of price calculations to previously unpriced resources, Sraffian theory has no definite advantage over neoclassical theory.

---

[21] Patterson 1998, p. 114.
[22] Ibid.
[23] Christensen 1989, p. 33.
[24] Patterson 1998, p. 113.
[25] Ibid.

(ii)   It is not clear that ecological economics should focus on flows rather than stocks. In the respective controversies over natural capital and entropy, for example, both stock and flow issues are prominent (see Chapters 3 to 5). Neoclassical theory does tend to subordinate production to its concern with 'optimal allocation of resources through exchange', and one form this takes is the use of an abstract 'production function' that fails to allow for the environmental (matter-energy) requirements of labour and capital.[26] But the production function approach does, however imperfectly, depict relations between stocks of resources and flows of productive services. This explains why England is able to formally extend neoclassical production and growth theory to incorporate irreplaceable natural capital.[27]

Moreover, given that one defining characteristic of capitalist economies is the generalisation of market exchange, it seems misguided to champion Sraffian theory based on its downgrading of exchange in favour of production. A superior view is that neoclassical and Sraffian theories each offer one-sided views of the economy, with the former overemphasising exchange at the expense of production (taking the point of view of the capitalist *rentier*) and the latter doing the reverse (taking the point of view of the entrepreneur or functioning industrial capitalist).[28] This reflects the absence from both theories of a critical analysis of capitalism's specific forms of valuation as rooted in capitalism's specific production relations. Except for Sraffian theory's greater ability to deal with the heterogeneity of capital, its conception of production is just as abstract, just as technical, as that of neoclassical theory. To treat production as a set of input/output coefficients relating different goods and services to each other, with no allowance for the specific social relations that structure the productive metabolism between people and nature, is merely to disaggregate, not qualitatively improve upon, the neoclassical production function approach.

(iii)   On joint production, we can be brief. Textbooks in advanced neoclassical microeconomics have long contained detailed treatments of this

---

[26] Gowdy 1991, p. 79; compare Georgescu-Roegen 1979a; Daly 1997.
[27] England 2000.
[28] Roosevelt 1977, pp. 444–52.

phenomenon.[29] Neoclassical economists routinely note the 'jointly produced' character of pollution and marketed commodities.[30] In arguing that 'the concept of joint production should be considered as one of the conceptual foundations of ecological economics', Baumgärtner, et al. draw upon 'a substantial body of both theory and applications . . . in the economics and business administration literature', and document the close connections between the neoclassical analyses of external effects and of joint production.[31] In short, there is nothing inherently Sraffian about joint production.

Equally serious questions dog the conflict-based rationales for adopting Sraffian techniques:

(iv)   As Martinez-Alier notes, that 'prices depend . . . on the distribution of income' is 'common ground to both conventional neoclassical and Sraffian economics'.[32] True, in neoclassical theory, distribution affects prices by changing the pattern of demands for goods and services, which in turn influences 'prices of production factors', whereas, for Sraffian theory, the causal chain is completely 'from the supply side'.[33] But the advantage of the Sraffian story over the neoclassical one is unclear. O'Connor and Martinez-Alier suggest that neoclassical 'general equilibrium methodology, although fairly useless for empirical analyses of the real march of the economy and its impact on ecosystems, can nevertheless be put to good didactic use to highlight . . . issues of unequal ecological distribution'.[34] There remains the fact that Sraffa's critique leaves the neoclassicals without a coherent theory of distribution outside of a one-good economy, but, even here, the only alternative offered by the Sraffians is to argue that distribution is an outcome of conflicts (see point (vi) below).

(v)   That Sraffian analysis can handle heterogeneous natural capital is only a plus insofar as one accepts natural capital as a viable and useful

---

[29] See, for example, Henderson and Quandt 1980, pp. 92–101.
[30] See, among many others, Mishan 1971, p. 102; Varian 1978, p. 204.
[31] Baumgärtner et al. 2001, p. 367.
[32] Martinez-Alier 1995b, p. 78.
[33] Ibid.
[34] O'Connor and Martinez-Alier 1998, p. 39.

category, a question on which ecological economists are deeply divided (see Chapters 3 and 4). Oddly, Martinez-Alier endorses Sraffian analysis of conflicts over natural capital while simultaneously criticising the conceptual foundations of natural-capital theory.[35] Sraffian theory does not resolve the incommensurability and common pool resource problems that he rightly says afflict natural capital. Sraffian models can demarcate different forms of natural capital, but, like neoclassical theory, they presume monetary commensurability of the ecological use-values embodied in natural-capital stocks. Neither theory explains the necessity of monetary exchange and valuation. Both theories presume that nature becomes 'capital' whenever it is 'appropriated', regardless of 'by whom'.[36] In other words, the didactic use of Sraffian natural-capital models to analyse ecological conflicts requires that one conflate capital with given use-values and limit the influence of social (including class) relations to the *distribution* of these use-values.

(vi) The distribution of income between wages and profits is a key parameter in Sraffian models, but it does not follow that these models are a useful tool for analysing distributional conflicts. In fact, the Sraffian model treats income distribution between workers and capitalists as an exogenous parameter 'determined from outside the system'.[37] Moreover, the Sraffian model does not explain the origins of the surplus that is the purported object of distributional conflict between workers and capitalists.[38] As O'Connor observes, Sraffian theorists, like 'classical political economists', treat 'distributional conflict in terms of *appropriation* of produced economic surplus'.[39] The *existence* of this produced surplus is taken as given from the technical conditions of production. On the social relations forcing workers to labour beyond the time needed to maintain the current level of production, the theory is silent. Class conflict is thereby relegated to distribution, and can play no role in production. No wonder the theory lacks a critical perspective on monetary

---

[35] Martinez-Alier 1995b; see also Martinez-Alier and O'Connor 1996.
[36] Martinez-Alier 1995b, p. 79.
[37] Sraffa 1960, p. 33.
[38] Roosevelt 1977, pp. 441–4.
[39] O'Connor 1993a, p. 398 (emphasis added).

valuation, that is, one rooted in the class relations of production and their exploitative character toward both labour and nature. If one takes production as a technical given and identifies capital with use-values, it is but one more small step to the notion that prices can be interpreted as qualitatively adequate indicators of conflicting use-values (see next two sections).

The provisional conclusion is that Sraffian analysis not only contains very little positive potential for enhancing analysis of ecological crises and conflicts, but actively constrains such analysis in significant ways. Like neoclassical theory, it throws a technical, ahistorical cloak over the social relations of production and their shaping of the combined exploitation of labour and nature. This makes it not very useful in specifying capitalist ecological crises and conflicts. As is shown next, the methodological shortcomings of eco-Sraffian theory appear in different analytical forms depending on the specific assumptions made about the marketisation of nature.

II. Perrings and the eco-Sraffian 'missing markets' perspective

Perrings notes that the original Sraffa model assumes that 'the economy functions independently of its environment', which 'implies that resources can be costlessly exacted from nature, and that residuals generated in the economy can be costlessly disposed of in nature'.[40] In other words, the Sraffa model ignores the 'conservation of mass condition' applicable to all physical processes.[41] Perrings's attempt to correct this shortcoming begins with two distinct, if overlapping, definitions of the economy/environment distinction.

Economy and environment

The first definition is a purely physical one based on Sraffa's distinction between 'basic' and 'non-basic' goods. For Sraffa, basic goods are those that enter, directly or indirectly, into the production of all other goods, while non-basics are 'not used, whether as instruments of production or as articles of

---

[40] Perrings 1986, p. 199.
[41] Ibid.

subsistence, in the production of others'.[42] To ecologise Sraffa, Perrings defines the environment as the systems that produce goods which are, from the standpoint of the economy's reproduction, essential and irreplaceable, that is, basic goods that cannot be produced by the economy itself.[43] The economy is thus unilaterally dependent on the environment in the sense that the former's reproduction relies on *exaction* of resources (basics) from the latter, but not vice versa:

> If, however, one process employs the output of another as an input but does not in turn supply inputs to the other directly or indirectly, the first process may be said to be unilaterally dependent on the second. . . . The relation between the two processes is then called an exaction. . . . Whenever a society employs a stock of resources appropriated from nature, it is making exactions on the system[s] that yield those resources. To use a very obvious example, a hunting community living 'off' a herd of buffalo may be said to be unilaterally dependent on that herd.[44]

Perrings sees the economy's unilateral exaction of basics from nature as the prime source of ecological conflicts, his rationale being that such 'exaction always implies force majeure'.[45] Because the environmental dependence of economies is often mediated by their dependence 'on other human societies that are themselves dependent on [environmental] systems', there are likely to be conflicts between societies over the terms of exaction.[46]

Perrings's second definition is more social. It locates the dividing line between economy and environment in terms of whether production and resource allocation are undertaken in response to the economy's 'social signals':

> At the most general level, a human economy may be defined as a physical system of production organized according to a social system of signals. . . . We

---

[42] Sraffa 1960, p. 7; see also Dobb 1973, pp. 259–60.

[43] Perrings 1985, pp. 835–9. Sraffa himself treated natural resources as a kind of converse non-basic: 'Being employed in production, but not themselves produced, they are the converse of commodities which, although produced, are not used in production' (Sraffa 1960, p. 74). Moreover, Sraffa's very brief analysis of reproduction prices with natural resources excluded all resources that do not yield rents ('"free" natural resources') (Sraffa 1960, p. 75).

[44] Perrings 1985, pp. 836, 838.

[45] Perrings 1985, p. 836.

[46] Perrings 1985, p. 845.

may define a social system of signals to be a set of mutually consistent indicators recognizable to and guiding the behavior of a particular society. . . . In all cases, though, it is the system of signals that sets an economy apart from the other systems of social production with which it interacts.[47]

An economy's social signals may include 'the price system' as well as 'a range of cultural or ideological codes of behavior'.[48] The reach of these signals defines the boundary between an economy and its environment. Also, the environment may include other societies from which basics are exacted, but which operate according to different sets of social signals. Perrings clearly sees the economy/environment boundary as a dividing line between controlled and uncontrolled aspects of economic life. The social signals are thus presumed to enable the various economic agents within a society to control their activities in a 'mutually consistent' way.[49] Elaborating the point, Perrings states that

the human economy is founded on activities that depend on the ability of human agents to manage the signals guiding the behavior of agents in other (subordinate) systems of production. . . . The limit of human control in such circumstances marks the dividing line between the economy and its environment.[50]

This controllability dimension is also clear from Perrings's critique of the 'Neumann or Sraffa models'. Here, he argues that

we cannot meaningfully represent the economy as a closed system . . . unless we believe that all processes in the global system are 'owned' and 'controlled' by economic agents. If this is not the case then the complement of the process of the economy will be the processes of the environment, and the time behavior of each depends on the links between them.[51]

Before delving further into Perrings's analysis, it is important to consider the difficulties with his two definitions of the economy/environment divide. Basically, both definitions employ an 'internal/external' metaphor to describe

---

[47] Perrings 1987, p. 3.
[48] Ibid.
[49] Ibid.
[50] Perrings 1987, p. 4.
[51] Perrings 1986, p. 200.

232 • Chapter Eight

economy-environment relations. Without further consideration of the social relations of production, however, this metaphor may not be adequate. Consider the case of one very basic good: the labour-power, or ability to work, of human beings. This resource is certainly essential to the economy's reproduction, but is it part of the environment or part of the economy? It is, arguably, both. Labour-power's reproduction is, in large part, a natural process not physically producible by the economy itself (test-tube babies notwithstanding), and this reproduction is not fully in response to the economy's social signals – at least, not under capitalism. Yet labour-power's reproduction is also at least partly dependent upon physical inputs and social signals from the economy. We cannot get any more specific without further information on the social relations of production.

Important issues are involved here. For example, in the Marxist view, the forced exaction of labour (specifically surplus labour) from labour-power is what defines individual societies as class societies; yet Perrings's first definition would treat such exploitation as the exploitation of one society by another society – viewing the capitalist and the worker (or the lord and the serf) as inhabitants of two different societies. The *internal contradictions* of class societies, including the possibility that their internal systems of 'social signals' may not after all be 'mutually consistent', are thus fogged over by Perrings's internal/external analogy, according to which 'the environment to an economy may include human as well as nonhuman systems of production, [and] coercive systems of production such as the slave, feudal, or corvee systems are directly analogous to the more familiar exploitation of nonhuman environments'.[52]

Indeed, Perrings's Sraffian conception of economy and environment does not qualitatively distinguish labour from other production inputs.[53] No mention is made of the distinction between labour-power and actual labour, let alone of the natural limits to the labour exaction process. Instead, as with other resources, labour exaction is represented by given input/output coefficients relating the labour input to other goods. This procedure precludes the specification of the forms of labour exaction and appropriation from nature associated with different (class and non-class) societies.

---

[52] Perrings 1987, p. xii.
[53] Perrings 1985, pp. 835–9, and 1986, pp. 201–2.

The notion of *unilateral* dependence of the economy on the environment may not be viable, either. Here, Perrings misses the tension between the very active influence of the economy (including non-basics production) on the environment in his own model versus the 'purely passive' character of non-basic goods in Sraffa's original analysis (the fact that such goods 'have no part in the determination of the system' of prices and profits).[54] The economy, through its exaction of basics from the environment, clearly alters the conditions of environmental basics production. Hence the situation is really *not* one of unilateral dependence of economy on environment: environmental conditions are dependent on the economy's pattern and level of activity. Moreover, since the economy's production is, by definition, driven by its social signals, the attendant 'negative output' of environmental basics, and other (possibly useful) environmental impacts, are driven by these same signals. In other words, Perrings's second, more social, definition of the economy/environment divide also breaks down. Economy and environment cannot be treated as separate systems whose interaction may be unilateral, but, instead, must be seen as a single system composed of two co-evolving subsystems.

In terms of Perrings's example of a hunting community living off buffalo, it should be obvious that the buffalo population, indeed the whole range of the herd's conditions of existence, are determined in large part by the exactive activities of the human community – and not just the exaction of buffalo but other activities involving land use, exaction of use-values from other species that co-evolve with the buffalo, etc. As such, the social signals to which the human community's exactive activities respond are important conditions of the buffalos' reproduction and development. Such co-production of economic and environmental conditions is all the more unavoidable insofar as basic goods include the *sinks* provided by the environment for the economy's waste residuals of matter and energy. As Perrings inversely phrases it, 'the status of the environment as a receptacle for the waste products generated in the economy' means that 'the economy makes both *exactions* on and *insertions* into the environment'.[55] That being the case, human economy 'produces nature' – to use Neil Smith's term – in the sense that its appropriation and

---

[54] Sraffa 1960, pp. 7–8.
[55] Perrings 1986, p. 201 (emphases in original).

expulsion of matter and energy inevitably alters environmental conditions.[56]

It is also unclear whether Perrings's two definitions of the economy/environment divide are consistent with each other. At minimum, their consistency requires that: (i) the production of all essential basics not producible by the economy be regulated (if at all) by signals completely independent of the economy's own social signals; *and* (ii) all goods and services produced within the economy (whether or not environmental basics enter into their production) are fully controllable in the sense that their production is regulated by a 'mutually consistent' set of social signals internal to the economy. Human labour-power does not seem to abide by either requirement insofar as it is a basic good whose production is largely (in Perrings's terms) environmental yet not fully independent of the economy's output and social signals. Requirement (i) is also violated by the simple observation that the environment (basics production) is not independent of the growth and development of the economy. There is also the question whether the economy's social signals can be relied upon to be mutually consistent – and this issue is crucial to Perrings's treatment of market systems (see below).

The eco-Sraffian 'natural economy'

To see how Perrings's framework leads to a 'missing markets' view of environmental crisis, one must first consider his algebraic treatment of 'natural economy'.[57] Natural economy is basically a catch-all term for all precapitalist economies. Perrings uses his conception of economic exaction from the environment to analyse 'the structural conditions that make the so-called natural or primitive systems antithetical to modern capitalist economy'.[58] Specifically, he seeks to determine 'the dynamic features' that 'explain why technological or institutional change should be so prescribed [limited] in this type of system'.[59]

From a brief review of the philosophical, historical, and economic literatures on the concept of natural economy, Perrings concludes that such economies share the following features:

---

[56] Smith 1984, Chapter 2.
[57] Perrings 1985.
[58] Perrings 1985, p. 829.
[59] Ibid.

All production is undertaken by a set of self-sufficient institutions, which in any given system are homogenous with respect to the technical fragmentation of the tasks undertaken (the technical division of labour), rights in property in the inputs advanced (the social division of labour), and output (through differential rates of capacity utilization). There are few if any transactions between such institutions, and the transactions that do take place have no effect on production decisions. Money may or may not be present, but the basic means of production are not bought and sold on the market. The systems tend to be stationary for long periods.[60]

In short, while the (limited) transactions among the self-sufficient units of natural economy may or may not be undertaken through markets and money, the appropriation of resources from nature is definitely not. Perrings uses the algebra of input/output analysis to formalise this situation where 'each of' the natural economy's 'several virtually self-contained subeconomies depends on exaction from a common resource', namely, the natural environment.[61] He considers two cases: one where the economy's internal units conduct input/output transactions amongst each other, and one where they do not. In both cases, the key feature is the unilateral dependence of all economic units on exactions from the environment.[62] In addition to conservation of mass, this formal analysis allows for depreciation of the products exacted from nature, consistent with the entropic dissipation of useful material forms (see Chapter 5).

Perrings formalises the conditions under which this 'system can converge to an equilibrium rate of growth'.[63] Not surprisingly, he finds that the individual and collective growth of the natural economy's sub-units is constrained by the growth of natural resources, and by the depreciation of these resources. Specifically, growth of the economy may exceed 'the maximum potential rate of subsystem(s) from which exactions are made only if the undepreciated

---

[60] Perrings 1985, pp. 834–5.
[61] Perrings 1985, p. 838.
[62] To simplify things, Perrings assumes that even if the individual economic units conduct transactions with each other, they do not use markets or money. Hence all intra-economy and economy-environment transactions are represented simply in the form of physical input/output matrices.
[63] Perrings 1985, pp. 840–1.

part of the products exacted compensates for the difference in the levels of output between the dependent [economic] and independent [environmental] subsystems'; otherwise 'the system will be constrained . . . and will not converge to equilibrium'.[64] For each individual (basic) resource exacted from the environment, 'The viability of the system . . . requires that the surplus generated in the process from which exactions are made is at least equal to the difference between the gross input of the resource in all other processes and the undepreciated part of that resource at the end of the previous period'.[65] This viability condition can be relaxed by innovations that slow down the depreciation of resources (for example, new maintenance or recycling techniques) or which increase the amount of economic goods (use-values) that can be produced per unit of basic inputs from the environment (increases in productive efficiency on the output side). Perrings also mentions the possibility of human interventions that increase the productivity of the environmental systems that produce basic resources.[66]

This analysis of a stylised natural economy contradicts the notion of the economy's unilateral dependence on the environment, upon which the analysis is supposedly based. Innovations to reduce depreciation and (especially) to increase the productivity of environmental 'subsystems' defy any 'one-way' conception of economy-environment interactions; and, even in the absence of such innovations, environmental conditions will be shaped by the pattern and level of resource exaction by the economy.

Perrings then uses his material viability condition to interpret the lack of technological and institutional dynamism of natural economy compared to capitalist economy. His explanation is that the environmental conditions faced by natural economies, including the rapid depreciation rates of their main food products, mean that they can only survive if they place cultural and institutional restraints on technological and institutional change – restraints ensuring that the level of exaction from nature does not endanger social reproduction. Perrings interprets these restraints as limits on the utilisation of productive capacity:

---

[64] Perrings 1985, p. 841.
[65] Ibid.
[66] Perrings 1985, p. 843.

Most important, if a system comprises dependent and independent sectors, and if productivity is greater in the former than the latter, it may converge to an equilibrium state in which there is no underutilization of capacity only if the rate of depreciation of the products exacted permits it. Because historically these have been food products with very high rates of depreciation, such systems have typically been constrained by the maximum sustainable rate of exaction on the independent sector to a level of activity that has left the dependent sector consistently underemployed. In the absence of innovation or contest over the extent of resources, the history of the dependent sector has been dominated by mechanisms that regulate the level of capacity utilization . . .[67]

Of course, the regulation of capacity utilisation, hence of exactions from the environment, by the internal mechanisms of natural economies violates Perrings's underlying assumption that environmental reproduction is independent of the economy's social signals. This tension may explain why Perrings interprets such regulation as a constraint on the realisation of human potential:

Primitive communities produce below capacity not because they aim low but because they are prevented by their social institutions from realizing their full potential. . . . Anyone considered to be an 'economic deviant' is constrained both physically and morally. . . . What emerges is a feature of natural or primitive economy that is quite general: for whatever reason, capacity is systematically underutilized.[68]

Perrings thus tries to salvage the environment's independence from the natural economy's internal social signals by arguing that these social signals are not consciously developed to maintain the community's ecological viability, but for some other (unspecified) reason. But this requires that the long-term reproduction of natural economies be seen as a Darwinian process in which the technologically and institutionally stagnant economies are selected out and survive while the more technologically and institutionally dynamic communities end up not being viable and disappear. Even if it were historically

---

[67] Perrings 1985, p. 842.
[68] Perrings 1985, p. 834.

accurate (which it is not), this approach would beg the question as to why technological and institutional dynamism in the context of natural economies has been associated with increased exactions from nature that imperil socio-economic reproduction.

In other words, the Darwinian interpretation only saves Perrings's concept of the economy/environment divide insofar as the environmental effects of the economy's social signals are arbitrarily limited to *intentional* effects. But, then, one must explain why the more technologically and institutionally dynamic communities unintentionally allow themselves to become environmentally unviable while the stagnant, backward communities manage to remain viable without realising it. Part of the difficulty here resides in Perrings's impoverished conception of how precapitalist economies regulate their exactions from nature. He treats their individual sub-units as homogenous, self-sufficient, and uninnovative. In the real world, we find that precapitalist systems have developed a variety of common property devices internally tailored to the variegated natural environments on which they depend for their reproduction. Often, as these devices have been passed down from one generation to the next in culturally embedded ways, they have been consciously developed to enhance communities' ability to live and prosper with nature (see Chapter 10).

Perrings interprets all precapitalist regulations of exaction from nature as restrictions on the realisation of human potential and 'capacity utilization'. These are, of course, normative terms that must be interpreted in historically relative ways. Is human development on the basis of culturally embedded regulations on exactions from the environment any less fulfilling of human potential than human development on the basis of capitalist market economy with its competitive, profit-driven exploitation of labour and nature? In the absence of a conception of the historical development of production relations as material-social relations, an affirmative answer to this question must employ the circular logic that acquisitive market-driven behaviour – Adam Smith's 'propensity to truck, barter, and exchange' – is a natural, universal form of the development of 'modern man'. In the real world, meanwhile, the reason why many natural economies have disappeared (despite their environmental viability) is the predatory imperialist operations of capital and its military functionaries; it has had very little to do with any inherent human drive to escape 'rigorous social restraint to inhibit contest over the resources of the independent system(s)'.[69]

Besides, if precapitalist economies do not exact as much from nature as capitalism does, this has less to do with the former's lower rate of capacity utilisation than with the relatively limited level of precapitalist productive capacity. And, if we want to explain the differences between capitalist and precapitalist productive capacities, we have to look to the class relations of production. What Perrings takes as a precapitalist underutilisation of productive capacity and human potential compared to capitalism is really capitalism's greater ability to exact forced labour from the direct producers and to use the resulting surplus products in ways that increase the economy's productive capacity. (As for underutilisation and outright waste of productive capacity, capitalism is much more guilty of these crimes than all previous systems combined.) Capitalism develops the productivity of labour to unprecedented levels due to its historically extreme social separation of the producers from the material conditions of production, and their combined development in the competitive pursuit of profit. The same separation and profit-driven development of labour and nature explains capitalism's unprecedented exactions from, and impacts on, the environment.[70] At the same time, capitalism's development of productive capacity creates a new potential for humanity to live in conscious collective harmony with nature on a world-scale in ways that cannot be realised by capitalism itself – through reduced work-time and a collectively planned development and utilisation of productive forces in pursuit of sustainable human development instead of competitive money-making.[71]

By not considering the specific production relations and common property systems by which natural economies have often successfully regulated their exactions from nature, Perrings puts them in a purely negative, 'backward' light, thereby tipping the scale in favour of market solutions to environmental problems. The impression he gives (however unintentionally) is that only market relations are consistent with the realisation of human potential.

---

[69] Perrings 1985, p. 844.
[70] Foster 1994; Burkett 1999a, Chapters 5–10.
[71] Burkett 2003a, and 2003c.

From natural economy to environmental externalities

That Perrings would solve environmental problems by extending markets to human exactions from nature becomes clearer when he 'considers the structure of the price system, and the role of prices in signaling resource scarcity'.[72] He 'develops a variant of the classical general equilibrium models of Sraffa and Neumann that locates the economy in a materially closed global system, and investigates the implications of the conservation of mass condition on the time behaviour of the system'.[73]

In this model, the non-market, cultural signals earlier considered under natural economy are fully replaced by market signals. Perrings thus states that 'to distinguish between the processes of the economy and those of the environment, I now identify a price system involving the construction of two . . . vectors', with the first vector showing positive prices for goods produced in the economy, and the second vector showing zero prices for 'the waste products of economic processes or unvalued environmental products'.[74] In other words, the boundary between economy and environment is defined by the reach of the economy's price signals. As Perrings stipulates, 'environmental resources' are those 'that do not have the status of commodities' and therefore 'lie outside the price system of the economy'.[75]

Perrings's model follows standard Sraffian practice by coupling a physical (input/output) production system with a price system. His physical system allows the resource 'residuals' left over from production to be either re-invested (akin to Sraffa's joint production of fixed capital) *or* disposed of (wasted). Conservation of mass means not only that 'high rates of growth in one subset of processes imply high rates of exaction on other processes', but also that 'the system will be subject to change resulting from the disposal of

---

[72] Perrings 1987, p. 10.

[73] Perrings 1986, p. 200. The main difference between the analyses of Von Neumann 1945–6 and Sraffa 1960 is that the former was mainly concerned with establishing the conditions under which a general equilibrium exists, whereas the latter aimed to show the dependence of reproduction prices (including the valuation of capital goods) on income distribution.

[74] Perrings 1986, p. 200.

[75] Perrings 1987, p. 11. The non-pricing of waste products is equivalent to a non-pricing of the 'sink' resources provided by the environment.

residuals in its environment'.[76] Whether taking the form of re-investment or waste, 'the disposal of [residuals] has the effect of changing the technology of the system'.[77] Within the economy, these effects are mediated by the price system. Here, Perrings assumes that each price (and sector profit rate) 'is an increasing function of the level of excess demand' for the economic good in question.[78] Also, he assumes that an increase in the price of a resource leads producers to economise on its use by altering the respective shares of resource residuals that are re-invested and wasted, which modifies the physical production system. In his words, 'the effect of a particular resource price on the demand for the resource' takes the form of a 'controlled application of the residuals to the system' of physical production that is 'triggered by changes in the control system outputs, the price signals'.[79]

Perrings argues that his conception of the regulative functions of the price system is broader than that of neoclassical theory:

> The price system is assumed not only to ration a given set of resources at a given moment in time, but to discriminate between resources that are subject to rights in property and those that are not, and to mediate the conflicting claims to the social product of distinct classes of economic agent. It thus admits a broader set of functions than is common in models built on strictly neoclassical foundations and allows a less restricted set of outcomes.[80]

This argument is curious, insofar as the zero pricing of external costs and benefits (due to incomplete property rights in the resources generating these costs and benefits) is central to the problems addressed by neoclassical environmental economics (see Chapter 2). Moreover, as the principles-level 'one dollar, one vote' argument shows, neoclassical economists are well aware that the price system – like all rationing systems – mediates conflicting claims to the social product. And the representative producers/consumers in Perrings's model are neither more nor less 'distinct' than those inhabiting neoclassical general equilibrium models. Certainly, the hypothesised feedback from resource

---

[76] Perrings 1986, p. 208.
[77] Perrings 1986, p. 205.
[78] Ibid.
[79] Perrings 1986, pp. 206–7.
[80] Perrings 1987, p. 10.

demands to resource prices to resource use is impeccably neoclassical.[81] Finally, Perrings's treatment of the individual production units as perfectly competitive price-takers, rather than monopolistic price-makers, is hardly alien to neoclassical analysis. Although he refers to his model's prices as 'observers and instruments of control', the real observer and operator of these instruments is nothing other than the invisible hand or auctioneer of neoclassical theory.[82] In line with standard neoclassical practice, Perrings does not specify the information gathering/dissemination technology that the invisible hand employs to come up with a mutually consistent set of price signals. Apparently, central planning ('optimal control') is costless so long as it is undertaken by the imaginary neoclassical auctioneer.

Although Perrings tries to distinguish his analysis from neoclassical theory, at other points he rightly characterises it as a variant of the neoclassical externalities approach to environmental problems. The source of these problems, according to Perrings, is that the price system's regulation of resource demands is limited to economic resources, while environmental resources remain unpriced. He sees 'external effects' as 'an inevitable and integral part of a system in which resources exist that are uncontrolled by economic agents, where control is a function of possession rather than property – of the ability to influence the output of the resource in question through the application of valorized [priced] inputs, rather than through legal title'.[83] It is, evidently, the *limited reach* of 'market prices in an interdependent economy-environment system' that makes them 'inadequate observers of the effects of economic activity on the relative scarcity of environmental resources', not any inherent ecological shortcomings of market pricing and monetary valuation.[84]

Nonetheless, Perrings suggests that his conception of environmental management as a 'problem of external effects' goes beyond neoclassical theory by consistently applying the 'conservation of mass condition' to the economy-

---

[81] Perrings himself notes that 'control theory has been applied to economy-environment problems' by neoclassical economists (Perrings 1986, p. 205). He distinguishes his own framework from the neoclassical approach by appealing to its endogenisation of technology. As the mushrooming field of 'new growth theory' shows, however, there is nothing non-neoclassical about feedbacks from the price system to technology.

[82] Perrings 1986, p. 205.

[83] Perrings 1987, p. 11.

[84] Perrings 1986, p. 200.

environment system.[85] Formally speaking, however, the key factor in Perrings's analysis is not conservation of mass, but rather the existence of 'unanticipated feedback effects' of productive activities on other productive activities stemming from the unpriced exactions of resources.[86] Any variant of such external effects could trigger price and technological adjustments that 'will not have determinate effects' on the economy-environment system, leading to further 'unanticipated feedback effects', and so on.[87] One does not need conservation of mass to establish 'the necessity of the system to be driven from one disequilibrium state to the next by persistent external effects that result from the unobservability and uncontrollability of the processes of the environment through the price system'.[88]

Perrings's main policy proposal is, thus, fully neoclassical. He suggests an environmental bond market as a mechanism for extending the invisible hand into the environment, thereby gaining 'social control of external effects'.[89] The bond prices paid by resource-users (equivalent to environmental user fees) would be geared to the level of social costs associated with the use of the bonded resources, measured on a worst-case basis. Revenues obtained from bond sales would fund research to improve the estimation of current and future environmental costs.[90]

The lack of critical value-form analysis causes Perrings's enquiry to bypass some fundamental questions. Most basically, he does not consider the non-pricing of environmental resources by market systems as a specific material-social relation growing out of a specific set of production relationships. To begin with, that such non-valuation takes the *form* of non-pricing of nature's gifts should tell us something about the market system. Adam Smith's mystical invisible hand notwithstanding, the market system can never adequately register the communal imperatives of social reproduction (environmental and otherwise) precisely because these imperatives are communal and hence cannot be priced – cannot be monetarily valued. The market system excludes the sustainable use of nature's gifts (and other communal imperatives) from

---

[85] Perrings 1987, p. 3, and 1986, p. 208.
[86] Perrings 1986, p. 207.
[87] Ibid.
[88] Perrings 1987, p. 11.
[89] Perrings 1987, pp. 164–5. The proposal follows Solow 1971.
[90] Perrings 1989.

explicit social signalling precisely because in this kind of system the inherent communality of social reproduction takes the alienated form of 'private' transactions among 'independent' property owners. And this anti-ecological form of socio-economic intercourse grows out of the social separation of the direct producers from necessary conditions of production – a separation that makes some of these conditions controllable by individual competing capitalists (Perrings's 'economic' resources) while the rest are freely appropriated and converted into conditions of competitive capital accumulation (Perrings's 'environmental' resources).

Perrings, by contrast, suggests that environmental crises can be resolved without even addressing the social relations of production. For him, these crises reduce to a 'problem of external effects [which] exists *because something has been left out or distorted in the description of the essential elements of reality summarized in the axiomatic structure of our models'.*[91] Environmental crises do not reflect the inherent contradictions of private, class-exploitative production and its market system, but, rather, 'fundamental flaws in *the axiomatic structure of the dominant models of the economic system'.*[92] To achieve a determinate and sustainable path of social reproduction, we need only extend *our models* so as to internalise the environment into the market's system of price signals. Presumably, enlightened policymakers (if they are listening) will do the rest. There is no need for the bloody chaos of class struggle.

There is just one problem: Perrings's model presumes that the goal is sustainable production of commodities by means of commodities; it says nothing about the sustainable development of human beings. In his model, the environment's only function is to serve as an input and sink for the production of commodities for a profit. His model says absolutely nothing about the market system as a form – a historically limited form – of human development. It treats the reproduction of labour (which is not distinguished from labour-power) as identical to the reproduction of all the other physical inputs to production.[93] And this labour's productive capabilities, as represented by technical input/output coefficients, are not formally distinguished from

---

[91] Perrings 1987, p. 3 [emphasis added].
[92] Ibid.
[93] 'The processes undertaken by households are registered in exactly the same way as the processes undertaken by any other institution . . .' (Perrings 1987, p. 11).

those of any other input. Hence the model says nothing about the alienation of the producers from the combined productive powers of nature and their own collective labour, and the connection between this alienation and the 'external effects' of production.

In other words, Perrings's analysis does not distinguish the environment as a condition of capitalist reproduction from the environment as a condition of human development. Consider his notion that the uncontrollable 'external effects' of economic activity can be alleviated by extending price signals into the environment. Even if this is true from the narrowly economic (that is, capitalist) point of view – and it requires an extraordinary leap of faith to ignore the information, uncertainty, and co-ordination problems associated with the application of market mechanisms to common pool resources – it says nothing about the effects of market-oriented activity on the environment as a condition of human development. And it does not explain the powerlessness of the producers vis-à-vis their own collective metabolism with nature, or why this metabolism can only be mediated by market relations.

The incompleteness of Perrings's economy-environment system is reflected in his technocratic conception of environmental crises and conflicts. For him, environmental crises reduce to the 'unanticipated feedback effects' on the production system stemming from the 'uncontrolled disposal of residuals'.[94] He relates neither these crises nor the resulting conflicts to the social relations of production that, although not specified by his Sraffian model, must, in reality, structure the physical production data and market exchanges. Instead, conflicts and their destabilising effects are conceived as zero-sum growth games between different sectors:

> There is no reason why a particular subset of processes within a materially closed system should not have a positive growth rate over some finite period, but it will necessarily be at the expense of some other set of processes in its environment. An expansion in the mass of resources at the command of a particular group of agents implies a contraction in the mass of resources at the disposal of some other group of agents. It also implies an expansion in the mass of wastes generated by the former. High rates of growth in one subset of processes imply high rates of exaction on other processes, and high rates of residuals disposals in both sets of processes. Consequently,

---

[94] Perrings 1986, p. 207.

high rates of growth in one subset of processes imply high rates of change in the system as a whole. Not only is the growth-oriented economy itself an unstable system, it is directly responsible for destabilizing the global system of which it is a part.[95]

This conception relegates conflicts to the realm of distribution of natural resources and economic outputs, just as standard Sraffian analysis limits conflicts to 'contests over the distribution of property (assets) and income' which may 'exacerbate the time variability of the system'.[96] In both cases, the nature and outcomes of these conflicts are determined outside the model, since the model itself says nothing about the social relations that define the conflicting agents and their interests vis-à-vis the physical production and price systems. For instance, to assume that conflicts can be reduced to differential growth contests is to presume that the growth of a sector or society (through growth of its exactive reproductive activities) is in the interests of that sector or society (or at least is seen as such by those wielding power within that sector or society). But this association of growth with success in conflicts needs to be explained – especially insofar as the relatively rapid growth of a sector or society may undermine its own conditions of existence. Where does such an irrational growth imperative come from?

The same basic difficulty afflicts Perrings's conception of the role of *force* in economy-environment relations and associated conflicts. His notion that exaction from nature 'always implies force majeure' has already been noted.[97] For Perrings, exaction is always involuntary for the exactee, whether the exactee be a non-human species or, instead, a society whose reproduction depends on the resources being exacted by another society:

> The concepts of exaction and insertion each imply actions that are not agreed to by all the parties concerned. That is, they imply the impositions of one agent or species on another – a relationship of domination and subordination between agents or species. To the extent that human economies depend on exactions from the environment, they depend on the subordination of the environment.[98]

---

[95] Perrings 1986, pp. 208–9.
[96] Perrings 1987, p. 11.
[97] Perrings 1985, p. 836.
[98] Perrings 1986, p. 201.

Elsewhere Perrings identifies *power* with this ability to forcefully exact resources:

> More particularly, exaction implies that the agents operating the process that makes use of the exacted product are more powerful than those operating the process that yields the exacted product. If this power relation is reversed, such that a particular product is imposed on another less powerful agent, the relation may be called an insertion.[99]

It is not clear why Perrings thinks that all exactions and insertions must be involuntary for either the exactees or the insertees. Presumably, whether this is the case will depend on the specific social relationships that structure the transactions involved. Also, there are different levels on which the distinction between 'forced' and 'voluntary' transactions can and should be addressed. For instance, the sale of a worker's labour-power, and the capitalist's exaction of labour from it, may seem completely voluntary insofar as nobody holds a gun to the worker's head and forces her to offer her services to a particular capitalist. Yet, in a structural sense, it is involuntary insofar as the worker must sell her labour-power and submit to the exaction of her labour in order to obtain the money needed to purchase necessary means of subsistence in capitalist society. Similar ambiguities apply to the submission of working people and communities to capitalist exactions from, and insertions into, the natural environment. They call for analysis of the material-social relations of production – an analysis precluded by Perrings's Sraffian approach, which grafts market signals onto physical production data without providing any class mediations between them. The shortcomings of Sraffian modelling cannot be overcome by importing abstract notions of force, power, and conflict that do not even distinguish between human and non-human species.[100]

---

[99] Perrings 1985, p. 849.

[100] This limitation is shared by Gale's 'broad and inclusive definition of power' as 'the production of (or the capacity to produce) effects' (Gale 1998, p. 136). It is not clear what is to be gained by identifying power with any kind of cause-effect relationship be it intentional or unintentional, animate or inanimate. For a taxonomy of different forms of power that goes beyond such vague generalities, see Boulding 1978, pp. 233–52.

III. O'Connor and conflicts over ecological capital

Like Perrings, O'Connor derives ecological conflicts directly from the environmental dependence of human production.[101] His starting point is 'ecological capital', understood as 'irreplaceable natural resources and environmental amenities', including 'stock natural resources' as well as 'the ecological systems that furnish renewable resource flows and life-support services'.[102] For O'Connor, ecological conflicts are an inevitable result of the fact that ecological capital is 'essential, scarce and depletable'.[103]

> Inevitably, therefore, we see conflicts of interests concerning the appropriation and use of ecological capital: conflicts between different societies and between groups within a society, over access to depletable natural resources, over reproduction or destruction of environmental amenities (and of the planetary life-support system) and, finally, conflicts over which cultural projects will or will not be served by appropriation of environmental resources and services. Such conflicts have always existed . . .[104]

Despite his reference to conflicts 'within a society', O'Connor's formal analysis deals only with conflicts between societies. But he goes beyond Perrings by extending the Sraffian framework to allow for the marketisation of ecological capital.

Ecological capital and the economy/environment distinction

O'Connor sees 'reproduction or accumulation of an "ecological capital" as a sort of *para-economy* activity' whose product may be sold on the market.[105] As with Perrings, the reproduction of ecological capital is defined as a non-industrial sphere – one that often supports the reproduction of 'non-industrial economies that are vulnerable to predation by an expanding modern economy'.[106] But, unlike Perrings, O'Connor allows for the marketing of ecological capital by non-industrial 'proprietors' for a profit.[107] He thus interprets

---

[101] O'Connor 1993a.
[102] O'Connor 1993a, p. 399.
[103] O'Connor 1993a, p. 400.
[104] Ibid.
[105] Ibid. (emphasis in original).
[106] O'Connor 1993a, p. 399.
[107] In fact, O'Connor (1993a, p. 399) applies the term 'ecological capital' not just to

'value system conflicts associated with incompatible uses of [ecological capital]', and the effects of these conflicts on the viability of industrial and ecological reproduction, in terms of alternative assumptions about the relative prices and rates of profit yielded by 'economic capital' (whose production is managed by modern industrial proprietors) and ecological capital.[108]

In other words, O'Connor drops Perrings's assumption that the market system's price signals do not reach into the environment. Perrings's analysis, in which environmental goods yield zero prices and zero profits, thus emerges as a special case of O'Connor's more general framework. Also, compared to Perrings, O'Connor's model has a more transparent specification of waste-disposal and its economic and ecological impacts. Unlike Perrings, however, O'Connor simplifies things by assuming that the technology of production does not change in response to price changes. In O'Connor's model, there is no feedback from the price system to the physical production system. Importantly, O'Connor's model follows Perrings in not distinguishing labour from other inputs, that is, not explicitly showing the exaction of labour from labour-power, let alone its specific social form. Hence, all of his references to 'values' denote either *prices* or *use-values*.

O'Connor begins his formal analysis by specifying a 'Four-Process, Four Resource Model', which is, really, a two-economy model in which each economy engages in waste-disposal activities.[109] Process 1, representing the modern industrial economy, produces an economic good (or 'economic capital') which can be used for consumption or as a means of producing itself. Inputs of both the economic good and ecological capital are needed to produce the economic good. Process 1 also produces waste (call it 'Waste 1') which can be disposed of using inputs of ecological capital as sinks. This waste-disposal process, overseen by the same proprietors who run Process 1, may be labelled Process 2. The reproduction of ecological capital, overseen by non-industrial proprietors, is represented by Process 3. In line with the 'basic' character of ecological capital, it is assumed that Process 3 is 'self-reproducing' in the sense that no economic goods enter into it.[110] Nonetheless, it is assumed that

---

environmental use-values but also to the (pre-modern, non-industrial) *societies* that oversee the reproduction of these use-values.

[108] O'Connor 1993a, p. 399.
[109] O'Connor 1993a, p. 404.
[110] O'Connor 1993a, p. 405.

the reproduction of ecological capital generates its own waste (call it 'Waste 3') whose disposal or 'treatment' in Process 4 (managed by non-industrial proprietors) does require some input of the economic good.[111] It is also assumed that all the productive transactions within and between sectors are defined by constant input/output coefficients.

Table 1

O'Connor's Two-Economy, Four-Process Model

Economy	Process	Outputs	Inputs
Industrial	1	economic good waste 1	economic good ecological capital
	2	disposal of waste 1	waste 1 ecological capital
Non-industrial	3	ecological capital waste 3	ecological capital (self-reproducing)
	4	treatment of waste 3	waste 3 economic good

Source: Based on O'Connor 1993a, p. 404.

This set-up is depicted in Table 1, which completes the formalisation by entering Waste 1 as an input into Process 2, and Waste 3 as an input into Process 4. Obviously, the key relation in this model is the using up of ecological capital in the production of the economic good – either as a direct input (Process 1) or as a sink for disposal of Waste 1 (Process 2). But there is scope for additional feedback effects from the non-industrial to the industrial economy, due to the need for the economic good as an input into the disposal of

---

[111] We are not told why economic goods are needed to treat Waste 3 but not to dispose of Waste 1.

Waste 3 (Process 4). The procedure followed by O'Connor is to consider various special cases of this four-process model, defined by: (i) the necessity or non-necessity of Processes 2 and/or 4, that is, by whether or not waste residuals are assumed to exist; (ii) the pricing or non-pricing of ecological capital and/or waste disposal services; (iii) the equalisation or non-equalisation of sectoral rates of profit, depending on whether free competition or power-conflicts determine prices and rates of return. Without going through all the details of the numerous cases considered by O'Connor, it is possible to communicate the general flavour of his results.

Ecological value system contests

O'Connor first considers a case that assumes away both Waste 1 and Waste 3, so that Processes 2 and 4 disappear. Moreover, he initially assumes that ecological capital is not priced, so that the modern industrial economy (Process 1) relies on *force majeure* (plunder) to appropriate ecological capital as a 'free gift' from the non-industrial economy.[112] This situation clearly parallels the assumptions made by Perrings and thus yields similar results.[113] If the industrial economy's 'maximum expansion rate' (as determined by Process 1's input/output coefficients with full re-investment of profits) exceeds the rate at which ecological capital reproduces itself in Process 3, then ecological capital will be 'progressively depleted'.[114] 'Economic activity will at a certain point come to a shuddering halt unless a substitute for [ecological capital] can be found'.[115]

Then, still abstracting from waste production and disposal, O'Connor turns to the case where ecological capital is produced for the market where it yields a positive price and rate of profit. O'Connor interprets this situation as one in which the industrial proprietors bribe the non-industrial proprietors to convince them to '"alienate" their [ecological] capital . . . and to allow it to be used in the service of economic capital accumulation'.[116] In this scenario, the positive profit on ecological capital represents 'a claim on some of the output at the end of the period of economic capital', so that 'para-economy

---

[112] O'Connor 1993a, pp. 407, 409.
[113] Compare Perrings 1986, and 1987, Part II.
[114] O'Connor 1993a, p. 407.
[115] Ibid.
[116] O'Connor 1993a, p. 409.

proprietors are . . . inducted progressively into participation in the expanding modern economy'.[117] Two sub-cases are considered here. The first assumes equalisation of the profit rates earned by Processes 1 and 3.[118] Here again, any excess of Process 1 growth over Process 3 growth results in 'ecological capital . . . being diverted away from Process 3', that is, 'predation of the ecological capital by the economy until eventual extinction of the [former]' and 'the modern economy itself will collapse once the traditional (ecological) capital is used up'.[119]

The second sub-case drops the assumption of profit rate equalisation in favour of the view that relative profit rates are the outcome of distributional conflicts between the industrial and non-industrial proprietors – conflicts that take on the character of 'a *military and/or political* process'.[120] Here, 'the rate(s) of return and relative prices that actually prevail can be thought of as kinds of distributional parameters indicating the outcome of the contest over purposes of productive activity and over appropriation of the surpluses'.[121] O'Connor considers various possibilities, all of which are taken as given. While exhibiting different distributions of profits between the industrial and non-industrial proprietors, they do not alter the basic dynamic in which – assuming limited growth of ecological capital compared to industry – industrial accumulation uses up the ecological capital until both economies are rendered extinct.[122] As O'Connor notes, even in the case where the relative price of ecological capital rises to the point where the rate of profit in Process 3 exceeds that in Process 1, the only effect is that

---

[117] O'Connor 1993a, p. 409.

[118] O'Connor does not specify the exact mechanism by which the rates of profit are equalised, although at one point he suggests, following Perrings (1987, p. 70) that non-substitutability of goods is sufficient to rule out such equalisation (O'Connor 1993a, pp. 414–15). This is actually a fundamental question given the likely barriers to penetration of profit-making capital into Process 3, which is supposed to be part of 'a "traditional" society geared to self-reproduction' (O'Connor 1993a, p. 409). In other words, the real issue underlying O'Connor's understandable scepticism on profit-rate equalisation is whether and how the internal socio-economic relations of this traditional society can be reconciled with production for the market and a profit.

[119] O'Connor 1993a, pp. 409–10. The bracketed 'former' replaces the word 'latter' which is clearly a slip.

[120] O'Connor 1993a, p. 414 (emphasis in original).

[121] O'Connor 1993a, p. 416.

[122] O'Connor 1993a, pp. 416–17.

Owners of ecological capital who sell it to the economy will come to own economic capital at a faster rate than in the 'equitable' situation (but this does nothing to diminish the impact of the eventual depletion of ecological capital).[123]

In expanding the analysis to include waste, O'Connor first brings Process 2 (industrial waste disposal) back onto the stage, while still suppressing Process 4 (ecological waste). So, now, the industrial economy uses up ecological capital not only as a direct input (Process 1) but also as a sink for its waste (Process 2). Any ecological capital used as a sink becomes 'wasteland' that is forever useless to both Process 1 and Process 3.[124] As before, this three-process set-up is first analysed under the assumption that the industrial economy appropriates ecological capital as an unpriced 'free gift' from the non-industrial economy, and, secondly, under the assumption that ecological capital is marketised – with equal and unequal rates of profit comprising two variants of the second case.

Since this set-up just adds another mode by which Process 1 depletes ecological capital, the results closely parallel those obtained for the two-process case reviewed above. Assuming that the industrial economy grows faster than ecological capital (and this situation is, to repeat, taken as given), 'the para-economy as a going concern' is once again 'progressively compromised and once the [ecological capital] is depleted the [industrial] economy no longer has a site for its waste disposal' (or the ecological inputs needed for Process 1).[125]

Finally, O'Connor considers the full four-process model which allows for ecological waste (Waste 3) and its treatment by the non-industrial economy's Process 4. Here, the non-industrial proprietors' need for the economic good as an input to *their* waste treatment process adds a new dimension to 'the emergence and bilateral resolution of the conflict over possession of resources'.[126] Now the non-industrial economy's growth may be indirectly constrained by the amount of the economic good available in trade, which is lower insofar as the industrial proprietors reinvest the economic good in Process 1. As

[123] O'Connor 1993a, p. 416.
[124] O'Connor 1993a, pp. 415–16.
[125] O'Connor 1993a, p. 413.
[126] O'Connor 1993a, p. 417.

before, various price-system outcomes are possible, depending on whether the industrial economy undertakes a forced plunder (zero-pricing) of ecological capital, or is, instead, constrained by military-political circumstances to offer a positive price and profit to the non-industrial proprietors. In any event, the exact terms of trade are likely to be determined by the relative power of the two sides rather than automatic profit-rate equalisation.[127] After all,

> from each individual economy's point of view, the more that must be paid for waste control, the greater the inhibition on growth. So there is a conflict of interests, a mutual stand-off between two groups of proprietors each wishing to sustain their distinct going concern as best they can.[128]

At this point, O'Connor simplifies things by assuming that the industrial economy's Processes 1 and 2 earn equal rates of profit, and that the non-industrial economy's Processes 3 and 4 also earn equal rates of profit. But he allows the industrial and non-industrial profit rates to differ from each other depending on exogenously given conflict outcomes. If one economy grows faster than the other, the latter's capital is depleted, which, in turn, undercuts the conditions required for the former's waste disposal activity. As a result, barring an accidental balance between the two economies' profitability and growth, their 'struggle over the reciprocal imposition of a waste-disposal burden' will lead to their mutual destruction:

> In this situation . . . a rate of return for one economy higher than that sustainable for the other will entail a real decumulation of the 'capital' of the other. In the present example, this occurs if either the para-economy or the economy exceeds zero-physical growth at the expense of the other. The effect of depleting the capital of the dominated system is, therefore, to deplete the wherewithal of the dominant system's own waste disposal. So victorious proprietors of the dominant system will, eventually, get buried under their own waste.[129]

---

[127] O'Connor 1993a, pp. 418, 421.
[128] O'Connor 1993a, p. 420.
[129] O'Connor 1993a, p. 421.

Limitations of O'Connor's analysis

Overall, O'Connor's analysis is a salutary reminder that conflicts over 'appropriation of produced economic surplus' are ultimately limited by the natural conditions that make production of such a surplus possible.[130] Unfortunately, O'Connor's Sraffian framework does not explain how this nature-based *possibility* of a surplus product is translated into an actuality, and how this leads to conflicts, in particular kinds of economies. To do that, he would have to move beyond his purely physical model of production and treat the economy as a definite material-social life process structured by historically specific class relations of production.[131] The physical possibility of a surplus product tells us nothing about the social arrangements compelling workers to labour beyond the time required to reproduce themselves, let alone about the structure and dynamics of conflict over this surplus labour *and* the distribution of the resulting surplus.

Because O'Connor's model lacks a treatment of the industrial economy's internal production relations as relations of class exploitation (it does not even distinguish human labourers from other inputs), it must take this economy's growth imperative as a given. Since the model does not explain this imperative, or how it is related to competition, it cannot explain why rational capitalists ('industrial proprietors') would pursue it to the point of their own destruction, or how they are able to get their employees to follow them down this suicidal path.

O'Connor's model also reminds us that nature is often caught in the deadly crossfires of socio-economic and military-political conflicts. The problem, however, is that without treating the conflictive nature of production relations as material (people-nature) and social (people-people) relations, there is no way to bring in any struggle for a more pro-ecological production. Without treating class exploitation and its basis in the alienation of the producers from necessary conditions of production including natural conditions ('ecological capital'), there is no apparent agency with either an interest in, or capability of, converting production and its natural basis from vehicles of competitive money-making into conditions of sustainable human development. To put it

---

[130] O'Connor 1993a, p. 398.
[131] Kennedy 1998.

bluntly, O'Connor's model suggests that the environment and human economy are both doomed if the environment is marketised, and equally doomed if the environment is not marketised. It cannot explain the material-social origins of this dilemma because it does not recognise capitalism's social separation of the producers from the necessary means of production and resultant conversion of natural conditions into conditions of exploitative capital accumulation whether or not they are marketised, that is, whether they are freely appropriated or purchased as commodities.[132] Because it does not treat capitalism's alienation of the worker and her labour as an alienation from nature, O'Connor's model misses the possibility that the disalienation of the worker may provide a potential avenue toward an ecologically sustainable system. Indeed, one could conclude from O'Connor's model that the workers in industrial economies are fully implicated, and have a (short-sighted) self-interest, in the depletion of ecological capital via the subjugation of non-industrial economies.

O'Connor's model can only depict the results of *inter*-economy, not *intra*-economy, conflicts. And lacking any specification of either society's internal production relations, his presumptions concerning the conflictual character of the relations between the two economies inevitably have an arbitrary flavour. For example, O'Connor interprets a positive price and profit on ecological capital as a form of 'coercion by the economy over the para-economy, where the latter's proprietors are making the best of a situation they did not choose to enter' – his logic being that 'the value accumulation' (hence the profit share appropriated by the non-industrial proprietors) 'is unsustainable'.[133] O'Connor does not indicate why the relationship is any less coercive for the

---

[132] Burkett 1999a, Chapter 6. Similarly, O'Connor and Martinez-Alier (1998, p. 38) first note that the free appropriation of natural conditions often results in 'cost-shifting onto local communities, onto "the taxpayer", and onto future generations'; and then observe that 'the creating of markets through defining rights and subsequent "capitalization" is not necessarily a step toward social justice and sustainability. On the contrary it may work as a doorway for dispossession and continued cost-shifting on a huge scale'. Their eco-Sraffian framework, informally adapted from O'Connor 1993a, renders them incapable of transcending this conundrum. They are unable to see that even freely appropriated nature is capitalised insofar as it is used as a condition of capital accumulation. In other words, the Sraffian failure to delve into production relations is here manifested in a conflation of nature's capitalisation with its marketisation.
[133] O'Connor 1993a, pp. 413–14.

industrial entrepreneurs and their employees for whom it is equally unsustainable and involuntarily entered. (After all, if the industrial economy does not gain access to the ecological capital, all its inhabitants will die.) Nor does he tell us whether the relationship would be non-coercive if it *were* sustainable (which, as far as we know from his model, is at least as likely an outcome).

Similarly, in considering the full model where the industrial and non-industrial economies require each others' outputs as means of their respective waste disposal operations, O'Connor interprets their mutual inability 'to operate independently' as 'a clear conflict of interests'.[134] His reasoning is that 'the requirement on the economy and on the para-economy to accommodate waste disposal from the other imposes on each of them an impairment of growth potential'.[135] He does not explain why any 'bargained solution . . . to establish exchange ratios for "transactions" of inputs needed for disposal of respective waste materials' must be constrained by an imperative to maximise growth.[136] Nor are we told why the industrial and non-industrial proprietors 'may have wholly distinct interests and objectives' even when they both produce commodities for a profit.[137] Indeed, according to the fully marketised version of the model, both economic and ecological capital have one function and one function only: to serve as inputs for the profitable production of commodities by means of commodities. That is why the model can only predict one kind of economic-environmental crisis: a general breakdown in commodity production due to the depletion of ecological capital. As O'Connor puts it, 'unless the ecological capital regenerates at a faster rate than it is depleted by being used as an input to production . . . or waste disposal . . . economic activity is doomed eventually to stagnate or collapse'.[138] Assuming that both industrial and non-industrial proprietors wish to avoid such a collapse, there would seem to be no long-term structural basis for a conflict of interest here.

The preceding difficulty points to problems with O'Connor's characterisation of the non-industrial economy. This economy is supposed to be 'a "traditional"

---

[134] O'Connor 1993a, p. 418.
[135] O'Connor 1993a, p. 419.
[136] O'Connor 1993a, p. 418.
[137] Ibid.
[138] O'Connor 1993a, p. 400.

society geared to self-reproduction', yet at various points it is assumed to gear its entire production to the market and profit-making.[139] The contradiction between generalised commodification and precapitalist production relations is swept under a technocratic rug. Considering 'which resources are valorized . . . as opposed to those deemed "free", and [on] which processes a rate of profit is to be assessed', O'Connor merely says that 'There can be no general rule on these matters', referring the reader to the technical Sraffian literature on 'traditional solution concepts'.[140] Apparently, anything goes once market relations are disconnected from production relations and overlaid onto physical production systems. Unfortunately, the only alternative to ecological marketisation offered by O'Connor's model is outright plunder by the industrial economy, so that his specifications run the danger of lending credence to that conservative interpretation of the 'tragedy of the commons' which falsely conflates communal property with open, unregulated access (see Chapter 10).

On the other hand, in applying prices and profit rates even to a non-industrial economy geared to self-reproduction, O'Connor seems to suggest that these market signals can serve as adequate indicators of all kinds of use-values including ecological ones. This view is implicit in O'Connor's treatment of 'rate(s) of return and relative prices . . . as kinds of distributional parameters indicating the outcome of the contest *over purposes of economic activity*', not just 'over appropriation of the surpluses'.[141] Here, the 'distinct use-values to the respective proprietor groups' are apparently reflected in the 'rates of *value* accumulation' associated with their respective processes.[142] The problem, in O'Connor's view, is that the non-industrial proprietors' use-values may not be priced *fairly*, due to their inadequate bargaining power against the industrial proprietors. Such unfair pricing will be exhibited in the 'non-equalisation of returns'; but a reduction of power inequality between the two sets of proprietors would lead to a fairer set of prices and profit-rates that presumably better represents the non-industrial economy's 'distinct use-values'.[143]

---

[139] O'Connor 1993a, p. 409.
[140] O'Connor 1993a, p. 403.
[141] O'Connor 1993a, p. 416 (emphasis added).
[142] O'Connor 1993a, p. 415 (emphasis in original).
[143] O'Connor 1993a, p. 415. This line of thinking leads inexorably to a politics of 'greening capitalism' that strives for an ecologically correct pricing of natural resources. See, for example, Sandler 1994; or Vlachou 2002, and 2003–4.

O'Connor even lapses into the position that the goal of capitalist production is the production of particular kinds of use-values, not the accumulation of value as represented by money. As already noted, he interprets the allocation of resources to waste-disposal activities as 'an impairment of growth potential' and hence as a source of conflict between industrial and non-industrial economies.[144] But this presumes that waste-disposal activities are not themselves part of 'economic growth', even though they may be undertaken for the market and yield a profit, that is, generate incomes for their proprietors and employees. If waste disposal generates income and appears as part of GDP, it no longer makes sense to argue that 'from each individual economy's point of view, the more that must be paid for waste control, the greater the inhibition on growth'.[145]

Furthermore, insofar as waste disposal can be profitably sold on the market, it is not clear why it necessarily represents a conflict of interest between the two economies; it could just as well provide an opportunity for the industrial and non-industrial proprietors to reap gains from trade based on the comparative advantages that their respective capital 'endowments' give them in the exploitation of their respective labour forces. As a distinctive going concern, capitalism does not care about the character of the use-values that it uses as vehicles of value accumulation. There are many commodities the demand for which is generated by the negative externalities of capitalist production, and which provide very lucrative opportunities for profit-making: air conditioners in overheated and polluted cities, burglar alarms, various pharmaceuticals, and so forth.[146] What is needed is a critical perspective on *capital*'s 'environmental defensive activities' and their inadequacies from the standpoint of sustainable human development, not their exclusion by *fiat* from the category of 'economic growth'.

---

[144] O'Connor 1993a, p. 419.
[145] O'Connor 1993a, p. 420.
[146] Rowe 2004.

Chapter Nine

Toward a Marxist Approach to Ecological Conflicts and Crises

With their emphasis on class exploitation and struggle, it is not surprising that Marxists have long recognised the conflictual nature of environmental problems.[1] The present chapter demonstrates how Marxist class analysis generates important insights into the systemic roots of environmental crises and conflicts. It is also suggested that this analytical power can be strengthened insofar as Marxists distinguish environmental crises of capital accumulation from crises in the natural conditions of human development.

The Marxist analyses discussed in this chapter have been mostly neglected not only by ecological economists but also by ecological Marxists.[2] They do, however, treat capitalism as a definite material-social life-process whose exploitation of labour and nature has definite historical limits. That is why these Marxist analyses point the way toward an approach that corrects the shortcomings of the frameworks surveyed in Chapters 7 and 8. As shown in Sections I–IV, the

---

[1] England 1987, Chapter 7.
[2] Martinez-Alier 1995b laments a purported Marxist neglect of ecology, but does not note the existence of any of the analyses surveyed in the present chapter. Nor are they cited in the recent survey of Marxist approaches by Adaman and Özkaynak 2002, or in the special ecological numbers of the Marxist journals *Science & Society* 1996 and *Capital & Class* 2000.

Marxists' inability to fulfill this analytical promise is mainly due to their presumption that environmental maintenance activities are a pure cost for capitalist production. Once it is recognised that environmental maintenance activities can present opportunities for profitable commodity production and investment, it becomes clear that one must distinguish capitalist environmental maintenance from the kind of maintenance that can promote sustainable human development.

Accordingly, Section V concludes the chapter by explaining how a more holistic Marxist analysis can distinguish capitalist sustainability from human developmental sustainability. The proposed extensions incorporate Marx's analysis of the co-evolutionary maldevelopment created by capitalism's metabolic rift between workers and nature, and the resulting special position of workers and their communities in the shift of production onto a healthier path through struggles to de-capitalise necessary conditions of production. By highlighting the basis of these struggles in capitalism's exploitative globalisation of production, this analysis leads into Chapter 10's discussion of communism as the struggle for sustainable human development.

I. Perelman on growth and environmental reproduction costs

Perelman argues that 'the same type of analysis which Marx used to analyze value theory offers the best approach for an analysis of environmental problems'.[3] What distinguishes Marx's value analysis from 'traditional price theory', in Perelman's view, is its recognition of 'the dual character of labor' as 'a use value (its capacity to produce) and an exchange value (wages)'.[4] More specifically, the use-value of labour-power includes its ability to labour beyond the time required to reproduce itself, so that 'capitalists are able to extract a surplus value from the production process'.[5]

Perelman suggests that 'a similar dual analysis' applies to natural resources. In particular, if one abstracts from rents, then the prices capitalists pay for natural resources are regulated by their values, that is, by the labour times

---

[3] Perelman 1974, p. 75.
[4] Ibid.
[5] Ibid.

required for their extraction. But such values have no correspondence with the cost of reproducing the resources in question, which may, in fact, be infinite insofar as the resources are irreplaceable. Moreover, even if these resources yield rents, in Marx's view such rents represent redistributions of surplus-value and are thus limited by value production. Hence, rents cannot resolve the gap between reproduction costs and extraction costs for natural resources.

'With natural resources', in short, 'the cost of reproduction is usually much more than the cost of extracting raw materials from nature (even allowing for rent as part of the extraction cost)'.[6] This difference 'creates a fictitious "surplus" in that the capitalist pays one price for resources while the actual cost of production or reproduction of such resources would be much higher'.[7] 'The effect of this duality', according to Perelman, 'is to make it profitable to deplete stocks of natural resources'.[8]

This analysis has much more radical implications than the neoclassical notion that environmental problems can be corrected through efficient pricing of 'external costs'. By distinguishing value from price, Perelman is able to show that resource prices are limited by value relations even with rents. Moreover, his analysis incorporates irreplaceable resources for which no monetary rent can adequately represent depletion costs as measured by (effectively infinite) reproduction costs.

As with Marx, Perelman's analysis does not ascribe value directly to natural resources. But it still recognises that natural resources are necessary conditions of value and surplus-value production, the reason being that the production of value is a material process undertaken by living human beings. When Perelman says that the gap between reproduction costs and extraction costs makes it profitable for capitalists to deplete natural resources, he does not mean that capitalists extract value directly from nature. Rather, he means that this gap makes it profitable for capitalists to extract natural resources *as conditions required for* the exploitation of labour-power and/or for the objectification of surplus labour in vendible use-values.

---

[6] Ibid.
[7] Ibid.
[8] Ibid.

Unfortunately, Perelman does not distinguish between reproduction costs from a capitalist point of view and reproduction costs from the standpoint of sustainable human development. The difficulty becomes apparent when he incorporates the gap between reproduction and extraction costs into a Von Neumann/Sraffa model of long-run growth, in which, given finite resources, 'the maximal [maximum sustainable] rate of growth is the one which expands the output of all goods by the same proportions'.[9] Perelman argues that the systemic underpricing of natural resources relative to their reproduction costs means that this sustainable growth path 'has a lower rate of growth and a lower rate of profit than other possible [short-run] growth paths', and that this makes 'the capitalist class very willing to deviate from this path'.[10] As a result, natural resources tend to be depleted to the point where 'even simple reproduction (the stationary state) is impossible, let alone expanded reproduction'.[11]

The reason why Perelman lapses into a simple environmental breakdown model is that his category of resource reproduction costs does not distinguish the resource requirements of capitalist production from the requirements of sustainable human development. Formally speaking, all that capitalism requires from the environment are conditions consistent with the reproduction of exploitable labour-power and the objectification of abstract labour in commodities. It does not require any reproduction of natural resources in their extant state, unless and insofar as such a reproduction is itself a requirement for the minimal conditions just mentioned. Indeed, the reproduction costs generated by capitalism – and this includes the imperfect substitution of new products and previously unexploited resources for depleted and degraded resources – provide many opportunities for profitable investment and production. Yet Perelman's formal model treats all resource reproduction costs as a drain on profits and growth.[12]

---

[9] Perelman 1974, p. 76. This balanced growth equilibrium is known as the Von Neumann ray (Von Neumann 1945–6); in terms of Sraffa's (1960) model, it corresponds to growth with constant input/output coefficients, equal sectoral profit rates, and full reinvestment of profits in all sectors.

[10] Perelman 1974, p. 76.

[11] Ibid.

[12] This is partly because the Von Neumann/Sraffa framework assumes away any possible shortage of profitable investments relative to savings or profits; hence there is no role for investments in resource reproduction as an offset to overaccumulation of capital.

Nor can the environmental requirements of sustainable human development be conceived simply in terms of the reproduction of extant natural resources, given the inevitable two-way relationship between human production and the environment. Rather, sustainable human development paths involve particular forms of co-evolution between economy and environment. Once this is recognised, it becomes clear that capitalist environmental conflicts are likely to concern not just the *amount* of money and resources that should be allocated to natural resource reproduction, but the *qualitative forms* that such reproductive activities should take. Should resource reproduction simply entail the minimum disposal, treatment, and recycling needed to create conditions for profitable growth and accumulation of capital (often represented by continued growth of real GDP)? Or should reproductive activities be dedicated to the goal of a sustainable development of human beings in healthy co-evolution with other species and the entire biosphere?

The Von Neumann/Sraffa model that Perelman deploys for illustrative purposes cannot distinguish sustainable growth of capitalism from sustainable development of human beings as a total material-social life-process. This model depicts a fully marketised economy that 'has settled down to an equilibrium position . . . a quasi-stationary state' in which 'the production of all goods remains in the same proportion although a uniform geometric rate of growth is allowed to the whole system'.[13] In this equilibrium, 'growth merely consists of replication and the economic system expands like a crystal suspended in a solution of its own salt'.[14] 'All possible techniques are known already . . . and nobody learns anything'.[15] Equilibrium growth proceeds 'without any recognizable aim (except accumulation as such)'.[16] The model, in short, 'can throw no direct light on problems of economic development and changes in the standard of living'.[17] It is 'the climax of "pure economics", the complete elimination of history'.[18]

Stated differently, the Von Neumann/Sraffa balanced growth framework does not treat capitalist commodity production as a definite material-social

---

[13] Champernowne 1945–6, p. 11.
[14] Ibid.
[15] Steindl 1990, p. 127.
[16] Ibid.
[17] Champernowne 1945–6, p. 11.
[18] Steindl 1990, p. 128.

life-process with its own laws of development, crisis, and conflict. Bypassing the economy's specific production relations, and treating the production system as qualitatively static, the framework can depict no evolution at all, let alone a dialectical, conflict- and crisis-driven evolution stemming from tensions between the system's growth requirements and sustainable human development. Its singular conception of breakdowns (deviations from the maximal growth path) says nothing about how a new life-process may develop out of the old via the midwife of class struggle over the conditions of production including natural wealth. It is hard to imagine a less adequate basis for analysing ecological conflicts and crises.

The limitations of Perelman's illustrative framework do not fully explain his undialectical treatment of reproduction costs, however. In treating the duality between labour's use-value and its exchange-value, Perelman emphasises the feature that 'the value of the produce of labor exceeds the exchange value of labor [as represented by the value of labour-power]'.[19] In other words, he focuses on the quantitative aspect of the labour dialectic. But this dialectic has a qualitative dimension as well.[20] The tension between labour as use-value and labour as exchange-value is really a tension between labour as a condition of human development versus labour as a condition of capital accumulation. It is a tension between use-value in the sense of human needs versus use-value as a mere vehicle for the pursuit of monetary value. And the same qualitative tension applies to natural resources: they are use-values for the *real* wealth of human reproduction and development; yet capital is concerned with these resources only insofar as they can serve as material conditions for the accumulation of value, of *abstract* wealth as represented by money. This tension is reflected in, but not captured fully by, the quantitative gap between the reproduction and extraction costs of natural resources. Hence, when Perelman argues that the Von Neumann/Sraffa model can be extended further to include 'the maintenance or expansion of natural resources . . . in our matrix of technology', and that one way of doing this is to treat 'the value of natural resources . . . as being equal to the labour cost of their reproduction', he bypasses the distinction between labour and nature as vehicles of capital

---

[19] Perelman 1974, p. 75.
[20] Sweezy 1981, pp. 21–7.

accumulation versus labour and nature as conditions and forms of co-evolutionary human development.[21] Insofar as his extended model is meant to depict a capitalist economy, it contradicts his assumption that capitalism undervalues natural resources relative to their reproduction costs. If the extended model is supposed to be a postcapitalist economy, then it under-identifies use-value as labour cost.

II. England on capitalist reproduction and environmental quality

England develops a two-sector model of capitalist growth in which production and technological change 'produce toxic, persistent wastes as well as marketable commodities'.[22] The model extends Marx's reproduction schemes to include the environmental impacts of production. It also moves beyond Marx's schemes by considering technological change and attendant reductions in the values of commodities, as well as the determination of total employment of labour. In fact, the effect of pollution on labour supply emerges as the centrepiece of his analysis.[23]

The two sectors in England's model produce means of production and consumption goods, respectively. Each sector requires a given quantity of labour and means of production per unit of output produced. It is assumed that a 'reserve army' of unemployed labour-power exists, so that labour supply is not a constraint on firms' production decisions. The real daily wage is thus assumed to be constant, at least initially. Both sectors emit a given amount of pollution per unit of output, and an additional given amount of pollution results from each unit of goods consumed by working-class households. (Capitalists do not consume in this model; on which more presently.) These pollutants are assumed to be homogenous and can thus be aggregated. The amount of pollution present in the environment at the end of any given production period is determined by total emissions during that period adjusted for any pollution remaining from previous periods. More specifically, it is assumed that a constant fraction of any pollution already in

---

[21] Perelman 1974, p. 76.
[22] England 1980, p. 164.
[23] However, England does not consider the monetary dimension of capitalist reproduction, which is central to Marx's analysis in Volume II of *Capital* (Burkett 2004).

the environment dissipates or 'decays' during each period.[24] The formal model does not include any feedback effects from pollution to production, but this assumption is eventually relaxed in an informal way.

Following traditional Marxist practice, England specifies the model's value magnitudes in terms of the number of hours of homogenous labour time embodied in the two sectors' respective outputs, including the labour embodied in their means of production.[25] Given the assumption that workers do not save, the surplus-value or profit appropriated by the capitalists in each sector is equal to the difference between total value produced (= total labour time expended by workers) and the value of the goods consumed by workers (= the value of wages). The capital advanced by each sector to purchase labour-power, which yields this profit, is thus termed *variable capital*. By contrast, the *constant capital* invested in means of production by each sector is merely transferred to the sector's output without adding to profits. This constant capital is still important, however, insofar as it is a necessary condition for the exploitation of labour-power. It also enters into the denominator of the *rate of profit* (surplus-value divided by the total capital invested).[26]

As with Marx's reproduction schemes, equilibrium requires certain balances in the exchanges within and across the two sectors, both in physical use-value terms and in terms of value magnitudes. Here, England simplifies things a bit by assuming that profits are fully re-invested in both sectors, that is, that capitalists do not consume.[27] Hence, the value of the total demand for consumption goods is equal to the combined total wages of both sectors (including any wages paid out of re-invested profits), which must be equal to the value of the consumption goods sector's output. Meanwhile, the value of the other sector's output of means of production must be equal to the combined value of both sectors' demands for these means of production (including the demands represented by re-invested profits). At the same time,

---

[24] England 1980, p. 165.
[25] Since both sectors are assumed to have the same production period which is equal to the turnover period for their means of production, the entire value of the means of production is transferred to the outputs during the production period.
[26] England 1980, p. 168.
[27] England further assumes that, for both sectors, the respective shares of profits invested in additional labour-power and means of production conform to the given input requirements per unit of output.

parallel equilibrium conditions must apply to the production and exchange of consumption goods and means of production in physical terms, that is, 'the physical supplies of both commodities . . . must be physically consumed during the present period'.[28] These conditions correspond to those derived in Marx's analysis of expanded reproduction.[29]

In this framework, the concentration of pollution in the environment

> depends on the propensities of sectoral techniques to produce waste emissions and on the durability of those emissions, on the scale of production in the current period, and on the concentration of pollutants inherited from earlier periods of history.[30]

Insofar as the growth of production is driven by the re-investment of the surplus-value extracted from workers by capitalists, this establishes a connection between capitalism's specific class relations and environmental degradation. As England puts it, any 'acceleration of capital accumulation' is 'accompanied by a larger flow of waste emissions and consequently lower degree of environmental quality'.[31] One need not treat anti-ecological 'growthmania' as a non-systemic cultural phenomenon. By its nature, 'capitalist development is a process in which value expands itself, and capitalists are the human agents whereby this self-expansion of value takes place'.[32]

England then informally extends his analysis to take account of two dimensions of capitalist technological change. First, he observes that capitalist development has tended to generate new kinds of 'waste emissions' that *persist* in their toxic forms well beyond their period of discharge and hence accumulate as environmental stocks of pollutants'.[33] Examples include plastics, very slowly decaying toxic chemicals of various kinds (pesticides, cleaning fluids, and so on), and nuclear waste. Moreover, the sheer scale of some pollutants means that they can no longer be dispersed or processed by the environment; they thus accumulate in ever greater quantities. An important example is 'the combustion of fossil fuels' which 'leads to the environmental accumulation of another pollutant . . . carbon dioxide'.[34]

---

[28] England 1980, p. 168.
[29] Marx 1981, Vol. II, Chapter 21.
[30] England 1980, p. 172.
[31] England 1980, p. 174.
[32] England 1980, p. 173.
[33] Ibid. (emphasis in original).
[34] Ibid.

Second, England suggests that capitalist technological change has tended to be labour saving, given the incentive of capitalists to counter 'periodic labour shortages' caused by overextensions of worktime and by 'various statutes limiting the duration of the working day'.[35] Labour-saving technological advance tends to 'increase both the total mass of surplus-value and the rate of profit' by reducing the value of the goods consumed by workers at any given real wage (in Marx's terms, by reducing the value of labour-power).[36]

> These technical innovations tended to cheapen wage goods, and hence each employed worker had to labour fewer hours in order to produce commodities equivalent in value to that of the wage goods he or she was simultaneously consuming. This increase in the rate of surplus-value attributable to labor-saving mechanisation constituted in Marx's vocabulary, the production of *relative* surplus-value and tended to bolster the value rate of profit.[37]

However, while labour-saving techniques may be directly profitable, they also 'require changes in the physical *composition* of the materials and energy sources' used in production.[38] This is where England links up the labour-saving dimension of technological change with its environmental impacts. As 'chemical fertilisers and pesticides . . . replace manure and natural pest controls in agriculture', and as 'nuclear power and fossil fuels . . . substitute for water wheels and wind mills as power sources' in industry, etc., it has become obvious that 'many of the particular materials and energy sources introduced by capitalists in recent decades to bolster labor productivity have resulted in increased *toxicity* and environmental *durability* of waste discharges'.[39] Capitalist labour-saving technology thus has 'the ominous, longer-term consequence that environmental stocks of toxic pollutants accumulate far more rapidly'.[40]

England argues that this toxic build-up could 'eventually lead to serious, persistent health problems for the working class', especially insofar as workers

---

[35] England 1980, pp. 173–4.
[36] England 1980, p. 174.
[37] England 1980, p. 173 (emphasis in original).
[38] England 1980, p. 174 (emphasis in original).
[39] Ibid.
[40] England 1980, p. 175.

are 'exposed to pollutants' in production, which, in turn, 'might substantially increase the quantity of medical care required to reproduce workers' laboring capacities'.[41] Depending on the bargaining strength of workers, this could lead to rising wage costs and declining profitability for capitalists.

> If workers demand and get compensatory health care or a shorter working day to escape occupational health hazards, their real wage rate will increase sharply and hence the rate of profit will ultimately tend to fall. . . . Hence, the myopic, competitive introduction of new technologies by individual capitalists could eventually lead to an ironic result – the undermining of the environmental foundation which is necessary for capital accumulation in future decades.[42]

England's analysis clearly foreshadows James O'Connor's 'second contradiction' approach which also emphasises the rising costs to capitalists stemming from various defensive expenditures against environmental degradation, with the extent and forms of such rising costs mediated by class conflicts in both private and public sectors.[43] Moreover, England connects environmental degradation with capitalism's characteristic form of technological advance: labour-saving mechanisation. As highlighted by Braverman, such mechanisation is a two-step dynamic in which work processes are first simplified into sub-processes that can be quantitatively monitored by managers, and the knowledge thus obtained then used to apply machinery to these sub-processes in ways that partially replace, and regulate the pace of, workers' labour.[44] Capitalism, arguably, applies a similar logic to nature. With the producers separated from natural conditions of production, capitalist managers and their scientific and technological functionaries are free to isolate and apply the particular forms of natural wealth that are most useful for the mechanisation of labour and the objectification of this labour in commodities.[45] The result? 'As labor became more homogenous, so did much of nature, which underwent a similar process of degradation'.[46] The development of non-biodegradeables and other persistent

---

[41] Ibid.
[42] Ibid.
[43] O'Connor 1998.
[44] Braverman 1974.
[45] Burkett 1999a, pp. 158–63.
[46] Foster 1994, p. 111.

forms of pollutants is merely the latest phase of this dual degradation of labour and nature.

Unfortunately, England's analysis also foreshadows O'Connor's treatment of the defensive activities instigated by environmental degradation as *pure costs* for capitalism. Both analyses neglect the possibility that such activities may represent profit-making opportunities for capitalist enterprise insofar as they can be converted into commodities produced by wage-labour.[47] This theoretical gap is particularly apparent in England's case, given that the medical-industrial complex (hospitals, pharmaceuticals, medical machinery, and so forth) is now a prime sector of accumulation for advanced capitalism.

This is not to say that capitalist medical-sector activity is not contradictory from a class perspective. The worldwide health-care financing crisis, spiralling dependencies on prescription drugs, and HIV/AIDS epidemics, all indicate the fundamental contradiction between medicine for profit and the requirements of public health. But capitalism is quite capable of functioning without universal, affordable, and quality health care, that is, without a labour force that is in good health throughout its ranks. All it requires is a sufficient supply of *exploitable* labour-power. Of course, the medical needs of a minority of mid- and upper-level managers and professionals may have to be reasonably well taken care of in order to avoid an immediate full-scale rebellion. For most purposes, however, a 'quick succession of unhealthy and short-lived generations will keep the labour market as well supplied as a series of vigorous and long-lived generations'.[48]

England suggests that declining health conditions will eventually lead workers to bargain for offsetting increases in wages and health benefits, thereby raising the capitalists' labour costs. This analysis ignores the regulation of wages by the rates of capital accumulation and labour-saving technological advance, via the reserve army of labour. Strangely, England motivates his discussion of labour-saving mechanisation by referring to its historical alleviation of labour shortages;[49] yet his model does not allow such mechanisation to replenish the reserve army of unemployed and thereby place downward pressure on wages.

---

[47] Burkett 1999a, pp. 195–96, and 1999b, pp. 53–4.
[48] Marx 1976b, p. 57.
[49] England 1980, p. 173.

Unlike Marx, who consistently distinguishes between the real wage and the value of labour-power, England follows the Sraffian practice of treating the real wage ('the physical quantities of various wage goods which workers require in order to reproduce their manual and mental capacities to labour') as the primary concern of class conflict.[50] And, except for his informal discussion of labour-cost problems due to pollution and declining health conditions, England assumes that this physical wage is a given, exogenous variable. As a result, his model has both the real wage and employment directly constrained by the supply of consumer goods rather than indirectly by the rate and technology of accumulation. We are told that 'the number of employed depends just on the daily real wage' because 'each employed worker must be paid enough money wages to purchase the daily bundle of consumer goods required to reproduce his or her laboring capacities'.[51] This Sraffian version of the old 'wage-fund' approach to labour demand and wages explains the strange result that labour-saving technological change has no impact on employment in England's model.[52]

In Marx's analysis of employment-wage dynamics, by contrast, the rate of accumulation and reserve army of unemployed keep wage increases confined within bounds that allow capitalist reproduction to continue. If accumulation takes off to the point where labour shortages and increases in wages occur, then, even without technological change, the rate of accumulation will slacken, thus increasing unemployment which places downward pressure on wages. Labour-saving technological change reinforces this regulative mechanism.[53]

Marx's analysis does not imply that workers' wage struggles are completely futile, however; it only establishes the inability of such distributive struggles to generate a crisis of capitalist reproduction. Insofar as labour productivity continues to rise, workers can successfully demand commensurate increases in wages and benefits without triggering a regulative decline in the rate of capital accumulation. Marx interprets these demands as efforts by workers to maintain the *value* of labour-power. But workers' ability to improve their compensation in line with the requirements of a healthy and sustainable

---

[50] England 1980, p. 164.
[51] England 1980, p. 171.
[52] England 1980, p. 174.
[53] Burkett 1998a, pp. 128–30.

human development is constrained by the system of capitalist reproduction itself, and this includes not just the regulative power of the rate of accumulation over the labour market but also the tensions between worker-community needs and the need of capital to shape and reshape health-care and other use-values into profit-making, not human-developmental, activities. In this sense, the primary revolutionary function of wage and benefit struggles is to build the solidarity and organisation needed to move toward 'an economic reconstruction of society . . . the ultimate abolition of the wages system'.[54]

III. England .on environmental quality and class conflict

In two subsequent contributions, England theorises how class conflict might influence the level of pollution generated by the capitalist economy.[55] Although both articles are informed by Marxist class categories, each of them employs a non-Marxist modelling device: the 1982 piece uses neoclassical production theory, and the 1986 piece a Sraffian framework. It is convenient to begin with the latter analysis, both because it is simpler than the former and because it illustrates once again the shortcomings of Sraffian methods for analysing environmental conflicts.

England's Sraffian/Marxist model has the economy producing a single product, corn. It is assumed that the production of each bushel of corn requires inputs of corn, labour, and natural resources. While corn and labour are bought and sold on the market, natural resources – including the use of the environment as a sink for wastes – are appropriated for free.[56]

The waste emitted from production is specified as follows: (i) a given amount of waste is generated per bushel of corn produced, and (ii) the amounts of corn and labour required to produce each bushel of corn 'vary inversely with [a] unit emission ceiling enforced by the state'.[57] It is also assumed that the emissions cap does not affect the *ratio* of corn to labour used in production. In other words, the respective productivities of corn and labour are positively and equally related to the amount of pollution emissions allowed by the

---

[54] Marx 1976b, pp. 61–2.
[55] England 1982, and 1986.
[56] England 1986, p. 236.
[57] England 1986, p. 237 (emphasis in original).

authorities. This is equivalent to the assumption that, in controlling their emissions in line with the legal ceiling, firms utilise a waste treatment or disposal technology in which the corn/labour ratio happens to be the same as in corn production itself.

Moreover, the model does not include any adverse impacts of pollution on either production or profits. As a result, a reduction of emissions (due to a lowering of the emissions ceiling by the state) appears as a pure cost to firms, that is, as a technologically neutral but unproductive expenditure of factor inputs on emissions control. Any such reduction of emissions will decrease the output or income available for distribution between wages and profits. In this sense, 'environmental policy is intimately tied to issues of income distribution'.[58]

The model's formal results thus take the form of an extension of the Sraffian 'wage-profit frontier'. As derived by Sraffa, this frontier shows an inverse relation between the wage rate and the rate of profit for a given physical production system.[59] In England's model, 'there are *many* wage-profit frontiers, each one corresponding to a different level of environmental protection'.[60] As emissions decrease, total production falls, so that 'lower and lower profit rates are obtainable at any particular wage rate'.[61] England interprets these results as suggesting that

> there is no single 'socially optimal' level of pollution. Rather, various social classes stand to gain the most from different and conflicting levels of environmental quality. The particular level of environmental quality actually enforced by the state will presumably reflect the relative political power of those various social classes and hence their respective capacities to influence government decisions on environmental protection.[62]

There are three problems with this interpretation. First, the model itself says nothing about how the relative power of classes is determined. This is a

---

[58] England 1986, p. 238.
[59] Sraffa 1960, pp. 22–3, 31–3.
[60] England 1986, p. 240 (emphasis in original).
[61] Ibid. 'Alternatively, one can argue that there are various combinations of the real wage and degree of environmental protection leading to the same rate of profit' (England 1986, p. 240).
[62] England 1986, p. 242.

general feature of Sraffian models: they 'explain' crucial variables as conflict outcomes without shedding any light on the structural factors that shape these conflicts. Second, and relatedly, England's model does not establish any basis for environmental conflicts between capitalists and workers. Taken by itself the model suggests that both classes should oppose the imposition of emissions ceilings by the state, insofar as such ceilings reduce both wages and profits for any given wage/profit ratio. This is because the model assumes that emissions-reduction uses up productive resources without adding to either the production of commodities or to income.

Stated differently, England's model assumes that waste treatment and disposal is not itself a commodity produced for profit.[63] As a result – and this is the third problem – the model does not distinguish pollution control for profit versus pollution control for human needs. This gravely weakens England's effort to relate the model to 'attempts by workers . . . to *impose* techniques of production on capitalists which improve environmental quality in the workplace and in working-class communities'.[64] Once we recognise that waste disposal and treatment may be profitable activities, then a key question becomes *what kinds* of pollution control (and of environmentally policies more broadly) are likely to be supported by capitalists and workers, respectively.

For instance, the kind of waste disposal that profitably relocates toxic wastes to high-poverty countries and regions does not qualify as sustainable production of use-values for human development; nor is it in the best interest of the working class even in the developed countries that generate the bulk of the wastes. By undermining environmental conditions in poor countries, it deepens their underdevelopment, poverty, and economic desperation, thereby fuelling workers' competitive race to the bottom under the pressure of transnational capital's control over investment, production, jobs, and (increasingly) state environmental and social policies.[65] What is needed is a change in production

---

[63] England (1986, p. 238) says that 'most emission control efforts are undertaken privately because of state regulations'. But he does not address the contradiction between the profitable sale of pollution-control services and his model's treatment of them as a deadweight loss.

[64] England 1986, p. 242 (emphasis in original).

[65] Brecher and Costello 1994.

technology toward greater quality and durability of the goods produced and less total waste generated by production itself. But such a change conflicts with the capitalist imperative to accumulate ever larger quantities of capital through the production and sale of commodities. That is why it can only occur in the context of workers and communities taking control of production and reorienting it toward sustainable human development.

By contrast with England's 1986 analysis, his 1982 article suggests that 'both workers and capitalists have an economic stake in the *imposition* of political limits on pollution'.[66] Nonetheless, it argues that workers and capitalists have 'a fundamental conflict of interests . . . over the *strictness* of pollution standards', with workers 'standing to gain more from stringent limits'.[67]

England develops this argument by extending a two-sector neoclassical aggregate supply and demand model to include pollution as well as the distinction between workers' wage income and capitalists' profit income. All variables in the model are expressed in real (inflation-adjusted) terms, so no changes in either relative prices or the overall price level are considered. Sector 1 produces a single commodity which can serve as either a consumption good or as an investment good, while Sector 2 produces waste treatment, recycling, and disposal services ('waste disposal' for short). Both sectors employ capital and labour inputs, and it is assumed that the economy's capital stock and labour force are 'fully employed and . . . can be instantaneously reallocated between the two sectors'.[68]

In addition, both sectors use 'environmental services' in the production of their respective outputs. These services are available for free, but their positive impact on production in each sector is negatively related to the level of pollution in the economy.[69] For both sectors, the negative effect of pollution on the productivity of environmental services is assumed to be 'nonlinear, i.e., negligible at low levels of pollution but increasingly severe with additional unit increases in its level'.[70] Pollution also has a positive and nonlinear impact on the rate of depreciation of the capital stock. In line with his 1980 analysis,

---

[66] England 1982, p. 39 (emphasis in original).
[67] Ibid.
[68] England 1982, p. 40.
[69] England 1982, pp. 39–40.
[70] England 1982, p. 40.

England also assumes that pollution has a negative and nonlinear impact on the supply of labour.

The pollution itself is generated by any expansion of Sector 1 production or of aggregate consumption, with the respective 'waste residual propensities' of production and consumption taken as given. At the same time, Sector 2's waste disposal services are defined in such a way that any increase of Sector 2 output represents a one-to-one reduction of the economy's pollution emissions. As England puts it, 'The output of the waste disposal sector is measured by the physical quantity of a homogenous waste material which is purified, recycled, or otherwise not discharged into the environment in a potentially costly form'.[71] Finally, the level of pollution is reduced by 'the (limited) ability of the environment to assimilate waste residuals costlessly', and this assimilation capacity is also taken as given.[72]

As in any aggregate supply and demand model with no government and no international trade, equilibrium requires that planned (gross) investment equals planned savings. Gross investment is equal to total Sector 1 output minus total consumption by workers and capitalists. Total planned savings are equal to workers' saving plus capitalist saving plus depreciation. Workers are assumed to save a given fraction of their wages and capitalists a given fraction of their profits. The distribution of net income (total income minus depreciation) is governed by a fixed ratio of profits to wages.[73]

Given full employment of capital and labour, the economy's possible equilibrium positions can be represented by a set of production possibilities frontiers showing different combinations of Sector 1 and Sector 2 output 'at various hypothetical levels of pollution'.[74] As pollution grows, the resultant

[71] England 1982, p. 39. This formulation may violate the second law thermodynamics. See Chapter 5's discussion of the controversy over complete recycling.
[72] England 1982, p. 40. England (1982, p. 44) says that his model 'assumes that unassimilated waste residuals do not persist in the environment after discharge'. But his pollution assimilation variable is actually equivalent to the pollution decay factor in his earlier analysis (England 1980, p. 167, equation 8). There is no reason why costless assimilation of waste could not apply to pollutants emitted in previous periods. Perhaps what prevents England from seeing this is the fact that the 1982 model is a one-period framework, whereas the 1980 model allows for 'a dynamic link between the present period and the previous period' (England 1980, p. 166).
[73] England 1982, p. 40.
[74] England 1982, p. 41. To avoid unnecessary complications, we define these frontiers in net output terms, that is, net of depreciation, unlike England (1982, p. 42) who first defines them in gross output terms and then adjusts his results for depreciation.

nonlinear impacts on environmental services, labour supply and depreciation cause the production possibilities frontier to move closer to the origin 'and increasingly dramatically so as additional unit increases in the level of pollution are hypothesized to take place'.[75] However, the actual feasibility of any given frontier depends on the assumption that 'sufficient waste disposal [is] undertaken to enforce the pollution level corresponding to that set of production possibilities'.[76] In other words, only one point on a given frontier is actually feasible: the one where Sector 2 output equals 'the amount of pollution abatement activity which would be necessary to realize a particular pollution ceiling'.[77]

According to England, this model represents a potential tradeoff from a capitalist perspective. Assuming that Sector 1 output is initially greater than or equal to the level at which the resulting pollution emissions can be fully assimilated by the environment, any further increases in production mean that 'more waste disposal output . . . would be required to counteract the greater volume of production- and consumption-related waste residuals'.[78] But, he says, any such increase in Sector 2 output means that less 'capital goods and labour skills . . . could be devoted to [Sector 1] commodity production'.[79] Given the nonlinear effects of pollution on production, England surmises that there is likely to be some intermediate level of pollution (and of Sector 2 activity) where Sector 1 output 'is at its maximum', which, he says, corresponds to maximum commodity output and (given the fixed profit/wage ratio) maximum profits.[80]

Drawing out the implications for environmental class conflict, England first argues that if the initial level of pollution happens to be greater than the intermediate level that maximizes Sector 1 output and profits, then 'no class conflict of interest would exist' since 'most workers and capitalists would stand to gain from the imposition of environmental standards'.[81] But if pollution happens to be lower than this intermediate level, 'proposals to tighten

---

[75] Ibid.
[76] England 1982, p. 41.
[77] Ibid.
[78] England 1982, p. 42.
[79] Ibid.
[80] England 1982, pp. 42–3.
[81] England 1982, p. 43.

environmental standards might provoke political disputes' because such a tightening entails a 'diversion of economic resources from commodity production'.[82] In this situation, 'the immediate improvements in environmental quality can come only at the expense of net commodity output foregone because of input transfers to waste disposal production'.[83] Workers, according to England, are more likely than capitalists to support such input transfers, the reason being that 'pollution affects workers' welfare in several other ways' besides reducing net commodity output.[84] Here, England cites not only adverse impacts on workers' health but also the possible accelerated depreciation of consumer durables, and declines in the aesthetic quality of affordable residential locations. In short, workers are more likely than capitalists to be 'willing to sacrifice a certain amount of commodity consumption in return for a sufficiently great improvement in environmental quality'.[85]

> The implication . . . is that a business coalition organized to maximize aggregate profits and a coalition of workers organized to maximize their collective welfare would differ politically over the desirable degree of strictness of environmental standards. Capitalists would prefer a higher level of pollution than that preferred by workers.[86]

This perspective is similar to the one in England's 1980 article, insofar as both analyses imply that environmental conflicts are not based simply on workers favouring pollution control and capitalists opposing it. In both analyses, pollution imposes economic costs on capitalists. In the 1980 article, pollution leads to rising labour costs, while the 1982 model also includes negative impacts on the environmental services used in production as well as accelerated capital depreciation. Hence, the respective analyses each represent increased pollution as a 'tradeoff' from a capitalist point of view: between increased profits from labour-saving technological change and the adverse labour supply effects of the resulting pollution (the 1980 analysis), or between increased pollution costs and reduced diversion of resources to waste disposal (the 1982 analysis). That the capitalist tradeoff dimension is developed more explicitly

---

[82] Ibid.
[83] Ibid.
[84] Ibid.
[85] England 1982, p. 43.
[86] England 1982, pp. 43–4.

in the 1982 article is a matter of presentation, not of analytical substance. In the 1986 Sraffian/Marxist analysis, on the other hand, the tradeoff dimension is completely absent due to the assumption that pollution control unambiguously reduces profits (for a given wage/profit ratio).

A crucial point here is that England's general perspective – as opposed to his formal models – does not reduce the effects of pollution on working-class welfare to changes in wages or private consumption levels.[87] Indeed, he emphasises that pollution's impacts on worker health and aesthetic well-being make class conflicts over the level of pollution control much more likely. The reason is obvious: for workers, labour-power and nature are conditions of human reproduction and development, whereas, for capital, they are just vehicles of competitive monetary accumulation.

As with England's 1980 and 1986 articles, however, his 1982 model formalises pollution and pollution control in a purely quantitative way, as a 'range of environmental quality targets' that are measured in terms of the levels of commodity production – net of waste disposal – that are consistent with their achievement.[88] This explains why class conflicts over the best level of pollution control are not structurally inevitable in his 1982 analysis, but, rather, depend on given assumptions about the technology of production, its pollution intensity, and the initial level of pollution compared to its profit-maximising level. It also explains why workers' environmental interests are reduced to a tradeoff between the production and consumption of commodities on the one hand, versus the (partly non-economic) benefits from reduced pollution on the other.

A more basic problem is that the neoclassical treatment of production causes England's 1982 model to fog over the alienation of workers from production and its natural conditions. As a result, his analysis side-steps the question of class conflicts over alternative forms (not just the level) of waste treatment/ recycling/disposal. It also bypasses the whole issue of waste *management* (through treatment, recycling, and disposal) versus waste *prevention* (through changes in production technologies, increased durability of goods, and a transformation of needs toward less matter-energy intensive needs). It avoids

[87] See also England 1987, pp. 120–2.
[88] England 1982, p. 39.

these questions partly by treating pollution and waste disposal in purely quantitative ways, but also by arbitrarily assuming that Sector 2's waste disposal activity generates no income, that is, does not take the form of commodity production for a profit. Instead, England assumes that the economy's gross value added (wages plus profits plus depreciation) is equal to the output of Sector 1.[89] This leads to much confusion in his argument that between the 'two extremes' of zero pollution and zero waste disposal activity, 'it is likely that gross commodity production would first rise and then decrease as environmental standards varied between their most stringent and most lenient values':[90]

> If pollution were prohibited entirely, the economy would enjoy its most extensive production possibilities since labor supply and environmental services would be at their respective maxima. Requiring zero pollution would also entail, however, the most extensive commitment of economic resources to pollution control activities. . . . If, on the other hand, no abatement were to take place, then the entire endowment of capital goods and labor skills in the economy could be devoted to commodity production. The size and productivity of this factor endowment would, however, be minimized by the relatively severe effects of pollution accompanying this resource allocation. As a result, production possibilities would be minimized by this choice of environmental policy.[91]

We are not told how Sector 2's waste disposal operations can enter into production possibilities, and employ both labour and capital which are bought and sold in markets, but not count as part of the system of commodity production. The closest England comes to an explanation is the following:

> The fact that net commodity output and aggregate profits are maximized at the same pollution standard reflects the fact that capitalists profit by hiring workers to produce commodities which can be appropriated for market sale, not by producing freely available goods such as environmental quality.[92]

---

[89] England 1982, p. 40, equation 10.
[90] England 1982, p. 42.
[91] Ibid.
[92] England 1982, pp. 42–3.

This statement ignores the fact that the model has Sector 2 'producing environmental quality' using labour and capital that are purchased on the market; hence environmental quality is *not* 'freely available'. It also directly contradicts England's observation that, between 1972 and 1978, 'current and capital account outlays on pollution abatement and control activities in the United States totalled $211 billion (in 1972 dollars)'.[93] England treats this expenditure as a pure cost, ignoring the fact that it also represents net value added and thus wages and profits for the enterprises producing the abatement and control activities. Using the same logic, one would have to exclude household and corporate expenditures on air conditioners, necessitated by overheated and polluted conditions in urban areas, from commodity production, value added, and income.

By treating waste disposal costs as a pure drain on commodity production and profits (ignoring the revenue side), England downgrades the possibility that capitalist waste management can profitably maintain the environmental quality needed to reproduce capitalism itself, even as it degrades the environment as a condition of human development. In effect, his formal model reduces the environmental use-value/exchange contradiction to a conflict between commodity production and environmental management. But, insofar as environmental management is itself a commodity produced for profit, the use-value/exchange-value contradiction appears as a contradiction between capitalist market-driven environmental management versus environmental management for sustainable human development. Environmental class conflict thus naturally extends to conflicts over alternative forms of waste disposal and prevention as determinants of the co-evolutionary development of humanity and nature.

IV. Weisskopf on environmental accumulation and legitimation crises

Weisskopf addresses crises in the natural and social environment using an informal model in which capital accumulation leads to some combination of environmental deterioration and rising 'real costs of social reproduction'.[94]

---

[93] England 1982, p. 43.
[94] Weisskopf 1991, p. 85.

The real costs take the form of 'maintenance activities' that are 'designed to prevent or counteract an intolerable augmentation of social tensions' and/or 'an intolerable decline in environmental quality'.[95] Weisskopf then defines 'real economic growth' as GNP growth net of environmental maintenance expenditures, depletion of non-renewable natural resources, *and* reductions in the quality of the natural and social environments.[96] He argues that capitalism's tendency to degrade its natural and social environments is registered in slow or even negative real economic growth, even with continued growth of production and income as measured by GNP.

Weisskopf projects two specific crisis scenarios out of the tendency for 'tensions to escalate over the way in which the burden of slow or negative real economic growth would be shared among different segments of society'.[97] The first scenario has 'growing pressures on the natural environment' reaching a point where 'the capacity of the environment to support continuing production might become severely impaired'.[98] Disruption of agriculture by global warming, or the depletion of oil and other nonrenewable resources, might '*reduce* the real output that can be produced with given inputs of labor and capital'.[99] This could threaten the growth in real per capita output and consumption needed 'for managing the social and economic tensions that would otherwise arise from the uneven and unstable pattern of economic development so characteristic of capitalism'.[100] 'Without the lubrication of long-run material growth, the potential tensions could easily get out of hand'.[101]

In the second crisis scenario, 'growing pressures on the natural environment are met by increasing expenditure on maintenance activities'.[102] According to Weisskopf,

> Such expenditures would require that a growing proportion of the real output generated by productive economic activity be withdrawn from activities contributing to an enhancement of people's welfare and be directed instead to activities preventing a decline in their welfare.[103]

---

95 Weisskopf 1991, pp. 85, 88.
96 Weisskopf 1991, pp. 82–4.
97 Weisskopf 1991, p. 85.
98 Weisskopf 1991, p. 84.
99 Ibid. (emphasis in original).
100 Weisskopf 1991, p. 85.
101 Ibid.
102 Ibid.
103 Ibid.

As a result, 'The true net output of the economy would grow more slowly, or possibly even decline, and the distribution of the burden of that decline would become a contentious issue'.[104]

Under either scenario, the actual crisis could take one of two forms: an accumulation crisis involving declining profits and investment, or, instead, a crisis of legitimation in which people increasingly demand a new kind of economic system dedicated more to human needs and less to profits. Which form is most prevalent will depend on the outcomes of distributional conflicts over the sharing of reductions in real material output per capita. Insofar as profits bear the burdens, the outcome will be an accumulation crisis. But, insofar as the burdens are borne by workers and communities while capital continues to accumulate, the crisis will be one of legitimation.[105] However, Weisskopf goes on to suggest that, insofar as a legitimation crisis only 'directly affects' the system's 'political structure', whereas in 'an accumulation crisis the economic structure of the capitalist system is directly affected', the latter is 'more certainly threatening to a capitalist society'.[106]

The two key distinctions in Weisskopf's framework are between measured (market-valued) and real (need-satisfying) economic growth, and between accumulation and legitimation crises. Both distinctions clearly imply that the environmental conditions required by capital accumulation differ from those needed for sustainable human development. Unfortunately, Weisskopf does not follow through on or develop this difference, and this weakens the power of his analysis. More specifically, he fails to distinguish those environmental maintenance activities/expenditures that reproduce the conditions of capital accumulation from those that reproduce and improve the environment as a

---

[104] Ibid.

[105] Weisskopf's framework is an adaptation of James O'Connor's 'fiscal crisis of the state' approach (O'Connor 1973). In O'Connor's analysis, government expenditures on 'social expenses' to alleviate various problems created by capital accumulation, together with ongoing government provision of the 'social capital' and 'social consumption' required for increasingly socialised capitalist production and labour-power reproduction, create a tendency for government expenditure to rise relative to GNP. The result is some combination of public-sector budgetary crises, accumulation problems, and legitimation crises. Weisskopf simplifies O'Connor's model by focusing on social expenses (or, as Weisskopf calls them, maintenance expenditures), bypassing the more pro-active role of social capital and social consumption expenditures in the capital accumulation process.

[106] Weisskopf 1991, pp. 89–90.

condition of human development. As a result, he treats maintenance expenditures (and the resulting reductions in real economic growth) as a singular quantitative burden that is shared among competing (capitalist and non-capitalist) claimants, without addressing conflicts over the forms of environmental maintenance activities. One aspect of this analytical gap is a failure to consider maintenance activities as opportunities for profitable capital accumulation, insofar as they can take the form of commodities produced by wage-labour. Conflicts are likely to arise between such profitable maintenance activities versus activities that, even if not privately profitable, help create and reproduce conditions for sustainable human development.

Rather than a Marxist deconstruction of the 'environmental maintenance' concept, Weisskopf's conception of real economic growth relies on a distinction between 'activities contributing to an enhancement of people's welfare' versus activities 'directed instead to . . . preventing a decline in their welfare'.[107] It is not clear if this distinction is a viable one, insofar as both labels could apply to virtually any commodified use-value entering into human reproduction under capitalism. For example, does an individual's purchase and use of an automobile enhance her welfare or prevent a decline in her welfare? The answer depends on whether one takes the spatial organisation of workplaces, residences, retailing and other facilities – and the availability of public transportation – as natural givens. Similar concerns would apply to air conditioners, personal computers, and other consumer appliances, especially with the planned obsolescence and 'keep up with the Jones's' effects connected with these commodities. Given the fundamental contradictions between human needs and production for profit, and between social production versus anarchic private competition and appropriation, virtually all household expenditures can be viewed as maintenance expenditures that, rather than enhancing welfare, prevent declines in welfare – and imperfectly at that.[108]

The root of Weisskopf's failure to develop a critical analysis of environmental maintenance lies in his narrowly economic interpretation of Marxian crisis

---

[107] Weisskopf 1991, p. 88.
[108] This applies even to food, where people's declining domestic self-sufficiency, due among other things to long worktimes and corporate marketing strategies, has created extremely unhealthy patterns of consumption in which food appears more as a debilitating narcotic than a culturally embedded source of life-renewal – especially in that most purely capitalist society, the United States.

theory.[109] Weisskopf sees concern about environmental deterioration and maintenance expenditures as more 'Polanyian' and 'Ricardian' than Marxian.[110] In Marx's view, however, the social separation of workers from necessary conditions of production, and the employment of these conditions and workers' labour-power to produce marketable commodities for a profit, are defining characteristics of capitalism. A consistent Marxist perspective threfore sees both accumulation crises *and* crises of legitimation as *always* environmental crises in the sense that they are an outgrowth of: (i) workers' alienation from production and its natural and social conditions, and (ii) the use of natural and social conditions to extract surplus-value from workers and to objectify this surplus-value in vendible commodities.[111]

Bypassing capitalist alienation and its close relationship with capitalist exploitation, Weisskopf reduces environmental crises to a quantitative 'decline in the availability of real economic benefits to be shared among the competing claimants'.[112] He misses the close connection between legitimation crises and capitalist alienation, in other words, the roots of the system's anti-human and anti-ecological priorities in the class relation between capital and labour. His narrowly economic conception of class manifests itself in the strange assertion that despite 'the deterioration of the natural environment and the social environment', when considered 'in terms of its ability to deliver the goods, modern capitalism appears to have a great deal of life left in it'.[113] Here, 'delivering the goods' is artificially separated from the whole realm of communal (natural and social) use-values, faithfully reproducing capitalism's own mystification of all non-market realms as somehow 'external' to capitalist reality.

Indeed, despite his vague appeals to Polanyi and Ricardo, Weisskopf's explanation of the system's environmental problems closely follows the 'externalities' perspective of neoclassical theory. Observing that 'environmental costs of production are largely external to the profit-maximizing calculus of individual firms', he suggests that 'the kind of comprehensive planning

---

[109] Burkett 1999a, Chapter 12.
[110] Weisskopf 1991, p. 86.
[111] Compare Foster 2000a.
[112] Weisskopf 1991, p. 85.
[113] Weisskopf 1991, pp. 71, 77.

necessary to ensure ecologically sound resource use is anathema to capitalist free marketeers'.[114] This perspective does not relate the apparently 'external' character of environmental costs to the system's class relations.[115] Nor does it adequately oppose the neoclassical view that the best solution is simply to extend market pricing to the environment. Weisskopf's preference for 'comprehensive planning' over the market is purely technocratic; he therefore phrases the resolution of environmental crises as a trade-off between individual rights (as represented by the market) and the collective good:

> To bring about a significant improvement in the natural and social environments, however, the socioeconomic system would have to be restructured to the point where its fundamental logic was transformed. . . . The sovereignty of the individual would have to yield much ground to the interests of the community, and effective mechanisms for making collective decisions democratically would need to be developed as viable alternatives to individual choice.[116]

In sum, Weisskopf associates the market with individual free choice and politics with collective choices that reduce individual sovereignty. He thus concludes that the movement toward a more sustainable economy must come at the expense of individual sovereignty – as if the capitalist market system, with its treadmill of work and commodified consumption, and its creation of an ever more stultifying environment, actually serves individual freedom and self-development. The purportedly inherent contradiction between individuality and community plays into the hands of capitalism's defenders especially insofar as individual sovereignty is identified with the market, and community interests with comprehensive state planning. Such are the limits of grafting the 'externalities' view of environmental problems onto a narrowly economistic interpretation of Marxism.

---

[114] Weisskopf 1991, p. 78.

[115] Similarly, as per the social environment, we are told that: 'The more complex and interrelated the social and economic system becomes, the more stress is put on social relations among people and the greater the difficulty of maintaining the social environment. This trend is surely intensified by market-oriented forms of capitalism, as compared with welfare-state systems' (Weisskopf 1991, pp. 87–8). Class relations are nowhere to be found.

[116] Weisskopf 1991, p. 91.

V. A more holistic Marxist perspective

A prominent theme in this and the preceding two chapters has been the failure of environmental crisis and conflict models to consistently distinguish crises of capital accumulation and crises of human development. Yet, this distinction is arguably implied by several important currents in ecological economics.

For example, among ecological economists it is now widely accepted that the concept of ecological 'carrying capacity . . . has an important normative and institutional component'.[117] It follows that any 'judgement of an environmental situation or the decision of limits . . . is influenced by value-judgements and institutional settings'.[118] This means, among other things, that 'sustainable development' is specific to the set of values and institutions whose reproduction is to be sustained. Kenneth Boulding's distinction between the 'cowboy' and 'spaceman' economies is relevant here.[119] While the cowboy perspective treats the global environment as infinitely large relative to the scale of economic activity, the spaceman perspective recognises that 'the earth has become a single spaceship, without unlimited resources of anything, either for extraction or for pollution, and in which, therefore, man must find his place in a cyclical ecological system'.[120] If one adds that capitalism can reproduce itself on the basis of a progressively degraded environment (on which more below), then it becomes clear that the cowboy/spaceman dichotomy mirrors the distinction between capitalist development and sustainable human development as alternative forms of economy-environment interaction. The co-evolutionary concept of 'Noösphere' allows us to take this distinction one step further.[121] Kenneth Stokes provides a useful description of this concept and its implications, based on the work of the Soviet scientist Vladimir Vernadsky:

> The term Noösphere is composed from two Greek words: 'noos', mind, and sphere, in the sense of an envelope of Earth. The emergence of the Noösphere refers to a stage in the evolution of the Biosphere in which man becomes

---

[117] Seidl and Tisdell 1999, pp. 401–2.
[118] Seidl and Tisdell 1999, p. 402.
[119] Boulding 1966.
[120] Boulding 1966, p. 9; compare Boulding 1978, p. 291.
[121] See Chapter 10 for further discussion of co-evolutionary approaches to sustainable development.

aware of his capacity to influence the further course of evolution. Moreover, it represents a stage in which the power of technological systems is restructured to renounce that form of rationality that has spawned the technological imperative – an unthinking destruction of nature – in favor of a substantive form of rationality that supports the cultivation of the inner aspirations of life. For Vernadsky, this conscious influence itself signaled a new era in the evolution of the Biosphere.[122]

Insofar as capitalism is the system that has produced the 'the unthinking destruction of nature' on a biospheric scale, the Noöspheric choice between destructive and life-affirming forms of rationality parallels the distinction between sustainable capitalism and sustainable human development.

The same distinction is evident in the growing body of theoretical and empirical work by ecological economists that questions whether increased consumption of commodities always increases the welfare of households. Lintott, for example, argues that 'once basic material needs are satisfied, it is an individual's relative, not absolute, consumption that counts for his or her welfare', so that 'in rich countries increases in consumption do not, in the aggregate, lead to improvements in overall welfare'.[123] Indeed, insofar as increased consumption is driven by households striving to maintain their relative consumption position, it may pressure households to increase their worktimes, placing them on a 'treadmill' of work and consumption that *reduces* their welfare.[124] The depletion and degradation of natural resources connected with the increased production, consumption, and disposal of commodities makes such a negative welfare impact all the more likely.

Bartolini and Bonatti develop this argument by observing that, in market economies, 'the growth mechanism is a substitution process based on the destruction of non-market goods'.[125] In their formal model, household welfare (utility) is related to the consumption of commodities and of non-market environmental use-values. But environmental use-values are degraded as more commodities are produced, due to the use of the environment as a sink for the pollution generated by producing firms. As the environment deteriorates,

---

122 Stokes 1994, p. 5.
123 Lintott 1998, p. 242.
124 Schor 1992.
125 Bartolini and Bonatti 2002, p. 3.

households respond by increasing their consumption of commodities, which requires that they increase their worktimes. (The increased private consumption could be described as a 'defensive expenditure' against the effects of pollution, urban overcrowding, and so on, on household welfare.) In this way, 'each household contributes to a further increase in aggregate production, thus causing additional damage to the [environment] and feeding the growth process'.[126] Put differently, 'growth is driven by its own destructive power', so that 'the declining endowment of free resources can boost economic growth'.[127] Economic growth, in the sense of increased production and consumption of commodities, thus winds up reducing household welfare, although institutions and cultural attitudes help determine the strength of this result. Hence, 'one could speculate that in a society dominated by a consumerist life-style and by a strong work ethic the level of market activities will be higher and the quality of the social assets will be lower than in a society in which consumerism and work ethic are weaker'.[128]

The distinction between systemic and human developmental crises is thus reasonably well grounded in ecological economics. But the analytical power and political resonance of this distinction have been held back by a lack of attention to the social relations of production, that is, by a failure to 'name the system'. To point out the ecological limitations of markets without reference to production relations is a bootless exercise insofar as pro-ecological forms of exchange, distribution, and valuation must be rooted in new kinds of production relationships by which workers and communities gain more effective control (limiting power) over their appropriation, processing, and circulation of natural wealth. Moreover, insofar as ecological conflicts concern irreconcilable claims on an economy's surplus product, their analysis requires

---

[126] Bartolini and Bonatti 2002, p. 2.
[127] Bartolini and Bonatti 2002, p. 3.
[128] Bartolini and Bonatti 2002, p. 2. Along the same lines, Magnani (2000, p. 432) suggests that increases in income inequality might lead to further increases in market activity at the expense of the environment 'by reducing the demand for pollution abatement'. Greater inequality, and attendant demonstration effects of consumption by affluent households, may increase desired private consumption levels among less affluent households relative to their willingness to pay for environmental protection. Magnani finds support for this hypothesis from data for OECD countries over the years 1980–91, which reveal negative correlations between income inequality measures and public research and development expenditures earmarked for environmental protection.

some explanation of the social *and* material origins, specific social forms, and *conflictual nature*, of this surplus product – none of which can be undertaken without a clear specification of the class relations of production. Finally, analysis of production relationships is needed to identify, and intervene on behalf of, the social agency (or agencies) capable of leading the movement toward a more sustainable and human developmental economic system.

The contribution of Marxism is clearest with regard to the origins and nature of the surplus product. The Marxist perspective recognises that all surplus production (production over and above that needed to maintain the current level of production) has a natural basis, namely, natural conditions enabling human labourers to produce more than they consume. At the most basic level, this boils down to environmental conditions that enable some workers to produce more food than is needed for their own survival. In this respect, at least, Marxist theory agrees with the physiocrats' insistence on the natural basis of all wealth (see Chapter 1). However, unlike the physiocrats, Marxists distinguish between this natural basis and the specific social forms of the surplus product. In class (exploitative) societies, the production of a surplus product involves *forced labour* on the part of the direct producers, that is, a situation in which workers involuntarily labour beyond the time needed to produce their means of subsistence. And workers' submission to this forced labour is underpinned by their social separation from control over necessary conditions of production, above all from the land. The most extreme form of such class separation is capitalism, in which workers are socially dislodged from productive access to necessary conditions of production outside the wage-labour relationship, so that forced labour takes the mystifying form of 'paid' labour beyond the time needed to produce the commodities purchased with wages.[129]

---

[129] Bartolini and Bonatti (2002, p. 3) observe that the market system's growth, 'fueled by a diminution of free consumption' of environmental goods, was historically enabled by 'the commercialization of land and leisure', that is, by the forcible separation of workers from the land and their conversion into wage-labourers purchasing commodified means of subsistence (compare Marx 1981, Vol. I, Chapters 26–33). Yet their formal model assumes that all households share equally in firms' profits, that is, that no class distinctions exist (Bartolini and Bonatti 2002, p. 7, equation 1d). The role of workers' alienation from the means of production is further hidden by their assumption that labour is the sole productive input (Bartolini and Bonatti 2002, p. 7, equation 3). As a result, they end up blaming environmentally destructive and welfare-detracting growth on culturally based co-ordination failures rather than the class relations of production.

The ecological potential of the Marxist perspective stems from the fact that it does not artificially separate a material realm of production from a social realm of exchange and distribution. Rather, it sees class relations as material-social relations, and therefore as specific forms of economy-environment interaction. Class-exploitation is seen as both a social and an environmental relation *of production*, one based on the producers' alienation from necessary conditions of production including natural conditions – and not simply as a problem of unequal distribution. Marketisation of exchange and distribution is itself seen as a material and social outgrowth of this underlying class relation. The commodification of wealth only reaches its full development on the basis of the commodification of labour-power.

Marketisation is not the only possible exchange-form of the wage-labour relation, however. Capitalist production also relies on *free appropriation* of environmental use-values possessing communal characteristics, insofar as these use-values serve as conditions for extracting the natural force of human labour-power and objectifying this force as surplus-value in commodities.[130] The exact pattern of wealth commodification and free appropriation is historically contingent on changes in productive technology, new product development, and the spatial outlay of production, all shaped by competitive struggles among capitalists and landowners both in markets and over the régime of property rights. The class struggle, too, shapes the extent to which natural wealth is commodified and explicitly converted into capital, as well as the extent to which capital's free appropriation of communal wealth is regulated on behalf of workers and communities.

At the heart of Marx's critique of capitalism, as Foster has demonstrated, is the metabolic rift between society and nature produced by the alienation of workers from the conditions of production and the development of these conditions as means of capital accumulation.[131] The combined simplification and degradation of labour and nature, mentioned earlier in this chapter, is a primary mechanism of this rift. Another mechanism is the division of labour between urban manufacturing industry and industrialised agriculture, which disrupts the circulation of matter and energy required for a healthy and

---

[130] Burkett 1999a, Chapter 6, and 1999c.
[131] Foster 2000a.

sustainable metabolic reproduction of human-natural eco-systems.[132] Nowadays the production and disposal of bio-nondegradeables, and biospheric disruptions such as the ozone and global warming problems, must be added to the growing list of metabolic rift mechanisms.[133]

All these mechanisms can be seen as outgrowths of the divergence between the material conditions required and produced by capital accumulation and the consciously co-evolutionary conditions that would be produced by an economic system dedicated to sustainable human development. Capitalist reproduction does not care about co-evolution; it only cares about its continued access to productive labour-power and material use-values enabling labour-power's exploitation (including conditions allowing labour to be objectified in vendible commodities). The co-evolutionary connection between these socially separated, human and extra-human, production inputs does not concern either the individual competing capitalist or the capitalist class as a whole: they are only concerned with how people and their environment can be used as inputs, and to create markets, for commodity production. Capitalists only broach environmental initiatives insofar as they are consistent with healthy profit-and-loss statements and maintenance of their economic and political power. As shown by Earth Day, the ideology of green capitalism, and big business and government (non)responses to global warming, there is no shortage of subterfuges and figleafs that capitalists and their functionaries can use to deflect attention from the fundamental contradiction between environmental health and the exploitative and competitive pursuit of abstract wealth.

Stated differently, the tension between the system's economic signals and the environment is not a matter of 'missing markets'. The problem is that the economic signals and incentives generated by the wage-labour relation do not, and cannot, encompass the requirements of a healthy and sustainable economy-environment interaction. They can only encompass the environmental requirements of value accumulation with all its ecological contradictions. No matter how efficient, complete, or undistorted the price system may be, there is no way that its one-dimensional measuring rod of money can be an adequate

---

[132] Marx 1981, Vol. I, Chapter 15, Section 10.
[133] Burkett 1999a, pp. 128–32; Clark and York 2004.

measure of, or guide to, the sustainable production of use-values by human labour enmeshed with nature. There is no way that the system can reverse its anti-ecological reduction of wealth to abstract labour, or the dominance of markets and money over life-values. A system based on exploitation of labour must also exploit nature. A more ecologically sensitive system would have to overcome the separation of workers and communities from the conditions of production and put sustainable human development, not money and capital, in command of production.

The social separation of workers from natural conditions, and the divergence of capitalism's material requirements from the co-evolutionary requirements of sustainable human development, are manifested in two distinct kinds of environmental crisis. In the first kind of crisis, capital accumulation is threatened by environmental constraints on supplies of its requisite material use-values. Examples include nineteenth-century cotton crises, as well as more recent oil and other materials-price shocks. The second kind of environmental crisis involves capitalism's degradation of the conditions of human development. As mentioned above, Marx studied this second kind of crisis in connection with the unhealthy circulations of matter produced by capitalism's spatial separation and industrial integration of manufacturing and agriculture. He also saw capital's tendency to deplete human labour-power through long and intensive working times as a direct threat to human reproduction and development.[134]

Marxists have analysed capitalism's historical dynamics in terms of the complex interactions between these two kinds of crisis on national and global scales. Westra suggests that the transition to 'mass consumption' capitalism can be understood as an outgrowth of the accumulation and human development crises associated with early industrial capitalism's extended and intensive working times.[135] Capitalists responded to working time legislation and labour-power shortages by stepping up the mechanisation of production. The resulting increases in labour productivity generated more massive streams of commodities to be sold *and* created a material basis for increases in real wages within a rising rate of exploitation, thereby creating the motivation

[134] Burkett 1999a, Chapter 10.
[135] Westra 2003.

and the means for developing mass working-class markets.[136] That increases in labour productivity were largely obtained through the installation of machine-systems reinforced the mass consumption imperative, seeing as how expanding sales were a condition for competitive accelerations in the turnover of such fixed capital stocks.[137]

In short, mechanised mass consumption capitalism was in large part the system's corrective, self-reproductive response to its own threat to one of its essential conditions: the natural force of human labour-power. But this response had its own ecological contradictions. In the context of competitive, profit-driven production, the development and application of machine-systems meant a quantitative leap in, and qualitatively new forms of, ecologically disruptive throughputs of materials and energy. New means of production and new consumer goods were developed simply and solely according to their potential profitability. The result was a new crisis in the conditions of human development. One prominent form of this crisis was the *waste crisis*. However, the most common response to this waste crisis, recycling, was limited by the producers' alienation from necessary conditions of production. Household recycling thus came to be defined largely as an individual environmental lifestyle choice having little bearing on the overall system of production.[138] It even became a growth industry in its own right, using up larger and larger flows of matter and energy in its own operations, and generating its own noxious forms of waste – such waste being for the most part conveniently located in underdeveloped countries and less affluent locales in the developed countries.[139] Indeed, the recycling industry has become a victim of its own capitalist success, with its profitability disrupted by periodic and secular patterns of overproduction of recycled materials. In short, recycling of household goods has been integrated into, and limited by, the system of mechanised mass production and consumption that is at the root of the waste problem. Little if anything has been done to inhibit the massive flows of

---

[136] Fine (1992, pp. 133–42) adds that the market for household consumer goods was shaped by the partial withdrawal of women and children from the wage-labour market under the combined influence of patriarchy, rising adult-male wages, and child-labour regulations.

[137] Compare Burkett 1999a, pp. 170–2.

[138] Horton 1995; Strasser 1999.

[139] Huws 1999.

matter-energy throughput associated with the competitive and profit-driven scrapping of machines and structures long before the end of their natural lives.[140]

On the world-historical level, Marxists have shown how the initial expansion of merchant, and then industrial, capital accumulation in the developed centres of the world capitalist system produced environmental crises of human development in the peripheral zones used as sources of raw materials. Variegated eco-systems in the periphery were plundered and converted into monocultural systems to disastrous effect. The case of the 'sugar frontier' is well described by Jason Moore:

> The sugar frontier was a fundamental moment of the transition to capitalism during the 'long' sixteenth century. It was the classic instance of capitalism's 'metabolic rift', whereby the nutrient cycling between town and country is progressively disrupted, leading to ecological exhaustion in the countryside and worsening 'pollution' in the cities. . . . The sugar frontier was such an intensively transformative historical structure because sugar monoculture rapidly exhausted soil fertility through a process of highly unequal, and very rapid, ecological exchange. . . . Nutrients were pumped out of one ecosystem in the periphery and transferred to another in the core. In essence, the land was progressively mined, until its relative exhaustion fettered profitability, whereupon capital was forced to seek out fresh lands, the incorporation of which inaugurated a new phase of capitalist development on a world scale.[141]

The sugar example illustrates a repeating pattern in the geographical development of the capitalist world-system: environmental crises of capital accumulation leading to new spatial expansions of capitalism and new capitalist appropriations of natural wealth, which, in turn, create new crises in the conditions of human development while setting the stage for future accumulation crises. As Moore puts it, 'capitalism's relationship to nature developed discontinuously over time as recurrent ecological crises have formed a decisive moment of world capitalist crisis, forcing successive waves of

---

[140] Horton 1997.
[141] Moore 2000b, pp. 413–14, 429.

restructuring over long historical time'.[142] An example analysed by Foster and
Clark is the crisis of mid-nineteenth-century 'British "high farming"'.[143] This
'early industrialized agriculture', developed on the basis of the forcible
separation of the peasantry from the land, 'robbed the soil of England of its
nutrients, and then sought to compensate for this by robbing other countries
of the means to replace them'.[144] More specifically, guano and nitrates were
imported from Peru and Chile, whose economies became trapped in the
familiar peripheral pattern of dependence on raw material exports and rising
external debt.[145]

For the native populations of the peripheral areas being conquered by
capitalism, the system's expansion was experienced as the most extreme and
brutal forms of metabolic rift: complete dispossession from formerly communal
lands, mass exterminations, and enslavement in monocultural production
and/or household servitude. 'The genocide inflicted on the indigenous
populations went hand in hand with the seizure of wealth in the new world'.[146]
As Marx described it:

> The discovery of gold and silver in America, the extirpation, enslavement
> and entombment in mines of the indigenous population of that continent,
> the beginnings of the conquest and plunder of India, and the conversion of
> Africa into a preserve for the commercial hunting of blackskins, are all things
> which characterize the dawn of the era of capitalist production. . . . The
> treatment of the indigenous population was, of course, at its most frightful

[142] Moore 2000a, p. 123. Elsewhere, in extending Fernand Braudel's world-historical framework to incorporate the Marxist metabolic rift approach, Moore (2003, p. 453) shows that 'merchant capital's imposition of monocultures on island political ecologies induced radical transformations of land, labour, and society. Ecology was implicated in imperialist expansion and social inequality. Socio-ecological contradictions in fur trade, in mining, and even in grain cultivation induced successive waves of restructuring and geographical expansion'.
[143] Foster and Clark 2004, p. 233.
[144] Ibid.
[145] Foster and Clark 2004, pp. 233–4. The conditions faced by the labourers employed in guano extraction were truly horrific: 'Loading the guano into ships required digging into deep mounds of excrement that covered rocky islands. Acrid dust penetrated the eyes, the nose, the mouth of a worker, and the stench was appalling. After slavery was abolished in 1854 tens of thousands of Chinese coolies were contracted for through Macau and Hong Kong. By 1875 some 80,000 were working under conditions of virtual slavery in the desert and islands of Peru' (Foster and Clark 2004, p. 234).
[146] Foster and Clark 2004, p. 232.

in plantation-colonies set up exclusively for the export trade, such as the West Indies, and in rich and well-populated countries, such as Mexico and India, that were given over to plunder. . . . The treasures captured outside Europe by undisguised looting, enslavement and murder flowed back to the mother-country and were turned into capital there.[147]

Through such violent and super-exploitative processes, capitalism 'progressively deepens the world-historical character of microlevel socio-ecologies in the interests of the ceaseless accumulation of capital, which generates geometrically rising pressures for ceaseless global expansion'.[148] The current era of 'globalisation' is just the latest example of this broader eco-historical dynamic of capital accumulation and imperialism.

Every phase of capitalist development entails a new, more expansive and more intensive, exploitative relation to the land. . . . As a consequence, capitalism's recurrent crises have called forth new and ever more ruthless forms of dominating the earth – thus we have moved from the colonization of the New World in the 16th century to the colonization of the genome in the 20th.[149]

The co-evolutionary, open-system dimension of Marxism is on full display in Moore's thermodynamic interpretation of world capitalist history:

The opening of the world-scale metabolic rift in the sixteenth century meant that capital could not survive as a 'closed cycle system', to borrow a phrase from ecology. . . . Capitalism's dependence on external resources rises over time, as it requires ever larger energy inputs in order to reproduce itself. As a result, the system experiences a geometrically increasing 'energy density' that today is fast approaching natural limits, as capital hogs an ever-larger share of the world's energy for itself, leaving an ever-smaller share for the planet's (nonhuman) residents. As long as capitalism did not encompass the entire globe, these natural limits could be overcome by geographical expansion and to a lesser extent by a shift to capital-intensive agriculture, although the possibility of the latter ultimately depended on the success of the former.[150]

---

[147] Marx 1981, Vol. I, pp. 915, 917–18.
[148] Moore 2003, p. 447.
[149] Moore 2001, pp. 136–7.
[150] Moore 2000b, pp. 429–30.

Although Marxist world-ecological perspectives have not yet been distilled into formal mathematical models of the type surveyed in the present and preceding chapters, they are sufficient to establish the exploitative character and historical limits of capitalism as a co-evolutionary life-process. They show how environmental crises of capital accumulation have been resolved in ways that deepen the metabolic rift between the producers and their material conditions. Marxist historiography thus supports the growing number of ecological economists who see capitalism's one-dimensional monetary measuring rod, and derivative 'adjustments' of prices and GDP, as hopelessly inadequate representations of environmental use-values.[151] Only direct and multi-dimensional measures of natural wealth and human health can properly inform the evaluation of capitalism's ecological contradictions as well as the movement toward a consciously noöspheric economy guided by life-values.

The Marxist metabolic rift approach adds a much-needed systemic dimension to non-Marxist co-evolutionary perspectives on the conflict between economic growth and sustainable life-values. This conflict can now be seen as not just an industrial or cultural problem, or even as a manifestation of the inadequate reach of market signals, but rather as an inherent outgrowth of the capitalistic alienation of the producers from necessary conditions of production. As such, it implicates the entire system of capitalist production and can only be overcome if this system is transformed at its very roots, through a disalienation of the conditions of production vis-à-vis the producers and their communities.

Marxism also provides a systemic perspective on the possibility of such a radical change in production relations. The very development of ecological and biospheric ways of thinking is itself largely a product of capitalism's development and socialisation of production into a globalised whole. Biospheric disruptions, and the evident need for noöspheric ways of thinking more in tune with life-values, are inseparable from capitalism's appropriation and encouragement of scientific discoveries, however distorted its productive applications of science have been from the standpoint of sustainable human development. But the positive life-potential of scientific knowledge and co-evolutionary thinking can only be realised insofar as life-values guide the whole system of production from its industrial base on through its

---

[151] See Chapters 2 and 4 for further discussion.

infrastructures of exchange, distribution, culture, and science itself. The only potential transformative agency that combines these productive and broader reproductive dimensions in its own life-activity is the working class and its communities.

The working class is the only agency whose everyday life-activities and (individual and collective) struggles are rooted in, but not limited to, capitalism's dominant form of productive activity: wage-labour and capital accumulation. It is the only systemically essential group that directly experiences the limitations of purely economic struggles over wages and working conditions as ways of achieving human development, given the increasingly communal and global character of the environmental problems produced by capitalist production. It is, therefore, the only agency capable not just of envisioning but of practically undertaking a planned and life-guided recombination of economic and environmental reproduction. But to lead this project it must struggle not just for a de-marketisation of production and its necessary conditions, but for its own collective taking, holding, and utilisation of these conditions and their conversion into means of sustaining human development. This includes a practical grasp of scientific knowledge.[152] Without such a thoroughgoing disalienation, which necessarily involves a long historical epoch of struggle, the de-marketisation of production will only lead to new forms of alienation and capitalisation, and new forms of the metabolic rift, as occurred, for instance, in the Soviet Union.

---

[152] Wallis 2004.

Chapter Ten

Marxism, Ecological Economics, and Sustainable Human Development

This chapter reconsiders the contribution Marxism can make to the debate over sustainable development within ecological economics. As noted in Chapter 4, although many ecological economists interpret sustainable development through the conceptual lens of 'natural capital', this approach has not been embraced by all members of the discipline. Accordingly, Section I of the present chapter maps out three broader dimensions or elements of sustainable development thinking in ecological economics: (i) the *common-pool* character of natural resources as conditions of human development now and in the future; (ii) the *co-evolutionary* approach to individual human beings, society, and nature; (iii) the need for, and functional requirements of, *common property* in natural resources. It is suggested that even though elements (ii) and (iii) share a common root in element (i), they have not been adequately integrated. Human developmental considerations, which are central to the co-evolutionary approach, have been largely absent from, or treated in non-holistic and/or non-evolutionary ways by, common property analyses. Meanwhile, co-evolutionary theorists have not paid nearly enough attention to the potential role of production relationships, specifically common property management, in sustainable development. This non-integration of basic elements in sustainable development theory partly reflects the ongoing influence of pro-market views as a reference point within ecological economics.

Based on Marx and Engels's writings on postcapitalist society, Section II illustrates how a Marxist focus on production relations as material-social relations can enhance the integration of the three basic dimensions of sustainable development. All-round human development is shown to be the central consideration in Marx and Engels's projections of communist property, planning, and non-market resource allocation. The co-evolutionary character of human development under Marx and Engels's communism is evidenced in its treatment of the land as a common-pool resource, its commitment to environmental management of land use in the interest of future generations, and its diversification of human needs and capabilities in less matter-energy intensive and more natural scientific and aesthetic directions. The chapter concludes by briefly linking the sustainable human development interpretation of communism with worker-community struggles in and against capitalism. This demonstrates once again the historical openness of the ecological-Marxist vision of institutions and policies.

I. Three dimensions of sustainable development

In the most general sense, 'sustainable development . . . can be interpreted as economic development that is consistent with long-term stable environmental quality and resource availability'.[1] As the 1987 Brundtland Report of the World Commission on Environment and Development puts it: 'Sustainable development is development that meets the needs of the present without compromising the ability of future generations to meet their own needs'.[2] This broad definition leaves room for a diversity of perspectives on the meaning of environmental quality and resource availability, and on *what kinds* of present and future needs should be satisfied. Hence, although *'sustainable development* has over a quite short period of time become the dominant concept in the study of interactions between the economy and the biophysical

---

[1] Mulder and Van Den Bergh 2001, p. 110.
[2] Quoted by Rao 2000, p. 85.

environment, as well as a generally accepted goal of environmental policy',
its theoretical and practical significance is still controversial.[3]

Within this diversity and controversy, however, it remains the case that the
starting point for all conceptions of sustainable development is a vision of
how natural limits could – in the absence of appropriate adjustments in
resource use – make development unsustainable. It is from this initial vision
of environmental constraints that different views on the behavioural and
institutional requirements of sustainable development are largely derived.
Accordingly, the present sketch begins by outlining how ecological economists
have specified the natural conditions and limits of economic development.

Nature as a common-pool resource for human development

As a meta-paradigm, ecological economics encompasses diverse views on the
natural limits to economic development. But one element shared by all these
perspectives is the treatment of the environment, in whole or in major part,
as a *common-pool* resource. The 'pool' aspect refers to the fact that the
overexploitation of natural resources reduces their availability now and in
the future.[4] Of course, overexploitation and, conversely, sustainable exploitation,
require specific definitions depending on the particular resources in question.
Mulder and Van Den Bergh, while recognising the conceptual problems this
involves, nonetheless refer to 'a broad consensus' that sustainable development

> means that economic activities should be consistent with . . . protection of
> ecosystem features and functions, preservation of biological diversity, a level
> of harmful emissions remaining below critical (assimilative) thresholds, and
> avoidance of irreversible damage to the environment and nature. Non-
> renewable resources pose some difficulties. . . . One can choose to reduce

---

[3] Mulder and Van Den Bergh 2001, p. 111 (emphasis in original). See Rao 2000 for
a useful survey of alternative conceptions of sustainable development. The conflicts
between pro-business and pro-ecological interpretations of sustainable development
are well documented by Jamison 2001 and Bond 2002.

[4] Feeny et al. 1990, p. 3. Common *pool* is not an altogether pleasing terminology
insofar as it may bring to mind the image of nature as an inventory-stock, similar to
the natural-capital analogy that was criticised in Chapter 4. We nonetheless employ
the term due to its use in the literature and because it is far superior to the phrase
'common property resources' that one often finds (Gordon 1954; Wade 1987). The
latter term conflates resource characteristics with property systems, generating much
confusion.

their use as much as possible, oriented towards a long-run goal of being completely independent of them. This can be based on investments in renewable alternatives (depending on the potential uses, e.g., supplying energy or materials) and technological progress in general (materials and energy efficiency increases in production and consumption).[5]

One's conception of sustainable resource exploitation is clearly influenced by one's presumptions about the feasibility of finding and/or manufacturing substitute resources. Broadly speaking, ecological economists are sceptical about such substitution possibilities.[6] For some, this scepticism is based on the ultimate scarcity of low-entropy matter and energy, or on other biospheric limits that may be broached by the matter-energy throughput produced by the economy (see Chapter 5). Others point out that the uniqueness of plant and animal species, and the complexity and interrelatedness of the eco-systems with which they co-evolve, effectively render these species and systems unreproducible once they have been eradicated and/or damaged by human production, consumption, and waste disposal. Moreover, if species and eco-systems have an intrinsic value *as they have co-evolved historically*, then they are irreplaceable from an ethical standpoint even if they could somehow be 'mimicked' by human industry.

Ultimately, however, the notions of resource overexploitation and substitution must be informed by the 'common' aspect of nature as a common-pool resource. As developed by ecological economists, this communal dimension involves more than just the fact that the overexploitation of natural resources reduces their availability. It also asserts that access to the resources in question, or to the (material and immaterial) goods and services produced by/with these resources, is a non-trivial element of the welfare of all human beings now or in the future. The presumption is that any closure of such access represents a reduction in the welfare of the people affected, and that this applies even if these people have not *heretofore* exercised such access – *so long as they might wish to in the future*. In other words, natural resources are 'public goods' insofar as their availability shapes and constrains the *life opportunities* of all human beings, even in those cases where a resource is not currently

[5] Mulder and Van Den Bergh 2001, p. 111.
[6] Costanza 1989.

used by all.[7] This view defines overexploitation as any depletion or damaging of resources that reduces peoples' life opportunities, taking the human manufacture of substitute resources into account. To qualify as sustainable, development must ensure a quantity and quality of natural resources sufficient to maintain non-decreasing life opportunities to all people within and across generations.[8]

From this perspective, the neoclassical notion of discounting the value of future consumption compared to current consumption arbitrarily excludes the life opportunity constraints imposed by resource overexploitation. Stated in terms of natural-capital theory, it presumes that manufactured capital can substitute for natural capital in a way that does not reduce the quantity, quality, and variety of human life opportunities. But, from the standpoint of ecological economics, such substitution is ultimately impossible; hence discounting merely translates resource overexploitation into an exploitation of future generations by current generations. In this sense, 'a positive discount rate goes against the very notion of environmental sustainability'.[9]

The life opportunities approach to sustainable development nicely encapsulates both the 'common' character and the dynamic diversity of environment as a condition for the development of all human beings. But it also calls for a vision of the *kinds* of life opportunities – the kinds of individual human development – that are consistent with ecological sustainability. And any such vision must have two sides: a positive side that sets out the basic elements of the pro-ecological 'good life' and of the movement toward it; and a proscriptive side that envisions how the exploitation of natural resources will be constrained so as to make possible improvements in life opportunities for all. Within ecological economics, co-evolutionary theorists have taken the lead in developing the positive side, while common property theorists have done the most to envision the proscriptive side.

---

[7] Phillips 1993, p. 109.
[8] Howarth 1997, pp. 574–6.
[9] Gowdy and Olsen 1994, p. 167. This critique of present-future discounting mirrors Herman Daly's critique of 'money fetishism', that is, of the notion that economic values can grow *ad infinitum* just like money earning interest in the bank (Daly 1992a, pp. 45, 186–7, 197–8).

Co-evolutionary sustainable human development

According to Mulder and Van den Bergh, co-evolutionary theory 'focuses the attention on irreversible, path-dependent change, and long-run mutual selection of environmental and economic processes and systems'.[10] Just as biologists conceptualise co-evolution 'based on reciprocal responses between two [or more] closely interacting species', ecological economists use it 'as a framework to study the interaction between economic and ecological processes, because of its emphasis on the dynamic feature of [their] mutual dependence'.[11] By contrast with 'mainstream economics', in which 'the economic system traditionally is depicted as a closed system ("circular flow")', the co-evolutionary perspective sees the economy as 'an open system, relying upon trade of matter and energy with the rest of the (economic and natural) world'.[12]

For co-evolutionary theory, moreover, the development of technologies and institutions is a crucial element of the economy-environment dynamic. In other words, the 'mutual selection' of economy and environment is not seen as a purely natural process. It is, rather, seen as largely driven by technological and institutional developments that are, in turn, shaped by conscious human and social purposes.[13] And these purposes are informed not just by human knowledge about environmental and economic processes, but also by human values which themselves co-evolve with the entire economy-environment dynamic.[14]

The problem, according to the co-evolutionary view, is that human values do not automatically develop in directions ensuring that technological and institutional changes, hence the co-evolution of economy and environment, proceed along a sustainable path, that is, one that ensures non-diminishing human life opportunities in the holistic and communal sense defined earlier. In this respect, it seems that the ability of human economy to influence the evolution of the environment has run ahead of the necessary adjustment of human values and purposes. As a result, human production is having all kinds of unforeseen eco-systemic and biospheric impacts, but technological

---

[10] Mulder and Van den Bergh 2001, p. 112.
[11] Mulder and Van den Bergh 2001, p. 117.
[12] Mulder and Van den Bergh 2001, p. 115.
[13] Boulding 1978, Chapters 6 and 10.
[14] Norgaard 1995.

and institutional developments for the most part still take the environment as an exogenous or given factor in the human life-process. What is needed is for human values themselves to become subject to conscious and collective human intervention, in the form of new visions and cultures of the good life that abide by the requirements of sustainability. Society needs to consciously produce human beings capable of living and developing within these requirements. Building upon and adapting previous technological and institutional developments, society must design and utilise technologies and institutions that can sustain fulfilling life opportunities, but this requires a cultural transition to human values that explicitly recognise eco-systems and the biosphere as co-evolutionary partners in human development.[15]

Mulder and Van Den Bergh thus argue that sustainable development theory 'must go beyond evolutionary theories of technical change' to include 'endogenous change of preferences'.[16] The neoclassical tradition of conducting analysis on the basis of given, fixed preferences is clearly inadequate to sustainable development as a co-evolutionary *human development* process, one that 'involves not just physical and environmental adaptation but psychological adaptation'.[17] And the needed changes in preferences involve more than the acceptance of 'changes in consumption that reduce environmental pressures'; they include positive utilities gained by individual human beings from pro-ecological 'technological niche development and management, sustainable technological regime-shifts, and the evolution of large technological systems and innovative networks'.[18] This, of course, presumes that human beings have the requisite technological knowledge and experience to appreciate such utilities. In sum, sustainable development theory must see 'value, knowledge, organizational, technological, and environmental subsystems co-evolving in response to changes in each other', while recognising the role of conscious

---

[15] For historical-intellectual background on the co-evolutionary vision, see Gowdy 1994a, Norgaard 1994, and Stokes 1994. Boulding (1978, pp. 78–82) provides a useful outline of different forms of co-evolution (mutual cooperation, parasitism, predation, etc.).

[16] Mulder and Van Den Bergh 2001, p. 112.

[17] Howe 1997, p. 605. For further discussion of endogenous preferences as an essential element of sustainable development theory, and of ecological economics more broadly, see Spash and Hanley 1995; Stern 1997; Norton, Costanza and Bishop 1998; Van Den Bergh, Ferrer-I-Carbonelli and Munda 2000.

[18] Mulder and Van Den Bergh 2001, pp. 123–4.

human purposes in steering the process (or failing to steer it) in sustainable directions, that is, directions that do not diminish human life opportunities.[19]

When criticising standard environmental economics, co-evolutionary theorists have focused largely on the tensions between sustainable development and the hedonistic individual motivations presumed by the neoclassical market model. Even if the market efficiently serves given preferences, that is, even if government policies are used to create artificial markets that price environmental resources in line with the individual utilities gained from their exploitation, this does not ensure sustainability – for the simple reason that 'sustainability is a matter of the distribution of assets across generations'.[20] More precisely, 'incorporating environmental values per se in decision-making will not bring about sustainability unless each generation is committed to transferring to the next sufficient natural resources and capital assets to make development sustainable'.[21] Sustainability analysis cannot take values and preferences as given data. Rather, it must envision, and operationalise *conscious social interventions* into, the co-evolutionary process that shapes these values and preferences. Insofar as advertising and other market institutions encourage people to discount the future in favour of the present, for example, this needs to be counteracted through education and other policies that encourage and reward more far-sighted and intergenerationally solidaristic behaviour.[22] This consideration is strengthened by the common-pool character of the environment:

> Some might argue that parent-offspring altruism should ensure sustained improvements in the human condition, obviating the need to consider sustainability as an explicit policy criterion. . . . [But] the welfare of future generations is likely to be a public good to a considerable extent, implying a significant role for collective action in effecting socially desired inter-generational transfers. Individuals clearly cannot provide for the climate of their offspring individually.[23]

In short, the standard market model fails insofar as 'the valuation of environmental services and how society cares for the future are interdependent.

---

[19] Norgaard 1995, p. 486.
[20] Howarth and Norgaard 1992, p. 473.
[21] Ibid.
[22] Norgaard 1995; Howe 1997.
[23] Howarth and Norgaard 1992, p. 475.

Valuation when there is too little caring for the future (i.e., too little asset transfer) will not lead to sustainability'.[24] The difficulty is accentuated insofar as ecological processes have characteristics (indivisibility, irreversibility, discontinuous 'threshold' effects, etc.) that 'preclude the marginal trade-offs assumed by neoclassical theory'.[25] When one adds ecological uncertainties to the mix, the need for a co-evolutionary approach, with an important place for conscious social interventions, becomes even more clear.[26]

The affinities between co-evolutionary theory and Marxism are clear enough. Both approaches emphasise the ecological shortcomings of market valuation and the need for collective actions to steer production onto a more sustainable course, in other words, one consistent with expanding human life opportunities. However, Marxists have not always been sufficiently sensitive to the crucial role of human values in economic development, or, perhaps even worse, have treated human values and human fulfilment as purely derivative elements of a socio-economic totality completely dominated by the economy in general and the forces of production in particular. Co-evolutionary theory is a useful reminder that sustainable development necessarily entails some positive vision of the good life – a vision insisting that human values and human fulfilment are not reducible to either monetary calculations or access to material goods.[27]

That said, it is also clear that co-evolutionary theory's commitment to collective action as an alternative to the market is weakened by its failure to grapple with the social relations of production. Just like ecological economics in general, it fails to root the shortcomings of market valuation and other anti-ecological aspects of capitalist production in the system's class relations, especially the social separation of the direct producers from necessary conditions of production (see Chapters 1–5). Likewise, the vision of a sustainable co-evolution of economy and environment needs to be informed by the necessity of disalienating the conditions of production vis-à-vis the producers. In effect, co-evolutionary theory emphasises the communality of nature as a condition of human development (expanding life opportunities), but this communality is not allowed to reach into the realm of production itself via an explicit

[24] Howarth and Norgaard 1992, p. 476.
[25] Gowdy and Olsen 1994, p. 163; compare Phillips 1993, pp. 109–10.
[26] Gowdy and Olsen 1994, pp. 169–70.
[27] Burkett 1997; Eagleton 2003.

socialisation of production and its necessary conditions. This is a crucial gap, insofar as it is precisely in and through the social relations of production that collective actions to regulate the exploitation of natural resources, and to develop appropriate technologies, education, and so forth, exert their effects on the economy's material dynamics. Production relations are a crucial mediator between the system of production and peoples' development as labouring creatures – labour being, of course, the central dimension of human productive interaction with the environment.

This failure to delve into production relationships helps explain co-evolutionary theory's over-reliance on autonomous changes in values as the key to sustainable development, in spite of its nominal insistence on the co-evolutionary character of value-formation. Hence, for Gowdy, the answer is to reject the 'preoccupation of modern economies with economic growth' and 'the extractive mentality'.[28] For Norgaard, salvation can only be attained if society rejects materialist philosophy in all its forms – a position that seems to contradict the materiality of human economy so central to co-evolutionary theory.[29] The use of values as a kind of *deus ex machina* is also reflected in a tendency to conflate the shortcomings of market valuation with the shortcomings of the neoclassical market model. Often, co-evolutionary theorists seem to suggest that the main impediment to economic sustainability is neoclassical-type thinking, with its allegiance to monetary values and its 'too little caring for the future'.[30] The struggle for sustainable development is thus reduced to a clash of alternative values and alternative theories, while struggles in the realm of production are relegated to the sidelines.

Common property as a 'third way' to sustainable development

Hardin's classic 'tragedy of the commons' analysis presumed that the only alternative to private or state property in natural resources was open, that is, unregulated, access.[31] This presumption is still very influential in neoclassical economics, where, combined with certain arguments regarding the efficiency

---

[28] Gowdy 1984, p. 397.
[29] Norgaard 1995.
[30] Howarth and Norgaard 1992, p. 476.
[31] Hardin 1968; see also Gordon 1954.

of private property compared to state property, it underpins the case for market-based environmental policies based on clear and well-enforced private property rights over natural resources. Nonetheless, in the decades since Hardin's analysis appeared, a growing wave of research has questioned the notion that the treatment of natural resources as commons must lead to their wanton overexploitation. Study after study has demonstrated the viability of common-property systems that regulate resource use while ensuring access rights to those whose survival and life opportunities depend on the resources in question.[32] These systems involve 'rights and obligations that defy a simple "public or private" categorization', thereby debunking the notion that 'common property is no property'.[33] Moreover, insofar as successful common-property management requires collective action to set up, maintain, and adjust access rights and obligations in line with environmental circumstances (see below), it runs counter to the influential hypothesis that individual incentives to 'free ride' generally undercut sustained collective efforts.[34]

How do common-property systems ensure sustainable patterns of resource exploitation? This question can be answered on formal and informal levels. Swaney sets out the formal aspect as follows: 'Common property is characterized by restrictions on who uses the resource, and when and how. Rights and responsibilities are assigned and, through some mechanism of social control, enforced'.[35]

More specifically, according to Aguilera-Klink, common-property systems normally have 'two fundamental characteristics':

1. Distribution of property rights in resources in which a number of owners are co-equal in their rights to use the resource. This means that their rights are not lost through non-use.
2. Potential resource users who are not members of a group of co-equal owners are excluded.[36]

Two qualifications to this specification are needed, however. First, the term 'owners' is somewhat inappropriate insofar as common-property user rights

---

[32] Ciriacy-Wantrup and Bishop 1975; Feeny et al. 1990; Swallow and Bromley 1995; Ostrom 1990, and 2000; Biel 2000, pp. 15–18.
[33] Usher 1993, p. 93; Quiggin 1988, p. 1074.
[34] Olson 1971; Wade 1987.
[35] Swaney 1990, p. 452.
[36] Aguilera-Klink 1994, p. 222.

in no way imply the kind of possession and alienability of the resource associated with private property. Second, many common property groups allow for provisional, and separately regulated, access to resources by non-members (for example, visitors from neighbouring communities).[37]

Still on the formal level, common-property systems 'include procedures for making decisions that affect the group as a whole, and methods for enforcing those decisions'.[38] These decision-making processes, and the user rights and responsibilities with which they are conjoined, typically 'act both to resolve conflict and to minimize the amount and cost of conflict'.[39] In short, 'conflicts [are] resolved and transgressors punished quickly, openly, and fairly'.[40]

On a less formal level, 'Common property frequently operates through tacit co-operation according to a culturally embedded set of rules'.[41] In hunting and gathering systems, for example, 'the structure and functioning of resource-regulating institutions are based on customs, taboos, and kinship rather than on formal relations such as legislation and court decisions which characterize "advanced societies"'.[42] Such informal validations often contain a large 'emphasis on sharing among members of the group . . . to discourage accumulation'.[43] Obviously, 'moral sanctions associated with the idea of community and of joint responsibility for carrying out decisions made jointly . . . play a larger role than in the case of private property'.[44] Common-property systems thus work better insofar as resource users have a real 'concern for other members of the commons'.[45]

However, moral sanctions and group harmony do not preclude conflicts among common-property users; hence the importance of rules and processes for conflict resolution that are clear, open, and fair. Experience seems to show that such transparency and evenhandedness are more likely insofar as 'divergences in the type and quantity of rights between individuals are

---

[37] Usher 1993, pp. 95–6.
[38] Quiggin 1988, p. 1080.
[39] Ibid.
[40] Swaney 1990, p. 454.
[41] Swaney 1990, p. 452.
[42] Ciriacy-Wantrup and Bishop 1975, p. 717.
[43] Ibid.
[44] Quiggin 1988, p. 1082.
[45] Swaney 1990, pp. 454–5.

minimized'.[46] 'Common interests are fostered through a *parity of conditions* for all users of the common property', especially 'universal access and benefit within the group'.[47] And a crucial aspect of this parity is that decisions regarding user rights and responsibilities, enforcement, and conflict resolution are broadly participatory, in the sense that all individuals affected by these decisions have a say in them, either directly or through what they view as their legitimate representatives.[48] Such 'universal involvement and consensus in management' has been most easily accomplished where 'management and production were not separate functions', that is, where 'management "data" included accumulated historical experience' directly grasped by all or most commons members – based on their own resource-using activities interacting with the cultural-knowledge systems in which common property systems are embedded.[49]

Their co-evolution with culture and productive practices helps explain why common-property systems exhibit 'a wide range of institutional arrangements and governance structures'.[50] Given the diversity of eco-systems and other common-pool resources, in terms of scale and the particular use-values they provide, it is not surprising that researchers have found complex and variegated 'common property regimes' that combine several common-property systems into 'a set of institutional arrangements that define the conditions of access to, and control over, a range of benefits arising from collectively-used natural resources'.[51] Ostrom, for example, notes that common property in larger-scale resources (such as, fisheries, water used for irrigation) is often organised into 'nested' associations of local users that co-operate in their 'appropriation, provision, monitoring, enforcement, conflict resolution, and governance activities'.[52] This jibes with Usher's observation that Canada's aboriginal systems 'combined principles of universal access and benefit within the group' with 'territorial boundaries that were permeable according to social rules'.[53]

[46] Quiggin 1988, pp. 1080–1.
[47] Swaney 1990, p. 454 (emphasis in original); Usher 1993, p. 95.
[48] Ostrom 1990, pp. 93–101; Chakraborty 2001, pp. 347–9.
[49] Usher 1993, pp. 95–6.
[50] Swallow and Bromley 1995, p. 100.
[51] Ibid.
[52] Ostrom 1990, p. 101.
[53] Usher 1993, p. 95.

Even within a particular locale, the plurality of use-values and divergent reproductive conditions within eco-systems have often led to the development of complex, internally differentiated common-property régimes. Based on observations from Indonesia and Vietnam, Adger and Luttrell argue that 'wetland resources tend to have unique property rights regimes due to their ecological characteristics, namely, their multiple-resource characteristics, the indivisible nature of these resources, and the seasonal and cyclical nature of different wetland resource components'.[54] 'Each wetland component tends to have different property rights regimes associated with it', that is, 'specific rights to utilise, control and exchange assets'.[55] Accordingly, the authors find it

> debatable whether a single model relevant to all wetlands can be developed, given the danger of over-generalization about an ecosystem with such an enormous cultural, institutional and biological diversity, without making the term wetland almost meaningless.[56]

In sum, the evidence suggests that common-property systems 'have played socially beneficial roles in natural resources management from economic pre-history up to the present'.[57] The range of resources that are still being managed as common property is impressive: Southeast Asian wetlands, forests in parts of India and Nepal, fisheries in Japan and other Pacific island nations, dams in Sri Lanka, canals in India, rangelands in various African countries, grazing lands in Britain and continental Europe, and groundwater in numerous countries.[58] An increasing number of analysts look to common-property systems for 'help in solving pressing resources problems in both the developed and the developing countries'.[59] Some see common property as the key to sustainable management of the *global* commons. Aguilera-Klink, for example, argues that

---

[54] Adger and Luttrell 2000, p. 75.
[55] Adger and Luttrell 2000, p. 79.
[56] Adger and Luttrell 2000, p. 77.
[57] Ciriacy-Wantrup and Bishop 1975, p. 713.
[58] Roster culled from Ciriacy-Wantrup and Bishop 1975, pp. 719–22; Wade 1987; Quiggin 1988, p. 1081; Feeny et al. 1990, p. 7; Swaney 1990, p. 452; Swallow and Bromley 1995, p. 100; Blair 1996; Adger and Luttrell 2000; Chakraborty 2001.
[59] Ciriacy-Wantrup and Bishop 1975, p. 713.

there is much more to the concept of common property than its mere application in the management of a natural resource. It is fundamental to the management of ecosystems. The planet earth can be considered to be an ecosystem or a set of interrelated systems for which sustainable management is possible only through the subscribing of world agreements – in the sense of restrictions of pure private rights – to apply certain principles. . . . It can be asserted, therefore, that common property as an institution has a promising future.[60]

This statement encapsulates the strengths and weaknesses of recent common-property analyses. The strengths are the recognition that private and state property are not the only resource-management alternatives, and that common property is often the most appropriate way to manage resources possessing common-pool characteristics. The weaknesses are the overriding focus on common property's ability to regulate and control resource appropriation, and the relative neglect of common property as a means of developing human beings. In effect, common property has been emphasised mainly from the proscriptive side of the sustainable development equation, while its role in enabling a 'good life' (improvements in human life opportunities) has been given short shrift. Unlike the co-evolutionary approach, in which the development of human capabilities and human fulfilment is, at least in part, an end in itself, the common-property literature treats human values and other positive human interactions mainly as instruments for restricting resource appropriation. The affirmation of common property as a form of human development is largely absent. This, arguably, represents a significant untapped analytical and political potential. After all, the literature has highlighted the complex and variegated forms taken on by common property as it has co-evolved with diverse eco-systems, as well as the role of grassroots participation in commons management based on culturally embedded knowledge and productive practices – which together suggest that common property could help generate a rich diversity of human life opportunities.

This failure to treat common-property relations as forms of human development is closely related to the literature's under-emphasis on class relations and class struggles *internal to* the societies engaging in common-

---

[60] Aguilera-Klink 1994, p. 227.

property management. There has been relatively little focus on how intra-community class structures may impede or facilitate the development of the egalitarian rights and obligations, and fair conflict-resolution procedures, needed for common-property management to work in a way that improves the life opportunities of all community members. The role of class struggle in the development and/or breakdown of commons management, in other words, class struggle as a form of human development in and through the transformation of social relations, tends to be downplayed. Instead, observed breakdowns of common-property systems are almost wholly and universally ascribed to exogenous external forces. As Ciriacy-Wantrup and Bishop put it:

> Such societies were capable of existing over long periods in equilibrium with their resources unless disturbed by unusual environmental changes or interference from the outside. . . . The most important outside interference with these societies has been contact with the market economy and other aspects of western culture.[61]

Swaney also argues that 'In many cases, both historical and contemporary, common property is destroyed by the extension of the market'.[62] Similarly, for Beaumont and Walker, 'Excessive herd sizes and attendant environmental degradation recently observed in Africa and India . . . are well-explained by externalities arising after breakdowns in common property restrictions, in the wake of land reforms'.[63]

Now, it may be true that common-property systems 'have inherent weaknesses in adapting to contact with the market', and that 'these weaknesses are not related to common ownership' as such.[64] But the importance of internal class relations in determining this non-adaptability is clearly implied by the mechanisms of externally-based destruction of common-property systems often cited in the literature. Contact with market systems may, for example, increase the opportunity cost to commons members of continued participation in common-property management.[65] Erstwhile communal and otherwise self-

---

[61] Ciriacy-Wantrup and Bishop 1975, p. 718.
[62] Swaney 1990, p. 453.
[63] Beaumont and Walker 1996, p. 56.
[64] Ciriacy-Wantrup and Bishop 1975, p. 718.
[65] Beaumont and Walker 1996, pp. 64–5.

sufficient producers may overexploit resources 'in order to acquire market products', including new technologies, or to pay monetary taxes imposed by colonisers.[66] Class-based inequalities in access to marketable resources may impede efforts by common-property holders to maintain their solidarity in the face of such dynamics. If wealthy members of a community see significant gains from a dissolution of the commons, they may even support a change in the legal environment that de-sanctions common property in favour of private property. Such was the case, of course, with the British enclosures.[67] Conversely, 'the more powerful are those who benefit from retaining the commons, and the weaker are those who favour sub-group enclosure or private property, the better the chances of success'.[68]

Once class interest has begun to dissolve common property, the immiseration of less affluent community members may force them to engage in further resource overexploitation. Even in cases where common-property management still effectively impedes overexploitation of commons, poorer community members may resort to (legal or illegal) overexploitation of state- or privately-owned resources to obtain their subsistence. Chakraborty, reporting on common-property forest systems in the Terai region of Nepal, observes that:

> The available evidence suggests that community forestry serves well to protect forests locally. However, the distributive conflict between the rich and the poor on the establishment of strong forest protection rules is eased by the fact that the latter resort to exploiting forests managed under state property.[69]

In all these ways, class relations may affect the resilience of common property in the face of external pressures. This is not just a theoretical issue: by clarifying the conditions needed to sustain common-property management, class analysis can assist the struggle against resource privatisation and marketisation. For example, neoclassical economists have been known to interpret secondary

---

[66] Ciriacy-Wantrup and Bishop 1975, p. 718.

[67] During the transition to a new régime, the 'instability in property rights' may encourage the forcible separation of less powerful users from the commons, and other forms of '"rent–seeking" behavior aimed at securing a reassignment of rights' favoring the wealthy (Quiggin 1988, p. 1077).

[68] Wade 1987, p. 104.

[69] Chakraborty 2001, p. 342.

resource overexploitation by impoverished peasants as evidence of the need for clearer private-property rights, when the true 'tragedy of the commons' is that class inequalities and resulting market and non-market incentives have prevented common property from functioning equitably and sustainably. Similarly, the inability of some common-property arrangements to survive contacts with private-market activity is often ascribed to the latter's inherently greater room for freedom and creativity. But the real problem may be the suppression of human capabilities and life-opportunities by class-based inequalities within formally communal-property systems. Rather than marketisation, such inequalities may call for political revolutions that rebalance the substantive distribution of individual rights within these systems.

The reason why the common-property literature has tended to downplay human development and class lies in its intellectual origins. This literature developed as a reaction to the pro-private-property arguments of neoclassical and other theorists – arguments that conflated common property with open access. Its overriding priority has thus been to demonstrate that common property can be a rational and efficient arrangement in the conventional economic sense. As a result, considerations of human development and grassroots empowerment have been largely displaced or treated as means to the end of neoclassical efficiency. Common property has typically been seen as a supportive infrastructure for the formal (private-market and state) economy – one that can fill in the gaps created by limited state capacities to enforce private-property rights, regulate markets, or directly manage resources especially in rural areas. In short, 'group rights to particular resources' and 'internal group dynamics' are treated simply as cost-effective tools for achieving 'efficient resource management outcomes' *within* an otherwise fully capitalist macro-structure.[70] As Wade puts it:

> One good reason for taking [common property] seriously is that collective action is likely to be much cheaper in terms of state resources. . . . Both private property regimes and state control regimes are expensive to make effective. Already over-stretched states in developing countries may not be able to provide the necessary resources to make them work across myriad micro-locations. A malfunctioning approximation to a formalized system of

---

[70] Swallow and Bromley 1995, p. 99.

state control or private property rights, based on a distant authority only dimly aware of local conditions, may be worse in terms of resource management than a strategy which aims to improve, or at least not impair, local systems of rules.[71]

Over the past decade, this kind of thinking has merged into a new wave of analyses that emphasise the contributions to the market economy made by various kinds of 'social capital', as captured in institutional terms by non-governmental organisations (NGOs) and non-market, non-state networks (political, cultural, and familial). Empirical proxies of social capital are now routinely entered as independent variables alongside labour and physical capital in statistical estimates of neoclassical growth models.[72] The timing of the social-capital explosion is no accident. It follows on the heels of neoliberal stabilisation and structural adjustment programmes implemented by the IMF-World Bank and allied governments in numerous Third-World and post-Soviet nations. Basically, common property and other elements of social capital are seen as cost-effective substitutes for state actions to clean up the socio-economic wreckage (poverty, unemployment, declining health and education conditions, environmental havoc, social and cultural dislocation, and so on) left behind by these programmes. The traditional shock-absorbing and safety-valve functions of the family for capitalism have been expanded to incorporate all non-market, non-government, relations that can help maintain the subsistence and productivity – and defuse the potential militancy – of exploited and systemically marginalised producers. In this broader context, the tensions between capitalist functionalisation and the anticapitalist character of communal property comprise a primary field of ecological struggles around the world.[73]

---

[71] Wade 1987, p. 105. Similarly, Blair (1996, p. 475), based on observations of forest management in India, suggests that common-property systems often outperform state property. The reason? 'Local user groups . . . can restrict membership and thus avoid free riders, and they can establish a close linkage in their members' minds between benefits and costs of participating in group discipline to maintain the resource'.

[72] Fine 2001, pp. 114–22.

[73] Biel 2000, pp. 244–5, 295–9; Fine 2001, Chapters 8 and 9.

II. Communism as sustainable human development

Although the evolutionary credentials of Marxism are well established,[74] its ability to address *co*-evolutionary considerations has been less appreciated by ecological economists. This is largely due, in my opinion, to the virtual non-recognition – even among many Marxists – of the vision of all-round human development that lies at the heart of Marx and Engels's communism. Debates over the 'economics of socialism' have instead concentrated on questions of information, incentives, and efficiency in resource allocation.[75] This focus on 'socialist calculation' has displaced the concern with communism as a form of sustainable human development.[76]

For Marx and Engels, the overriding imperative of communism is the free development of individual human beings as social individuals. They insist that 'the association of individuals . . . puts the conditions of the free development and movement of individuals under their control – conditions which were previously left to chance and had acquired an independent existence over against the separate individuals'.[77] Communism's 'all-round realisation of the individual' presumes that 'the impact of the world which stimulates the real development of the abilities of the individual is under the control of individuals themselves'.[78] And, instead of opportunities for individual development being obtained mainly at the expense of others, as in class societies, the future 'community' will provide 'each individual [with] the means of cultivating his gifts in all directions; hence personal freedom becomes possible only within the community'.[79] In short, Marx and Engels foresee communism as 'an association, in which the free development of each is a condition for the free development of all'.[80]

Disalienation, common property, and non-market allocation

The most basic feature of communism in Marx and Engels's projection is its overcoming of capitalism's social separation of the producers from necessary

---

[74] Dugger and Sherman 2000; Dickens 2004, pp. 66–73.
[75] Lange and Taylor 1964; *Science & Society* 1992, and 2002.
[76] A notable exception is Lebowitz 2002.
[77] Marx and Engels 1976, p. 89.
[78] Marx and Engels 1976, p. 309.
[79] Marx and Engels 1976, p. 86.
[80] Marx and Engels 1968, p. 53.

conditions of production. Communism is the 'historical reversal' of 'the separation of labour and the worker from the conditions of labour, which confront him as independent forces'.[81] This disalienation entails a decommodification of labour-power plus a new set of common property rights in the conditions of production.[82] Communism replaces 'capitalist property with a *higher form* of the archaic type of property, i.e. communist property'.[83]

For Marx and Engels, the *common* dimension of communist property is closely bound up with *individual* all-round human development as both means and end of the development of productive forces. They do not envision mechanised productive forces standing above, and determining the life opportunities of, workers and their communities. Instead, they see human beings individually and collectively taking, holding, operating and developing these productive forces in ways that improve human capabilities and life opportunities holistically defined. It is in this holistic, human-developmental sense that they see 'the human being himself' as 'the main force of production'.[84] In this view, 'forces of production and social relations' are 'two different sides of the development of the social individual'.[85] The highly socialised production bequeathed by capitalism means that 'individuals must appropriate the existing totality of productive forces, not only to achieve self-activity, but, also, merely to safeguard their very existence'.[86]

In order to be an effective vehicle of all-round human development, communism must be an 'appropriation of the total productive forces by the united individuals'; but it must not reduce individuals to minuscule, interchangeable cogs in a giant collective machine operating outside their control in an alienated pursuit of 'production for the sake of production'.[87] It must enhance the development of *human* productive forces capable of grasping and controlling social production in line with 'the development of the richness of human nature as an end in itself'.[88] Although communist

---

[81] Marx 1971, pp. 271–2. See also Marx 1976b, p. 39.
[82] Engels 1939, p. 221; Marx 1968, p. 580, and 1971, p. 525.
[83] Marx 1989b, p. 363 (emphasis in original).
[84] Marx 1973, p. 190.
[85] Marx 1973, p. 706.
[86] Marx and Engels 1976, p. 96.
[87] Marx and Engels 1976, p. 97.
[88] Marx 1968, pp. 117–18.

'appropriation [has] a universal character corresponding to . . . the productive forces', it also promotes 'the development of the individual capacities corresponding to the material instruments of production'.[89] Because these instruments 'have been developed to a totality and . . . only exist within a universal intercourse', their effective appropriation requires 'the development of a totality of capacities in the individuals themselves'.[90] In short, 'the genuine and free development of individuals' under communism shapes, and, in turn, is shaped by, 'the universal character of the activity of individuals on the basis of the existing productive forces'.[91]

Accordingly, although it 'does not re-establish *private* property' in the means of production, communism 'does indeed establish individual property on the basis of the achievements of the capitalist era: namely co-operation and the possession in common of the land and the means of production'.[92] 'The *alien property* of the capitalist' is 'abolished by converting his property into the property . . . of the *associated, social individual*'.[93] Communist property thus affirms each individual's access to the conditions and results of production as needed to become a 'totally developed individual'.[94] In addition to the right to participate in the planning and management of production (see below), there are three specific individual rights in communist property that work in the direction of all-round human development.

First, communism protects the individual's right to a share in the total product for her private consumption.[95] In this sense, 'social ownership extends to the land and the other means of production, and private ownership to the products, that is, the articles of consumption'.[96] Naturally, social ownership must also apply to certain other deductions over and above those earmarked for 'replacing and increasing . . . means of production'.[97] There must, for example, be 'a reserve fund for production and consumption'.[98] Further

---

[89] Marx and Engels 1976, p. 96.
[90] Ibid.
[91] Marx and Engels 1976, p. 465.
[92] Marx 1981, Vol. I, p. 929 (emphasis added).
[93] Marx 1994, p. 109 (emphases in original).
[94] Marx 1981, Vol. I, p. 618.
[95] Marx and Engels 1968, p. 49.
[96] Engels 1939, p. 144; compare Marx 1981, pp. 172–3.
[97] Engels 1979, p. 28.
[98] Engels 1979, p. 28; see also Marx 1966, p. 7, and 1981, Vol. III, p. 1016.

deductions are required for 'general costs of administration', for 'the communal satisfaction of needs, such as schools, health services, etc.', and for 'funds for those unable to work'.[99] But after these deductions, the remaining 'part of the means of consumption . . . is divided among the individual producers of the co-operative society'.[100]

In terms of the distribution of individuals' consumption claims, Marx and Engels envision a two-phase process. For 'the first phase of communist society as it is when it has just emerged after prolonged birth pangs from capitalist society', they suggest that 'the share of each individual producer in the means of subsistence' is likely to be 'determined by his labour-time'.[101] But in the second, 'higher phase of communist society', labour-based consumption claims can and should 'be fully left behind and society inscribe on its banners: from each according to his ability, to each according to his needs!'[102] In this higher phase, the 'mode of distribution . . . allows *all* members of society to develop, maintain and exert their capacities in all possible directions'.[103] In other words, 'the worker's own individual consumption' is 'expanded to the scale . . . required for the full development of individuality'.[104]

The second way in which communist property promotes individual human development is by assuring all individuals access to the expanded social services – education, health care, utilities, and old-age pensions – that are financed by deductions from the total product prior to its distribution among individuals. In this way, 'what the producer is deprived of in his capacity as a private individual benefits him directly or indirectly in his capacity as a member of society'.[105] Such social consumption will be 'considerably increased in comparison with present-day society and it increases in proportion as the new society develops'.[106] Its human development dimension is evident from the projected expansion of 'technological education, both theoretical and practical . . . in the schools of the workers', including 'an early combination

---

[99] Marx 1966, p. 7.
[100] Marx 1966, pp. 7–8.
[101] Marx 1966, p. 10, and 1981, Vol. I, p. 172.
[102] Marx 1966, p. 10; compare Marx and Engels 1976, p. 566.
[103] Engels 1939, p. 221 (emphasis in original).
[104] Marx 1981, Vol. III, pp. 1015–16.
[105] Marx 1966, p. 8.
[106] Marx 1966, p. 7.

of productive labour with education' – presuming, of course, 'a strict regulation of the working time according to the different age groups and other safety measures for the protection of children'.[107] An important function of this holistic education will be to 'convert science from an instrument of class rule into a popular force'.[108]

Third, communist property includes the individual's right to progressively shorter working time. This 'reduction of the working day' will facilitate human development by giving individuals more free time in which to enjoy the 'material and intellectual advantages . . . of social development'.[109] Free time is 'time . . . for the free intellectual and social activity of the individual'.[110] As such,

> free time, *disposable time*, is wealth itself, partly for the enjoyment of the product, partly for free activity which – unlike labour – is not dominated by the pressure of an extraneous purpose which must be fulfilled, and the fulfilment of which is regarded as a natural necessity or a social duty.[111]

Accordingly, with communism 'the measure of wealth is . . . not any longer, in any way, labour time, but rather disposable time'.[112]

Communism pursues this enhancement of human wealth by replacing market allocation with a 'collective production' in which 'society distributes labour-power and means of production between the various branches of industry'.[113] With 'the means of production held in common', production 'becomes production by freely associated men, and stands under their conscious and planned control'.[114] The 'many different forms of labour-power' are expended 'in full self-awareness as one single social labour force . . . in accordance with a definite social plan [which] maintains the correct proportions between the different functions of labour and the various needs of the association'.[115]

---

[107] Marx 1981, Vol. I, p. 619, and 1966, p. 22.
[108] Marx 1985, p. 162.
[109] Marx 1981, Vol. III, pp. 958–9.
[110] Marx 1981, Vol. I, p. 667.
[111] Marx 1971, p. 257 (emphasis in original).
[112] Marx 1973, p. 708.
[113] Marx 1981, Vol. II, p. 434.
[114] Marx 1981, Vol. I, pp. 171, 173.
[115] Marx 1981, Vol. I, pp. 171–2.

As noted earlier, debates over the 'economics of socialism' have focused on technical issues of allocative efficiency ('socialist calculation'). Marx and Engels themselves often emphasised communism's superior allocative capabilities compared to capitalism. For example, Marx asserted that with communism, 'united co-operative societies are to regulate national production upon a common plan, thus taking it under their own control, and putting an end to the constant anarchy and periodic convulsions which are the fatality of capitalist production'.[116] Nonetheless, for Marx and Engels, the main significance of communist planning does not lie in greater social control and efficiency, but rather in its role as an enabler and effect of the human developmental impulses unleashed by the new system of common property rights – with its security of subsistence, expanding social services including theoretical and practical education, and increases in free time. The reason communism is 'a society organised for co-operative working on a planned basis' is 'to ensure all members of society the means of existence and the full development of their capacities'.[117] This assurance is incompatible with market- and profit-driven production, under which 'individuals are subsumed under social production; social production exists outside them as their fate'.[118]

Marx and Engels's argument is that the market's alienation of individuals (and society as a whole) from direct, common control over production is an outgrowth of the basic wage-labour relation. It is capitalism's social separation of the producers from conditions of production that creates the situation in which production is carried out in independently organised enterprises guided by market signals.[119] That is why Marx insists that communism is 'a form of production diametrically opposed to the production of commodities'.[120] The elimination of the commodity-form and the overcoming of workers' social separation from necessary conditions of production are two aspects of the same phenomenon, with the latter aspect being primary. Communism's disalienation of production takes the form of labour being 'directly socialized labour', with no need to engage in monetary exchanges in order to establish

---

[116] Marx 1985, p. 76.
[117] Engels 1939, p. 167.
[118] Marx 1973, p. 158.
[119] Marx 1970, pp. 84–5, and 1973, pp. 171–2.
[120] Marx 1981, Vol. I, p. 188.

a reproductive social division of labour.[121] As Marx says, the market is only 'the bond natural to individuals within specific limited relations of production'; and the 'alien and independent character' of this bond 'vis-à-vis individuals proves only that the latter are still engaged in the creation of the conditions of their social life, and that they have not yet begun, on the basis of these conditions, to live it'.[122]

In summary, communism's system of directly social labour is seen as co-evolving with the producers' individual and collective development as human beings. This makes sense given the considerable human-resource requirements of 'cooperative labour . . . developed to national dimensions'.[123] These requirements appear even more formidable when one considers that this system is not to be governed by any centralised state power, but instead 'starts with the self-government of the communities'.[124] State bureaucracies are to be replaced by workers' associations, and any communal officials (including judges) will be not only elected but subject to immediate recall and compensated no more than the average working person.[125] From this angle, communism can be defined as 'the people acting for itself by itself', or 'the reabsorption of the state power by society as its own living forces instead of as forces controlling and subduing it'.[126] In this reabsorption of alienated power, the development of human capacities and needs will shape the evolution of the association's planning capabilities including its management of the natural conditions of production.

Managing the commons communally

Marx and Engels were deeply concerned with capitalism's environmental crisis tendencies.[127] Accordingly, they emphasised the need for postcapitalist society to responsibly manage its natural conditions. This explains their insistence on the extension of common property to the land and other 'sources

---

[121] Marx 1981, Vol. I, p. 188; see also Marx 1973, p. 158; Engels 1939, pp. 337–8.
[122] Marx 1973, p. 162.
[123] Marx 1974a, p. 80.
[124] Marx 1989a, p. 519.
[125] Marx 1985, pp. 71–7, 153–7; compare Ollman 1979, pp. 58–62.
[126] Marx 1985, pp. 130, 153.
[127] Burkett 1999a, Chapters 9–10; Foster 2000a, Chapter 5.

of life'.[128] In Marx and Engels's projection, communism 'reestablishes, now on a rational basis, no longer mediated by serfdom, overlordship and the silly mysticism of [private] property, the intimate ties of man with the earth, since the earth ceases to be an object of huckstering'.[129] This 'common property' in land 'does not mean the restoration of the old original common ownership, but the institution of a far higher and more developed form of possession in common'.[130]

Nonetheless, there are two functional parallels between Marx and Engels's conception of communist property in land and the common-property resource systems surveyed in Section I. First, in neither case does common property confer any right – individual or collective – to overexploit land and other natural conditions. Marx and Engels recognised that the land is not just a particular resource but the basic source of 'the whole gamut of permanent conditions of life required by the chain of human generations'.[131] They therefore argued that all conventional notions of land 'ownership' – involving rights of individuals to exploit and alienate the land as they see fit – would no longer apply under communism, which would instead rely on a communal system of user rights and responsibilities.[132] Communist property will, of course, give all individuals the right to participate in the productive utilisation of the land and its products as conditions of their reproduction and all-round development. But this individual right operates within communism's 'conscious and rational treatment of the land as permanent communal property, as the inalienable condition for the existence and reproduction of the chain of human generations'.[133] There can be little doubt that Marx and Engels, like most ecological economists, would reject the notion of a positive discount rate applied to future non-access to common-pool resources.

The second parallel between observed common-property systems and Marx and Engels's projection is the practical empowerment of community members, based on the deep embedding of common-property institutions in cultural and productive practices. Marx and Engels see the producers wielding the

---

[128] Marx 1966, p. 5.
[129] Marx 1964, p. 103.
[130] Engels 1939, p. 151.
[131] Marx 1981, Vol. III, p. 754.
[132] Marx 1981, Vol. III, p. 911.
[133] Marx 1981, Vol. III, p. 949.

scientific knowledge needed to self-manage their labour processes including their use of natural conditions. Communism's emphasis on theoretical and practical education is quite relevant in this connection. Here, Marx and Engels see the diffusion and further development of scientific knowledge taking the form of new combinations of natural and social science.[134] Although this evolving unity of natural and social science is a logical corollary of the co-evolution of nature and humanity,[135] the realisation of both unities is a function of communism's disalienation of the conditions of production and their conversion into conditions of human development. Only then will people become genuinely

> conscious of the internal relations between what are today called 'natural'
> and 'social' worlds, . . . treating the hitherto separate halves as a single
> totality. In learning about either society or nature, the individual will recognize
> that he is learning about both.[136]

Or, as Engels straightforwardly puts it, people will 'not only feel but also know their oneness with nature'.[137]

This conscious 'reconciliation of mankind with nature and with itself' depends above all on communism's 'increase of free time' and its use 'for the full development of the individual' capable of 'the grasping of his own history as a *process*, and the recognition of nature (equally present as practical power over nature) as his real body'.[138] Through the practical-intellectual development of the producers during free time *and* working time, communist labour's 'social character is posited . . . not in a merely natural, spontaneous form, but as an activity regulating all the forces of nature'.[139] As Marx says,

> Free time – which is both idle time and time for higher activity – has naturally
> transformed its possessor into a different subject, and he then enters into

---

[134] Marx 1964, p. 143; Marx and Engels 1976, p. 34.
[135] For Marx and Engels (1976, p. 45), nature and society are not 'two separate "things"'; rather, humanity has 'an historical nature and a natural history'. While insisting that 'the nature that preceded human history . . . today no longer exists', they recognise the ongoing importance of 'natural instruments of production' in the use of which 'individuals are subservient to nature' (Marx and Engels 1976, pp. 46, 71).
[136] Ollman 1979, p. 76.
[137] Engels 1964a, p. 183. Marx (1964, p. 137) thus defines communism as 'the unity of being of man with nature'.
[138] Engels 1964b, p. 204; Marx 1973, p. 542 (emphasis in original).
[139] Marx 1973, p. 612.

the direct production process as this different subject. This process is then both discipline, as regards the human being in the process of becoming; and, at the same time, practice, experimental science, materially creative and objectifying science, as regards the human being who has become, in whose head exists the accumulated knowledge of society.[140]

The ecological significance of free time as a measure of communist wealth cannot be overestimated. Rising labour productivity need not increase matter-energy throughput insofar as the producers are compensated by reductions in working time instead of increases in *material* consumption. Moreover, to the extent that the human needs developed and satisfied during expanded free time are less matter-energy intensive, their increasing weight in total needs reduces the pressure of production on the natural environment, *ceteris paribus*. Such eco-friendly activities can include not only the accumulation of productive and other scientific knowledge, but other self-educational and artistic pursuits. In fact, Marx and Engels foresee the producers using their newfound material security and expanded free time to engage in a variety of intellectual and aesthetic forms of self-development.[141] This partial de-entropification of human needs and human development should be enhanced by the greater opportunities communism affords for people to become informed participants in and shapers of economic, political, and cultural life.

Of course, the inherent unity of humanity and nature means that it will still be necessary for communist society to 'wrestle with nature to satisfy [its] needs, to maintain and reproduce [its] life'.[142] This makes it all the more essential

> that socialized man, the associated producers, govern the human metabolism with nature in a rational way, bringing it under their collective control instead of being dominated by it as a blind power; accomplishing it with the least expenditure of energy and in conditions most worthy and appropriate for their human nature.[143]

---

[140] Marx 1973, p. 712. Compare Marx 1971, p. 257.
[141] Marx 1973, p. 287; Marx and Engels 1976, p. 53.
[142] Marx 1981, Vol. III, p. 959.
[143] Ibid.

Such a 'real conscious mastery of Nature' presumes that the producers have 'become masters of their own social organization'.[144] But it does not presume that humanity has overcome all natural limits; nor does it presume that the associated producers have attained complete technological control over natural forces:

> Freedom does not consist in the dream of independence of natural laws, but in the knowledge of these laws, and in the possibility this gives of systematically making them work towards definite ends. This holds good in relation both to the laws of external nature and to those which govern the bodily and mental existence of men themselves – two classes of laws which we can separate from each other at most only in thought but not in reality. . . . Freedom therefore consists in the control over ourselves and over external nature which is founded on natural necessity.[145]

It is in this prudential sense that Marx foresees the associated producers 'direct[ing] production from the outset so that the yearly grain supply depends only to a very minimum on the variations in the weather; the sphere of production – the supply- and the use-aspects thereof – is rationally regulated'.[146] For example, 'perpetual relative overproduction', that is, 'production on a greater scale than is needed for the simple replacement and reproduction of the existing wealth', is simply a judicious way of insuring against 'destruction by way of extraordinary natural events, fire, flood, etc.'.[147] 'Within capitalist society', by contrast, uncontrollable natural conditions impart a needless 'anarchic element' to social reproduction.[148] Communism's pre-emptive planning for unpredictable natural events illustrates how 'real human freedom' can only be based on 'an existence in harmony with the established laws of nature'.[149]

---

[144] Engels 1939, p. 309.
[145] Engels 1939, p. 125.
[146] Marx 1975, p. 188.
[147] Marx 1981, Vol. II, pp. 256–7, 544. See also Marx 1966, p. 7, and 1971, pp. 357–8.
[148] Marx 1981, Vol. II, p. 545.
[149] Engels 1939, p. 126.

III. Sustainable human development, class struggle, and ecological economics

Marx and Engels's vision of communism integrates the common-pool resource, co-evolution, and common-property dimensions of sustainable development. And this vision combines natural-scientific and social-scientific thinking in a practical-intellectual way that is quite consistent with the interdisciplinary character of ecological economics. At the same time, that Marx and Engels do not provide a detailed blueprint of the future society means that their vision leaves room for a variety of institutional and cultural developments consistent with its basic principle of sustainable human development based on disalienation of the conditions of production. In this sense, their communism abides by ecological economists' commitment to methodological pluralism and historical openness.

Of course, Marx and Engels did not envision communism in this way so that they could gain entry into the discipline of ecological economics. They had pressing political reasons for putting forth an inclusive and historically open framework of principles rather than a blueprint. A rigid blueprint would violate the requirement that 'the emancipation of the working classes must be conquered by the working classes themselves'.[150] It would foreclose the self-development of the working class through political debates, conflicts, and trial-and-error experiences of struggle, thereby impeding the germination and growth of a worker-community-centred revolutionary movement. As Alan Shandro explains, Marx and Engels understood the working class 'as a unity in diversity, as a political community'.[151] That is why they saw communism not as a 'master plan' but 'as a means of organizing the workers' movement and structuring and guiding debate in and around it'.[152]

This approach is consistent with the difficult and prolonged character of the transition to communism in Marx and Engels's view. After all, this transition involves the conversion of natural and social conditions of production from alienated conditions of class exploitation into conditions of sustainable human development, and that is not something that can be accomplished overnight. Communist production is not simply inherited from capitalism; it requires

---

[150] Marx 1974b, p. 82.
[151] Shandro 2000, p. 21.
[152] Shandro 2000, pp. 22–3.

'long struggles, through a series of historical processes, transforming circumstances and men'.[153] Among these transformed circumstances will be 'a new social organization of production, or rather the delivery (setting free) of the social forms of production . . . of their present class character, and their harmonious national and international co-ordination'.[154]

Any detailed blueprint of the outcome of this global-epochal transition would be utterly utopian in the most dogmatic and abstract sense of the term. The real-world struggle for 'the conditions of free and associated labour . . . will be again and again relented and impeded by the resistance of vested interests and class egotisms', and this is precisely why its exact achievements (and setbacks) cannot be predetermined.[155] The transition to a communal system of sustainable human development is by nature a highly path-dependent co-evolutionary process. One crucial aspect of this path dependency, in Marx and Engels's view, is that communism's human developmental preconditions will be generated in large part by the revolutionary struggle itself. As stated in *The German Ideology*, communist

> appropriation . . . can only be effected through a union, which by the character of the proletariat itself can only be a universal one, and through a revolution, in which, on the one hand, the power of the earlier mode of production . . . is overthrown, and, on the other hand, there develops the universal character and the energy of the proletariat, which are required to accomplish the appropriation, and the proletariat moreover rids itself of everything that still clings to it from its previous position in society.[156]

The demand for more equitable and environmentally sustainable life opportunities is central to the growing worldwide rebellion against dominant economic institutions (transnational corporations, the IMF-World Bank, and WTO). But this movement needs a framework for the debate, reconciliation, and realisation of alternative human development strategies guided by life values – not by the market, private profit, and other forms of exploitation and oppression. The classical-Marxist vision of communism as disalienation of production in service of human development still has much to contribute to this needed framework.

---

[153] Marx 1985, p. 76.
[154] Marx 1985, p. 157.
[155] Ibid.
[156] Marx and Engels 1976, p. 97.

References

Aaheim, Asbjørn and Karine Nyborg 1995, 'On the Interpretation and Applicability of a "Green National Product"', *Review of Income and Wealth*, 41, 1: 57–71.

Ackerman, Frank and Lisa Heinzerling 2004, *Priceless*, New York: New Press.

Adaman, Fikret and Begüm Özkaynak 2002, 'The Economics-Environment Relationship', *Studies in Political Economy*, 69: 109–35.

Adger, W. Neil and Cecilia Luttrell 2000, 'Property Rights and the Utilization of Wetlands', *Ecological Economics*, 35, 1: 75–89.

Aguilera-Klink, Federico 1994, 'Some Notes on the Misuse of Classic Writings in Economics on the Subject of Common Property', *Ecological Economics*, 9, 3: 221–8.

Åkerman, Maria 2003, 'What Does "Natural Capital" Do?', *Environmental Values*, 12, 4: 431–48.

Altvater, Elmar 1990, 'The Foundations of Life (Nature) and the Maintenance of Life (Work)', *International Journal of Political Economy*, 20, 1: 10–34.

Altvater, Elmar 1993, *The Future of the Market*, London: Verso.

Altvater, Elmar 1994, 'Ecological and Economic Modalities of Time and Space', in *Is Capitalism Sustainable?*, edited by Martin O'Connor, New York: Guilford.

Altvater, Elmar. 2003, 'Is there an Ecological Marxism?', Lecture at the Virtual University of CLACSO – Consejo Latinoamericano de las Ciencias Sociales.

Amir, Shmuel 1998, 'The Role of Thermodynamics for Ecological Economics', *Ecological Economics*, 27, 2: 213–14.

Amiran, Edoh K. and Daniel A. Hagen 2003, 'Willingness To Pay and Willingness To Accept: How Much Do They Differ? Comment', *American Economic Review*, 93, 1: 458–64.

Anand, Paul 2000, 'Decisions vs. Willingness-to-Pay in Social Choice', *Environmental Values*, 9, 4: 419–30.

Arrow, Kenneth J. 1963, *Social Choice and Individual Values*, Second Edition, New Haven: Yale University Press.

Arrow, Kenneth, Bert Bolin, Robert Costanza, Partha Dasgupta, Carl Folke, C.S. Holling, Bengt-Owe Jansson, Simon Levin, Karl-Göran Mäler, Charles Perrings and David Pimentel 1995, 'Economic Growth, Carrying Capacity, and the Environment', *Science*, 268 (April 28): 520–1.

Ayres, Robert U. 1997, 'Comments on Georgescu-Roegen', *Ecological Economics*, 22, 3: 285–7.

Ayres, Robert U. 1998, 'Eco-Thermodynamics: Economics and the Second Law', *Ecological Economics*, 26, 2: 189–209.

Ayres, Robert U. 1999, 'The Second Law, the Fourth Law, Recycling and Limits to Growth', *Ecological Economics*, 29, 3: 473–83.

Ayres, Robert U. and Allen V. Kneese 1969, 'Production, Consumption, and Externalities', *American Economic Review*, 59, 2: 282–97.

Ayres, Robert, Geraldo Ferrer and Tania Van Leynseele 1997, 'Eco-Efficiency, Asset Recovery and Remanufacturing', *European Management Journal*, 15, 5: 557–74.

Baksi, Pradip 1996, 'Karl Marx's Study of Science and Technology', *Nature, Society, and Thought*, 9, 3: 261–96.

Baksi, Pradip 2001, 'MEGA IV/31: Natural Science Notes of Marx and Engels, 1877–1883', *Nature, Society, and Thought*, 14, 4: 377–90.

Banzhaf, H. Spencer 2000, 'Productive Nature and the Net Product', *History of Political Economy*, 32, 3: 517–51.

Barry, John 1999, 'Marxism and Ecology', in *Marxism and Social Science*, edited by Andrew Gamble, David Marsh, and Tony Tant, Urbana: University of Illinois Press.

Barry, John 2001, 'Justice, Nature and Political Economy', *Economy and Society*, 30, 3: 381–94.

Bartolini, Stefano and Luigi Bonatti 2002, 'Environmental and Social Degradation as the Engine of Economic Growth', *Ecological Economics*, 43, 1: 1–16.

Baumgärtner, Stefan, Harald Dyckhoff, Malte Faber, John Proops and Johannes Schiller 2001, 'The Concept of Joint Production and Ecological Economics', *Ecological Economics*, 36, 3: 365–72.

Beaumont, Paul M. and Robert T. Walker 1996, 'Land Degradation and Property Regimes', *Ecological Economics*, 18, 1: 55–66.

Benton, Ted 1989, 'Marxism and Natural Limits: An Ecological Critique and Reconstruction', *New Left Review*, I, 178: 51–86.

Bergström, S. 1993, 'Value Standards in Sub-Sustainable Development: On Limits of Ecological Economics', *Ecological Economics*, 7, 1: 1–18.

Berkes, Fikret and Carl Folke 1992, 'A Systems Perspective on the Interrelations Between Natural, Human-Made and Cultural Capital', *Ecological Economics*, 5, 1: 1–8.

Biancardi, C., A. Donati and S. Ulgiati 1993a, 'On the Relationship Between the Economic Process, the Carnot Cycle and the Entropy Law', *Ecological Economics*, 8, 1: 7–10.

Biancardi, C., E. Tiezzi and S. Ulgiati 1993b, 'Complete Recycling of Matter in the Frameworks of Physics, Biology and Ecological Economics', *Ecological Economics*, 8, 1: 1–5.

Biel, Robert 2000, *The New Imperialism*, London: Zed Books.

Binswanger, Mathias 1993, 'From Microscopic to Macroscopic Theories: Entropic Aspects of Ecological and Economic Processes', *Ecological Economics*, 8, 3: 209–34.

Blair, Harry W. 1996, 'Democracy, Equity and Common Property Resource Management in the Indian Subcontinent', *Development and Change*, 27, 3: 475–99.

Bond, Patrick 2000, *Cities of Gold, Townships of Coal*, Trenton: Africa World Press.

Bond, Patrick 2002, *Unsustainable South Africa: Environment, Development and Social Protest*, London: Merlin.

Boucher, Douglas H. 1996, 'Not with a Bang but a Whimper', *Science & Society*, 60, 3: 279–89.

Boulding, Kenneth E. 1966, 'The Economics of the Coming Spaceship Earth', in *Environmental Quality in a Growing Economy*, edited by Henry Jarrett, Baltimore: Johns Hopkins Press.

Boulding, Kenneth E. 1978, *Ecodynamics*, Beverly Hills: Sage.

Boyce, James K. 1994, 'Inequality as a Cause of Environmental Degradation', *Ecological Economics*, 11, 3: 169–78.

Boyce, James K. 2002, *The Political Economy of the Environment*, Cheltenham: Edward Elgar.

Boyce, James K. 2004, 'Green and Brown? Globalization and the Environment', *Oxford Review of Economic Policy*, 20, 1: 105–28.

Boyce, James K., Andrew R. Klemer, Paul H. Templet and Cleve E. Willis 1999, 'Power Distribution, the Environment, and Public Health: A State-Level Analysis', *Ecological Economics*, 29, 1: 127–40.

Bramwell, Anna 1989, *Ecology in the Twentieth Century*, New Haven: Yale University Press.

Braverman, Harry 1974, *Labor and Monopoly Capital*, New York: Monthly Review Press.

Brecher, Jeremy and Tim Costello 1994, *Global Village or Global Pillage*, Boston: South End Press.

Brennan, Teresa 1997, 'Economy for the Earth', *Ecological Economics*, 20, 2: 175–85.

Bromley, Daniel W. 1995, 'Property Rights and Natural Resource Damage Assessments', *Ecological Economics*, 14, 2: 129–35.

Brown, Thomas C. and Robin Gregory 1999, 'Why the WTA-WTP Disparity Matters', *Ecological Economics*, 28, 3: 323–35.

Buchanan, James M. and Gordon Tullock 1975, 'Polluters' Profits and Political Response: Direct Controls Versus Taxes', *American Economic Review*, 65, 1: 139–47.

Burkett, Paul 1996a, 'On Some Common Misconceptions About Nature and Marx's Critique of Political Economy', *Capitalism, Nature, Socialism*, 7, 3: 57–80.

Burkett, Paul 1996b, 'Value, Capital and Nature: Some Ecological Implications of Marx's Critique of Political Economy', *Science & Society*, 60, 3: 332–59.

Burkett, Paul 1997, 'Nature in Marx Reconsidered', *Organization & Environment*, 10, 2: 164–83.

Burkett, Paul 1998a, 'A Critique of Neo-Malthusian Marxism', *Historical Materialism*, 2: 118–42.

Burkett, Paul 1998b, 'Labor, Eco-Regulation, and Value', *Historical Materialism*, 3: 119–44.

Burkett, Paul 1999a, *Marx and Nature*, New York: St. Martin's Press.

Burkett, Paul 1999b, 'Fusing Red and Green', *Monthly Review*, 50, 9: 47–56.

Burkett, Paul 1999c, 'Nature's "Free Gifts" and the Ecological Significance of Value', *Capital & Class*, 68: 89–110.

Burkett, Paul 2000, 'Marxism and Ecology: A Comment on Lipietz', *Capitalism, Nature, Socialism*, 11, 2: 90–6.

Burkett, Paul 2003a, 'Marx's Vision of Communism and Sustainable Human Development', Paper Presented at the Conference on the Work of Karl Marx and Challenges for the 21st Century, Havana, Cuba, May 5–8, 2003 (web-published by *Cuba Siglo XXI*, No. XXVIII, April 2003: <http://www.nodo50.org/cubasigloXXI/index.htm>).

Burkett, Paul 2003b, 'The Value Problem in Ecological Economics', *Organization & Environment*, 16, 2: 137–67.

Burkett, Paul 2003c, 'Ecology and Marx's Vision of Communism', *Socialism and Democracy*, 17, 2: 41–72.

Burkett, Paul 2003d, 'Natural Capital, Ecological Economics, and Marxism', *International Papers in Political Economy*, 10, 3: 1–61.

Burkett, Paul 2003–4, 'Nature and Value Theory: Airing Out the Issues', *Science & Society*, 67, 4: 452–62.

Burkett, Paul 2004, 'Marx's Reproduction Schemes and the Environment', *Ecological Economics*, 49, 4: 457–67.

Burkett, Paul 2005, 'Entropy in Ecological Economics: A Marxist Intervention', *Historical Materialism*, 13, 1: 117–52.

Burkett, Paul and John Bellamy Foster 2006, 'Metabolism, Energy, and Entropy in Marx's Critique of Political Economy: Beyond the Podolinsky Myth', *Theory and Society*, forthcoming.

Burness, Stuart, Ronald Cummings, Glenn Morris and Inja Paik 1980, 'Thermodynamic and Economic Concepts as Related to Resource-Use Policies', *Land Economics*, 56, 1: 1–9.

Burness, H.S. and R.G. Cummings 1986, 'Thermodynamic and Economic Concepts as Related to Resource-Use Policies: Reply', *Land Economics*, 62, 3: 323–4.

Campos, Daniel G. 2002, 'Assessing the Value of Nature: A Transactional Approach', *Environmental Ethics*, 24, 1: 57–74.

Capital & Class 2000, 'Environmental Politics: Analyses and Alternatives', 72.

Carnot, Sadi 1977 [1824], *Reflections on the Motive Power of Fire*, Gloucester, MA.: Peter Smith.

Carson, Rachel L. 1951, *The Sea Around Us*, New York: Oxford University Press.

Castro, Carlos J. 2004, 'Sustainable Development: Mainstream and Critical Perspectives', *Organization & Environment*, 17, 2: 195–225.

Cavlovic, Therese E., Kenneth H. Baker, Robert P. Berrens and Kishore Gawande 2000, 'A Meta-Analysis of Environmental Kuznets Curve Studies', *Agricultural and Resource Economics Review*, 29, 1: 32–42.

Chakraborty, Rabindra Nath 2001, 'Stability and Outcomes of Common Property

Institutions in Forestry: Evidence from the Terai Region in Nepal', *Ecological Economics*, 36, 2: 341–53.

Champernowne, D.G. 1945–6, 'A Note on J. v. Neumann's Article on "A Model of Economic Equilibrium"', *Review of Economic Studies*, 13, 1: 10–18.

Christensen, Paul P. 1989, 'Historical Roots for Ecological Economics', *Ecological Economics*, 1, 1: 17–36.

Christensen, Paul P. 1994, 'Fire, Motion, and Productivity: The Proto-Energetics of Nature and Economy in François Quesnay', in *Natural Images in Economic Thought*, edited by Philip Mirowski, Cambridge: Cambridge University Press.

Churchill, Ward 1993, *Struggle for the Land*, Monroe: Common Courage Press.

Ciorcirlan, Cristina E. and Bruce Yandle 2003, 'The Political Economy of Green Taxation in OECD Countries', *European Journal of Law and Economics*, 15, 3: 203–18.

Ciriacy-Wantrup, S.V. 1947, 'Capital Returns from Soil Conservation Practices', *Journal of Farm Economics*, 29, 4: 1181–96.

Ciriacy-Wantrup, S.V. and Richard C. Bishop 1975, '"Common Property" as a Concept in Natural Resources Policy', *Natural Resources Journal*, 15, 4: 713–27.

Clark, Brett and John Bellamy Foster 2001, 'William Stanley Jevons and *The Coal Question'*, *Organization & Environment*, 14, 1: 93–8.

Clark, Brett and Richard York 2004, 'Carbon Metabolism: Global Capitalism, Climate Change, and the Biospheric Rift', Paper Presented at the Annual Meetings of the American Sociological Association, San Francisco, 14–17 August.

Clark, Colin 1973, 'The Economics of Overexploitation', *Science*, 181 (17 August): 630–4.

Clark, Judy, Jacquelin Burgess and Carolyn M. Harrison 2000, '"I Struggled With This Money Business": Respondents' Perspectives on Contingent Valuation', *Ecological Economics*, 33, 1: 45–62.

Cleveland, Cutler J. 1987, 'Biophysical Economics', *Ecological Modelling*, 38: 47–73.

Cleveland, Cutler J. 1999, 'Biophysical Economics', in *Bioeconomics and Sustainability*, edited by John Gowdy and Kozo Mayumi, Northampton, MA.: Edward Elgar.

Cleveland, Cutler J., Robert Costanza, Charles A.S. Hall and Robert Kaufmann 1984, 'Energy and the U.S. Economy', *Science*, 225 (31 August): 890–7.

Cleveland, Cutler J. and Mathias Ruth 1997, 'When, Where, and By How Much Do Biophysical Limits Constrain the Economic Process?', *Ecological Economics*, 22, 3: 203–23.

Converse, A.O. 1996, 'On Complete Recycling', *Ecological Economics*, 19, 3: 193–4.

Converse, A.O. 1997, 'On Complete Recycling, 2', *Ecological Economics*, 20, 1: 1–2.

Copeland, Brian R. and M. Scott Taylor 2004, 'Trade, Growth, and the Environment', *Journal of Economic Literature*, 42, 1: 7–71.

Costanza, Robert 1980, 'Embodied Energy and Economic Valuation', *Science*, 210 (12 December): 1219–24.

Costanza, Robert 1981a, 'Embodied Energy, Energy Analysis, and Economics', in *Energy, Economics, and the Environment*, edited by Herman E. Daly and Alvaro F. Umaña, Boulder: Westview.

Costanza, Robert 1981b, 'Reply: An Embodied Energy Theory of Value', in *Energy, Economics, and the Environment*, edited by Herman E. Daly and Alvaro F. Umaña, Boulder: Westview.

Costanza, Robert 1989, 'What Is Ecological Economics?', *Ecological Economics*, 1, 1: 1–7.

Costanza, Robert 2003, 'Ecological Economics is Post-Autistic', *Post-Autistic Economics Review*, 20: 6–8.

Costanza, Robert and Herman E. Daly 1992, 'Natural Capital and Sustainable Development', *Conservation Biology*, 6, 1: 37–46.

Costanza, Robert, Ralph d'Arge, Rudolf de Groot, Stephen Farber, Monica Grasso, Bruce Hannon, Karin Limburg, Shahid Naeem, Robert V. O'Neill, Jose Paruelo, Robert G. Raskin, Paul Sutton and Marjan van den Belt 1997, 'The Value of the World's Ecosystem Services and Natural Capital', *Nature* (15 May): 253–60.

Craig, Paul P. 2001, 'Energy Limits on Recycling', *Ecological Economics*, 36, 3: 373–84.

Daly, Herman E. 1968, 'On Economics as a Life Science', *Journal of Political Economy*, 76, 2: 392–406.

Daly, Herman E. 1974, 'The Economics of the Steady State', *American Economic Review*, 64, 2: 15–21.

Daly, Herman E. 1981, 'Postscript: Unresolved Problems and Issues for Further Research', in *Energy, Economics, and the Environment*, edited by Herman E. Daly and Alvaro F. Umaña, Boulder: Westview.

Daly, Herman E. 1986, 'Thermodynamic and Economic Concepts as Related to Resource-Use Policies: Comment', *Land Economics*, 62, 3: 319–22.

Daly, Herman E. 1990, 'Toward Some Operational Principles of Sustainable Development', *Ecological Economics*, 2, 1: 1–6.

Daly, Herman E. 1991, 'Elements of Environmental Macroeconomics', in *Ecological Economics*, edited by Robert Costanza, New York: Columbia University Press.

Daly, Herman E. 1992a, *Steady-State Economics*, Second Edition, London: Earthscan.

Daly, Herman E. 1992b, 'Allocation, Distribution, and Scale', *Ecological Economics*, 6, 3: 185–93.

Daly, Herman E. 1992c, 'Is the Entropy Law Relevant to the Economics of Natural Resource Scarcity? – Yes, of Course It Is!', *Journal of Environmental Economics and Management*, 23, 1: 91–5.

Daly, Herman E. 1994a, 'Fostering Environmentally Sustainable Development: Four Parting Suggestions for the World Bank', *Ecological Economics*, 10, 3: 183–7.

Daly, Herman E. 1994b, 'Operationalizing Sustainable Development By Investing in Natural Capital', in *Investing in Natural Capital*, edited by AnnMari Jansson, Monica Hammer, Carl Folke and Robert Costanza, Washington, DC.: Island Press.

Daly, Herman E. 1994c, 'Reply', *Ecological Economics*, 10, 2: 90–1.

Daly, Herman E. 1997, 'Georgescu-Roegen Versus Solow/Stiglitz', *Ecological Economics*, 22, 3: 261–6.

Daly, Herman E. 1999, 'Reply to Marcus Stewen', *Ecological Economics*, 30, 1: 1–3.

Daly, Herman E. and John B. Cobb 1989, *For the Common Good*, Boston: Beacon Press.

Dasgupta, P.S. and G.M. Heal 1979, *Economic Theory and Exhaustible Resources*, Cambridge: Cambridge University Press.

Dasgupta, Susmita, Benoit Laplante, Hua Wang and David Wheeler 2002, 'Confronting the Environmental Kuznets Curve', *Journal of Economic Perspectives*, 16, 1: 147–68.

Deléage, Jean-Paul 1994, 'Eco-Marxist Critique of Political Economy', in *Is Capitalism Sustainable?*, edited by Martin O'Connor, New York: Guilford.

Diamond, Peter A. and Jerry A. Hausman 1994, 'Contingent Valuation: Is Some Number Better than No Number?', *Journal of Economic Perspectives*, 8, 4: 45–64.

Dickens, Peter 2004, *Society and Nature*, Cambridge: Polity Press.

Dinda, Soumyananda 2004, 'Environmental Kuznets Curve Hypothesis: A Survey', *Ecological Economics*, 49, 4: 431–55.

Dobb, Maurice 1973, *Theories of Value and Distribution Since Adam Smith*, Cambridge: Cambridge University Press.

Dobson, Andrew 1999, 'Introduction', in *Fairness and Futurity*, edited by Andrew Dobson, Oxford: Oxford University Press.

Douguet, Jean-Marc and Martin O'Connor 2003, 'Maintaining the Integrity of the French *Terroir*: A Study of Critical Natural Capital in its Cultural Context', *Ecological Economics*, 44, 2–3: 233–54.

Drepper, Friedhelm R. and Bengt Å. Månsson 1993, 'Intertemporal Valuation in an Unpredictable Environment', *Ecological Economics*, 7, 1: 43–67.

Dugger, William M. and Howard J. Sherman 2000, *Reclaiming Evolution*, London: Routledge.

Eagleton, Terry 2003, *After Theory*, New York: Basic Books.

Ekins, Paul 1997, 'The Kuznets Curve for the Environment and Economic Growth: Examining the Evidence', *Environment and Planning A*, 29, 5: 805–30.

Ekins, Paul, Carl Folke and Rudolf De Groot 2003, 'Identifying Critical Natural Capital', *Ecological Economics*, 44, 2–3: 159–63.

El Serafy, Salah 1991, 'The Environment as Capital', in *Ecological Economics*, edited by Robert Costanza, New York: Columbia University Press.

El Serafy, Salah 1997, 'Green Accounting and Economic Policy', *Ecological Economics*, 21, 3: 217–29.

Engels, Frederick 1939 [1878], *Anti–Dühring*, New York: International Publishers.

Engels. Frederick 1964a [1925], *Dialectics of Nature*, Moscow: Progress Publishers.

Engels, Frederick 1964b [1844], 'Outlines of a Critique of Political Economy', in *Economic and Philosophical Manuscripts of 1844*, by Karl Marx, New York: International Publishers.

Engels, Frederick 1978 [1882], 'The Mark', in *Collected Works, Karl Marx and Frederick Engels*, Volume 24, New York: International Publishers.

Engels, Frederick 1979 [1872], *The Housing Question*, Moscow: Progress Publishers.

England, Richard W. 1980, 'Environmental Quality in a Marxian Model of Reproduction', *Journal of Economic Studies*, 7, 3, 164–78.

England, Richard W. 1982, 'Workers, Capitalists, and Environmental Policy: An Economic Analysis', *The American Economist*, 26, 2: 39–45.

England, Richard W. 1986, 'Production, Distribution, and Environmental Quality: Mr. Sraffa Interpreted as an Ecologist', *Kyklos*, 39, 2: 230–44.

England, Richard W. 1987, 'Ecology, Social Class, and Political Conflict', in *Economic Processes and Political Conflicts*, edited by Richard W. England, New York: Praeger.

England, Richard W. 1994, 'On Economic Growth and Resource Scarcity: Lessons from Nonequilibrium Thermodynamics', in *Evolutionary Concepts in Contemporary Economics*, edited by Richard W. England, Ann Arbor: University of Michigan Press.

England, Richard W. 1998a, 'Measurement of Social Well-Being: Alternatives to Gross Domestic Product', *Ecological Economics*, 25, 1: 89–103.

England, Richard W. 1998b, 'Should We Pursue Measurement of the Natural Capital Stock?', *Ecological Economics*, 27, 3: 257–66.

England, Richard W. 2000, 'Natural Capital and the Theory of Economic Growth', *Ecological Economics*, 34, 3: 425–31.

Fairlie, Simon 1992, 'Long Distance, Short Life: Why Big Business Favors Recycling', *The Ecologist*, 22, 6: 276–83.

Farber, Stephen C., Robert Costanza and Matthew A. Wilson 2002, 'Economic and Ecological Concepts for Valuing Ecosystem Services', *Ecological Economics*, 41, 3: 375–92.

Feeny, David, Fikret Berkes, Bonnie J. McCay and James M. Acheson 1990, 'The Tragedy of the Commons: Twenty-Two Years Later', *Human Ecology*, 18, 1: 1–19.

Fermi, Enrico 1956 [1937], *Thermodynamics*, New York: Dover.

Fine, Ben 1992, *Women's Employment and the Capitalist Family*, London: Routledge.

Fine, Ben 2001, *Social Capital versus Social Theory*, London: Routledge.

Fine, Ben 2002, '"Economic Imperialism": A View from the Periphery', *Review of Radical Political Economics*, 34, 2: 187–201.

Fischer-Kowalski, Marina 1997, 'Society's Metabolism', in *The International Handbook of Environmental Sociology*, edited by Michael Redclifte and Graham Woodgate, Cheltenham: Edward Elgar.

Folke, Carl, Monica Hammer, Robert Costanza and AnnMari Jansson 1994, 'Investing in Natural Capital', in *Investing in Natural Capital*, edited by AnnMari Jansson, Monica Hammer, Carl Folke, and Robert Costanza, Washington, DC.: Island Press.

Foster, John 1997, 'Introduction: Environmental Value and the Scope of Economics', in *Valuing Nature?*, edited by John Foster, London: Routledge.

Foster, John Bellamy 1994, *The Vulnerable Planet*, New York: Monthly Review Press.

Foster, John Bellamy 1995, 'Marx and the Environment', *Monthly Review*, 47, 3: 108–23.

Foster, John Bellamy 1996, 'Sustainable Development of What?', *Capitalism, Nature, Socialism*, 7, 3: 129–32.

Foster, John Bellamy 2000a, *Marx's Ecology*, New York: Monthly Review Press.

Foster, John Bellamy 2000b, 'The Ecological Tyranny of the Bottom Line', in *Reclaiming the Environmental Debate*, edited by Richard Hofrichter, Cambridge, MA.: MIT Press.

Foster, John Bellamy 2001, 'Review of "Environmental Politics: Analyses and Alternatives"', *Historical Materialism*, 8: 461–77.

Foster, John Bellamy and Paul Burkett 2000, 'The Dialectic of Organic/Inorganic Relations', *Organization & Environment*, 13, 4: 403–25.

Foster, John Bellamy and Paul Burkett 2001, 'Marx and the Dialectic of Organic/Inorganic Relations', *Organization & Environment*, 14, 4: 451–62.

Foster, John Bellamy and Paul Burkett 2004, 'Ecological Economics and Classical Marxism: The "Podolinsky Business" Reconsidered', *Organization & Environment*, 17, 1: 32–60.

Foster, John Bellamy and Brett Clark 2004, 'Ecological Imperialism', in *Socialist Register 2004: The New Imperial Challenge*, edited by Leo Panitch and Colin Leys, New York: Monthly Review Press.

Gale, Fred P. 1998, 'Theorizing Power in Ecological Economics', *Ecological Economics*, 27, 2: 131–8.

Georgescu-Roegen, Nicholas 1954, 'Choice, Expectations and Measurability', *Quarterly Journal of Economics*, 68, 4: 503–34.

Georgescu-Roegen, Nicholas 1971, *The Entropy Law and the Economic Process*, Cambridge, MA.: Harvard University Press.

Georgescu-Roegen, Nicholas 1973, 'The Entropy Law and the Economic Problem', in *Economics, Ecology, Ethics*, edited by Herman E. Daly, San Francisco: W.H. Freeman.

Georgescu-Roegen, Nicholas 1975, 'Energy and Economic Myths', *Southern Economic Journal*, 41, 3: 347–81.

Georgescu-Roegen, Nicholas 1976, *Energy and Economic Myths*, New York: Pergamon.

Georgescu-Roegen, Nicholas 1979a, 'Comments on the Papers by Daly and Stiglitz', in *Scarcity and Growth Reconsidered*, edited by V. Kerry Smith, Baltimore: Johns Hopkins University Press.

Georgescu-Roegen, Nicholas 1979b, 'Energy Analysis and Economic Valuation', *Southern Economic Journal*, 45, 4: 1023–58.

Georgescu-Roegen, Nicholas 1981, 'Energy, Matter, and Economic Valuation: Where Do We Stand?', in *Energy, Economics, and the Environment*, edited by Herman E. Daly and Alvaro F. Umaña, Boulder: Westview.

Giampietro, Mario and David Pimentel 1991, 'Energy Efficiency: Assessing the Interaction Between Humans and Their Environment', *Ecological Economics*, 4, 2: 117–44.

Gordon, H. Scott 1954, 'The Economic Theory of a Common Property Resource: The Fishery', *Journal of Political Economy*, 62, 2: 124–42.

Gowdy, John M. 1984, 'Marx and Resource Scarcity', *Journal of Economic Issues*, 18, 2: 393–400.

Gowdy, John M. 1988, 'The Entropy Law and Marxian Value Theory', *Review of Radical Political Economics*, 20, 2–3: 34–40.

Gowdy, John M. 1991, 'Bioeconomics and Post Keynesian Economics', *Ecological Economics*, 3, 1: 77–87.

Gowdy, John M. 1994a, *Coevolutionary Economics*, Boston: Kluwer.

Gowdy, John M. 1994b, 'The Social Context of Natural Capital', *International Journal of Social Economics*, 21, 8: 43–55.

Gowdy, John M. 1997, 'The Value of Biodiversity: Markets, Society, and Ecosystems', *Land Economics*, 73, 1: 25–41.

Gowdy, John and Peg R. Olsen 1994, 'Further Problems with Neoclassical Environmental Economics', *Environmental Ethics*, 16, 2: 161–71.

Gowdy, John M. and Jon D. Erickson 2005, 'The Approach of Ecological Economics', *Cambridge Journal of Economics*, 29, 2: 207–22.

Griese, Anneliese and Gerd Pawelzig 1995, 'Why Did Marx and Engels Concern Themselves with Natural Science?', *Nature, Society, and Thought*, 8, 2: 125–37.

Grove, William Robert 1864 [1846], *On the Correlation of Physical Forces*, in *The Correlation and Conservation of Forces*, edited by Edward L. Youmans, New York: D. Appleton and Co.

Guha, Ramachandra and Juan Martinez-Alier 1997, *Varieties of Environmentalism*, London: Earthscan.

Gustafsson, Bo 1998, 'Scope and Limits of the Market Mechanism in Environmental Management', *Ecological Economics*. 24, 2–3: 259–74.

Gutés, Maite Cabeza 1996, 'The Concept of Weak Sustainability', *Ecological Economics*, 17, 3: 147–56.

Hanemann, W. Michael 1991, 'Willingness to Pay and Willingness to Accept: How Much Can They Differ?', *American Economic Review*, 81, 3: 635–47.

Hanley, Nick 2000, 'Macroeconomic Measures of "Sustainability"', *Journal of Economic Surveys*, 14, 1: 1–30.

Hanley, Nick, Jason F. Shogren and Ben White 1997, *Environmental Economics in Theory and Practice*, Oxford: Oxford University Press.

Hannon, Bruce M. 1973, 'An Energy Standard of Value', *Annals of the American Academy of Political and Social Science*, 410: 139–53.

Hannon, Bruce M. 1998, 'How Might Nature Value Man?', *Ecological Economics*, 25, 3: 265–79.

Hannon, Bruce M. 2001, 'Ecological Pricing and Economic Efficiency', *Ecological Economics*, 36, 1: 19–30.

Hardin, Garrett 1968, 'The Tragedy of the Commons', *Science*, 162: 1243–8.

Harris, Stuart 1996, 'Economics of the Environment: A Survey', *Economic Record*, 72: 154–71.

Harrison, Carolyn, Jacquelin Burgess and Judy Clark 1999, 'Capturing Values for Nature', in *Locality and Identity*, edited by Jane Holder and Donald McGillivray, Aldershot: Ashgate.

Harte, M.J. 1995, 'Ecology, Sustainability, and Environment as Capital', *Ecological Economics*, 15, 2: 157–64.

Hartwick, John M. 1977, 'Intergenerational Equity and the Investing of Rents from Exhaustible Resources', *American Economic Review*, 67, 5: 972–4.

Harvey, David 1996, *Justice, Nature and the Geography of Difference*, Oxford: Blackwell.

Hay, Peter 2002, *Main Currents in Western Environmental Thought*, Bloomington: Indiana University Press.

Hayward, Tim 1994, *Ecological Thought: An Introduction*, Cambridge: Polity Press.

Hayward, Tim 1997, 'Introduction', in *Justice, Property and the Environment*, edited by Tim Hayward and John O'Neill, Aldershot: Ashgate.

Henderson, James M. and Richard E. Quandt 1980, *Microeconomic Theory*, Third Edition, New York: McGraw-Hill.

Herlitz, Lars 1961, 'The Tableau Économique and the Doctrine of Sterility', *Scandinavian Economic History Review*, 9, 1: 3–55.

Hermann, Ludimar 1875 [1863], *Elements of Human Physiology*, Fifth Edition, London: Smith and Elder.

Hinterberger, Friedrich, Fred Luks and Friedrich Schmidt-Bleek 1997, 'Material Flows vs. "Natural Capital"', *Ecological Economics*, 23, 1: 1–14.

Holland, Alan 1994, 'Natural Capital', in *Philosophy and the Natural Environment*, edited by Robin Attfield and Andrew Belsey, Cambridge: Cambridge University Press.

Holland, Alan 1999, 'Sustainability: Should We Start from Here?', in *Fairness and Futurity*, edited by Andrew Dobson, Oxford: Oxford University Press.

Hornborg, Alf 1998, 'Towards an Ecological Theory of Unequal Exchange', *Ecological Economics*, 25, 1: 127–36.

Horton, Stephen 1995, 'Rethinking Recycling', *Capitalism, Nature, Socialism*, 6, 1: 1–19.

Horton, Stephen 1997, 'Value, Waste and the Built Environment: A Marxian Analysis', *Capitalism, Nature, Socialism*, 8, 2: 127–39.

Howarth, Richard B. 1997, 'Sustainability as Opportunity', *Land Economics*, 73, 4: 569–79.

Howarth, Richard B. and Richard B. Norgaard 1992, 'Environmental Valuation under Sustainable Development', *American Economic Review*, 82, 2: 473–7.

Howe, Charles W. 1997, 'Dimensions of Sustainability', *Land Economics*, 73, 4: 597–607.

Huesemann, Michael H. 2001, 'Can Pollution Problems Be Effectively Solved By Environmental Science and Technology?', *Ecological Economics*, 37, 2: 271–87.

Hueting, Roefie 1996, 'Three Persistent Myths in the Environmental Debate', *Ecological Economics*, 18, 2: 81–8.

Hughes, Jonathan 2000, *Ecology and Historical Materialism*, Cambridge: Cambridge University Press.

Huppes, Gjalt and Robert A. Kagan 1989, 'Market-Oriented Regulation of Environmental Problems in the Netherlands', *Law & Policy*, 11, 2: 215–39.

Huws, Ursula 1999, 'Material World: The Myth of the Weightless Economy', in *Socialist*

Register 1999: Global Capitalism Versus Democracy, edited by Leo Panitch and Colin Leys, New York: Monthly Review Press.

Jacobs, Michael 1997, 'Environmental Valuation, Deliberative Democracy and Public Decision-Making Institutions', in *Valuing Nature?*, edited by John Foster, London: Routledge.

Jacobs, Michael 1999, 'Sustainable Development as a Contested Concept', in *Fairness and Futurity*, edited by Andrew Dobson, Oxford: Oxford University Press.

Jamison, Andrew 2001, *The Making of Green Knowledge*, Cambridge: Cambridge University Press.

Jansson, AnnMari, Monica Hammer, Carl Folke and Robert Costanza (eds.) 1994, *Investing in Natural Capital*, Washington, DC.: Island Press.

Joffe-Waite, Benjamin 2005, 'China's Computer Wasteland', *The Progressive*, January: 30–3.

Johnston, Josée 2003, 'Who Cares about the Commons?', *Capitalism, Nature, Socialism*, 14, 4: 1–41.

Jordan, Andrew, Rudiger K.W. Wurzel and Anthony R. Zito 2003, '"New" Environmental Policy Instruments: An Evolution or a Revolution in Environmental Policy?', *Environmental Politics*, 12, 1: 201–24.

Jorgensen, Bradley S., Geoffrey J. Syme, Brian J. Bishop, and Blair E. Nancarrow 1999, 'Protest Responses in Contingent Valuation', *Environmental and Resource Economics*, 14, 1: 131–50.

Judson, D.H. 1989, 'The Convergence of Neo-Ricardian and Embodied Energy Theories of Value and Price', *Ecological Economics*, 1, 3: 262–81.

Kåberger, Tomas and Bengt Månsson 2001, 'Entropy and Economic Processes – Physics Perspectives', *Ecological Economics*, 36, 1: 165–79.

Kaplowitz, Michael D. and John P. Hoehn 2001, 'Do Focus Groups and Individual Interviews Reveal the Same Information for Natural Resource Valuation?', *Ecological Economics*, 36, 2: 237–47.

Kaufmann, Robert 1987, 'Biophysical and Marxist Economics', *Ecological Modelling*, 38, 1–2: 91–105.

Kaufmann, Robert 1992, 'A Biophysical Analysis of the Energy/Real GDP Ratio', *Ecological Economics*, 6, 1: 35–56.

Kennedy, David 1998, 'A Clarification of Marx's Theory of Crisis', *Critique*, 30–1: 49–70.

Keynes, John Maynard 1964 [1936], *The General Theory of Employment, Interest, and Money*, New York: Harcourt Brace.

Khalil, Elias L. 1990, 'Entropy Law and Exhaustion of Natural Resources: Is Nicholas Georgescu-Roegen's Paradigm Defensible?', *Ecological Economics*, 2, 2: 163–78.

Kirchgassner, Gebhard and Friedrich Schneider 2003, 'On the Political Economy of Environmental Policy', *Public Choice*, 115, 3: 369–96.

Knetsch, Jack L. and J.A. Sinden 1984, 'Willingness to Pay and Compensation Demanded: Experimental Evidence of an Unexpected Disparity in Measures of Value', *Quarterly Journal of Economics*, 99, 3: 507–21.

Konrad, Rachel 2005, 'High-Tech Pollution', *Terre Haute Tribune Star*, 21 April: A6.

Kopp, Raymond J., Paul R. Portney and Diane E. DeWitt 1990, 'International Comparisons of Environmental Regulation', in *Environmental Policy and the Cost of Capital*, Washington, DC.: American Council for Capital Formation.

Krohn, Wolfgang and Wolf Schäfer 1983, 'Agricultural Chemistry: The Origin and Structure of a Finalized Science', in *Finalization in Science*, edited by Wolf Schäfer, Boston: D. Reidel.

Kuhn, Thomas S. 1970 [1962], *The Structure of Scientific Revolutions*, Second Edition, Chicago: University of Chicago Press.

Kümmel, Reiner 1994, 'Energy, Entropy – Economy, Ecology', *Ecological Economics*, 9, 3: 194–6.

Kuznets, Simon 1955, 'Economic Growth and Income Inequality', *American Economic Review*, 45, 1: 1–28.

Lange, Oskar and Fred M. Taylor 1964, *On the Economic Theory of Socialism*, New York: McGraw-Hill.

Lawn, Phillip A. 1999, 'On Georgescu-Roegen's Contribution to Ecological Economics', *Ecological Economics*, 29, 1: 5–8.

Lazear, Edward P. 2000, 'Economic Imperialism', *Quarterly Journal of Economics*, 115, 1: 99–146.

Lebowitz, Michael A. 1992, *Beyond 'Capital'*, New York: St. Martin's Press.

Lebowitz, Michael A. 2002, 'Karl Marx: the Needs of Capital vs. the Needs of Human Beings', in *Understanding Capitalism: Critical Analysis from Karl Marx to Amartya Sen*, edited by Douglas Dowd, London: Pluto Press.

Lee, Frederic S. and Steve Keen 2004, 'The Incoherent Emperor: A Heterodox Critique of Neoclassical Microeconomic Theory', *Review of Social Economy*, 62, 2: 169–99.

Leff, Enrique 1995, *Green Production*, New York: Guilford.

Leff, Enrique 1996, 'Marxism and the Environmental Question', in *The Greening of Marxism*, edited by Ted Benton, New York: Guilford.

Linder, Marc (in collaboration with Julius Sensat, Jr.) 1977, *Anti-Samuelson*, Volume Two, New York: Urizen Books.

Lintott, John 1996, 'Environmental Accounting: Useful to Whom and For What?', *Ecological Economics*, 16, 3: 179–90.

Lintott, John 1998, 'Beyond the Economics of More', *Ecological Economics*, 25, 3: 239–48.

Lipietz, Alain 2000, 'Political Ecology and the Future of Marxism', *Capitalism, Nature, Socialism*, 11, 1: 69–85.

Lohmann, Larry 1998, 'Whose Value is Speaking? How Opinion Polling and Cost-Benefit Analysis Synthesize New "Publics"', *Cornerhouse Briefing*, 7 (May).

Lotspeich, Richard 1998, 'Comparative Environmental Policy: Market–Type Instruments in Industrialized Capitalist Countries', *Policy Studies Journal*, 26, 1: 85–104.

Lozada, Gabriel A. 1991, 'A Defense of Nicholas Georgescu-Roegen's Paradigm', *Ecological Economics*, 3, 2: 157–60.

Magnani, Elisabetta 2000, 'The Environmental Kuznets Curve, Environmental Protection Policy and Income Distribution', *Ecological Economics*, 32, 3: 431–43.

Månsson, Bengt Å. 1994, 'Recycling of Matter: A Response', *Ecological Economics*, 9, 3: 191–2.

Martinez-Alier, Juan 1987, *Ecological Economics*, Oxford: Basil Blackwell.

Martinez-Alier, Juan 1995a, 'The Environment as a Luxury Good or "Too Poor to be Green"?', *Ecological Economics*, 13, 1: 1–10.

Martinez-Alier, Juan 1995b, 'Political Ecology, Distributional Conflicts, and Economic Incommensurability', *New Left Review*, I, 211: 70–88.

Martinez-Alier, Juan 1995c, 'Distributional Issues in Ecological Economics', *Review of Social Economy*, 53, 4: 511–28.

Martinez-Alier, Juan 2003, 'Marxism, Social Metabolism, and Ecologically Unequal Exchange', Paper Presented at the Conference on World System Theory and the Environment, Lund University, Sweden, September.

Martinez-Alier, Juan and J.M. Naredo 1982, 'A Marxist Precursor of Ecological Economics: Podolinsky', *Journal of Peasant Studies*, 9, 2: 207–24.

Martinez-Alier, Juan and Martin O'Connor 1996, 'Ecological and Economic Distribution Conflicts', in *Getting Down to Earth*, edited by Robert Costanza, Olman Seguara, and Juan Martinez-Alier, Washington, DC.: Island Press.

Martinez-Alier, Juan, Giuseppe Munda and John O'Neill 1998, 'Weak Comparability of Values as a Foundation for Ecological Economics', *Ecological Economics*, 26, 3: 277–86.

Marx, Karl 1939 [1878], 'From the *Critical History*', in Part II, Chapter X of *Anti-Dühring*, by Frederick Engels, New York: International Publishers.

Marx, Karl 1955 [1844], 'Contribution to the Critique of Hegel's Philosophy of Right: Introduction', in *Marx and Engels on Religion*, Moscow: Progress Publishers.

Marx, Karl 1963 [1956], *Theories of Surplus Value*, Part I, Moscow: Progress Publishers.

Marx, Karl 1964 [1932], *Economic and Philosophical Manuscripts of 1844*, New York: International Publishers.

Marx, Karl 1966 [1890–1], *Critique of the Gotha Program*, New York: International Publishers.

Marx, Karl 1967 [1867], *Capital*, Volume I, New York: International Publishers.

Marx, Karl 1968 [1959], *Theories of Surplus Value*, Part II, Moscow: Progress Publishers.

Marx, Karl 1971 [1962], *Theories of Surplus Value*, Part III, Moscow: Progress Publishers.

Marx, Karl 1973 [1939–41], *Grundrisse*, New York: Vintage.

Marx, Karl 1974a [1864], 'Inaugural Address of the International Working Men's Association', in *The First International and After*, edited by David Fernbach, New York: Random House.

Marx, Karl 1974b [1871], 'Provisional Rules', in *The First International and After*, edited by David Fernbach, New York: Random House.

Marx, Karl 1975 [1930], 'Notes on Wagner', in *Texts on Method*, edited by Terrell Carver, Oxford: Basil Blackwell.

Marx, Karl 1976a [1924], 'Wages', in *Collected Works, Karl Marx and Frederick Engels*, Volume 6, New York: International Publishers.

Marx, Karl 1976b [1898], *Value, Price and Profit*, New York: International Publishers.

Marx, Karl 1977 [1933], 'Results of the Immediate Process of Production', in *Capital*, Volume I, by Karl Marx, New York: Vintage.

Marx, Karl 1981 [1867–94], *Capital*, Volumes I–III, New York: Vintage.

Marx, Karl 1985 [1871], 'The Civil War in France', in *Marx and Engels on the Paris Commune*, Moscow: Progress Publishers.

Marx, Karl 1989a [1926], 'Notes on Bakunin's Book *Statehood and Anarchy*', in *Collected Works, Karl Marx and Frederick Engels*, Volume 24, New York: International Publishers.

Marx, Karl 1989b [1924], 'Drafts of the Letter to Vera Zasulich', and 'Letter to Vera Zasulich (8 March 1881)', in *Collected Works, Karl Marx and Frederick Engels*, Volume 24, New York: International Publishers.

Marx, Karl 1991 [1976–82], 'Economic Manuscript of 1861–63, Continuation', in *Collected Works, Karl Marx and Frederick Engels*, Volume 33, New York: International Publishers.

Marx, Karl 1994 [1976–82], 'Economic Manuscript of 1861–63, Conclusion', in *Collected Works, Karl Marx and Frederick Engels*, Volume 34, New York: International Publishers.

Marx, Karl forthcoming [1880], 'Le Travail et la Conservation de l'Energie. Par. S. Podolinsky' (excerpt-notes), in *Historisch-Kritische Gesamtausgabe*, edited by Kevin B. Anderson, David Norman Smith, Norair Ter-Akopian, Georgi Bagaturia and Jürgen Rojahn, Berlin: Akademie-Verlag.

Marx, Karl and Frederick Engels 1968 [1848], 'Manifesto of the Communist Party', in *Selected Works, Karl Marx and Frederick Engels* (One Volume), London: Lawrence and Wishart.

Marx, Karl and Frederick Engels 1975, *Selected Correspondence*, Moscow: Progress Publishers.

Marx, Karl and Frederick Engels 1976 [1932], *The German Ideology*, Moscow: Progress Publishers.

Marx, Karl and Frederick Engels 1985, *Collected Works*, Volume 41, New York: International Publishers.

Marx, Karl and Frederick Engels 1992, *Collected Works*, Volume 46. New York: International Publishers.

Mayumi, Kozo 1991, 'Temporary Emancipation from Land', *Ecological Economics*, 4, 1: 35–56.

Mayumi, Kozo 1993, 'Georgescu-Roegen's "Fourth Law of Thermodynamics", the Modern Energetic Dogma, and Ecological Salvation', in *Trends in Ecological Physical Chemistry*, edited by L. Bonati, U. Cosentino, M. Lasagni, G. Moro, D. Pitea and A. Schiraldi, Amsterdam: Elsevier.

Mayumi, Kozo 2001, *The Origins of Ecological Economics*, London: Routledge.

Mayumi, Kozo and Mario Giampietro 2004, 'Entropy in Ecological Economics', in *Modelling in Ecological Economics*, edited by John L.R. Proops, Cheltenham: Edward Elgar.

McKibben, Bill 1990, *The End of Nature*, New York: Anchor Books.

Meadows, D.H., D.L. Meadows, J. Randers and W. Behrens 1972, *The Limits to Growth*, New York: Universe Books.

Meek, Ronald L. 1973 [1956], *Studies in the Labor Theory of Value*, Second Edition. London: Lawrence & Wishart.

Mesarovic, Mihajlo and Eduard Pestel 1975, *Mankind at the Turning Point*, London: Hutchinson.

Metroeconomica 2001, 'Symposium on Exhaustible Resources and Sraffian Analysis', 52, 3: 239–328.

Middleman, Stanley 1997, *An Introduction to Mass and Heat Transfer*, New York: John Wiley & Sons.

Mirowski, Philip 1988, 'Energy and Energetics in Economic Theory', *Journal of Economic Issues*, 22, 3: 811–30.

Mishan, E.J. 1971, *Cost-Benefit Analysis: An Introduction*, New York: Praeger.

Moore, Jason W. 2000a, 'Environmental Crises and the Metabolic Rift in World-Historical Perspective', *Organization & Environment*, 13, 2: 123–57.

Moore, Jason W. 2000b, 'Sugar and the Expansion of the Early Modern World Economy', *Review*, 23, 3: 409–33.

Moore, Jason W. 2001, '*Marx's Ecology* and the Environmental History of World Capitalism', *Capitalism, Nature, Socialism*, 12, 3: 134–39.

Moore, Jason W. 2003, 'Capitalism as World-Ecology: Braudel and Marx on Environmental History', *Organization & Environment*, 16, 4: 431–58.

Morton, John Chalmers 1859, 'On the Forces Used in Agriculture', *Journal of the Society of the Arts*, 9 December: 53–68.

Mulder, Peter and C.J.M. Van Den Bergh 2001, 'Evolutionary Economic Theories of Sustainable Development', *Growth and Change*, 32, 1: 110–34.

Munda, G., P. Nijkamp and P. Rietveld 1995, 'Monetary and Non-Monetary Evaluation Methods in Sustainable Development Planning', *Économie Appliquée*, 48, 2: 143–60.

Neefjes, Koos 1999, 'Ecological Degradation: A Cause for Conflict, A Concern for Survival', in *Fairness and Futurity*, edited by Andrew Dobson, Oxford: Oxford University Press.

Nelson, Anitra 2001, 'The Poverty of Money: Marxian Insights for Ecological Economists', *Ecological Economics*, 36, 3: 499–511.

Nelson Espeland, Wendy 1999, 'Value-Matters', Paper Presented at the Conference on 'The Cost-Benefit Analysis Dilemma: Strategies and Alternatives', Yale University, 8–10 October.

Neumayer, Eric 2000, 'Scarce or Abundant? The Economics of Natural Resource Availability', *Journal of Economic Surveys*, 14, 3: 307–35.

Neumayer, Eric 2004, 'The Environment, Left-Wing Political Orientation and Ecological Economics', *Ecological Economics*, 51, 3–4: 167–75.

Nicholson, Walter 1985, *Microeconomic Theory*, Third Edition, New York: Dryden Press.

Norgaard, Richard B. 1986, 'Thermodynamic and Economic Concepts as Related to Resource-Use Policies: Synthesis', *Land Economics*, 62, 3: 325–8.

Norgaard, Richard B. 1989a, 'The Case for Methodological Pluralism', *Ecological Economics*, 1, 1: 37–57.

Norgaard, Richard B. 1989b, 'Three Dilemmas of Environmental Accounting', *Ecological Economics*, 1, 4: 303–14.

Norgaard, Richard B. 1994, *Development Betrayed, the End of Progress and a Coevolutionary Revisioning of the Future*, London: Routledge.

Norgaard, Richard B. 1995, 'Beyond Materialism: A Coevolutionary Reinterpretation of the Environmental Crisis', *Review of Social Economy*, 53, 4: 475–92.

Norton, Bryan G. 1995, 'Evaluating Ecosystem States: Two Competing Paradigms', *Ecological Economics*, 14, 2: 113–27.

Norton, Bryan G. and Michael A. Toman 1997, 'Sustainability: Ecological and Economic Perspectives', *Land Economics*, 73, 4: 553–68.

Norton, Bryan, Robert Costanza and Richard C. Bishop 1998, 'The Evolution of Preferences', *Ecological Economics*, 24, 2–3: 193–211.

Nunes, Paulo A.L.D. and Jeroen C.J.M. Van der Bergh 2001, 'Economic Valuation of Biodiversity: Sense or Nonsense?', *Ecological Economics*, 39, 2: 203–22.

O'Connor, James 1973, *The Fiscal Crisis of the State*, New York: St. Martin's Press.

O'Connor, James 1998, *Natural Causes*, New York: Guilford.

O'Connor, Martin 1993a, 'Value System Contests and the Appropriation of Ecological Capital', *Manchester School*, 61, 4: 398–424.

O'Connor, Martin 1993b, 'Entropic Irreversibility and Uncontrolled Technological Change in Economy and Environment', *Journal of Evolutionary Economics*, 3, 4: 285–315.

O'Connor, Martin 1994, 'On the Misadventures of Capitalist Nature', in *Is Capitalism Sustainable?*, edited by Martin O'Connor, New York: Guilford.

O'Connor, Martin and Juan Martinez-Alier 1998, 'Ecological Distribution and Distributed Sustainability', in *Sustainable Development: Concepts, Rationalities, and Strategies*, edited by Sylvie Faucheux, Martin O'Connor and Jan van der Straaten, Boston: Kluwer.

Ollman, Bertell 1979, *Social and Sexual Revolution*, Boston: South End Press.

Olson, Mancur 1971, *The Logic of Collective Action*, Cambridge, MA.: Harvard University Press.

O'Neill, John 1997, 'King Darius and the Environmental Economist', in *Justice, Property and the Environment*, edited by Tim Hayward and John O'Neill, Aldershot: Ashgate.

O'Neill, John 2002, 'Socialist Calculation and Environmental Valuation', *Science & Society*, 66, 1: 137–51.

O'Neill, John 2004, 'Ecological Economics and the Politics of Knowledge: the Debate Between Hayek and Neurath', *Cambridge Journal of Economics*, 28, 3: 431–47.

Ostrom, Elinor 1990, *Governing the Commons*, Cambridge: Cambridge University Press.

Ostrom, Elinor 2000, 'Collective Action and the Evolution of Social Norms', *Journal of Economic Perspectives*, 14, 3: 137–58.

Parkinson, Eric 1999, 'Talking Technology', *Journal of Technology Education*, 11, 1: 60–73: <http://scholar.lib.vt.edu/ejournals/JTEv11n1/parkinson.html>.

Parlato, Valentino and Giovanna Ricoveri 1996, 'The Second Contradiction in the Italian Experience', in *The Greening of Marxism*, edited by Ted Benton, New York: Guilford.

Patterson, Murray 1998, 'Commensuration and Theories of Value in Ecological Economics', *Ecological Economics*, 25, 1: 105–25.

Pearce, David W. and Giles D. Atkinson 1993, 'Capital Theory and the Measurement of Sustainable Development: An Indicator of "Weak" Sustainability', *Ecological Economics*, 8, 2: 103–8.

Pearce, David W. and Giles D. Atkinson 1995, 'Measuring Sustainable Development', in *Handbook of Environmental Economics*, edited by Daniel W. Bromley, Oxford: Blackwell.

Pearce, David W., Giles D. Atkinson and W. Richard Dubourg 1994, 'The Economics of Sustainable Development', *Annual Review of Energy and Environment*, 19: 457–74.

Pepper, David 1996, *Modern Environmentalism*, London: Routledge.

Perelman, Michael 1974, 'An Application of Marxian Theory to Ecological Economics', *Review of Radical Political Economics*, 6, 3: 75–7.

Perelman, Michael 2003, 'Myths of the Market: Economics and the Environment', *Organization & Environment*, 16, 2: 168–226.

Perrings, Charles 1985, 'The Natural Economy Revisited', *Economic Development and Cultural Change*, 33, 4: 829–50.

Perrings, Charles 1986, 'Conservation of Mass and Instability in a Dynamic Economy-Environment System', *Journal of Environmental Economics and Management*, 13, 3: 199–211.

Perrings, Charles 1987, *Economy and Environment*, Cambridge: Cambridge University Press.

Perrings, Charles 1989, 'Environmental Bonds and Environmental Research in Innovative Activities', *Ecological Economics*, 1, 1: 95–110.

Phillips, Paul 1993, 'Red and Green: Economics, Property Rights, and the Environment', in *Green On Red: Evolving Ecological Socialism*, edited by Jesse Vorst, Ross Dobson and Ron Fletcher, Winnipeg: Fernwood.

Podolinsky, Sergei 1880, 'Le Socialisme et l'Unité des Forces Physiques', *La Revue Socialiste*, 8: 353–65.

Podolinsky, Sergei 1881, 'Il Socialismo e l'Unità delle Forze Fisiche', *La Plebe*, 14, 3: 13–6 and 14, 4: 5–15.

Podolinsky, Sergei 1883, 'Menschliche Arbeit und Einheit der Kraft', *Die Neue Zeit*, 1, 9: 413–24 and 1, 10: 449–57.

Podolinsky, Sergei 1991, *Human Labor and Its Relation to the Distribution of Energy*, Moscow: Noosfera (in Russian).

Podolinsky, Sergei 2004, 'Socialism and the Unity of Physical Forces' (translated by Angelo Di Salvo and Mark Hudson), *Organization & Environment*, 17, 1: 61–75.

Polanyi, Karl 1944, *The Great Transformation*, Boston: Beacon Press.

Portney, Paul R. 1994, 'The Contingent Valuation Debate: Why Economists Should Care', *Journal of Economic Perspectives*, 8, 4: 3–17.

Prakash, Aseem and Anil K. Gupta 1994, 'Are Efficiency, Equity, and Scale Independent?', *Ecological Economics*, 10, 2: 89–90.

Prigogine, Ilya and Isabelle Stengers 1984, *Order Out of Chaos*, New York: Bantam Books.

Proops, John L.R. 1987, 'Entropy, Information and Confusion in the Social Sciences', *Journal of Interdisciplinary Economics*, 1, 4: 225–42.

Proops, John L.R. 1989, 'Ecological Economics: Rationale and Problem Areas', *Ecological Economics*, 1, 1: 59–76.

Prugh, Thomas (with Robert Costanza, John H. Cumberland, Herman E. Daly, Robert Goodland and Richard B. Norgaard) 1995, *Natural Capital and Human Economic Survival*, White River Junction: USEE Press.

Quesnay, François 1963a [1763], 'Rural Philosophy (extract)', in *The Economics of Physiocracy: Essays and Translations*, edited by Ronald L. Meek, Cambridge, MA.: Harvard University Press.

Quesnay, François 1963b [1766], 'Dialogue on the Work of Artisans', in *The Economics of Physiocracy: Essays and Translations*, edited by Ronald L. Meek, Cambridge, MA.: Harvard University Press.

Quesnay, François 1963c [1766], 'Analysis', in *The Economics of Physiocracy: Essays and Translations*, edited by Ronald L. Meek, Cambridge, MA.: Harvard University Press.

Quesnay, François 1963d [1767], 'General Maxims for the Economic Government of an Agricultural Kingdom', in *The Economics of Physiocracy: Essays and Translations*, edited by Ronald L. Meek, Cambridge, MA.: Harvard University Press.

Quiggin, John 1988, 'Private and Common Property Rights in the Economics of the Environment', *Journal of Economic Issues*, 22, 4: 1071–87.

Rao, P.K. 2000, *Sustainable Development*, Oxford: Blackwell.

Rebane, Karl K. 1995, 'Energy, Entropy, Environment: Why Is Protection of the Environment Objectively Difficult?', *Ecological Economics*, 13, 2: 89–92.

Rees, William E. 1999, 'Consuming the Earth', *Ecological Economics*, 29, 1: 23–7.

Rees, William E. and Mathis Wackernagel 1999, 'Monetary Analysis: Turning a Blind Eye on Sustainability', *Ecological Economics*, 29, 1: 47–52.

Roosevelt, Frank 1977, 'Cambridge Economics as Commodity Fetishism', in *The Subtle Anatomy of Capitalism*, edited by Jesse Schwartz, Santa Monica: Goodyear.

Rosdolsky, Roman 1977, *The Making of Marxs 'Capital'*, London: Pluto Press.

Rosewarne, Stuart 1995, 'On Ecological Economics', *Capitalism, Nature, Socialism*, 6, 3: 105–15.

Rowe, Jonathan 2004, 'The Growth Consensus Unravels', in *Real World Macro*, Twenty-First Edition, edited by Daniel Fireside, John Miller, Amy Offner and the *Dollars and Sense* Collective, Cambridge, MA.: Economic Affairs Bureau, Inc.

Saad-Filho, Alfredo 2002, *The Value of Marx*, London: Routledge.

Salleh, Ariel 1997, *Ecofeminism as Politics*, London: Zed Books.

Sandler, Blair 1994, 'Grow or Die: Marxist Theories of Capitalism and the Environment', *Rethinking Marxism*, 7, 2: 38–57.

Savornin Lohman, Lex de 1994, 'Economic Incentives in Environmental Policy: Why are They White Ravens?', in *Economic Incentives and Environmental Policies*, edited by Hans Opschoor and Kerry Turner, Boston: Kluwer.

Schor, Juliet B. 1992, *The Overworked American: The Unexpected Decline of Leisure*, New York: Basic Books.

Schwartzman, David 1996, 'Solar Communism', *Science & Society*, 60, 3: 307–31.

Science & Society 1992, 'Socialism: Alternative Views and Models', 56, 1: 2–108.

Science & Society 1996, 'Marxism and Ecology', 60, 3: 258–379.

Science & Society 2002, 'Building Socialism Theoretically: Alternatives to Capitalism and the Invisible Hand', 66, 1: 3–158.

Scruggs, Lyle A. 1998, 'Political and Economic Inequality and the Environment', *Ecological Economics*, 26, 3: 259–75.

Seidl, Irmi and Clem A. Tisdell 1999, 'Carrying Capacity Reconsidered', *Ecological Economics*, 31, 3: 395–408.

Shabi, Rachel 2002, 'The E-Waste Land', *Guardian* (On-Line edition), November 30.

Shandro, Alan 2000, 'Karl Marx as a Conservative Thinker', *Historical Materialism*, 6: 3–25.

Shogren, Jason F., Joseph A. Herriges and Ramu Govindasamy 1993, 'Limits to Environmental Bonds', *Ecological Economics*, 8, 2: 109–33.

Skirbekk, Gunnar 1994, 'Marxism and Ecology', *Capitalism, Nature, Socialism*, 5, 4: 95–104.

Smith, Fred L. 1995, 'Markets and the Environment: A Critical Reappraisal', *Contemporary Economic Policy*, 13, 1: 62–73.

Smith, Neil 1984, *Uneven Development*, Oxford: Blackwell.

Solow, Robert M. 1971, 'The Economist's Approach to Pollution Control', *Science*, 173: 498–503.

Solow, Robert M. 1974a, 'The Economics of Resources or the Resources of Economics', *American Economic Review*, 64, 2: 1–14.

Solow, Robert M. 1974b, 'Intergenerational Equity and Exhaustible Resources', *Review of Economic Studies*, 41 (Symposium on the Economics of Exhaustible Resources): 29–45.

Solow, Robert M. 1976, 'Is the End of the World at Hand?', in *Great Debates in Economics*, Volume I, edited by Richard T. Gill, Pacific Palisades: Goodyear.

Solow, Robert M. 1986, 'On the Intergenerational Allocation of Resources', *Scandinavian Journal of Economics*, 88, 1: 141–9.

Spash, Clive L. 1999, 'The Development of Environmental Thinking in Economics', *Environmental Values*, 8, 4: 413–35.

Spash, Clive L. 2000a, 'Ecosystems, Contingent Valuation and Ethics', *Ecological Economics*, 34, 2: 195–215.

Spash, Clive L. 2000b, 'Ethical Motives and Charitable Contributions in Contingent Valuation', *Environmental Values*, 9, 4: 453–79.

Spash, Clive L. and Nick D. Hanley 1995, 'Preferences, Information, and Biodiversity Preservation', *Ecological Economics*, 12, 3: 191–208.

Sraffa, Piero 1960, *Production of Commodities By Means of Commodities*, Cambridge: Cambridge University Press.

Steedman, Ian 1977, *Marx After Sraffa*, London: New Left Books.

Steindl, Josef 1990, 'Ideas and Concepts of Long Run Growth', in *Economic Papers, 1941–88*, by Josef Steindl, New York: St. Martin's Press.

Stern, David I. 1997, 'Limits to Substitution and Irreversibility in Production and Consumption', *Ecological Economics*, 21, 3: 197–215.

Stern, David I. 1999, 'Is Energy Cost an Accurate Indicator of Natural Resource Quality?', *Ecological Economics*, 31, 3: 381–94.

Stern, David I., Michael S. Common and Edward B. Barbier 1996, 'Economic Growth and Environmental Degradation: The Environmental Kuznets Curve and Sustainable Development', *World Development*, 24, 7: 1151–60.

Sterrer, Wolfgang 1993, 'Human Economics: A Non-Human Perspective', *Ecological Economics*, 7, 3: 183–202.

Stevens, Thomas A., Jaime Echeverria, Ronald J. Glass, Tim Hager and Thomas A. More 1991, 'Measuring the Existence Value of Wildlife: What Do CVM Estimates Really Show?', *Land Economics*, 67, 4: 390–400.

Stewen, Marcus 1998, 'The Interdependence of Allocation, Distribution, Scale and Stability', Ecological Economics, 27, 2: 119–30.

Stiglitz, Joseph 1974, 'Growth with Exhaustible Natural Resources: Efficient and Optimal Growth Paths', Review of Economic Studies, 41 (Symposium on the Economics of Exhaustible Resources): 123–37.

Stirling, Andrew 1997, 'Multi-Criteria Mapping', in Valuing Nature?, edited by John Foster, London: Routledge.

Stokes, Kenneth M. 1994, Man and the Biosphere: Toward a Co-Evolutionary Political Economy, Armonk: M.E. Sharpe.

Strasser, Susan 1999, Waste and Want, New York: Henry Holt.

Svedsäter, Henrik 2003, 'Economic Valuation of the Environment: How Citizens Make Sense of Contingent Valuation Questions', Land Economics, 79, 1: 122–35.

Swallow, Brent M. and Daniel W. Bromley 1995, 'Institutions, Governance and Incentives in Common Property Regimes for African Rangelands', Environmental and Resource Economics, 6, 2: 99–118.

Swaney, James A. 1990, 'Common Property, Reciprocity, and Community', Journal of Economic Issues, 24, 2: 451–62.

Sweezy, Paul 1981, 'Marxian Value Theory and Crises', in The Value Controversy, by Ian Steedman, et al., London: Verso.

Thaler, Richard 1980, 'Toward a Positive Theory of Consumer Choice', Journal of Economic Behavior and Organization, 1, 1: 39–60.

Tietenberg, Tom 1996, Environmental and Natural Resource Economics, Fourth Edition, New York: Harper Collins.

Tinbergen, Jan 1970, On the Theory of Economic Policy, Amsterdam: North-Holland.

Torras, Mariano 2002, 'Environmental Damage and the Mismeasure of Poverty and Inequality: Applications to Indonesia and the Philippines', Asian Development Review, 19, 2: 90–103.

Torras, Mariano 2006, 'The Impact of Power Equality, Income, and the Environment on Human Health: Some Inter-Country Comparisons', International Review of Applied Economics, in press.

Torras, Mariano and James K. Boyce 1998, 'Income, Inequality, and Pollution: A Reassessment of the Environmental Kuznets Curve', Ecological Economics, 25, 2: 147–60.

Townsend, Kenneth M. 1992, 'Is the Entropy Law Relevant to the Economics of Natural Resource Scarcity? Comment', Journal of Environmental Economics and Management, 23, 1: 96–100.

Tsuchida, Atsushi and Takeshi Murota 1987, 'Fundamentals in the Entropy Theory of Ecocycle and Human Economy', in Environmental Economics: The Analysis of a Major Interface, edited by G. Pillet and T. Murota, Geneva: R. Leimgruber.

Turgot, Anne Robert Jacques 1898, Reflections on the Formation and Distribution of Riches, New York: Macmillan.

Tyndall, John 1863, Heat Considered as a Mode of Motion, London: Longman, Green & Co.

Underwood, Daniel A. and Paul G. King 1989, 'On the Ideological Foundations of Environmental Policy', Ecological Economics, 1, 4: 315–34.

Usher, Peter 1993, 'Aboriginal Property Systems in Land and Resources', in Green On Red: Evolving Ecological Socialism, edited by Jesse Vorst, Ross Dobson and Ron Fletcher, Winnipeg: Fernwood.

Van Den Bergh, Jeroen C.J.M., Ada Ferrer-I-Carbonelli and Giuseppe Munda 2000, 'Alternative Models of Individual Behavior and Implications for Environmental Policy', Ecological Economics, 32, 1: 43–61.

Van Ness, H.C. 1983 [1969], Understanding Thermodynamics, New York: Dover.

Varian, Hal R. 1978, Microeconomic Analysis, New York: Norton.

Vatn, Arild 2000, 'The Environment as a Commodity', Environmental Values, 9, 4: 493–509.

Vatn, Arild and Daniel W. Bromley 1994, 'Choices without Prices without Apologies', Journal of Environmental Economics and Management, 26, 2: 129–48.

Veblen, Thorstein 1990 [1919], *The Place of Science in Modern Civilization*, New Brunswick: Transactions Publishers.

Verbruggen, Harmen 1994, 'Environmental Policy Failures and Environmental Policy Levels', in *Economic Incentives and Environmental Policies*, edited by Hans Opschoor and Kerry Turner, Boston: Kluwer.

Victor, Peter A. 1991, 'Indicators of Sustainable Development: Some Lessons from Capital Theory', *Ecological Economics*, 4, 3: 191–213.

Vlachou, Andriana 2002, 'Nature and Value Theory', *Science & Society*, 66, 2: 169–201.

Vlachou, Andriana 2003–4, 'Reply to Critics', *Science & Society*, 67, 4: 468–80.

Vogel, Michael P. 1999, *Environmental Kuznets Curves*, Berlin: Springer-Verlag.

Von Neumann, J. 1945–6, 'A Model of General Economic Equilibrium', *Review of Economic Studies*, 13, 1: 1–9.

Wackernagel, Mathis and William E. Rees 1996, *Our Ecological Footprint*, Gabriola Island: New Society Publishers.

Wackernagel, Mathis, Larry Onisto, Patricia Belló, Alejandro Callejas Linares, Ina Susana López Falfán, Jesus Méndez Garcia, Ana Isabel Suárez Guerrero and Ma. Guadalupe Suárez 1999, 'National Natural Capital Accounting with the Ecological Footprint Concept', *Ecological Economics*, 29, 3: 375–90.

Wade, Robert 1987, 'The Management of Common Property Resources', *Cambridge Journal of Economics*, 11, 2: 95–106.

Wallis, Victor 2004, 'Technology, Ecology, and Socialist Renewal', *Capitalism, Nature, Socialism*, 15, 2: 35–46.

Ward, Kevin M. and John W. Duffield 1992, *Natural Resource Damages: Law and Economics*, New York: John Wiley.

Weeks, John 1989, *A Critique of Neoclassical Macroeconomics*, New York: St. Martin's Press.

Weisskopf, Thomas E. 1991, 'Marxian Crisis Theory and the Contradictions of Late Twentieth-Century Capitalism', *Rethinking Marxism*, 4, 4: 70–93.

Westra, Richard 2003, 'What is the "Value" of the Human Life-World? A Japanese Approach to Ecological Integrity', Paper Presented at the Conference on Global Ecological Integrity, Human Rights, and Human Responsibilities, Urbino, Italy, 27 June–1 July.

Williamson, A.G. 1993, 'The Second Law of Thermodynamics and the Economic Process', *Ecological Economics*, 7, 1: 69–71.

Willig, Robert D. 1976, 'Consumer's Surplus Without Apology', *American Economic Review*, 66, 4: 589–97.

Willis, Robert 1851, *A System of Apparatus for the Use of Lecturers and Experimenters in Mechanical Philosophy*, London: John Weale.

World Bank 2003, *World Development Report 2003: Sustainable Development in a Dynamic World*, Oxford: Oxford University Press.

Young, Jeffrey T. 1991, 'Is the Entropy Law Relevant to the Economics of Natural Resource Scarcity?', *Journal of Environmental Economics and Management*, 21, 2: 169–79.

Young, Jeffrey T. 1994, 'Entropy and Natural Resource Scarcity: A Reply to the Critics', *Journal of Environmental Economics and Management*, 26, 2: 210–13.

Index

HISTORICAL MATERIALISM BOOK SERIES

ISSN 1570–1522

1. ARTHUR, C.J. The New Dialectic and Marx's *Capital*. ISBN 90 04 12798 4 (2002, hardcover), 90 04 13643 6 (2004, paperback)
2. LÖWY, M. The Theory of Revolution in the Young Marx. 2003. ISBN 90 04 12901 4
3. CALLINICOS, A. Making History. Agency, Structure, and Change in Social Theory. 2004. ISBN 90 04 13627 4
4. DAY, R.B. Pavel V. Maksakovsky: The Capitalist Cycle. An Essay on the Marxist Theory of the Cycle. Translated with Introduction and Commentary. 2004. ISBN 90 04 13824 2
5. BROUÉ, P. The German Revolution, 1917-1923. 2005. ISBN 90 04 13940 0
6. MIÉVILLE, C. Between Equal Rights. A Marxist Theory of International Law. 2005. ISBN 90 04 13134 5
7. BEAUMONT, M. Utopia Ltd. Ideologies of Social Dreaming in England 1870-1900. 2005. ISBN 90 04 14296 7
8. KIELY, R. The Clash of Globalisations. Neo-Liberalism, the Third Way and Anti-Globalisation. 2005. ISBN 90 04 14318 1
9. LIH, L.T. Lenin Rediscovered: *What Is to Be Done?* in Context. 2006. ISBN 90 04 13120 5
10. SMITH, T. Globalisation. A Systematic Marxian Account. 2006. ISBN 90 04 14727 6
11. BURKETT, P. Marxism and Ecological Economics. Toward a Red and Green Political Economy. 2006. ISBN 90 04 14810 8